interchange

FIFTH EDITION

2

Teacher's Edition

Jack C. Richards
with Jonathan Hull and Susan Proctor

CAMBRIDGE
UNIVERSITY PRESS

CAMBRIDGE
UNIVERSITY PRESS

University Printing House, Cambridge CB2 8BS, United Kingdom

One Liberty Plaza, 20th Floor, New York, NY 10006, USA

477 Williamstown Road, Port Melbourne, VIC 3207, Australia

314–321, 3rd Floor, Plot 3, Splendor Forum, Jasola District Centre, New Delhi – 110025, India

79 Anson Road, #06–04/06, Singapore 079906

Cambridge University Press is part of the University of Cambridge.

It furthers the University's mission by disseminating knowledge in the pursuit of education, learning and research at the highest international levels of excellence.

www.cambridge.org
Information on this title: www.cambridge.org/9781108407090

First published 1991
Second edition 1998
Third edition 2005
Fourth edition 2013

20 19 18 17 16 15 14 13 12 11 10 9 8 7 6 5 4 3

Printed in Malaysia by Vivar Printing

A catalogue record for this publication is available from the British Library

ISBN	9781316620236	Student's Book 2 with Online Self-Study
ISBN	9781316620250	Student's Book 2A with Online Self-Study
ISBN	9781316620328	Student's Book 2B with Online Self-Study
ISBN	9781316620342	Student's Book 2 with Online Self-Study and Online Workbook
ISBN	9781316620366	Student's Book 2A with Online Self-Study and Online Workbook
ISBN	9781316620373	Student's Book 2B with Online Self-Study and Online Workbook
ISBN	9781316622698	Workbook 2
ISBN	9781316622704	Workbook 2A
ISBN	9781316622711	Workbook 2B
ISBN	9781108407090	Teacher's Edition 2
ISBN	9781316622285	Class Audio 2 CDs
ISBN	9781316623992	Full Contact 2 with Online Self-Study
ISBN	9781316624005	Full Contact 2A with Online Self-Study
ISBN	9781316624029	Full Contact 2B with Online Self-Study
ISBN	9781108403061	Presentation Plus 2

Additional resources for this publication at www.cambridge.org/interchange

Contents

Plan of Book 2

Pronunciation/Listening	Writing/Reading	Interchange Activity
Intonation in statements with time phrases Listening to people talk about changes	Writing a paragraph describing a person's past, present, and possible future "Aquaviva: Fighting for a Future": Reading about a town's attempt to attract new residents	"Cause and effect": Agreeing and disagreeing with classmates **PAGE 123**
Unreleased and released /t/ and /d/ Listening to people talk about their job preferences	Writing a an online cover letter for a job application "Global Work Solutions": Reading about understanding cultural differences in an international company	"You're hired.": Interviewing for a job **PAGE 124**
The letter *o* Listening to descriptions of monuments; listening for information about a country	Writing an introduction to an online city guide Reading about unusual museums	"True or false?": Sharing information about famous works **PAGE 125**
Contrastive stress in responses Listening to stories about unexpected experiences	Writing a description of a recent experience "Breaking Down the Sound of Silence": Reading about an unusual rock band	"It's my life.": Playing a board game to share past experiences **PAGE 126**
Emphatic stress Listening for opinions; listening to a movie review	Writing a movie review "The Real Art of Acting": Reading about unpleasant experiences actors put themselves through	"It was hilarious!": Asking classmates' opinions about movies, TV shows, and celebrities **PAGE 127**
Pitch Listening to people talk about the meaning of signs	Writing a list of rules "Understanding Idioms": Reading about idioms and their meaning	"Casual observers": Interpreting body language **PAGE 128**
Reduction of *have* Listening to people talk about predicaments; listening to a call-in radio show	Writing a blog post asking for advice "TOPTIPS.COM": Reading an online advice forum	"Tough choices": Deciding what to do in a difficult situation **PAGE 130**
Reduction of *had* and *would* Listening for excuses	Writing a report about people's responses to a survey "A Good Excuse for a Day Off Work": Reading about taking a sick day	"Just a bunch of excuses": Discussing calendar conflicts and making up excuses **PAGES 129, 131**

Informed by teachers

Teachers from all over the world helped develop *Interchange Fifth Edition*. They looked at everything – from the color of the designs to the topics in the conversations – in order to make sure that this course will work in the classroom.
We heard from 1,500 teachers in:

- Surveys
- Focus Groups
- In-Depth Reviews

We appreciate the help and input from everyone. In particular, we'd like to give the following people our special thanks:

Jader Franceschi, **Actúa Idiomas,** Bento Gonçalves, Rio Grande do Sul, Brazil
Juliana Dos Santos Voltan Costa, **Actus Idiomas,** São Paulo, Brazil
Ella Osorio, **Angelo State University,** San Angelo, TX, US
Mary Hunter, **Angelo State University,** San Angelo, TX, US
Mario César González, **Angloamericano de Monterrey, SC,** Monterrey, Mexico
Samantha Shipman, **Auburn High School,** Auburn, AL, US
Linda, **Bernick Language School,** Radford, VA, US
Dave Lowrance, **Bethesda University of California,** Yorba Linda, CA, US
Tajbakhsh Hosseini, **Bezmialem Vakif University,** Istanbul, Turkey
Dilek Gercek, **Bil English,** Izmir, Turkey
Erkan Kolat, **Biruni University, ELT,** Istanbul, Turkey
Nika Gutkowska, **Bluedata International,** New York, NY, US
Daniel Alcocer Gómez, **Cecati 92,** Guadalupe, Nuevo León, Mexico
Samantha Webb, **Central Middle School,** Milton-Freewater, OR, US
Verónica Salgado, **Centro Anglo Americano,** Cuernavaca, Mexico
Ana Rivadeneira Martínez and Georgia P. de Machuca, **Centro de Educación Continua – Universidad Politécnica del Ecuador,** Quito, Ecuador
Anderson Francisco Guimerães Maia, **Centro Cultural Brasil Estados Unidos,** Belém, Brazil
Rosana Mariano, **Centro Paula Souza,** São Paulo, Brazil
Carlos de la Paz Arroyo, Teresa Noemí Parra Alarcón, Gilberto
Bastida Gaytan, Manuel Esquivel Román, and Rosa Cepeda Tapia, **Centro Universitario Angloamericano,** Cuernavaca, Morelos, Mexico
Antonio Almeida, **CETEC,** Morelos, Mexico
Cinthia Ferreira, **Cinthia Ferreira Languages Services,** Toronto, ON, Canada
Phil Thomas and Sérgio Sanchez, **CLS Canadian Language School,** São Paulo, Brazil
Celia Concannon, **Cochise College,** Nogales, AZ, US
Maria do Carmo Rocha and CAOP English team, **Colégio Arquidiocesano Ouro Preto – Unidade Cônego Paulo Dilascio,** Ouro Preto, Brazil
Kim Rodriguez, **College of Charleston North,** Charleston, SC, US
Jesús Leza Alvarado, **Coparmex English Institute,** Monterrey, Mexico
John Partain, **Cortazar,** Guanajuato, Mexico
Alexander Palencia Navas, **Cursos de Lenguas, Universidad del Atlántico,** Barranquilla, Colombia
Kenneth Johan Gerardo Steenhuisen Cera, Melfi Osvaldo Guzman Triana, and Carlos Alberto Algarín Jiminez, **Cursos de Lenguas Extranjeras Universidad del Atlantico,** Barranquilla, Colombia
Jane P Kerford, **East Los Angeles College,** Pasadena, CA, US
Daniela, **East Village,** Campinas, São Paulo, Brazil
Rosalva Camacho Orduño, **Easy English for Groups S.A. de C.V.,** Monterrey, Nuevo León, Mexico
Adonis Gimenez Fusetti, **Easy Way Idiomas,** Ibiúna, Brazil
Eileen Thompson, **Edison Community College,** Piqua, OH, US
Ahminne Handeri O.L Froede, **Englishouse escola de idiomas,** Teófilo Otoni, Brazil
Ana Luz Delgado-Izazola, **Escuela Nacional Preparatoria 5, UNAM,** Mexico City, Mexico
Nancy Alarcón Mendoza, **Facultad de Estudios Superiores Zaragoza, UNAM,** Mexico City, Mexico
Marcilio N. Barros, **Fast English USA,** Campinas, São Paulo, Brazil
Greta Douthat, **FCI Ashland,** Ashland, KY, US
Carlos Lizárraga González, **Grupo Educativo Anglo Americano, S.C.,** Mexico City, Mexico
Hugo Fernando Alcántar Valle, **Instituto Politécnico Nacional, Escuela Superior de Comercio y Administración-Unidad Santotomás, Celex Esca Santo Tomás,** Mexico City, Mexico
Sueli Nascimento, **Instituto Superior de Educação do Rio de Janeiro,** Rio de Janeiro, Brazil
Elsa F Monteverde, **International Academic Services,** Miami, FL, US
Laura Anand, **Irvine Adult School,** Irvine, CA, US
Prof. Marli T. Fernandes (principal) and Prof. Dr. Jefferson J. Fernandes (pedagogue), **Jefferson Idiomass,** São Paulo, Brazil
Herman Bartelen, **Kanda Gaigo Gakuin,** Tokyo, Japan
Cassia Silva, **Key Languages,** Key Biscayne, FL, US
Sister Mary Hope, **Kyoto Notre Dame Joshi Gakuin,** Kyoto, Japan
Nate Freedman, **LAL Language Centres,** Boston, MA, US
Richard Janzen, **Langley Secondary School,** Abbotsford, BC, Canada

Christina Abel Gabardo, **Language House,** Campo Largo, Brazil
Ivonne Castro, **Learn English International,** Cali, Colombia
Julio Cesar Maciel Rodrigues, **Liberty Centro de Línguas,** São Paulo, Brazil
Ann Gibson, **Maynard High School,** Maynard, MA, US
Martin Darling, **Meiji Gakuin Daigaku,** Tokyo, Japan
Dax Thomas, **Meiji Gakuin Daigaku,** Yokohama, Kanagawa, Japan
Derya Budak, **Mevlana University,** Konya, Turkey
B Sullivan, **Miami Valley Career Technical Center International Program,** Dayton, OH, US
Julio Velazquez, **Milo Language Center,** Weston, FL, US
Daiane Siqueira da Silva, Luiz Carlos Buontempo, Marlete Avelina de Oliveira Cunha, Marcos Paulo Segatti, Morgana Eveline de Oliveira, Nadia Lia Gino Alo, and Paul Hyde Budgen, **New Interchange-Escola de Idiomas,** São Paulo, Brazil
Patrícia França Furtado da Costa, Juiz de Fora, Brazil
Patricia Servín
Chris Pollard, **North West Regional College SK,** North Battleford, SK, Canada
Olga Amy, **Notre Dame High School,** Red Deer, Canada
Amy Garrett, **Ouachita Baptist University,** Arkadelphia, AR, US
Mervin Curry, **Palm Beach State College,** Boca Raton, FL, US
Julie Barros, **Quality English Studio,** Guarulhos, São Paulo, Brazil
Teodoro González Saldaña and Jesús Monserrrta Mata Franco, **Race Idiomas,** Mexico City, Mexico
Autumn Westphal and Noga La`or, **Rennert International,** New York, NY, US
Antonio Gallo and Javy Palau, **Rigby Idiomas,** Monterrey, Mexico Tatiane Gabriela Sperb do Nascimento, **Right Way,** Igrejinha, Brazil
Mustafa Akgül, **Selahaddin Eyyubi Universitesi,** Diyarbakır, Turkey
James Drury M. Fonseca, **Senac Idiomas Fortaleza,** Fortaleza, Ceara, Brazil
Manoel Fialho S Neto, **Senac – PE,** Recife, Brazil
Jane Imber, **Small World,** Lawrence, KS, US
Tony Torres, **South Texas College,** McAllen, TX, US
Janet Rose, **Tennessee Foreign Language Institute,** College Grove, TN, US
Todd Enslen, **Tohoku University,** Sendai, Miyagi, Japan
Daniel Murray, **Torrance Adult School,** Torrance, CA, US
Juan Manuel Pulido Mendoza, **Universidad del Atlántico,** Barranquilla, Colombia
Juan Carlos Vargas Millán, **Universidad Libre Seccional Cali,** Cali (Valle del Cauca), Colombia
Carmen Cecilia Llanos Ospina, **Universidad Libre Seccional Cali,** Cali, Colombia
Jorge Noriega Zenteno, **Universidad Politécnica del Valle de México,** Estado de México, Mexico
Aimee Natasha Holguin S., **Universidad Politécnica del Valle de México UPVM,** Tultitlàn Estado de México, Mexico
Christian Selene Bernal Barraza, **UPVM Universidad Politécnica del Valle de México,** Ecatepec, Mexico
Lizeth Ramos Acosta, **Universidad Santiago de Cali,** Cali, Colombia
Silvana Dushku, **University of Illinois Champaign,** IL, US
Deirdre McMurtry, **University of Nebraska – Omaha,** Omaha, NE, US
Jason E Mower, **University of Utah,** Salt Lake City, UT, US
Paul Chugg, **Vanguard Taylor Language Institute,** Edmonton, Alberta, Canada
Henry Mulak, **Varsity Tutors,** Los Angeles, CA, US
Shirlei Strucker Calgaro and Hugo Guilherme Karrer, **VIP Centro de Idiomas,** Panambi, Rio Grande do Sul, Brazil
Eleanor Kelly, **Waseda Daigaku Extension Centre,** Tokyo, Japan
Sherry Ashworth, **Wichita State University,** Wichita, KS, US
Laine Bourdene, **William Carey University,** Hattiesburg, MS, US
Serap Aydın, Istanbul, Turkey
Liliana Covino, Guarulhos, Brazil
Yannuarys Jiménez, Barranquilla, Colombia
Juliana Morais Pazzini, Toronto, ON, Canada
Marlon Sanches, Montreal, Canada

Additional content contributed by Kenna Bourke, Inara Couto, Nic Harris, Greg Manin, Ashleigh Martinez, Laura McKenzie, Paul McIntyre, Clara Prado, Lynne Robertson, Mari Vargo, Theo Walker, and Maria Lucia Zaorob.

The Fifth Edition of *Interchange*

Interchange, the world's favorite English course, has a long tradition of teaching students how to speak confidently. Millions of people all over the world attest to its effectiveness.

What Makes *Interchange* Special?

Jack C. Richards' communicative methodology: Refined over years and in countless classrooms, the *Interchange* approach is rooted in solid pedagogy.

Flexible units: Instructors can change the order of the activities in each unit, keeping lessons fresh and students engaged. Additional photocopiable activities and a full video program give teachers even more freedom to make *Interchange* their own.

Students speak right from the start: The solid research and winning content give students the confidence to speak early and often.

What's New in the Fifth Edition?

50% new content: Readings, listenings, conversations, and Snapshots have been updated throughout the books.

Improved exercises for listenings and readings: We listened to teachers' requests for greater variety in the activities that accompany the listenings and readings.

New digital tools: Self-study for every student available online. An online workbook with fun games.

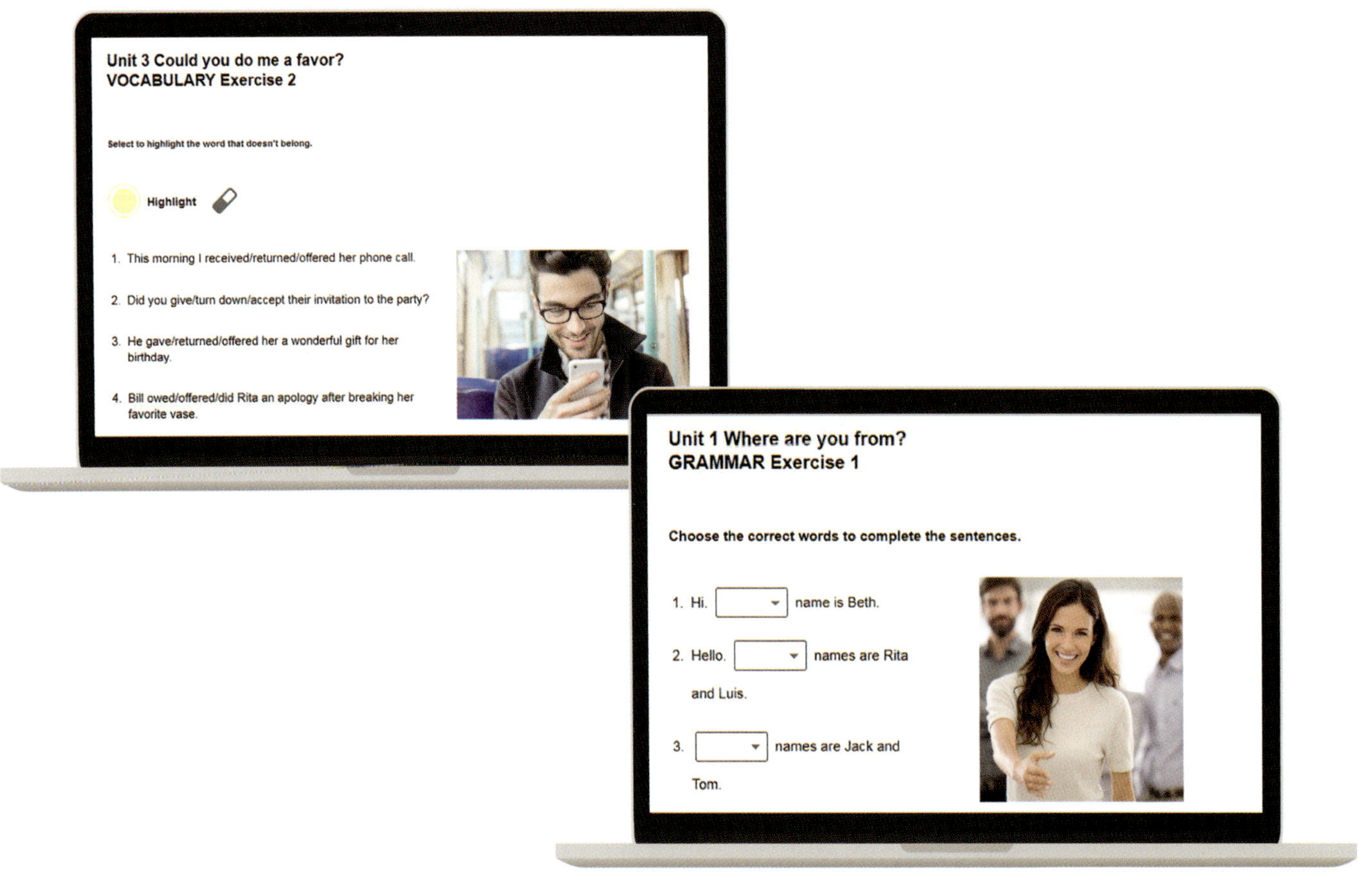

Student's Book overview

Every unit in *Interchange Fifth Edition* contains two cycles, each of which has a specific topic, grammar point, and function. The units in Level 2 contain a variety of exercises, including a Snapshot, Conversation, Perspectives, Grammar focus, Pronunciation, Discussion (or Speaking), Word power, Listening, Writing, Reading, and Interchange activity. The sequence of these exercises differs from unit to unit. Here is a sample unit from Level 2.

Cycle 1 (Exercises 1–7)

Topic: holidays and special occasions
Grammar: relative clauses of time
Function: describe celebrations and annual events

8 Time to celebrate!

▸ Discuss holidays and special occasions
▸ Describe celebrations, annual events, and customs

1 SNAPSHOT

HOLIDAYS AND FESTIVALS

Day of the Dead
November 2nd
Mexicans make playful skeleton sculptures and bake *pan de muerto* – bread of the dead.

Thanksgiving
November
In the United States, families get together, have a traditional meal, and give thanks for life and health.

Saint Patrick's Day
March 17th
People of Irish background wear green to celebrate their culture with parades, dancing, parties, and special foods.

Chinese New Year
January or February
Chinese people celebrate the lunar new year with fireworks and dragon dances.

Do you celebrate these or similar holidays in your country?
What other special days do you have?
What's your favorite holiday or festival?

2 WORD POWER Ways to celebrate

A Which word or phrase is not usually paired with each verb? Put a line through it. Then compare with a partner.

1. eat	candy	sweets	~~a mask~~
2. give	presents	a celebration	money
3. go to	decorations	a wedding	a party
4. have a	picnic	beach	meal
5. play	games	candles	music
6. send	cards	flowers	a barbecue
7. visit	relatives	food	close friends
8. watch	a birthday	a parade	fireworks
9. wear	costumes	invitations	traditional clothes

B **PAIR WORK** Do you do any of the things in part A as part of a cultural or family celebration? When? Tell your partner.

50

Snapshot

- Introduces the unit or cycle topic
- Presents vocabulary for discussing the topic
- Uses real-world information
- Provides personalized guided discussion questions

Word power

- Presents vocabulary related to the unit topic
- Provides practice with collocations and categorizing vocabulary
- Promotes freer, more personalized practice

Perspectives

- Provides structured listening and speaking practice
- Introduces the meaning and use of the cycle's grammar, useful expressions, and discourse
- Presents people's opinions and experiences about a topic

Grammar focus

- Includes audio recordings of the grammar
- Provides controlled grammar practice in realistic contexts, such as short conversations
- Provides freer, more personalized speaking practice

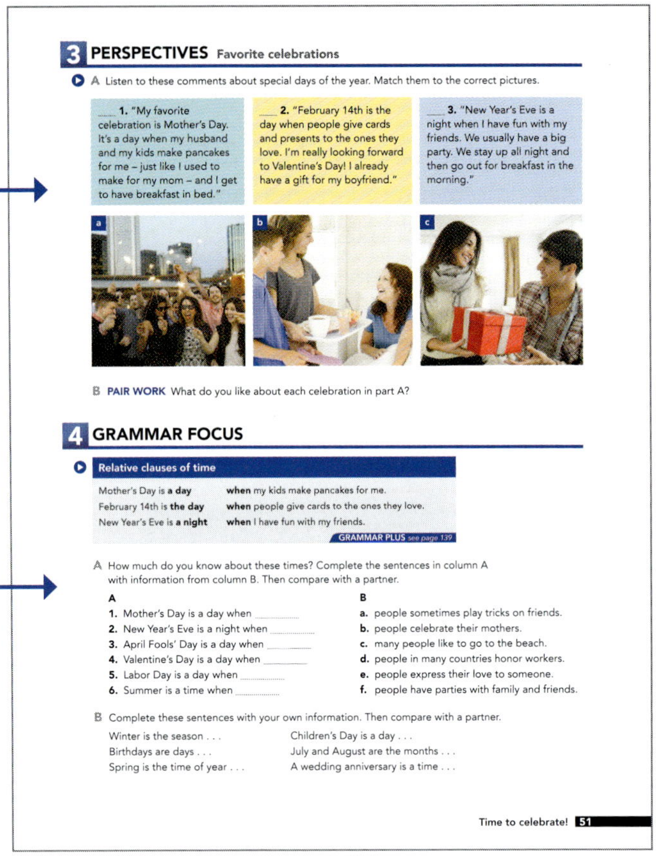

3 PERSPECTIVES Favorite celebrations

A Listen to these comments about special days of the year. Match them to the correct pictures.

___ 1. "My favorite celebration is Mother's Day. It's a day when my husband and my kids make pancakes for me – just like I used to make for my mom – and I get to have breakfast in bed."

___ 2. "February 14th is the day when people give cards and presents to the ones they love. I'm really looking forward to Valentine's Day! I already have a gift for my boyfriend."

___ 3. "New Year's Eve is a night when I have fun with my friends. We usually have a big party. We stay up all night and then go out for breakfast in the morning."

a b c

B PAIR WORK What do you like about each celebration in part A?

4 GRAMMAR FOCUS

Relative clauses of time

Mother's Day is **a day**	**when** my kids make pancakes for me.
February 14th is **the day**	**when** people give cards to the ones they love.
New Year's Eve is **a night**	**when** I have fun with my friends.

GRAMMAR PLUS see page 139

A How much do you know about these times? Complete the sentences in column A with information from column B. Then compare with a partner.

A	B
1. Mother's Day is a day when ______	a. people sometimes play tricks on friends.
2. New Year's Eve is a night when ______	b. people celebrate their mothers.
3. April Fools' Day is a day when ______	c. many people like to go to the beach.
4. Valentine's Day is a day when ______	d. people in many countries honor workers.
5. Labor Day is a day when ______	e. people express their love to someone.
6. Summer is a time when ______	f. people have parties with family and friends.

B Complete these sentences with your own information. Then compare with a partner.

Winter is the season . . .
Birthdays are days . . .
Spring is the time of year . . .
Children's Day is a day . . .
July and August are the months . . .
A wedding anniversary is a time . . .

Time to celebrate! 51

5 LISTENING Time for Carnival!

Carnival in Brazil

A Listen to Vanessa talk about her trip to Carnival in Brazil. Write three facts about Carnival that she mentions.

B Listen again and answer these questions about Vanessa's experience.

Why did she have to book her hotel six months early?
What happened when Vanessa got lost?
What was her favorite thing about Carnival? Why?

C PAIR WORK Think of another famous celebration that is similar to Carnival. Describe it to the class. They will try to guess the celebration.

6 SPEAKING Favorite holidays

A PAIR WORK Choose your three favorite holidays. Tell your partner why you like each one.

A: I really like Independence Day.
B: What do you like about it?
A: It's a day when we watch parades and fireworks.
B: Do you do anything special?
A: We usually have a barbecue. My father makes burgers, and my mother makes her special potato salad.

B CLASS ACTIVITY Take a class vote. What are the most popular holidays in your class?

7 WRITING An online entry

A Write an entry for a travel website about a festival or celebration where you live. When is it? How do people celebrate it? What should a visitor see and do?

Obon is an annual event when Japanese people commemorate their ancestors. They visit and clean the graves of their dead relatives. People put candles in lanterns and float them on rivers. There are neighborhood dances at parks, gardens, and . . . read more

B PAIR WORK Read your partner's entry. What do you like about it? Can you suggest anything to improve it?

52 Unit 8

Listening

- Provides pre-listening focus tasks or questions
- Develops a variety of listening skills, such as listening for main ideas and details
- Includes post-listening speaking tasks

Speaking

- Provides communicative tasks that help develop oral fluency
- Includes pair work, group work, and class activities

Writing

- Provides a model writing sample
- Develops skills in writing different texts, such as blogs and email messages
- Reinforces the vocabulary and grammar in the cycle or unit

Cycle 2 (Exercises 8–13)

Topic: weddings and traditions
Grammar: adverbial clauses of time
Function: describe customs

Conversation

- Provides structured listening and speaking practice
- Introduces the meaning and use of Cycle 2 grammar, useful expressions, and discourse
- Uses pictures to set the scene and illustrate new vocabulary

Pronunciation

- Provides controlled practice in recognizing and producing sounds linked to the cycle grammar
- Promotes extended or personalized pronunciation practice

8 CONVERSATION A traditional wedding

A Listen and practice.

JULIA Is this a picture from your wedding, Anusha?
ANUSHA Yes. We had the ceremony in India.
JULIA And was this your wedding dress?
ANUSHA Yes. It's a sari, actually. In India, when women get married, they usually wear a brightly colored sari, not a white dress.
JULIA It's beautiful! So, what are weddings like in India?
ANUSHA Well, in some traditions, after the groom arrives, the bride and groom exchange garlands of flowers. We did that. But we didn't do some other traditional things.
JULIA Oh? Like what?
ANUSHA Well, before the wedding, the bride's female relatives usually have a party to celebrate. But I'm an only child, and I don't have any female cousins, so we skipped that.
JULIA That makes sense. You know, I have heard about this one tradition . . . When the groom takes off his shoes, the bride's sisters steal them! I guess you didn't do that, either?
ANUSHA Oh, no, we did that part. My mom stole them!

B Listen to the rest of the conversation.
What does Anusha say about her wedding reception?

9 PRONUNCIATION Stress and rhythm

A Listen and practice. Notice how stressed words and syllables occur with a regular rhythm.

When women get married, they usually wear a brightly colored sari.

B Listen to the stress and rhythm in these sentences. Then practice them.

1. After the groom arrives, the bride and groom exchange garlands of flowers.
2. Before the wedding, the bride's female relatives usually have a party to celebrate.
3. When the groom takes off his shoes, the bride's sisters steal them.

Time to celebrate! 53

10 GRAMMAR FOCUS

Adverbial clauses of time

When women get married,	they usually wear a brightly colored sari.
After the groom arrives,	the bride and groom exchange garlands of flowers.
Before the wedding,	the bride's female relatives usually have a party to celebrate.

GRAMMAR PLUS *see page 139*

A What do you know about wedding customs in North America? Complete these sentences with the information below.

1. Before a man and woman get married, they usually ____
2. When a couple gets engaged, the man often ____
3. Right after a couple gets engaged, they usually ____
4. When a woman gets married, she usually ____
5. When guests go to a wedding, they almost always ____
6. Right after a couple gets married, they usually ____

a. wears a long white dress and a veil.
b. go on a short trip called a "honeymoon."
c. give the bride and groom gifts or some money.
d. gives the woman an engagement ring.
e. begin to plan the wedding.
f. date each other for a year or more.

B PAIR WORK What happens when people get married in your country? Tell your partner by completing the statements in part A with your own information. Pay attention to stress and rhythm.

11 INTERCHANGE 8 It's worth celebrating.

How do your classmates celebrate special occasions? Go to Interchange 8 on page 122.

12 SPEAKING My personal traditions

A GROUP WORK How do you usually celebrate the dates below? Share your personal traditions with your classmates.

your birthday New Year's Eve your country's national day your favorite holiday

A: On my birthday, I always wear new clothes, and I often have a party. What about you?
B: I usually celebrate my birthday with my family. We have a special meal and some relatives come over.
C: I used to celebrate my birthday at home, but now I usually go out with friends.

B CLASS ACTIVITY Tell the class the most interesting traditions you talked about in your group. Do you share any common traditions? Did you use to celebrate those dates the same way when you were younger?

54 Unit 8

Grammar focus

- Presents examples from the previous conversation
- Provides controlled grammar practice in realistic contexts, such as short conversations

Speaking

- Provides communicative tasks that help develop oral fluency
- Recycles grammar and vocabulary in the cycle
- Includes pair work, group work, and class activities

Reading

- Presents a variety of text types
- Introduces the text with a pre-reading task
- Develops a variety of reading skills, such as reading for main ideas, reading for details, and inferencing
- Promotes discussion that involves personalization and analysis

13 READING

A Skim the article. Which of these phrases could be a title for this article?

The best New Year's resolutions   New Year's traditions around the world
How to host a New Year's Eve party

It's midnight on New Year's Eve. Clocks are striking twelve as people welcome in the coming year and say goodbye to the old. It's a time when people wish for good luck in the future and forget bad things in the past. Around the world, people do different things to help their wishes come true. Some of them might surprise you.

Food is often central to New Year's customs. In Ireland, they hit the walls and doors of their houses with loaves of bread. They hope this will make good luck enter the house and bad luck leave it. The Spanish and the Mexicans eat twelve grapes in twelve seconds – one for luck in each of the coming months. Eating grapes so fast isn't easy, but it's fun and often messy!

Colors are important, too. Brazilians, for example, choose their clothes very carefully – for peace they wear white, yellow might bring success, and red means love is in the air! The Chinese believe red brings good luck, so they like to dress in this color, too. They also give family members and friends red envelopes containing money.

Some people destroy things on New Year's Eve because they want to forget the past. In Ecuador and Colombia, people make a dummy and fill it with sawdust, newspaper, or old clothes. They dress it, put a mask on it, and name it after someone famous or a friend or family member. Then they burn it.

And some customs have no reason at all; they just develop over time. On New Year's Eve in Germany, several TV stations show a short black-and-white movie called *Dinner for One*. It's a comedy in English, starring English actors. Nobody knows why they do this, not even the Germans!

B Read the article. Check (✓) True or False for each statement about New Year's customs. Then correct each false statement.

	True	False	
1. In Ireland, people eat loaves of bread for good luck.	☐	☐	
2. They eat apples for good luck in Spain.	☐	☐	
3. In China, people change the color of their doors.	☐	☐	
4. In Colombia, they burn a doll with old things inside.	☐	☐	
5. In Germany, people watch *Dinner for One* because it's about New Year's Eve.	☐	☐	

C What do the underlined words in the article refer to? Write the correct word.

1. them ______ 3. one ______ 5. they ______
2. this ______ 4. They ______

D What do people in your country do for the New Year? What is your favorite New Year's tradition?

Time to celebrate! 55

In the back of the book

Interchange activity

- Expands on the unit topic, vocabulary, and grammar
- Provides opportunities to consolidate new language in a creative or fun way
- Promotes fluency with communicative activities such as discussions, information gaps, and games

INTERCHANGE 8 It's worth celebrating.

A CLASS ACTIVITY How do your classmates celebrate special occasions? Go around the class and ask the questions below. If someone answers "yes," write down his or her name. Ask for more information and take notes.

Question	Name	Notes
1. Have you ever given someone a surprise party?		
2. What's the best gift you have ever received?		
3. Do you ever wear traditional clothes?		
4. Have you bought flowers for someone special recently?		
5. Do you like to watch parades?		
6. Does your family have big get-togethers?		
7. Has someone given you money recently as a gift?		
8. Will you celebrate your next birthday with a party?		
9. Do you ever give friends birthday presents?		
10. What's your favorite time of the year?		
11. Do you ever celebrate a holiday with fireworks?		

A: Have you ever given someone a surprise party?
B: Yes. Once we gave my co-worker a surprise party on his birthday.
A: How was it?
B: It was great. He never suspected that we were planning it, so he was really surprised. And he was very happy that we got his favorite cake!

B PAIR WORK Compare your information with a partner.

122 INTERCHANGE 8

Grammar plus

- Explores the unit grammar in greater depth
- Practices the grammar with controlled exercises
- Can be done in class or assigned as homework

UNIT 8

1 Relative clauses of time page 51

- Relative clauses with *when* describe the word *time* or a noun that refers to a period of time, such as *day, night, month,* and *year.*

Combine the two sentences using *when.*

1. Thanksgiving is a holiday. Entire families get together.
   Thanksgiving is a holiday when entire families get together.
2. It's a wonderful time. People give thanks for the good things in their lives.
3. It's a day. Everyone eats much more than usual.
4. I remember one particular year. The whole family came to our house.
5. That year was very cold. It snowed all Thanksgiving day.
6. I remember another thing about that Thanksgiving. My brother and I baked eight pies.

2 Adverbial clauses of time page 54

- An adverbial clause of time can come before or after the main clause. When it comes before the main clause, use a comma. When it comes after the main clause, don't use a comma: When Ginny and Tom met, they both lived in San Juan. BUT: Ginny and Tom met when they both lived in San Juan.
- The words *couple* and *family* are collective nouns. They are usually used with singular verbs: When a couple **gets** married, they often receive gifts. (NOT: When a couple **get** married, they often receive gifts.)

Combine the two sentences using the adverb in parentheses. Write one sentence with the adverbial clause before the main clause and another with the adverbial clause after the main clause.

1. Students complete their courses. A school holds a graduation ceremony. (after)
   a. *After students complete their courses, a school holds a graduation ceremony.*
   b. *A school holds a graduation ceremony after students complete their courses.*
2. Students gather to put on robes and special hats. The ceremony starts. (before)
   a.
   b.
3. Music plays. The students walk in a line to their seats. (when)
   a.
   b.
4. School officials and teachers make speeches. Students get their diplomas. (after)
   a.
   b.
5. The ceremony is finished. Students throw their hats into the air and cheer. (when)
   a.
   b.

Unit 8 Grammar plus 139

Online Self-study overview

Interchange Fifth Edition online Self-study provides students with hundreds of additional exercises to practice the language taught in the Student's Book on their own, in the classroom, or in the lab.

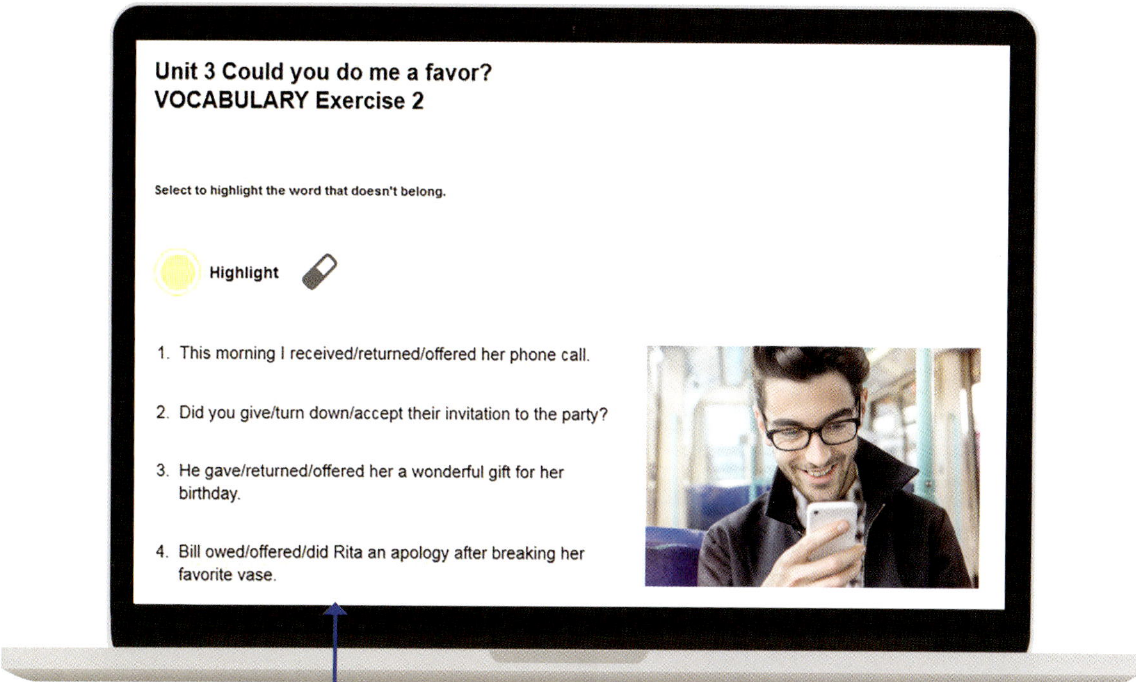

Interactive exercises

Hundreds of interactive exercises provide hours of additional:

- vocabulary practice
- grammar practice
- listening practice
- speaking practice
- reading practice

The complete *Interchange* video program

The entire *Interchange* video program for this level is included online with exercises that allow the students to watch and check comprehension themselves.

Online Workbook overview

The *Interchange Fifth Edition Online Workbook* provides additional activities to reinforce what is presented in the corresponding Student's Book. Each *Online Workbook* includes:

- A variety of interactive activities which correspond to each Student's Book lesson, allowing students to interact with workbook material in a fresh, lively way.
- Instant feedback for hundreds of activities, challenging students to focus on areas for improvement.
- Simple tools for teachers to monitor students' progress such as scores, attendance, and time spent online, providing instant information.

The *Interchange Fifth Edition Online Workbooks* can be purchased in two ways:

- as an institutional subscription,
- as part of a Student's Book with Online Workbook Pack.

Games

- Fun, interactive, self-scoring activities in the Online Workbooks offer a fresh change of pace.

Workbook overview

Interchange Fifth Edition provides students with additional opportunities to practice the language taught in the Student's Book outside of the classroom by using the Workbook that accompanies each level.

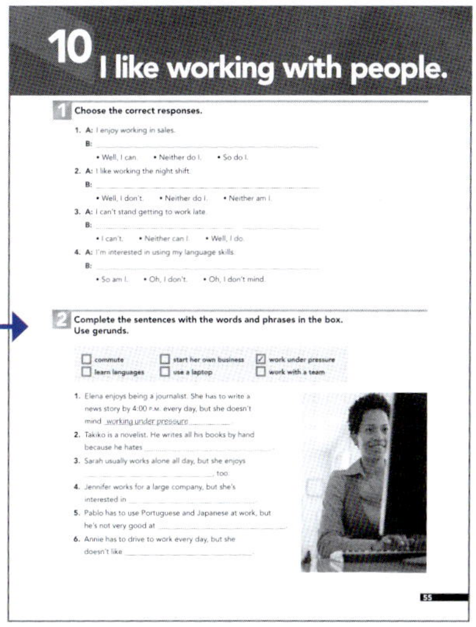

10 I like working with people.

1 Choose the correct responses.

2 Complete the sentences with the words and phrases in the box. Use gerunds.

Grammar

- Reinforces the unit grammar through controlled practice

Vocabulary

- Provides vocabulary practice based on the unit topic

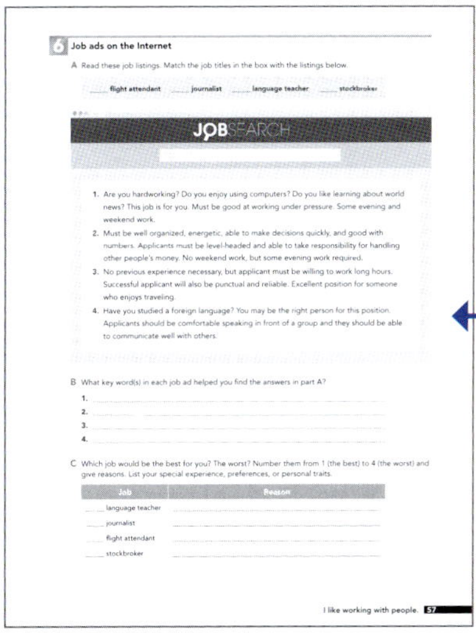

6 Job ads on the Internet

Reading

- Gives additional reading practice based on the theme of the unit
- Introduces the text with a pre-reading task
- Reinforces reading skills used in the Student's Book

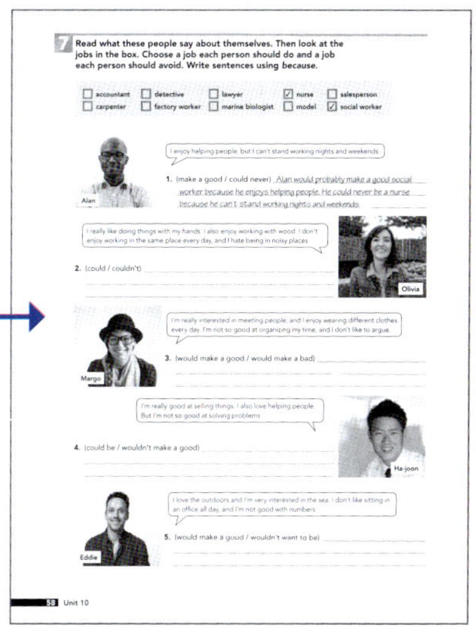

7 Read what these people say about themselves. Then look at the jobs in the box. Choose a job each person should do and a job each person should avoid. Write sentences using because.

Writing

- Promotes freer, more personalized practice
- Reinforces the vocabulary and grammar in the unit

Teacher's Edition overview

The Teacher's Editions provide complete support for teachers who are using *Interchange Fifth Edition*. They contain Supplementary Resources Overview charts to help teachers plan their lessons (for more information see page xx), Language summaries, Workbook answer keys, Audio scripts, Fresh ideas, and Games. They also include detailed teaching notes for the units and Progress checks in the Student's Books.

Teaching notes

- Learning objectives for each exercise
- Step-by-step lesson plans
- Audio scripts
- Answers and Vocabulary definitions
- Stimulating and fun Games to review or practice skills such as grammar and vocabulary
- Alternative ways to present and review exercises in the Fresh ideas
- Tips that promote teacher training and development
- Options for alternative presentations or expansions
- Suggestions for further practice in other *Interchange Fifth Edition* components and online
- Suggestions for regular assessment using quizzes and tests

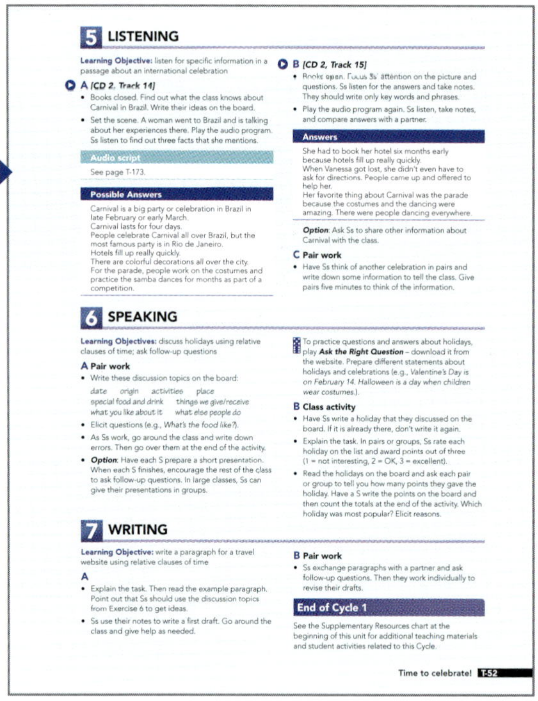

5 LISTENING

Learning Objective: listen for specific information in a passage about an international celebration

A *[CD 2, Track 14]*

- Books closed. Find out what the class knows about Carnival in Brazil. Write their ideas on the board.
- Set the scene. A woman went to Brazil and is talking about her experiences there. Play the audio program. Ss listen to find out three facts that she mentions.

Audio script

See page T-173.

Possible Answers

Carnival is a big party or celebration in Brazil in late February or early March.
Carnival lasts for four days.
People celebrate Carnival all over Brazil, but the most famous party is in Rio de Janeiro.
Hotels fill up really quickly.
There are colorful decorations all over the city.
For the parade, people work on the costumes and practice the samba dances for months as part of a competition.

B *[CD 2, Track 15]*

- Books open. Focus Ss' attention on the picture and questions. Ss listen for the answers and take notes. They should write only key words and phrases.
- Play the audio program again. Ss listen, take notes, and compare answers with a partner.

Answers

She had to book her hotel six months early because hotels fill up really quickly.
When Vanessa got lost, she didn't even have to ask for directions. People came up and offered to help her.
Her favorite thing about Carnival was the parade because the costumes and the dancing were amazing. There were people dancing everywhere.

Option: Ask Ss to share other information about Carnival with the class.

C **Pair work**

- Have Ss think of another celebration in pairs and write down some information to tell the class. Give pairs five minutes to think of the information.

6 SPEAKING

Learning Objectives: discuss holidays using relative clauses of time; ask follow-up questions

A **Pair work**

- Write these discussion topics on the board:
  date origin activities place
  special food and drink things we give/receive
  what you like about it what else people do
- Elicit questions (e.g., *What's the food like?*).
- As Ss work, go around the class and write down errors. Then go over them at the end of the activity.
- ***Option***: Have each S prepare a short presentation. When each S finishes, encourage the rest of the class to ask follow-up questions. In large classes, Ss can give their presentations in groups.

To practice questions and answers about holidays, play ***Ask the Right Question*** – download it from the website. Prepare different statements about holidays and celebrations (e.g., *Valentine's Day is on February 14. Halloween is a day when children wear costumes.*).

B **Class activity**

- Have Ss write a holiday that they discussed on the board. If it is already there, don't write it again.
- Explain the task. In pairs or groups, Ss rate each holiday on the list and award points out of three (1 = not interesting, 2 = OK, 3 = excellent).
- Read the holidays on the board and ask each pair or group to tell you how many points they gave the holiday. Have a S write the points on the board and then count the totals at the end of the activity. Which holiday was most popular? Elicit reasons.

7 WRITING

Learning Objective: write a paragraph for a travel website using relative clauses of time

A

- Explain the task. Then read the example paragraph. Point out that Ss should use the discussion topics from Exercise 6 to get ideas.
- Ss use their notes to write a first draft. Go around the class and give help as needed.

B **Pair work**

- Ss exchange paragraphs with a partner and ask follow-up questions. Then they work individually to revise their drafts.

End of Cycle 1

See the Supplementary Resources chart at the beginning of this unit for additional teaching materials and student activities related to this Cycle.

Time to celebrate! T-52

Complete Assessment Program

The complete assessment program contains oral and written quizzes and tests. It includes PDF and Microsoft Word versions of all quizzes, mid-term and final tests, the placement test program, audio, audio scripts, and answer keys.

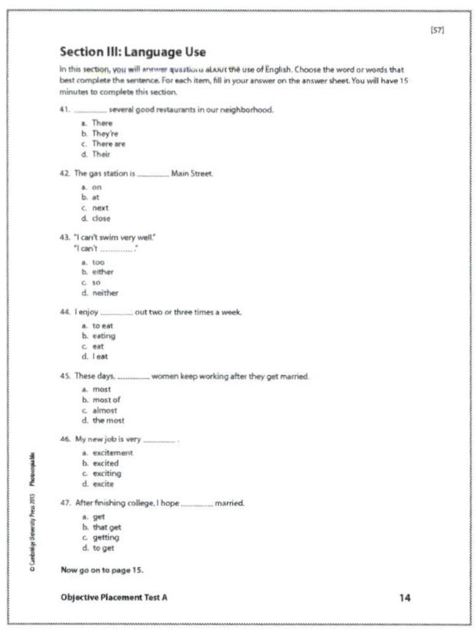

[57]

Section III: Language Use

In this section, you will answer questions about the use of English. Choose the word or words that best complete the sentence. For each item, fill in your answer on the answer sheet. You will have 15 minutes to complete this section.

41. ________ several good restaurants in our neighborhood.
    a. There
    b. They're
    c. There are
    d. Their

42. The gas station is ________ Main Street.
    a. on
    b. at
    c. next
    d. close

43. "I can't swim very well."
    "I can't ________."
    a. too
    b. either
    c. so
    d. neither

44. I enjoy ________ out two or three times a week.
    a. to eat
    b. eating
    c. eat
    d. I eat

45. These days, ________ women keep working after they get married.
    a. most
    b. most of
    c. almost
    d. the most

46. My new job is very ________.
    a. excitement
    b. excited
    c. exciting
    d. excite

47. After finishing college, I hope ________ married.
    a. get
    b. that get
    c. getting
    d. to get

Now go on to page 15.

© Cambridge University Press 2013 Photocopiable

Objective Placement Test A 14

Presentation Plus overview

Interchange Presentation Plus is a complete classroom presentation package, combining the contents of the Student's Book, the class audio, and the video program for each level of the series into a convenient one-stop presentation solution. It can be used with all types of interactive whiteboards or with just a projector and a computer to present *Interchange* core materials in the classroom in a lively and engaging way.

Presentation Plus simplifies several of the teaching tasks that take place in the classroom.

You can use Presentation Plus to display the answers for the exercises in an uncomplicated way, zoom in on a page to more efficiently focus students' attention on an activity or image, and even annotate pages for future lessons.

cambridge.org/interchange

Go online for offers a variety of materials to assist with your teaching of the series. Here you will find practical articles, correlations, language summaries, overviews of supplementary materials, ideas for games and extra activities, as well as a number of downloadable worksheets for projects and extra practice of vocabulary, grammar, listening, writing, and speaking.

Supplementary Resources Overviews

Indicate all the activities available in the various ancillary components that can be used after each exercise in the Student's Book units for extra practice, review, and assessment.

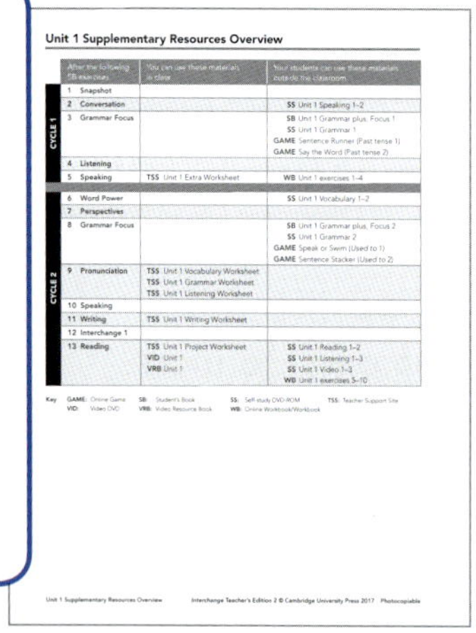

Unit 1 Supplementary Resources Overview

	After the following SB exercises	You can use these materials in class	Your students can use these materials outside the classroom
CYCLE 1	1 Snapshot		
	2 Conversation		SS Unit 1 Speaking 1–2
	3 Grammar Focus		SB Unit 1 Grammar plus, Focus 1 SS Unit 1 Grammar 1 GAME Sentence Runner (Past tense 1) GAME Say the Word (Past tense 2)
	4 Listening		
	5 Speaking	TSS Unit 1 Extra Worksheet	WB Unit 1 exercises 1–4
CYCLE 2	6 Word Power		SS Unit 1 Vocabulary 1–2
	7 Perspectives		
	8 Grammar Focus		SB Unit 1 Grammar plus, Focus 2 SS Unit 1 Grammar 2 GAME Speak or Swim (Used to 1) GAME Sentence Stacker (Used to 2)
	9 Pronunciation	TSS Unit 1 Vocabulary Worksheet TSS Unit 1 Grammar Worksheet TSS Unit 1 Listening Worksheet	
	10 Speaking		
	11 Writing	TSS Unit 1 Writing Worksheet	
	12 Interchange 1		
	13 Reading	TSS Unit 1 Project Worksheet VID Unit 1 VRB Unit 1	SS Unit 1 Reading 1–2 SS Unit 1 Listening 1–3 SS Unit 1 Video 1–3 WB Unit 1 exercises 5–10

Key GAME: Online Game SB: Student's Book SS: Self-study DVD-ROM TSS: Teacher Support Site
VID: Video DVD VRB: Video Resource Book WB: Online Workbook/Workbook

Unit 1 Supplementary Resources Overview Interchange Teacher's Edition 2 © Cambridge University Press 2017 Photocopiable

Downloadable worksheets

- Offer extra speaking opportunities
- Provide guidance for projects and extra practice of grammar, vocabulary, listening, and writing

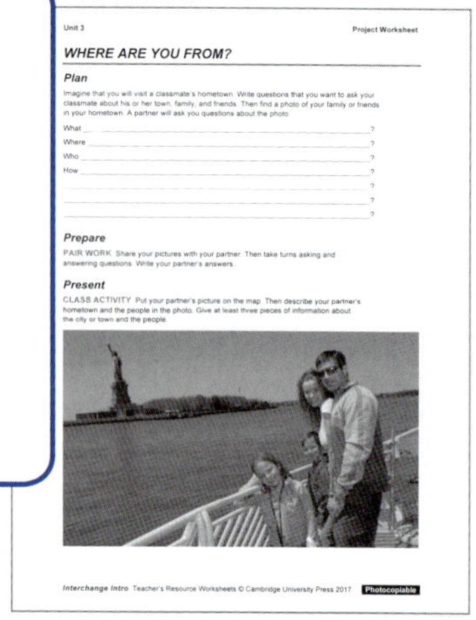

Unit 3 Project Worksheet

WHERE ARE YOU FROM?

Plan

Imagine that you will visit a classmate's hometown. Write questions that you want to ask your classmate about his or her town, family, and friends. Then find a photo of your family or friends in your hometown. A partner will ask you questions about the photo.

What ______________________?
Where ______________________?
Who ______________________?
How ______________________?

Prepare

PAIR WORK Share your pictures with your partner. Then take turns asking and answering questions. Write your partner's answers.

Present

CLASS ACTIVITY Put your partner's picture on the map. Then describe your partner's hometown and the people in the photo. Give at least three pieces of information about the city or town and the people.

Interchange Intro Teacher's Resource Worksheets © Cambridge University Press 2017 Photocopiable

Video program overview

The *Interchange* Video Program is designed to complement the Student's Books. Each video provides further practice related to the topics, language, and vocabulary introduced in the corresponding unit of the Student's Book.

PROGRAM COMPONENTS

Video

The sixteen videos in each level's video program complement Units 1 through 16 of the corresponding Student's Book. There are a variety of genres: dramatized stories, documentaries, interviews, profiles, and travelogues.

Video Resource Book

The Video Resource Book contains the following:

- engaging **photocopiable worksheets** for students
- detailed **teaching notes** for teachers
- answer keys for the student worksheets
- complete video transcripts

TEACHING A TYPICAL VIDEO SEQUENCE

The **worksheets** and **teaching notes** for each video are organized into four sections: *Preview, Watch the video, Follow-up*, and *Language close-up*. The unit-by-unit teaching notes in the Video Resource Book give detailed suggestions for teaching each unit.

Preview

The *Preview* activities build on each other to provide students with relevant background information and key vocabulary that will assist them in better understanding the video.

Watch the video

The carefully sequenced *Watch the video* activities first help students focus on gist and then guide them in identifying important details and language. These tasks also prepare them for *Follow-up* speaking activities.

Follow-up

The *Follow-up* speaking activities encourage students to extend and personalize information by voicing their opinions or carrying out communicative tasks.

Language close-up

Students finish with the *Language closeup*, examining and practicing the particular language structures and functions presented in the video.

Introduction to the CEFR

Introduction to the Common European Framework of Reference (CEFR)

The overall aim of the Council of Europe's Common European Framework of Reference (CEFR) is to provide objective criteria for describing and assessing language proficiency in an internationally comparable manner. The Council of Europe's work on the definition of appropriate learning objectives for adult language learners dates back to the '70s. The influential Threshold series (J. A. van Ek and J. L. M. Trim, Cambridge University Press, 1991) provides a detailed description in functional, notional, grammatical, and sociocultural terms, of what a language user needs to be able to do in order to communicate effectively in the sort of situations commonly encountered in everyday life. Three levels of proficiency are identified, called Waystage, Threshold, and Vantage (roughly corresponding to Elementary, Intermediate, and Upper Intermediate).

The Threshold series was followed in 2001 by the publication of the Common European Framework of Reference, which describes six levels of communicative ability in terms of competences or "can do" statements: A1 (Breakthrough), A2 (Waystage), B1 (Threshold), B2 (Vantage), C1 (Effective Operational Proficiency), and C2 (Mastery). Based on the CEFR descriptors, the Council of Europe also developed the European Language Portfolio, a document that enables learners to assess their language ability and to keep an internationally recognized record of their language learning experience.

Interchange Fifth Edition and the Common European Framework of Reference

The table below shows how *Interchange Fifth Edition* correlates with the Council of Europe's levels and with some major international examinations.

	CEFR	Council of Europe	Cambridge ESOL	IELTS	TOEFL iBT	TOEIC
Interchange						
Level Intro	A1	Breakthrough				120+
Level 1	A2	Waystage				225+
Level 2						
	B1	Threshold	KET (Key English Test)	4.0–5.0	57–86	550+
Level 3			PET (Preliminary English Test)			
Passages						
Level 1	B2	Vantage	FCE (First Certificate in English)	5.5–6.5	87–109	785+
Level 2	C1	Effective Operational Efficiency	CAE (Certificate in Advanced English)	7.0–8.0	110–120	490+ (Listening) 445+ (Reading)

Source: http://www.cambridgeesol.org/about/standards/cefr.html

Essential teaching tips

Classroom management

Error correction

- During controlled practice accuracy activities, correct students' wrong use of the target language right away, either by correcting the error yourself or, whenever possible, having the student identify and / or correct the error. This way, the focus is on accuracy, and students can internalize the correct forms, meaning, and use of the language.
- During oral fluency activities, go around the room and take notes on errors you hear. Do not interrupt students. Instead, take notes of their errors in the use of target language and write these errors on the board. Encourage students to correct them first. Be sure to point out and praise students for language used correctly as well.

Grouping students

It is good to have students work in a variety of settings: individually, in pairs, in groups and as a class. This creates a more student-centered environment and increases student talking time.

- The easiest and quickest way to put students in pairs is to have two students sitting close to one another work together. This is good for when students need to have a quick discussion or check answers.
- To ensure students don't always work with the same partner and / or for longer activities, pair students by name, e.g., Maria work with Javier.
- One way to put students in groups is to give them a number from 1 to 4, and then have all number 1s work together, all number 2s work together, and so forth.

Instructions

- Give short instructions and model the activity for the students.
- Check your instructions, but avoid asking, Do you understand? Instead ask concept questions such as, Are you going to speak or write when you do this activity?

Monitoring

- Make sure you go around the room and check that the students are doing the activity and offer help as necessary.
- Monitor closely during controlled practice, but don't make yourself too accessible during fluency activities; otherwise, students may rely on you to answer questions rather than focus on communicating their ideas to their partner or group.

Teaching lower-level students

- Teach the Classroom Language on page xxiii and put useful language up in the classroom, so the students get used to using English.
- Don't rush. Make sure all the students have had enough time to practice the material.
- Do a lot of repetition and drilling of the new target language.
- Encourage students to practice and review target language by doing activities in the Workbook and Self-study.
- Elicit answers from your students and involve them in the learning process. Even though they are beginners, they may have a passive knowledge of English. Find out what they already know by asking them questions.
- Use the optional activities within the Teaching Notes and the Supplementary Resources Overview charts at the beginning of each unit in this Teacher's Edition to add variety to your lessons.

Teaching reading and listening

- Reading and Listening texts are meant to help the students become better readers / listeners, not to test them. Explain to your students why they need to read or listen to a text several times.
- Adapt the reading speed to the purpose of the reading. When the students read for gist, encourage them to read quickly. When students read for detail, give them more time.

Classroom Language Student questions

Unit 1 Supplementary Resources Overview

	After the following SB exercises	You can use these materials in class	Your students can use these materials outside the classroom
CYCLE 1	1 Snapshot		
	2 Conversation		**SS** Unit 1 Speaking 1–2
	3 Grammar Focus		**SB** Unit 1 Grammar plus, Focus 1 **SS** Unit 1 Grammar 1 **GAME** Sentence Runner (Past tense 1) **GAME** Say the Word (Past tense 2)
	4 Listening		
	5 Speaking	**TSS** Unit 1 Extra Worksheet	**WB** Unit 1 exercises 1–4
CYCLE 2	6 Word Power		**SS** Unit 1 Vocabulary 1–2
	7 Perspectives		
	8 Grammar Focus		**SB** Unit 1 Grammar plus, Focus 2 **SS** Unit 1 Grammar 2 **GAME** Speak or Swim (*Used to* 1) **GAME** Sentence Stacker (*Used to* 2)
	9 Pronunciation	**TSS** Unit 1 Vocabulary Worksheet **TSS** Unit 1 Grammar Worksheet **TSS** Unit 1 Listening Worksheet	
	10 Speaking		
	11 Writing	**TSS** Unit 1 Writing Worksheet	
	12 Interchange 1		
	13 Reading	**TSS** Unit 1 Project Worksheet **VID** Unit 1 **VRB** Unit 1	**SS** Unit 1 Reading 1–2 **SS** Unit 1 Listening 1–3 **SS** Unit 1 Video 1–3 **WB** Unit 1 exercises 5–10

Key **GAME:** Online Game **SB:** Student's Book **SS:** Online Self-study **TSS:** Teacher Support Site
VID: Video DVD **VRB:** Video Resource Book **WB:** Online Workbook/Workbook

My Plan for Unit 1

Use the space below to customize a plan that fits your needs.

With the following SB exercises	I am using these materials in class	My students are using these materials outside the classroom

With or instead of the following SB section	I am using these materials for assessment

1 Good memories

- Ask questions to get to know people
- Discuss childhoods

1 SNAPSHOT

MyNeighbors

Isabel Austin
Lakewood

About

Hometown: Chicago, Illinois, U.S.A.

Employer: Lancaster Medical Center

Interests: I like to go to the movies and play video games. I also enjoy meeting people and cooking for friends.

Email: isabelaustin@cambridge.org

MyNeighbors

Nicolás Rodriguez
Lakewood

About

Hometown: Buenos Aires, Argentina

Employer: Lakewood Recreation Center

Interests: I love skiing, swimming, camping – anything outdoors. Right now, I'm learning to skateboard.

Email: nico_rodriguez@cup.org

Nicolás and Isabel are neighbors. Do you think they could be friends?
What social media sites do you belong to? Which one is your favorite?
Create your own online profile and share it with your classmates. What things do you have in common?

2 CONVERSATION Where did you learn to skateboard?

A Listen and practice.

Isabel: Oh, I'm really sorry. Are you OK?
Nico: I'm fine. But I'm not very good at this.
Isabel: Neither am I . . . . Hey, I like your shirt. Are you from Argentina?
Nico: Yes, I am, originally. I was born there.
Isabel: Did you grow up there?
Nico: Yes, I did, but my family moved here 10 years ago, when I was in middle school.
Isabel: And where did you learn to skateboard?
Nico: Here in the park. I only started about a month ago.
Isabel: Well, it's my *first* time. Can you give me some lessons?
Nico: Sure. Just follow me.
Isabel: By the way, my name is Isabel.
Nico: And I'm Nico. Nice to meet you.

B Listen to the rest of the conversation. What are two more things you learn about Isabel?

1 Good memories

Cycle 1, Exercises 1–5

By the end of Cycle 1, students will be able to use past-tense questions with *did* and *was/were* to ask people about their past. By the end of Cycle 2, students will be able to discuss their childhoods using *used to*.

1 SNAPSHOT

Learning Objective: discuss social networking

- Books closed. Introduce the topic of meeting people. Ask: "Do people use the Internet to make new friends in your country? What do you think about social networking? What do you think about online friends?"
- Books open. Ss look at two examples of online profiles of two neighbors. Ask: "What kind of information did these people include?" (Answer: basic information like location, hometown, work, likes and interests, and contact information)
- ***Option:*** Ss work in pairs. Student A reads the information on the left, and Student B reads the information on the right. Then partners exchange information about the people.
- Ss work in pairs or groups to discuss the questions. Go around the class and give help as needed.
- If necessary, review the structures "they both . . ." and "so does (s)he."
- ***Option:*** The third task, creating an online profile, could be assigned as homework or turned into a project.
- Ss compare their profiles with classmates. They discuss what they have in common.

2 CONVERSATION

Learning Objective: use the simple past in a conversation between two people meeting for the first time

A *[CD 1, Track 1]*

TIP
To help focus Ss' attention on the picture rather than the text, ask them to bring a small card (such as an index card) to class. Ss then use the card to cover the text.

- Ss cover the text with a card and look at the picture. Ask them to guess some information (e.g., "Where are these people? What are they doing? What has just happened? Do they know each other?"). Don't give the answers yet.
- Play the audio program. Ss listen and check their predictions. (Answer: Two strangers were skating in the park and crashed into each other.)
- Ask Ss to listen for three facts about Nico's background. Play the audio program again. Ss listen and take notes.
- Check Ss' answers. (Answers: He's from Argentina. He was born and grew up there. His family moved ten years ago, when he was in middle school.)
- Point out how Nico gives additional information (e.g., *Yes, I am, . . . I was born . . . Yes, I did, but . . .*). Tell Ss they will practice this.

  Play the audio program again. Ss listen and read silently. Go over any vocabulary that they find difficult.
- Ss practice the conversation in pairs. Go around the class and encourage Ss to be enthusiastic and to have fun.

! For more practice exchanging personal information, try ***Say It with Feeling!*** – download it from the website. Ss use gestures and emotions here, such as surprise when bumping into each other, hand gestures when saying "Here in the park," and a handshake when introducing themselves.

TIP
If time is an issue, ask only one or two pairs to act out the conversation.

B *[CD 1, Track 2]*

- Read the instructions and the question. Tell Ss not to worry about understanding every word. Then play the rest of the audio program. Ss listen to find the answers.

  (Note: Because *Interchange Fifth Edition* Student's Book 2 contains longer listening materials than Student's Book 1, the audio scripts appear at the back of this Teacher's Edition.)

Audio script

See page T-168.

Answer

Isabel works in a hospital. She's a computer specialist.

3 GRAMMAR FOCUS

Learning Objective: use *was/were* and *did* to ask and answer questions

[CD 1, Track 3]

Past tense questions

- Books closed. Write these questions on the board. Ask Ss to complete them:

  1. Where _______________ you born?
  2. When _______________ you move to Los Angeles?
- Focus Ss' attention on the Grammar Focus box. Then ask them to check their answers.
- Ask: "What is the difference between the left and right columns?" (Answer: Left column contains questions with *be;* right column contains questions with *did.*)
- Point out that we say "to *be* born" (not "to born") and "to die" (not "to be died").
- Elicit the rule for the two types of questions:

  To be: Wh- + ***was/were*** + subject + (rest)?
  Other verbs: Wh- + ***did*** + subject + verb + (rest)?
- Books open. Focus Ss' attention on the Grammar Focus box. Play the audio program to present the questions and statements.
- ***Option:*** Play the audio program again. Divide the class into two groups: One group repeats the questions, and the other repeats the responses. For additional practice, Ss switch roles.

A

- Read the instructions and model the task with the first question. Ss complete the exercise individually and then go over answers in pairs.
- Elicit Ss' responses to check answers.

Answers

1. A: Your English is very good. When **did** you begin to study English?
   B: I **began/started** in middle school.
   A: What **did** you think of English class at first?
   B: I **thought** it was a little difficult, but fun.
2. A: Where **were** you born?
   B: I **was** born in Mexico.
   A: **Did** you grow up there?
   B: No, I **didn't**. I **grew** up in Canada.
3. A: Where **did** you meet your best friend?
   B: We **met** in high school.
   A: Do you still see each other?
   B: Yes, but not very often. She **moved** to South Korea two years ago.
4. A: **Did** you have a favorite teacher when you **were** a child?
   B: Yes, I **did**. I **had** a very good teacher named Mr. Potter.
   A: What **did** he teach?
   B: He **taught** math.

- Ss practice the conversations in pairs. Then they switch roles and practice again.

! For another way to practice this conversation, try ***Look Up and Speak!*** – download it from the website.

B *Pair work*

- Read the instructions. Model the task with one or two Ss by asking them these questions in part A: "Where were you born? Did you grow up there?"
- Ss work in pairs to take turns asking the questions and responding with their own information.
- Go around the class and give help as needed. Note any common grammatical problems. After pairs finish, go over the errors you noticed.

4 LISTENING

Learning Objective: listen for details in interviews with immigrants

A *[CD 1, Track 4]*

- As a topic warm-up, ask Ss questions about immigrants (e.g., "Are there many immigrants where you live? Where are they from? What do you think they miss? What do you think they find difficult?").
- Set the scene. Ss are going to hear interviews with two immigrants. Play the audio program. Ss listen to find out why they moved to the U.S.A. (Answer: 1. Enrique: to study business; Jessica: to go to high school and improve her English)

Audio script

See page T-168.

B *[CD 1, Track 5]*

- Present the questions in the chart. Point out that Ss need to write only key words and phrases, not full sentences. Play the audio program again. Ss listen and complete the chart.
- After Ss compare answers in pairs, check answers by asking some Ss to write their responses on the board.

Answers

	Enrique	Jessica
1.	not spending time with family	the school system
2.	food	family and the music

C *Group work*

- Divide Ss into groups so they can answer the question orally. Have one S from each group present the answers to the class.

3 GRAMMAR FOCUS

Past tense

Where **were** you born?	When **did** you **move** to Los Angeles?
I **was** born in Argentina.	I **moved** here 10 years ago. I **didn't speak** English.
Were you born in Buenos Aires?	**Did** you **take** English classes in Argentina?
Yes, I **was**.	Yes, I **did**. I **took** classes for a year.
No, I **wasn't**. I **was** born in Córdoba.	No, I **didn't**. My aunt **taught** me at home.

GRAMMAR PLUS *see page 132*

A Complete these conversations. Then practice with a partner.

1. **A:** Your English is very good. When ______________ you begin to study English?
   B: I ______________ in middle school.
   A: What ______________ you think of English class at first?
   B: I ______________ it was a little difficult, but fun.
2. **A:** Where ______________ you born?
   B: I ______________ born in Mexico.
   A: ______________ you grow up there?
   B: No, I ______________. I ______________ up in Canada.
3. **A:** Where ______________ you meet your best friend?
   B: We ______________ in high school.
   A: Do you still see each other?
   B: Yes, but not very often. She ______________ to South Korea two years ago.
4. **A:** ______________ you have a favorite teacher when you ______________ a child?
   B: Yes, I ______________. I ______________ a very good teacher named Mr. Potter.
   A: What ______________ he teach?
   B: He ______________ math.

B **PAIR WORK** Take turns asking the questions in part A. Give your own information when answering.

4 LISTENING Why did you move?

A Listen to interviews with two immigrants to the United States. Why did they move to the U.S.A.?

B Listen again and complete the chart.

	Enrique	Jessica
1. What were the most difficult changes?		
2. What do they miss the most?		

C **GROUP WORK** Enrique and Jessica talk about difficult changes. What could be some positive things about moving to a city like New York?

5 SPEAKING Tell me about yourself.

A PAIR WORK Check (✓) six questions below and add your own questions. Then interview a classmate you don't know very well. Ask follow-up questions.

- ☐ Where were your grandparents born?
- ☐ Where did they grow up?
- ☐ Did you see them a lot when you were young?
- ☐ Who's your favorite relative?
- ☐ ________________

- ☐ When did you first study English?
- ☐ Can you speak other languages?
- ☐ What were your best subjects in middle school?
- ☐ What subjects didn't you like?
- ☐ ________________

A: Where were your grandparents born?
B: My grandfather was born in Brazil, but my grandmother was born in Colombia.
A: Really? Where did they first meet?

useful expressions

Oh, that's interesting.
Really? Me, too!
Wow! Tell me more.

B GROUP WORK Tell the group what you learned about your partner. Then answer any questions.

"Vera's grandfather was born in Brazil, but her grandmother was born in . . ."

6 WORD POWER

A Complete the word map. Add two more words of your own to each category. Then compare with a partner.

- ✓ amusement park
- beach
- cat
- collect comic books
- fish
- play video games
- playground
- stickers
- teddy bear
- toy cars
- turtle
- watch cartoons

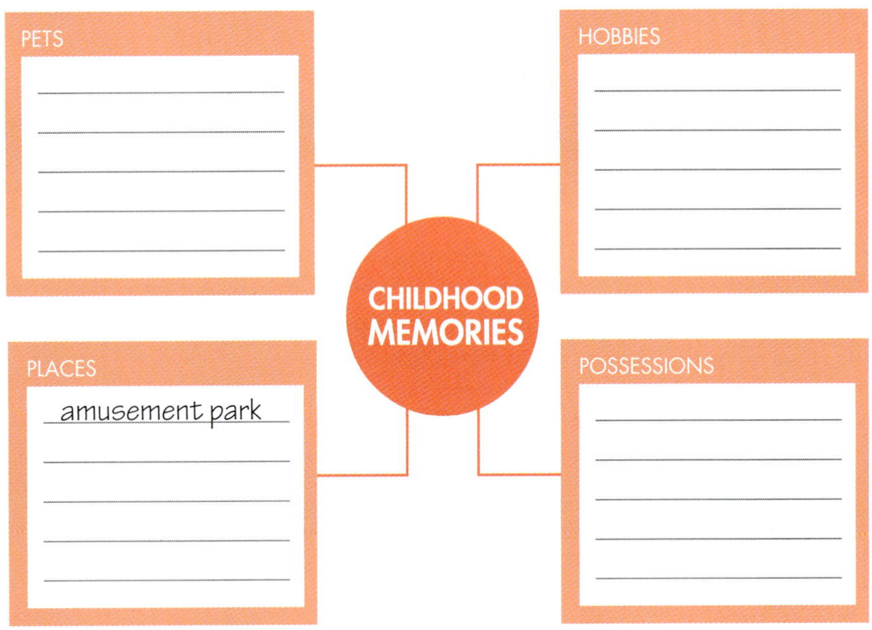

B PAIR WORK Choose three words from the word map and use them to describe some of your childhood memories.

A: I loved to watch cartoons when I was a kid.
B: Me, too. What was your favorite?
A: I liked anything with superheroes in it. What about you?

5 SPEAKING

Learning Objectives: discuss past experiences using questions with *was/were* and *did*; ask follow-up questions; give additional information

A *Pair work*

- Have Ss silently read the instructions and questions. Then let them choose six questions to ask a classmate.
- Model the task with a S.

  T: Hi, my name's ______________.
  S: Hello. I'm ______________. Nice to meet you.
  T: Nice to meet you, too. So, where were your grandparents born?
  S: My grandfather was born in Brazil, but my grandmother was born in Colombia.
- Ss work in pairs, preferably with a partner they don't know very well. Remind Ss to ask follow-up questions and give additional information. Point out the *useful expressions* box.
- While Ss are interviewing each other, go around the class and give help as needed.

! For a new way to practice exchanging personal information, try the ***Onion Ring*** – download it from the website.

B *Group work*

- Read the instructions and the example sentence. Have Ss form groups.
- Have Ss take turns telling the group three interesting things they learned about their partner and answering any questions.
- ***Option:*** Ss introduce their partner from part A to the class.

End of Cycle 1

See the Supplementary Resources chart at the beginning of this unit for additional teaching materials and student activities related to this Cycle.

Cycle 2, Exercises 6–13

6 WORD POWER

Learning Objective: use vocabulary for discussing childhood memories

A

- Read the instructions and focus Ss' attention on the word map. Then ask Ss to look at the vocabulary list and help them with the first word. Ask: "Is *beach* an example of a pet, hobby, place, or possession?" (Answer: place)
- Ss complete the word map individually. Remind them to add two more words to each category. Let them use their dictionaries if they want.
- Elicit answers from the class. Write additional words on the board and encourage Ss to add them to their own maps. Explain the meaning and pronunciation of any new vocabulary.

Answers

Pets	**Hobbies**
cat	collect comic books
fish	play video games
turtle	watch cartoons
Places	**Possessions**
amusement park	stickers
beach	teddy bear
playground	toy cars

B *Pair work*

- Go over the task and the example conversation.
- Model the task with one or two Ss.
- After Ss choose three words from the word map, have them form pairs and take turns talking about some of their childhood memories. Go around the class and give help as needed.
- ***Option:*** If possible, have Ss bring photos or mementos from their childhood to share with the class.

For more practice with childhood vocabulary and past tense verbs, play the ***Chain Game*** – download it from the website. Start like this:

S1: Many years ago, I collected comic books.
S2: Many years ago, S1 collected comic books and I had a cat.

7 PERSPECTIVES

Learning Objectives: discuss childhood habits; identify *used to* in context

TIP
The objective of the Perspectives section is to show Ss how a new structure is used. Don't expect them to produce the new language until it is presented in the Grammar Focus section.

A *[CD 1, Track 6]*

- Books closed. Write this sentence on the board:

  When I was a kid, I never used to play sports, but now I like to keep fit.

- Explain that *used to* refers to something that you regularly did in the past but do not do anymore.
- Elicit examples of activities that Ss regularly did in the past but don't do anymore (e.g., *be afraid of the dark, talk in class, play with dolls*).
- Books open. Explain the task. Ss silently read the statements and check (✓) those that are true for them.
- Go around the class and give help as needed. Explain any new vocabulary.

Vocabulary
fit: in good health; in shape
messy: untidy; not neat

- Play the audio program. Ss listen and raise their hand every time they hear a statement that is true about them. Find out which changes are most common in their lives.
- ***Option:*** Have Ss study some of the verbs and their collocations (e.g., *keep fit, follow politics, care about appearance*).

B *Pair work*

- Read the instructions and the example sentences. Ss work in pairs to discuss the changes. Point out that there are no right or wrong answers.

8 GRAMMAR FOCUS

Learning Objective: form questions, statements, negatives, and short answers with *used to*

[CD 1, Track 7]

- Focus Ss' attention on the statements in the Perspectives section. Check that they understand the meaning of *used to*. If helpful, point out that *used to* refers to an activity that takes place over an extended period of time. We can't say, "I used to go to the movies last Saturday."
- Have Ss find some examples in the Perspectives section of affirmative statements with *used to* (Answers: 2, 6, 7), and negative statements with *used to* (Answers: 1, 3, 4, 5). Then elicit the rules for forming affirmative and negative structures with *used to*:

  Affirmative: subject + *used to* + verb + (rest)
  I used to be (neat and organized . . .)

  Negative: subject + *didn't* + *use to* + verb + (rest)
  I didn't use to collect . . .

- Point out that while *never* is used in negative statements, it follows the rule for the affirmative structure.

  subject + *never* + *used to* + verb + (rest)
  I never used to play . . .

- Play the audio program. Ss listen and silently read the Grammar Focus box. Then point out how questions are formed (*did* + *use to*), and elicit examples from the class.

A

- Read the instructions and model the task with the first question. Have Ss complete the exercise individually and then go over answers in pairs.

Answers

1. Did . . . use to; used to
2. Did . . . use to; didn't use to; used to
3. did . . . use to; used to
4. did . . . use to; didn't use to

TIP
To encourage Ss to use English as they work in pairs, have them look at the Classroom Language on page v. If possible, write the phrases on posters and display them on the classroom walls.

B

- Explain the task. Ss first work individually to write four sentences about themselves with *used to*. Then Ss work in pairs, taking turns reading their sentences to each other.
- Encourage pairs to correct each other's sentences as needed. Tell Ss they will practice their sentences again in Exercise 9, part B.
- ***Option:*** Read some sentences written by Ss. Ask the class to guess who wrote the sentences.

For more practice with new vocabulary and *used to*, play ***Mime*** – download it from the website. Ss act out statements from the Perspectives section or make up their own.

7 PERSPECTIVES When I was a kid . . .

A Listen to these statements about changes. Check (✓) those that are true about you.

☐ **1.** "When I was a kid, I never used to play sports, but now I like to keep fit."
☐ **2.** "I used to go out with friends a lot, but now I don't have any free time."
☐ **3.** "When I was younger, I didn't use to collect anything, but now I do."
☐ **4.** "I didn't use to be a good student, but now I love to study and learn new things."
☐ **5.** "I never used to follow politics, but now I read the news online every morning."
☐ **6.** "I used to be really neat and organized, but now I'm very messy."
☐ **7.** "I used to care a lot about my appearance. Now, I'm too busy to care about how I look."

B **PAIR WORK** Look at the statements again. Which changes are positive? Which are negative?

"I think the first one is a positive change. It's good to exercise."

8 GRAMMAR FOCUS

Used to

***Used to* refers to something that you regularly did in the past but don't do anymore.**

Did you **use to** collect things?
Yes, I **used to** collect comic books.
No, I **didn't use to** collect anything, but now I collect old records.

What sports **did** you **use to** play?
I **used to play** baseball and volleyball.
I **never used to** play sports, but now I play tennis.

GRAMMAR PLUS *see page 132*

A Complete these questions and answers. Then compare with a partner.

1. **A:** ___Did___ you ___use to___ have any pets when you were a kid?
   B: Yes, I ______________ have a white cat named Snowball.
2. **A:** ______________ you and your classmates ______________ play together after school?
   B: No, we ______________ play during the week. We ______________ study a lot.
3. **A:** What music ______________ you ______________ listen to?
   B: I ______________ listen to rock a lot. Actually, I still do.
4. **A:** What hobbies ______________ you ______________ have when you were little?
   B: I ______________ have any hobbies, but now I play chess every week.

B How have you changed? Write sentences about yourself using *used to* or *didn't use to*. Then compare with a partner. Who has changed the most?

your hairstyle
your hobbies
your taste in music
the way you dress

I used to wear my hair much longer.
I didn't use to have a beard.

9 PRONUNCIATION *Used to*

A Listen and practice. Notice that the pronunciation of ***used to*** and ***use to*** is the same.

When I was a child, I **used to** play the guitar.
I **used to** have a nickname.
I didn't **use to** like scary movies.
I didn't **use to** study very hard at school.

B **PAIR WORK** Practice the sentences you wrote in Exercise 8, part B. Pay attention to the pronunciation of ***used to*** and ***use to***.

10 SPEAKING Memories

A **PAIR WORK** Add three questions to this list. Then take turns asking and answering the questions. Ask follow-up questions.

1. What's your favorite childhood memory?
2. What sports or games did you use to play when you were younger?
3. Did you use to have a nickname?
4. Where did you use to spend your vacations?
5. Is your taste in food different now?
6. ______________________________
7. ______________________________
8. ______________________________

B **CLASS ACTIVITY** Tell the class two interesting things about your partner.

11 WRITING We used to have a lot of fun.

A Write a paragraph about things you used to do as a child. Use some of your ideas from Exercise 10.

> I grew up in a small town, and my friends and I used to play outside a lot. We used to play all kinds of games. My favorite was hide-and-seek. We also used to ride our bikes to a beautiful lake near our school . . .

B **GROUP WORK** Share your paragraphs and answer any questions.
Did you and your classmates use to do the same things?
Do kids today do the same things you used to do?

12 INTERCHANGE 1 We have a lot in common.

Find out more about your classmates. Go to Interchange 1 on page 114.

9 PRONUNCIATION

Learning Objective: sound more natural when pronouncing *used to* and *use to*

A *[CD 1, Track 8]*

- Play the audio program. Point out the reduction of *used to* /juːs·tu/: The *d* in *used* is silent, so the pronunciation of *used to* and *use to* is the same. *To* sounds like "tuh."
- Play the audio program again. This time, have Ss listen and repeat each sentence using the reduced pronunciation of *used to*.

B *Pair work*

- Explain the task. Focus Ss' attention on their sentences from Exercise 8B. Ss work in pairs, taking turns reading the sentences and paying close attention to the pronunciation of *used to*. Have them work with a different partner from the one they had in Exercise 8B.
- Go around the class and listen to Ss' pronunciation. If they are having any difficulty, model the correct reduced sounds again.
- ***Option:*** For more practice, have Ss pronounce the statements from Exercise 7.

10 SPEAKING

Learning Objective: discuss childhood memories

A *Pair work*

- Explain the task. Ss write three more questions to ask each other. Tell them that they may work individually or in pairs on this initial task.
- Pairs take turns asking and answering the questions. If Ss feel a question is too personal, tell them to make up an answer or to say "I'm sorry, but I'd rather not answer that."

B *Class activity*

- Ss take turns telling the class two interesting things they learned about their partner.

For more speaking practice, play ***Just One Minute*** – download it from the website.

11 WRITING

Learning Objective: write a paragraph about childhood with *used to*
(Note: Writing exercises can be done in class or assigned as homework.)

A

- Have Ss silently read the example paragraph. Elicit some topics that Ss may wish to include in their own paragraphs (e.g., *family, houses, games, and hobbies*). Write the topics on the board.
- Tell the class to use their questions, notes, and ideas from Exercise 10 as additional topics (e.g., *sports* and *vacations*). Add these to the list on the board.
- Explain the task. Ss write a draft paragraph about their childhood. Encourage them to start by brainstorming ideas for each topic they choose to include. Then they should use that information to write a first draft.
- While Ss are writing their first drafts, go around the class and give individual feedback on the content and organization of each one's draft. Alternatively, have them work in pairs to give each other comments on what is good and what could be improved. Have Ss revise their paragraphs in class or as homework.

! For another way to help Ss plan their paragraphs, try ***Mind Mapping*** – download it from the website.

B *Group work*

- Read the instructions. Ss take turns reading their paragraphs in groups and answering any questions. Ss talk about what they have in common.
- ***Option:*** Collect the paragraphs and give Ss written comments. You could also post their paragraphs on a wall or bulletin board for others to read.
- ***Option:*** Turn this into a project. Have Ss include photos of their childhood, write poems or songs, or find out what else happened the year they were born.

12 INTERCHANGE 1

See page T-114 for teaching notes.

13 READING

Learning Objectives: scan a biographical article for key facts; identify meaning from context

A

- Books closed. Ask Ss to work in pairs to brainstorm what they know about the artist Frida Kahlo.

To help activate Ss' schema, play ***Prediction Bingo*** – download it from the website.

- Books open. Focus Ss' attention on the title of the reading. Ask: "What do you think a life in paintings means?" (Possible answer: Her paintings tell her life's story.)
- Ss scan the text quickly, ignoring words they don't know. They should simply look for the answers to the questions. (Answers: Kahlo was from Mexico. She was involved in a bus accident when she was eighteen. She married Mexican painter Diego Rivera.)

TIP
To encourage Ss to read quickly and focus on the task, give them a time limit.

B

- Ss read the article individually. Tell them not to use their dictionaries. Instead, encourage them to circle or highlight any words they can't guess from the context of the article.
- Explain the task. Ss find each word in the text and guess its meaning from context. Go over answers with the class.

Answers

1. a. courage	4. d. cast
2. f. tragedy	5. b. recognize
3. e. destiny	6. c. injury

- Elicit or explain any new vocabulary.

Vocabulary
illness: a disease or sickness
take up: start to do
body cast: a hard protector for the whole body after you break many bones
self-portrait: a painting an artist makes of him/herself
achievement: success
eyebrow: the strip of hair growing above a person's eye

C

- Explain the task and Ss work individually to answer the questions. Go around the class and give help as needed.
- Check answers as a class.

Answers

1. She played soccer and took up boxing. (She exercised.)
2. She started painting to entertain herself during her illness.
3. Because she was often alone and she knew herself very well.
4. Kahlo compared her marriage to the bus accident.
5. She couldn't have children because of the bus accident and her bad health.
6. She wore traditional Mexican clothes and had a traditional braided hairstyle. She had thick eyebrows.

- ***Option:*** Have Ss write a time line of Frida's life from the information given. (Possible answer: She was born in 1907, had polio in 1913, had an accident in 1925, got married in 1929, she died in 1954).

D *Group work*

- Ss discuss Frida's life. Encourage Ss to ask follow-up questions.
- ***Option:*** Ask Ss to think about other artists who are considered different from what society expects.

For more practice with past tense questions, play ***Twenty Questions*** – download it from the website. Have Ss use famous people to play the game.

Possible answers

Kahlo did sports that most girls didn't do. She had a career as a painter despite her illness. She didn't remove hair from her face like other women did.

End of Cycle 2

See the Supplementary Resources chart at the beginning of this unit for additional teaching materials and student activities related to this Cycle.

13 READING

A Scan the article. Where was Kahlo from? What happened when she was 18? Who did she marry?

A Life in Paintings: The Frida Kahlo Story

Mexican painter Frida Kahlo (1907–1954) was both a talented artist and a woman of great courage. Her paintings tell an amazing story of tragedy and hope.

At the age of six, Kahlo developed polio, and she spent nine months in bed. The illness damaged her right leg forever. Most girls didn't use to play sports back then, but Kahlo played soccer and took up boxing. Exercising helped Kahlo get stronger. Kahlo even dreamed of becoming a doctor one day.

At 18, Kahlo was in a terrible bus crash, and her destiny changed. She wore a full body cast for months because her injuries were so bad. But again, Kahlo refused to give up. She entertained herself by painting self-portraits. She said, "I paint myself because I'm often alone, and because I am the subject I know best."

Kahlo suffered from very bad health the rest of her life, but she continued to paint. Other artists began to recognize her talent – an unusual achievement for a woman at the time. In 1929, she married famous Mexican painter Diego Rivera, but their marriage was troubled. Kahlo once said, "There have been two great accidents in my life . . . Diego was by far the worst."

Kahlo became pregnant three times. Unfortunately, because of her injuries from the bus accident and her generally poor health, none of her babies survived childbirth. This sadness almost destroyed Kahlo. Her paintings often show a broken woman, both in heart and body.

When she traveled, Kahlo always attracted attention. She dressed in long traditional Mexican skirts, wore her hair in long braids, and let her thick eyebrows grow naturally. She chose to look different, and people noticed her beauty everywhere she went.

Kahlo died at the age of 47 in the house where she was born. Her life was short, but extraordinary. Her paintings still amaze people with their honesty and originality.

B Read the article. Then circle the following words in the article and match them to the definitions below.

1. courage ______
2. tragedy ______
3. destiny ______
4. cast ______
5. recognize ______
6. injury ______

a. ability to control your fear in a difficult situation
b. accept that something is good or valuable
c. damage to a person's body
d. a special hard case that protects a broken bone
e. the things that will happen in the future
f. very sad event or situation

C Answer the questions.

1. What did Kahlo do to get healthier after her childhood illness?
2. Why did Kahlo start painting?
3. Why did Kahlo often do self-portraits?
4. What did Kahlo compare her marriage to?
5. Why couldn't Kahlo have children?
6. What was unusual about Kahlo's appearance?

D **GROUP WORK** What was unusual about Kahlo's life? When do you think it's good to be different from what people expect?

Unit 2 Supplementary Resources Overview

	After the following SB exercises	You can use these materials in class	Your students can use these materials outside the classroom
CYCLE 1	1 Word Power	**TSS** Unit 2 Vocabulary Worksheet **TSS** Unit 2 Extra Worksheet	**SS** Unit 2 Vocabulary 1–2 **GAME** Spell or Slime (Compound nouns)
	2 Perspectives		
	3 Grammar Focus		**SB** Unit 2 Grammar plus, Focus 1 **SS** Unit 2 Grammar 1 **GAME** Say the Word (Expressions of quantity 1) **GAME** Sentence Stacker (Expressions of quantity 2)
	4 Listening	**TSS** Unit 2 Listening Worksheet	
	5 Discussion		
	6 Writing	**TSS** Unit 2 Writing Worksheet	**WB** Unit 2 exercises 1–4
CYCLE 2	7 Snapshot		
	8 Conversation		**SS** Unit 2 Speaking 1–2
	9 Grammar Focus	**TSS** Unit 2 Grammar Worksheet	**SB** Unit 2 Grammar plus, Focus 2 **SS** Unit 2 Grammar 2 **GAME** Sentence Runner (Indirect questions from Wh-questions)
	10 Pronunciation		
	11 Speaking		
	12 Interchange 2		
	13 Reading	**TSS** Unit 2 Project Worksheet **VID** Unit 2 **VRB** Unit 2	**SS** Unit 2 Reading 1–2 **SS** Unit 2 Listening 1–3 **SS** Unit 2 Video 1–3 **WB** Unit 2 exercises 5–8

With or instead of the following SB section	You can also use these materials for assessment
Units 1–2 Progress Check	**ASSESSMENT PROGRAM** Units 1–2 Oral Quiz **ASSESSMENT PROGRAM** Units 1–2 Written Quiz

Key **GAME:** Online Game **SB:** Student's Book **SS:** Online Self-study **TSS:** Teacher Support Site
VID: Video DVD **VRB:** Video Resource Book **WB:** Online Workbook/Workbook

My Plan for Unit 2

Use the space below to customize a plan that fits your needs.

With the following SB exercises	I am using these materials in class	My students are using these materials outside the classroom

With or instead of the following SB section	I am using these materials for assessment

2 Life in the city

- Discuss transportation and public services
- Ask questions about visiting cities

1 WORD POWER Compound nouns

A Match the words in columns A and B to make compound nouns. (More than one combination may be possible.)

subway + station = subway station

A	B
bicycle	center
bus	garage
green	jam
parking	lane
recycling	light
street	space
subway	stand
taxi	station
traffic	stop
train	system

traffic jam

green space

B **PAIR WORK** Which of these things can you find where you live?

A: There are a lot of bus lanes. **B:** Yes. But there isn't a subway system.

2 PERSPECTIVES City services

A Listen to these opinions about city services. Match them to the correct pictures.

a

b

c

YOUR VOICE COUNTS!

_____ 1. The streets are dark and dangerous. I don't think there are enough police officers. And we need more streetlights.

_____ 2. There's too much pollution from cars, motorcycles, and old buses. In cities with less pollution, people are healthier.

_____ 3. There should be fewer cars, but I think that the biggest problem is parking. There just isn't enough parking.

B **PAIR WORK** Does your city or town have similar problems? What do you think is the biggest problem?

2 Life in the city

Cycle 1, Exercises 1–6

In Unit 2, students discuss city life. By the end of Cycle 1, students will be able to discuss city issues and public services using expressions of quantity and compound nouns. By the end of Cycle 2, students will be able to ask indirect questions.

1 WORD POWER

Learning Objective: use compound nouns to discuss transportation

- ***Option:*** To introduce the topic of this cycle (transportation and other public services in a city), ask: "How many hours do you spend traveling each day? How do you get around the city? Do you ever get stuck in traffic? What do you do to stay calm?"

A

- Ask Ss: "What do we call a police officer who is a man? What do we call the car he drives? What do we call his dog?" (Answers: a policeman, a police car, a police dog)
- Write these words on the board and explain that they are compound nouns, or nouns that consist of two or more words. Point out that some compound nouns are written as one word and others are written as two separate words.
- Use the example answer to model the task. Help Ss make a compound noun using the first word in column A (*bicycle*). Point out that more than one combination is sometimes possible.
- Ss work individually or in pairs to complete the task before looking in a dictionary.
- Elicit answers and ask Ss to write them on the board.

Answers

bicycle: bicycle lane, bicycle stand
bus: bus lane, bus station, bus stop, bus system
green: green space
parking: parking garage, parking space
recycling: recycling center, recycling system
street: streetlight
subway: subway station, subway stop, subway system
taxi: taxi lane, taxi stand
traffic: traffic jam, traffic light
train: train station, train stop, train system

TIP
Encourage Ss to keep a vocabulary notebook.

B *Pair work*

- Ss work in pairs to discuss which things in part A can be found where they live. Go around the class and give help as needed.

TIP
To help Ss remember the new vocabulary, make a vocabulary box. Ask them to write the new words on slips of paper and put the slips into a shoebox or container. Review a few of these words during each class. Write a check (✓) on the slip if Ss are able to recall the word. When a slip has three checkmarks, remove it from the box.

To review the new vocabulary, play ***Picture It!*** – download it from the website.

2 PERSPECTIVES

Learning Objective: identify expressions of quantity in context

A *[CD 1, Track 9]*

- Books closed. Write these questions on the board:
  A. Which speaker says the biggest problem is parking?
  B. Which speaker says the streets are dark and dangerous?
  C. Which speaker says there is too much pollution?
- Play the audio program. Ss listen and decide which speaker made each statement. (Answers: A. 3, B. 1, C. 2)
- Books open. Have Ss look at the comments made by each speaker and match each opinion to the correct picture. (Answers: 1. c, 2. a, 3. b)
- Explain that *too much* means "more than we want." Ask: "Which things do the speakers think there are *too much* of?" (Answer: pollution, cars) Then ask: "What things do the speakers think there are *not enough* of?" (Answers: police officers, streetlights, parking)

For another way to teach this Perspectives, try ***Running Dictation*** – download it from the website.

B *Pair work*

- Explain the task. Ss work in pairs to decide on the biggest problem. Then elicit answers from the class.
- ***Option:*** Prepare some pictures about city issues to bring to class. Ask Ss to identify the problem and suggest a possible solution.

3 GRAMMAR FOCUS

Learning Objective: use expressions of quantity with count and noncount nouns

[CD 1, Track 10]

Count/noncount nouns

- Elicit or explain the differences between count and noncount nouns:

  Count nouns have a plural form – usually with *-s* – because they are considered separate and countable things (e.g., *a car, two cars*).
  Noncount nouns do not have a plural form because they are impossible to separate and count (e.g., *traffic*, but not *one traffic, two traffics*).

- Draw two columns on the board with the headings: *Count nouns* and *Noncount nouns*. Ask Ss to find examples of each in the Perspectives section. Then elicit answers and write them on the board.

For more practice with count and noncount nouns, play ***Run for It!*** – download it from the website. Prepare a list of sentences with missing nouns. Then write each missing noun on a sign and post the signs on the classroom walls.

Too much/many; less/fewer

- Write this on the board:

  Count nouns: there are + too many/few, fewer
  Noncount nouns: there is + too much/little, less

- ***Option:*** Do a quick substitution drill. Ask Ss to use information about their city.

  T: Streetlights.
  S1: There are too few streetlights.
  T: Pollution.
  S2: There is too much pollution.

- Point out the first two sentences in the Grammar Focus box. Elicit sentences that mean the same:

  There are too many cars. (Answer: There should be fewer cars.)
  There is too much pollution. (Answer: There should be less pollution.)

- ***Option:*** Ask Ss to change the other sentences so that they mean the same.

More/(not) enough

- Ss read the *more/(not) enough* examples in the Grammar Focus box. Answer any questions they have.
- Play the audio program to present the information.

A

- Read the instructions and model the task with the first two sentences. Ss work individually and then compare answers in pairs. Elicit answers.

Answers

1. We need **more** public schools.
2. There are **too many** accidents.
3. There are**n't enough/too few** public parks.
4. There is **too much** noise all the time.
5. There is**n't enough/too little** recycling in our city.
6. The government should build **more/less** affordable housing.
7. The city needs **more/fewer** bicycle lanes.
8. There are**n't enough/too few** free Wi-Fi hotspots.

B *Pair work*

- Read the instructions and elicit some answers for the first item. Ss work in pairs to write sentences. Ss will use their sentences again in Exercise 6B.

4 LISTENING

Learning Objective: listen for details in a passage about traffic problems

A *[CD 1, Track 11]*

- Books closed. Ask: "What are some problems people normally have in a big city?" Elicit responses.
- Set the scene. Two neighbors are talking about some problems their city has. Play the audio program. Ss listen and mark statements true or false.

Audio script

See page T-168.

Answers

1. False 2. True 3. False 4. False 5. True

B *[CD 1, Track 12]*

- Read the instructions and draw Ss' attention to the model answer for statement 1. Play the audio program again. Ss listen and correct statements 3 and 4 in the chart. Go over answers with the class.

Possible answers

1. He starts his new job tomorrow.
3. In summer, there are too many tourists.
4. People ride their bikes a lot.

C *Pair work*

- Have Ss discuss possible solutions. Help students having difficulty. Ask Ss to tell the class about what they discussed.

3 GRAMMAR FOCUS

Expressions of quantity

With count nouns	With noncount nouns
There are **too many** cars.	There is **too much** pollution.
There should be **fewer** cars.	There should be **less** pollution.
We need **more** streetlights.	We need **more** public transportation.
There aren't **enough** police officers.	There isn't **enough** parking.

GRAMMAR PLUS *see page 133*

A Complete these statements about city problems. Then compare with a partner. (More than one answer may be possible.)

1. We need ______________ public schools.
2. There are ______________ accidents.
3. There are ______________ public parks.
4. There is ______________ noise all the time.
5. There is ______________ recycling in our city.
6. The government should build ______________ affordable housing.
7. The city needs ______________ bicycle lanes.
8. There are ______________ free Wi-Fi hotspots.

B **PAIR WORK** Write sentences about the city or town you are living in. Then compare with another pair.

1. The city should provide more . . .
2. We have too many . . .
3. There's too much . . .
4. There isn't enough . . .
5. There should be fewer . . .
6. We don't have enough . . .
7. There should be less . . .
8. We need more . . .

4 LISTENING It'll take forever.

A Listen to a city resident talk to her new neighbor about the city. Check (✓) True or False for each statement.

	True	False	
1. Jacob already started his new job downtown.	☐	☑	*He starts his new job tomorrow.*
2. The city needs more buses.	☐	☐	
3. There aren't enough tourists in the city.	☐	☐	
4. Not many people ride bikes in the city.	☐	☐	
5. Sophia offers to lend Jacob her bike.	☐	☐	

B Listen again. For the false statements, write the correct information.

C **PAIR WORK** What things can a city do to improve the problems that Sophia mentions? Does your city have similar problems?

5 DISCUSSION Rate your city.

A GROUP WORK Which of these services are available in your city or town? Discuss what is good and bad about each one.

_____ recycling system	_____ parks and green spaces	_____ affordable housing
_____ transportation system	_____ Wi-Fi service	_____ recreational and sports facilities

B GROUP WORK How would you rate the services where you live? Give each item a rating from 1 to 5.

1 = terrible 2 = needs improvement 3 = average 4 = good 5 = excellent

A: I'd give the parks a 4. There are enough parks, but they aren't always clean.

B: I think a rating of 4 is too high. There aren't enough green spaces in many areas of the city . . .

6 WRITING A social media post

A Read this post about traffic in the city on a social networking page.

B Use your statements from Exercise 3, part B, and any new ideas to write a post about a local issue.

C GROUP WORK Take turns reading your messages. Do you have any of the same concerns?

Posted by Michelle K
Today at 5:30

I'm tired of this city. There's too much traffic, and it's getting worse. It used to take me 15 minutes to get to class. Today it took me more than 30 minutes during rush hour! There should be more subway lines. I think people want to use public transportation, but we need more . . .

comment

7 SNAPSHOT

Common Tourist Questions

- ☐ What's the best way to see the city?
- ☐ How much do taxis cost?
- ☐ Which hotel is closest to the airport?
- ☐ Where should I go shopping?
- ☐ What festivals or events are taking place?
- ☐ Where can I buy a SIM card for my phone?
- ☐ Where's a good place to meet friends?
- ☐ Where can I get a city guide?
- ☐ What museums should I see?
- ☐ What are some family-friendly activities?

Check (✓) the questions you can answer about your city.
What other questions could a visitor ask about your city?
Talk to your classmates. Find answers to the questions you didn't check.

5 DISCUSSION

Learning Objectives: discuss services using expressions of quantity; give reasons to support opinions

A *Group work*

- Write these expressions on the board:

  It's terrible/not bad/OK/pretty good/excellent.
  I think it's better/worse than it used to be.
  In my opinion, it's getting better/worse.
  On the positive side, . . . ; On the other hand, . . . ;
  The problem is that . . .
- Model the task with the first item (*recycling system*). Ask Ss to think about things like quantity, quality, cost, location, frequency, comfort, and awareness. Remind Ss to use the new language from the Grammar Focus.
- Ss discuss the other services in groups.

B *Group work*

- Read the instructions. Then explain the rating system and any unknown vocabulary.
- Ss work in groups with classmates who live, work, or go to school in the same city or town.
- Go around the class and give help as needed. Then have groups take turns explaining their ratings to the rest of the class.
- ***Option:*** Take a poll. Ask each group to announce how many points they gave each service. Add up the total points to see which services are best and worst.

6 WRITING

Learning Objective: write an online complaint post

A

- Ask: "Have you ever posted a complaint on social media?" If someone has, tell the others to ask that S questions.
- Ss silently read the example posting. Explain any new vocabulary and stylistic issues (e.g., say: "The writer begins with a story and then gives suggestions.").

B

- Ss brainstorm ideas for a post. They can work individually or, if they are going to write about the same city's traffic problems, in pairs or small groups.
- Ss use their brainstorming ideas and notes from Exercise 3B to write a first draft. Go around the class and make general comments about content or organization. Give individual feedback or encouragement as needed. Alternatively, sit in one place and encourage Ss to come to you to get help.

C *Group work*

- Ss work in small groups to take turns reading their social media posts.
- ***Option:*** Have Ss give each other suggestions on ways to improve their posts. Then have them revise their work into a final draft.
- ***Option:*** Collect the posts and display them on a wall or bulletin board for others to read. Encourage Ss to post their ideas in an appropriate online location.

End of Cycle 1

See the Supplementary Resources chart at the beginning of this unit for additional teaching materials and student activities related to this Cycle.

Cycle 2, Exercises 7–13

7 SNAPSHOT

Learning Objective: ask and answer common tourist questions

- Books closed. Ask Ss to brainstorm information about tourists who visit the city where Ss live. Ask: "Where are they from? Where do they stay? What places do they visit? Where do they eat?"
- Books open. Ss silently read the questions in the Snapshot. Go over any new vocabulary.
- Ss check (✓) the questions they can answer about their city. Then they brainstorm additional questions that visitors might ask and discuss possible answers to these questions.
- Have Ss work in small groups to find answers to all the questions.

8 CONVERSATION

Learning Objective: use indirect questions in a conversation about schedules and locations

A *[CD 1, Track 13]*

- Books closed. Write these focus questions on the board:

  _____ *Where are the restrooms?*
  _____ *Where is the nearest ATM?*
  _____ *Where can I catch a bus downtown?*
  _____ *How often do the buses run?*

- Ask: "In what order does Rachel want to know these things?" Then play the audio program. Ss listen and order the questions. Elicit answers. (Answers: 4, 1, 2, 3)
- Books open. Play the audio program again. Ss listen for the answers to Rachel's questions. Go over answers with the class. (Answers: 1. down the street, across from the café 2. follow the signs for "Public Transportation" 3. every 10 minutes or so 4. inside)
- Elicit or explain any new vocabulary.

Vocabulary

ATM: automated teller machine; a machine that automatically provides cash
sign: a symbol that gives information or instructions
restroom: a public toilet

- Ss practice the conversation in pairs. Ask them to act it out, standing up as if at a counter.

B *[CD 1, Track 14]*

- Play the second part of the audio program. Have Ss listen and check (✓) the information that Rachel asks for. Then have Ss compare answers in pairs.

Audio script

See page T-169.

Answers

the cost of the bus fare; the location of a bookstore

9 GRAMMAR FOCUS

Learning Objectives: change *Wh*-questions into indirect questions; ask and answer indirect questions

[CD 1, Track 15]

- Write one of these words and phrases on nine cards:

  ATM   Do you know   Can you tell me   do
  how often   is   run   they   where   the nearest

- Ask a S to read Rachel's first question from the board (*Where is the nearest ATM?*). Then ask four Ss to come to the front of the class. Give Ss the relevant cards (e.g., *Where, is, the nearest, ATM*). Have Ss stand in order and hold the cards for the rest of the class to see:

  S1: *Where*   S2: *is*   S3: *the nearest*   S4: *ATM*

- Now focus Ss' attention on the conversation and ask them to find her exact question (*Do you know where the nearest ATM is?*). Give another S the *Do you know* card and ask the S to stand with the others to form a question like Rachel's original one:

  S5: *Do you know*   S1: *where*   S3: *the nearest*
  S4: *ATM*   S2: *is*

- Ask: "What happened to the question?" (Answer: The word order changed.)
- Repeat the activity for Wh-questions with *do*. Ask four volunteers to stand in line holding up these cards:

  S1: *How often*   S2: *do*   S3: *they*   S4: *run*

- Give another S the *Can you tell me* card and ask the Ss to form Rachel's original question. Make sure S2 puts down the *do* card or steps out of line.
- Play the audio program. Have Ss listen and read along.
- ***Option:*** For extra practice, have Ss turn the questions in the Snapshot into indirect questions.

A

- Read the instructions. Use the first item to model the task. Then have Ss work individually to complete the task. After Ss go over their answers in pairs, elicit answers from the class.

Possible answers

Answers begin with:
Could/Can you tell me . . . or *Do you know . . .*
1. . . . where I can rent a car?
2. . . . how much a city tour costs?
3. . . . how early the stores open?
4. . . . where the nearest Wi-Fi hotspot is?
5. . . . how much a taxi to the airport costs?
6. . . . what time the post office opens?
7. . . . where an inexpensive hotel in this area is?
8. . . . how late the nightclubs stay open?

B *Pair work*

- Ss work in pairs to discuss the answers to the questions they wrote in part A.

8 CONVERSATION Do you know where . . . ?

A Listen and practice.

Rachel: Excuse me. Do you know where the nearest ATM is?

Clerk: There's one down the street, across from the café.

Rachel: Great. And do you know where I can catch a bus downtown?

Clerk: Sure. Just look for the signs for "Public Transportation."

Rachel: OK. And can you tell me how often they run?

Clerk: They run every 10 minutes or so.

Rachel: And just one more thing. Could you tell me where the restrooms are?

Clerk: Right inside. Do you see where that sign is?

Rachel: Oh. Thanks a lot.

B Listen to the rest of the conversation. Check (✓) the information that Rachel asks for.

- ☐ the cost of the bus fare
- ☐ the cost of a city guide
- ☐ the location of a taxi stand
- ☐ the location of a bookstore

9 GRAMMAR FOCUS

Indirect questions from Wh-questions

Wh-questions with *be*	**Indirect questions**
Where is the nearest ATM?	Could you tell me **where the nearest ATM is**?
Where are the restrooms?	Do you know **where the restrooms are**?
Wh-questions with *do*	**Indirect questions**
How often do the buses run?	Can you tell me **how often the buses run**?
What time does the bookstore open?	Do you know **what time the bookstore opens**?
Wh-questions with *can*	**Indirect questions**
Where can I catch the bus?	Do you know **where I can catch the bus**?

GRAMMAR PLUS *see page 133*

A Write indirect questions using these Wh-questions. Then compare with a partner.

1. Where can I rent a car?
2. How much does a city tour cost?
3. How early do the stores open?
4. Where's the nearest Wi-Fi hotspot?
5. How much does a taxi to the airport cost?
6. What time does the post office open?
7. Where's an inexpensive hotel in this area?
8. How late do the nightclubs stay open?

B **PAIR WORK** Take turns asking and answering the questions you wrote in part A.

A: Do you know where I can rent a car?
B: You can rent one at the airport.

10 PRONUNCIATION Syllable stress

A Listen and practice. Notice which syllable has the main stress in these two-syllable words.

● •	• ●
subway	garage
traffic	police

B Listen to the stress in these words. Write them in the correct columns. Then compare with a partner.

		● •	• ●
buses	improve	______	______
bookstore	provide	______	______
event	public	______	______
hotel	taxis	______	______

11 SPEAKING The best of our town

A Complete the chart with indirect questions.

	Name:
1. Where's the best area to stay? "*Do you know where the best area to stay is* ?"	
2. What's the best way to see the city? " ?"	
3. How late do the buses run? " ?"	
4. How much do people tip in a restaurant? " ?"	
5. What's a good restaurant to try the local food? " ?"	
6. What are the most popular attractions? " ?"	
7. Where can I hear live music? " ?"	

B **PAIR WORK** Use the indirect questions in the chart to interview a classmate about the city or town where you live. Take notes.

A: Do you know where the best area to stay is?
B: It depends. You can stay near . . .

C **CLASS ACTIVITY** Share your answers with the class. Who knows the most about your city or town?

12 INTERCHANGE 2 Top travel destinations

Discuss ways to attract tourists to a city. Go to Interchange 2 on page 115.

10 PRONUNCIATION

Learning Objective: sound more natural by using syllable stress in two-syllable words

A *[CD 1, Track 16]*

- Point out that the bubbles over the words show the different stress patterns in two-syllable words. The larger bubble means that syllable has the main stress.
- Play the audio program. Ss listen and practice.

B *[CD 1, Track 17]*

- Model the task with the first word. Have Ss write *buses* in the first column.
- Have Ss listen to the audio program and write the words in the correct column.
- ***Option:*** Change the order of the task. First, Ss guess in which column each word belongs, and then they listen to the audio program and check their answers.
- After Ss compare answers in pairs, elicit answers from the class.

Answers

● •	• ●
buses	improve
bookstore	provide
public	event
taxis	hotel

For more practice with syllable stress, play ***Tic-Tac-Toe*** – download it from the website.

- ***Option:*** To prepare Ss for the next activity, have them find the syllable pattern for these words: *city, people, local, music.* (Answer: All belong in the first column.)

11 SPEAKING

Learning Objective: discuss one's city or town using indirect questions

A

- Explain the task. Ss find out how much they know about their city or town by asking and answering questions about it.
- Ask Ss to give you the indirect question for each direct question in the chart. Then have Ss write the questions in the chart. Check answers by asking individual Ss to read their questions.

Answers

Answers begin with:
Could/Can you tell me . . . or *Do you know . . .*
1. . . . where the best area to stay is?
2. . . . what the best way to see the city is?
3. . . . how late the buses run?
4. . . . how much people tip in a restaurant?
5. . . . what a good restaurant to try the local food is?
6. . . . what the most popular attractions are?
7. . . . where I can hear live music?

TIP
To make sure you include everyone, write each S's name on a slip of paper. Put the slips in a pile on your desk. After asking a S a question, remove the slip with that S's name. Continue until you have asked each S a question. Alternatively, keep track of participation by checking names on a class list.

B *Pair work*

- Model the task with a few Ss. Write these useful expressions on the board:

  Let me think . . .
  That's an easy/a difficult question!
  I know this one.
  Sorry. I have no idea.
  I'm not sure, but I think . . .
- Have Ss complete the task in pairs. Remind Ss to give additional information when possible.
- Go around the class and listen for correct questions and good intonation. Take notes on any difficulties Ss have. After the pairs finish, go over errors with the class.

C *Class activity*

- Elicit answers from the class. Who knows the most about their city?
- ***Option:*** Ss work in pairs to ask questions about places their partner has visited on vacation. Ss can use the questions from Exercise 11A or their own ideas.

! For a new way to practice indirect questions, try ***Question Exchange*** – download it from the website.

12 INTERCHANGE 2

See page T-115 for teaching notes.

13 READING

Learning Objective: skim and read for details in article about cities

A

- Books closed. As a class, brainstorm what makes a city good to live in (e.g., *public transportation, being safe and clean, free healthcare and daycare, entertainment*). Write Ss' ideas on the board. Then tell Ss they are going to learn about the cities with the happiest residents.
- Books open. Go over the task. Ss skim quickly to find the words that are mentioned in the article (Answers: transportation, natural areas, safety, entertainment, schools)

B

- Ss silently read the article and decide which picture matches each paragraph. Ask Ss to explain their answers.

Answers

1. b 2. d 3. c 4. a

- Go over some vocabulary with the class. Ask if the Ss know any of these cities and which one they would like to live in and why.

Vocabulary

healthcare: the set of treatments provided for illness
daycare: a place that takes care of children while the parents are at work
commute: travel between work and home
earn: get money for work

- ***Option:*** To check if the Ss really understood the vocabulary, have Ss tell the class about the article from memory, without reading. Make sure they use the new vocabulary to talk about the four cities.

C

- Go over the comments to make sure Ss understand them. Ss work individually to answer the questions.
- ***Option:*** For more speaking practice, divide the class into pairs. Have each partner state whether they agree or disagree with each comment. Ask the Ss to give reasons for their answers.

Answers

1. d	3. b	5. c	7. a
2. b	4. a	6. d	8. b

D *Pair work*

- Ss discuss the comments in pairs. Have Ss ask follow-up questions about the problems and possible solutions in their city or town. Ask Ss how the problems are similar or different.
- ***Option:*** Have pairs share some of their ideas with the rest of the class. For similar problems, discuss who has the best solution.

End of Cycle 2

See the Supplementary Resources chart at the beginning of this unit for additional teaching materials and student activities related to this Cycle.

13 READING

A Skim the article. Which of the following things does it mention?

transportation **natural areas** **safety** **entertainment** **schools** **housing**

The World's Happiest Cities

Search

Home About Articles Community Traveling Food Booking

When author Dan Buettner went looking for the world's happiest people on four different continents, he found some really great places to live!

___ a. Singapore

With a population of 5.1 million, Singapore is really crowded, and people work very long hours. Yet 95 percent of Singapore residents say they are happy. Subway trains almost always arrive on time. The police are good at their jobs and always ready to help. People in Singapore love that their city is so clean and safe.

___ b. Aarhus, Denmark

Although people pay an incredible 68 percent of their salaries in taxes here, they get lots of services for free: healthcare, education, and daycare for young children. The city has lots of entertainment options too, like museums, shopping, and nightlife. For those who love nature, it's only a 15-minute bike ride to incredible beaches and forests.

___ c. San Luis Obispo, California, U.S.A.

People here smile and feel happy more than in any other American city. Most people travel less than 10 minutes to work, and there are lots of bike lanes, so commuting is easy. Residents share their joy with others, too. Almost 25 percent of people in San Luis Obispo volunteer to help people in their free time.

___ d. Monterrey, Mexico

Although many of its people don't earn high salaries, they still feel rich. People in Monterrey have strong family relationships and very busy social lives. They also have a positive attitude about life – they laugh and stay strong even in times of trouble.

Adapted from http://www.rd.com/advice/travel/the-4-happiest-cities-on-earth

1

2

3

4

B Read the article. Match the paragraphs (a–d) to the pictures (1–4).

C Read the comments from residents of these four cities. Which city do you think they live in? Write the letter.

1. "I spend a lot of time with my relatives." _____
2. "A lot of what I earn goes to the government, but I don't mind." _____
3. "I can see great art in my city." _____
4. "I often have to spend eleven hours or more in the office." _____
5. "I help children with their homework after school for free." _____
6. "I try to be cheerful, even when things are going badly." _____
7. "I take the train to work, and I'm never late." _____
8. "On weekends, I can get out of the city without taking the car." _____

D **PAIR WORK** Which sentences in part C are true for you and your city or town? How would you improve the place where you live?

3 SURVEY

Learning Objective: demonstrate one's ability to express opinions about cities and towns, and to agree and disagree

A

- Ask a S to read the survey topics aloud. Then have Ss complete the survey by checking (✓) the appropriate boxes. Point out that answers are the Ss' opinions.
- Ss complete the task individually.

B *Group work*

- Explain the task and have three Ss read the example conversation. Remind Ss to choose three ways to improve the city.
- Divide the class into small groups. Set a time limit of about ten minutes. Go around the class and make notes on common errors, especially expressions of quantity. When time is up, write the errors on the board and elicit corrections.
- ***Option:*** Ask one S from each group to write the group's suggestions on the board. Then have the class vote on which three ideas are the best.

4 ROLE PLAY

Learning Objective: demonstrate one's ability to ask for and give information about a city or town

- Divide the class into two groups, A and B. Explain that Student A is a visitor to his or her city or town and Student B is a front-desk clerk at a hotel. Based on the topics given, each Student A should write some indirect questions to ask about the city.
- While each Student A is writing questions, go over the useful expressions with Ss in group B. Remind them how a hotel clerk might begin and end the conversation (e.g., *Can I help you? Have a nice day!*).
- Students A and B form pairs. If possible, have them stand on either side of a desk, which will represent the hotel's front-desk counter. Set a time limit of about ten minutes.
- During the role play, go around the class and listen. When time is up, suggest ways the conversations could be improved, such as giving more information or asking follow-up questions. Give examples of good communication that you heard.
- Ss change roles and try the role play again.

WHAT'S NEXT?

Learning Objective: become more involved in one's learning

- Focus Ss' attention on the Self-assessment again. Ask: "How well can you do these things now?"
- Ask Ss to underline one thing they need to review. Ask: "What did you underline? How can you review it?"
- If needed, plan additional instruction, activities, or reviews based on Ss' answers.

3 SURVEY Are there enough parks?

A What do you think about these things in your city or town? Complete the survey.

	Not enough	OK	Too many/Too much
free shows and concerts	☐	☐	☐
places to go dancing	☐	☐	☐
parks and green spaces	☐	☐	☐
places to go shopping	☐	☐	☐
noise	☐	☐	☐
places to sit and have coffee	☐	☐	☐
public transportation	☐	☐	☐
places to meet new people	☐	☐	☐

B **GROUP WORK** Compare your opinions and suggest ways to make your city or town better. Then agree on three improvements.

A: How would you make our city better?

B: There should be more shows and concerts. There aren't enough free activities for young people.

C: I disagree. There should be more schools. We don't need more entertainment.

4 ROLE PLAY Can I help you?

Student A: Imagine you are a visitor in your city or town. Write five indirect questions about these categories. Then ask your questions to the hotel front-desk clerk.

Transportation	Sightseeing
Hotels	Shopping
Restaurants	Entertainment

Student B: You are a hotel front-desk clerk. Answer the guest's questions.

A: Excuse me.

B: Can I help you?

Change roles and try the role play again.

useful expressions

Let me think. Oh, yes, . . .
I'm not really sure, but I think . . .
Sorry, I don't know.

WHAT'S NEXT?

Look at your Self-assessment again. Do you need to review anything?

Unit 3 Supplementary Resources Overview

	After the following SB exercises	You can use these materials in class	Your students can use these materials outside the classroom
CYCLE 1	1 **Word Power**	**TSS** Unit 3 Vocabulary Worksheet	**SS** Unit 3 Vocabulary 1–2
	2 **Perspectives**	**TSS** Unit 3 Extra Worksheet	
	3 **Grammar Focus**	**TSS** Unit 3 Listening Worksheet	**SB** Unit 3 Grammar plus, Focus 1 **SS** Unit 3 Grammar 1 **GAME** Say the Word (Evaluations and comparisons)
	4 **Pronunciation**		**GAME** Name the Picture (Adjectives describing homes)
	5 **Listening**		
	6 **Writing**		**WB** Unit 3 exercises 1–4
CYCLE 2	7 **Snapshot**		
	8 **Conversation**		**SS** Unit 3 Speaking 1–2
	9 **Grammar Focus**	**TSS** Unit 3 Grammar Worksheet **TSS** Unit 3 Writing Worksheet	**SB** Unit 3 Grammar plus, Focus 2 **SS** Unit 3 Grammar 2 **GAME** Say the Word (Evaluations and comparisons; *Wish*) **GAME** Word Keys (*Wish*)
	10 **Speaking**		
	11 **Interchange 3**		
	12 **Reading**	**TSS** Unit 3 Project Worksheet **VID** Unit 3 **VRB** Unit 3	**SS** Unit 3 Reading 1–2 **SS** Unit 3 Listening 1–3 **SS** Unit 3 Video 1–3 **WB** Unit 3 exercises 5–8

Key
GAME: Online Game
VID: Video DVD
SB: Student's Book
VRB: Video Resource Book
SS: Online Self-study
WB: Online Workbook/Workbook
TSS: Teacher Support Site

My Plan for Unit 3

Use the space below to customize a plan that fits your needs.

With the following SB exercises	I am using these materials in class	My students are using these materials outside the classroom

With or instead of the following SB section	I am using these materials for assessment

3 Making changes

- Compare houses and apartments
- Discuss life changes

1 WORD POWER Homes

A These words are used to describe houses and apartments. Which are positive (**P**)? Which are negative (**N**)?

bright	_____	dingy	_____	private	_____
comfortable	_____	expensive	_____	quiet	_____
convenient	_____	huge	_____	run-down	_____
cramped	_____	inconvenient	_____	safe	_____
dangerous	_____	modern	_____	small	_____
dark	_____	noisy	_____	spacious	_____

cramped

B **PAIR WORK** Tell your partner two positive and two negative features of your house or apartment.

"I live in a nice neighborhood. It's safe and very convenient. However, the apartment is a little cramped and kind of expensive."

2 PERSPECTIVES How's your new apartment?

A Listen to a family talk about their new apartment. Which opinions are about the building or the neighborhood? Which are about the apartment?

1. I don't like living in an apartment. We don't have as much privacy as we had in our old place.
2. I just can't sleep at night. The neighbors make too much noise. The building isn't as quiet as our old one.
3. The new apartment is too dark and too hot. There aren't enough windows.
4. Our new apartment isn't big enough for our family. We don't have a big kitchen anymore, so cooking is difficult.
5. The location is just as convenient as the old one, but there aren't as many good restaurants around.

B **PAIR WORK** Look at the opinions again. Talk about similar problems you have.

A: My next-door neighbors make too much noise. They have parties every Saturday.
B: My brother has the same problem. His neighbor's band practices all weekend!

3 Making changes

Cycle 1, Exercises 1–6

By the end of Cycle 1, students will be able to evaluate and compare houses and apartments using *too* and comparatives. By the end of Cycle 2, students will be able to discuss changes in their lives using *I wish*.

1 WORD POWER

TIP
To show the purpose of activities, write the objectives on the board. As you complete each activity, check (✓) that objective so Ss know what they've learned.

Learning Objective: describe houses and apartments using positive and negative adjectives

- Have Ss discuss their ideal home in pairs. Tell them to think about location, size, view, facilities, and features (e.g., *I'd like a really big house on the beach. I'd like to have three bedrooms and . . .*).
- ***Option:*** Divide Ss into three groups and assign each group a column of vocabulary words. Ss look up the assigned words in a dictionary. Then Ss regroup and explain the meanings.

A

- Go over the instructions and explain the task.
- Ss work individually to complete the task. Tell them to guess about any words they don't know.
- When Ss finish, let them check their dictionaries.
- ***Option:*** Model the pronunciation of the adjectives in the list and have Ss repeat each word.

Vocabulary
cramped: having very little space; too small
dingy: dark and unattractive
run-down: old and in poor condition
spacious: large; with lots of extra room

- After Ss compare answers in pairs, go over answers as a class.

Answers

bright	P	comfortable	P
convenient	P	cramped	N
dangerous	N	dark	N
dingy	N	expensive	N
huge	P	inconvenient	N
modern	P	noisy	N
private	P	quiet	P
run-down	N	safe	P
small	N	spacious	P

For a new way to practice the vocabulary, try ***Vocabulary Steps*** – download it from the website. Choose six positive words. Ss order the words according to what is most important to them.

To review vocabulary, play ***Picture It!*** – download it from the website.

B *Pair work*

- Go over the instructions and read the example sentences aloud. Remind Ss that *however, though,* and *but* are all used to show contrast.
- Ss do the activity in pairs. Go around the class and give help as needed.

2 PERSPECTIVES

Learning Objectives: discuss houses and apartments; identify evaluations and comparisons in context

A *[CD 1, Track 19]*

- Books closed. Ask: "Have you ever moved? How is your house or apartment different from your old one? What makes a good neighborhood, building, or apartment/house?" Have Ss discuss the issue in pairs.
- Divide Ss into three groups: neighborhood, building, or apartment/house. Each group writes down three characteristics of a bad neighborhood, building, or apartment/house. After three minutes, have the groups exchange papers and discuss which characteristic they find worse. Go around the class and monitor Ss' comparisons and evaluations. Don't correct their language yet.
- Books open. Ss look at the statements to see which ones match what they listed. Explain the meaning of any new words.
- Elicit which items are about the building (2), neighborhood (5), and apartment (1, 3, 4).
- Play the audio program. Ss listen and read silently.

For another way to teach this Perspectives, try ***Running Dictation*** – download it from the website.

B *Pair work*

- Explain the task. Have Ss go over the list of opinions again and talk about their experiences. Give help as needed.
- ***Option:*** Play the audio program. Pause after each sentence and have Ss raise their hands if they had a similar problem. Determine which problems are most common.

3 GRAMMAR FOCUS

Learning Objective: use adjectives and nouns to evaluate and compare

[CD 1, Track 20]

Evaluations with adjectives and nouns

- Explain the difference between evaluations and comparisons: Both are judgments, but a comparison evaluates one thing against another.
- Have Ss circle the examples of *enough* and *too* in Exercise 2. Ask: "Is the adjective before or after *enough/too*?" (Answer: before *enough*, after *too*) Then write this on the board:

  1. *Enough* goes after the adjective (big + *enough*).
     The apartment isn't big enough.
     Enough goes before the noun (*enough* + closets).
     Houses don't have enough closets.
  2. *Too* always goes before the adjective (*too* + small).
     Apartments are too small for pets.

TIP
Use a different color for each structure. This helps visual Ss remember them.

- Do a quick substitution drill to practice these structures. Start with evaluations with adjectives, and then switch to evaluations with nouns:
  T: The kitchen isn't big enough. Bedroom.
  S: The bedroom isn't big enough.
  T: There aren't enough closets. Windows.
  S: There aren't enough windows.
- ***Option:*** Begin part A at this point.

Comparisons with adjectives and nouns

- Point out the new structures and have Ss find examples in Exercise 2. For a challenge, have Ss determine the rules. Then write this on the board:

  1. *as* + adjective (+ *as*)
     The location is just as convenient as the old one.
     The building isn't as quiet as our old one.
  2. *as many* + count noun (+ *as*)
     We don't have as many bedrooms as we had.
     There aren't as many good restaurants around.
  3. *as much* + noncount noun (+ *as*)
     We don't have as much privacy as we had in our old place.

- Do another substitution drill using the information on the board and the sentences in the boxes.
- Play the audio program.
- ***Option:*** Begin part B at this point.

A

- Go over the instructions. Ss look at the two pictures and the ads. Model the first two sentences using *too*.
- Ss work individually to complete the task. Remind them to use words from Exercise 1. Go around the class and give help as needed. Have Ss compare their answers in pairs before you go over them as a class.

Answers

1. It's too far from downtown./The house is too far from downtown./It's too inconvenient.
2. It's too inconvenient.
3. It doesn't have enough bathrooms.
4. It's too expensive./The rent is too high.
5. The apartment isn't modern enough./It's not modern enough./It's not new enough.
6. There aren't enough bedrooms.
7. It's too small.
8. There aren't enough parking spaces./There isn't enough parking.

B

- Read the task and example sentences. Remind Ss that all answers must follow one of these three patterns: *as* + adjective + *as*, *as many* + count noun + *as*, *as much* + noncount noun + *as*.
- Ss work individually to complete the task. Have Ss who finish early write their sentences on the board.

Possible answers

The apartment isn't as big as the house.
The house isn't as noisy as the apartment.
The apartment doesn't have as many bedrooms as the house.
The apartment isn't as expensive as the house.
The house has (just) as many bathrooms as the apartment.
The apartment isn't as modern as the house.
The apartment isn't as spacious as the house.
The house isn't as convenient as the apartment.
The apartment isn't as private as the house.
The apartment doesn't have as many parking spaces/as much parking as the house.

C *Group work*

- Go over the instructions and the example conversation. Then model the task with one or two Ss.
- As Ss work in small groups, go around the class and give help as needed.
- Elicit opinions and reasons from the class.

For more practice with evaluations and comparisons, play ***Concentration*** – download it from the website. Ss match cards with the same meaning (e.g., *It's too small.* and *It's not big enough.*).

3 GRAMMAR FOCUS

Evaluations and comparisons

Evaluations with adjectives
Our apartment is**n't** big **enough** for our family.
This apartment is **too** hot.

Comparisons with adjectives
The building is**n't as** quiet **as** our old one.
The location is **just as** convenient **as** the old one.

Evaluations with nouns
There are**n't enough** windows.
The neighbors make **too much** noise.

Comparisons with nouns
We do**n't** have **as many** bedrooms **as** we used to.
We do**n't** have **as much** privacy **as** we had.

GRAMMAR PLUS *see page 134*

A Imagine you are looking for a house or an apartment to rent. Read the two ads. Then rewrite the opinions using the words in parentheses. Compare with a partner.

3 bedrooms, 1 bathroom; in quiet suburb 20 miles from downtown; 2-car garage; $1500 per month.

2 bedrooms, 1 bathroom; downtown, near subway; 1 parking space; built in 1920; $900 per month.

1. The house is 20 miles from downtown. (too)
2. It's not convenient enough. (too)
3. It has only one bathroom. (not enough)
4. The rent is very high. (too)
5. The apartment is too old. (not enough)
6. There are only two bedrooms. (not enough)
7. It's not spacious enough. (too)
8. There's only one parking space. (not enough)

It's too far from downtown.

B Write comparisons of the house and the apartment using these words and *as . . . as*. Then compare with a partner.

big	noisy
bedrooms	expensive
bathrooms	modern
spacious	convenient
private	parking spaces

The apartment isn't as big as the house.
The apartment doesn't have as many bedrooms as the house.

C **GROUP WORK** Which would you prefer to rent: the house or the apartment? Why?

A: I'd choose the apartment. The house isn't close enough to public transportation.
B: I'd rent the house because the apartment is too small.

4 PRONUNCIATION Unpronounced vowels

A Listen and practice. The vowel immediately after a stressed syllable is sometimes not pronounced.

● •	● • •
aver̸age	comf̸ortable
diff̸erent	int̸er̸esting
sep̸arate	veg̸etable

B Write four sentences using some of the words in part A. Then read them with a partner. Pay attention to unpronounced vowels.

Today, the average house is much smaller than 50 years ago.

5 LISTENING A home away from home

A Listen to Josh describe a "capsule hotel." Check (✓) True or False for each statement.

	True	False	
1. Tokyo sometimes feels too noisy.	☐	☑	*Sometimes it feels too big.*
2. A capsule hotel is not as convenient as a regular hotel.	☐	☐	
3. Inside every capsule there is a TV, a radio, and an alarm clock.	☐	☐	
4. The capsule is a good option if you're busy and tired.	☐	☐	
5. Josh would recommend a capsule hotel to anyone.	☐	☐	

B Listen again. For the false statements, write the correct information.

C **GROUP WORK** Where else do you think a capsule hotel would be popular? Why?

6 WRITING My new home

A Imagine you've just moved to this apartment. Write an email to a friend comparing your old home to your new one.

Reply Forward

Hi Chloe,
How's everything? I have some great news. We just moved to a new apartment! Do you remember our old apartment? It was too small, and I didn't have enough space for my things. My new bedroom is spacious, and I have a separate area to study in. The apartment also has a balcony. It isn't very big, but now we can have breakfast outdoors on Sundays. The . . .

B **PAIR WORK** Read each other's emails. How are your descriptions similar? different?

4 PRONUNCIATION

Learning Objective: sound more natural when saying words with unpronounced vowels

A *[CD 1, Track 21]*

- Books closed. Write the words *average* and *different* on the board. Ask: "How many syllables do these words have?" Elicit answers, but don't say if they are right or wrong.
- Explain that although they are written with three syllables, we only hear two. Play the first two words on the audio program.
- Books open. Give Ss a minute to read part A. Then play the rest of the audio program.

B

- Explain the task and model the example sentence. Have Ss write their own sentences.
- Ss practice their sentences in pairs. Go around the class and listen in. If necessary, model the words and let Ss repeat.

5 LISTENING

Learning Objective: listen for the main idea and details in a passage about a unique building

A *[CD 1, Track 22]*

- Ask the class if anyone knows what a capsule hotel is. If not, explain the meaning of the word *capsule* (a small container). Have them predict which adjectives describe a capsule hotel.

TIP
To develop Ss' top-down listening skills, encourage them to make predictions before playing the audio program.

- Explain the task and read the five statements. Then play the audio program. Ss check (✓) whether the statements are True or False.

Answers

True statements: 3, 4 False statements: 1, 2, 5

Audio script

See page T-169.

B *[CD 1, Track 23]*

- Play the audio program again. This time, Ss listen for details. Let Ss compare their answers in pairs before you go over them as a class.

Answers

1. Sometimes it feels too big.
2. A capsule hotel is just as convenient as a regular hotel.
5. He wouldn't recommend a capsule hotel to people who can't relax in small, cramped spaces.

C *Group work*

- Ss form pairs and discuss the questions. Encourage them to explain their opinions.

6 WRITING

Learning Objective: write a descriptive email using adjectives and nouns for comparison

A

- Have Ss read the instructions and the example email silently.
- Direct Ss' attention to the picture. Elicit information about the apartment floor plan: spacious bedroom, one bathroom, large living room, modern kitchen, small balcony, only one closet in bedroom.
- As a class, Ss brainstorm ways to compare this apartment to their current home (e.g., *(not) enough bedrooms/bathrooms/windows, cramped – spacious, dark – bright.*).
- Elicit other ways that Ss might compare a new apartment to their current home (e.g., *dangerous – safe, only one parking space – two parking spaces*).
- Have Ss select at least three comparisons for their email. Then Ss write an email.

TIP
If you are going to grade Ss' writing, be sure to let them know what you expect of them.

B *Pair work*

- Ss exchange papers with another classmate. Then they read each other's emails and ask questions.

End of Cycle 1

See the Supplementary Resources chart at the beginning of this unit for additional teaching materials and student activities related to this Cycle.

7 SNAPSHOT

Learning Objective: discuss life improvements using *wish*

- Books closed. Ask Ss to brainstorm some common wishes people have about their lives (e.g., *earn more money*).
- Books open. Ss read the Snapshot and compare the wishes with their predictions.
- Explain the task. Ss check the things they would like to do individually and then tell a partner. Have Ss discuss the questions in pairs or groups.
- Go around the class and give help as needed. Then ask pairs or groups if they discovered anything interesting. Don't expect Ss to produce expressions with *wish* correctly. Instead, notice how they express their ideas.

8 CONVERSATION

Learning Objective: use the verb *wish* in a conversation about wanting life changes

A *[CD 1, Track 24]*

- Ss cover the text and look at the picture. Ask: "Do you think the men are friends? Strangers? Brothers? Where are they? How old do you think they are? What do you think they are talking about?" Accept any reasonable answers.
- Books closed. Play the audio program. Ss listen to find out if the two men are friends or strangers and what they are talking about. (Answers: friends; Dylan is complaining about living with his parents.)
- Write these focus questions on the board:

  True or false?
  1. Dylan hates living at home.
  2. Dylan's parents are always asking him to be home early.
  3. Dylan thinks his life is difficult.
  4. Dylan is going to move out of his parents' house soon.
- Play the audio program again. Ss listen and answer the questions on the board. Then check answers. (Answers: 1. F 2. T 3. T 4. F)
- ***Option:*** Ask Ss to listen for examples of additional information that Dylan gives.
- Elicit or explain any new vocabulary.

Vocabulary
criticize: express disagreement or disapproval
room and board: accommodation and meals (=a place to stay and food to eat)

- Ask Ss to think about the two men's personalities and the kinds of gestures and facial expressions they would use. Then play the audio program and have Ss listen for the emotions expressed by the speakers.
- Books open. Ss practice the conversation in pairs.

TIP
To find out how your Ss learn best, try different methods (e.g., listen and repeat, listen and read silently, listen and mouth the words). Then ask your Ss which method(s) they find most useful.

! For another way to practice this conversation, try ***Say It with Feeling!*** – download it from the website.

- ***Option:*** Have a class discussion about living with parents. Is Dylan's life easy or difficult? Should a son help his parents around the house? Should parents worry about an adult son? Should Dylan pay for his room and board?

B *[CD 1, Track 25]*

- Read the instructions aloud. Then play the second part of the audio program. Have Ss listen to Harry's wishes. Then elicit responses from the class.

Audio script
See page T-170.

Answer
Harry would like to change jobs and live somewhere more exciting.

! For another way to practice *wish* and other expressions, try ***Substitution Dialog*** – download it from the website. Use only the first half of the dialog, until ". . . parents are like that!" Ss replace these underlined expressions with:

1. <u>living with your parents?</u>/working at the bank?/studying?/ . . .
2. <u>my own apartment</u>/a different job/a career/ . . .
3. <u>parents</u>/co-workers/teachers / . . .
4. <u>be home before midnight</u>/make photocopies/write long compositions/ . . .
5. <u>worrying about me</u>/nagging me /giving me so much homework/ . . .

7 SNAPSHOT

MAKE A WISH

- ☐ Have a healthier lifestyle
- ☐ Start my own business
- ☐ Enjoy life more
- ☐ Add more hours to the day
- ☐ Do volunteer work
- ☐ Go back to school
- ☐ Improve my personality
- ☐ Move to a new home
- ☐ Make new friends
- ☐ Spend more time with my family

Check (✓) some of the things you would like to do. Then tell a partner why.
Which of these wishes would be easy to achieve? Which would be difficult or impossible?
What other things would you like to change about your life? Why?

8 CONVERSATION I wish I could.

A Listen and practice.

Harry: So, are you still living with your parents, Dylan?
Dylan: Yes, I am. But sometimes I wish I had my own apartment.
Harry: Why? Don't you like living at home?
Dylan: It's OK, but my parents are always asking me to come home early. I wish they'd stop worrying about me.
Harry: Yeah, parents are like that!
Dylan: Plus, they don't like my friends, and they won't stop criticizing them. I wish life weren't so difficult.
Harry: So, why don't you move out?
Dylan: Hey, I wish I could, but where else can I get free room and board?

B Listen to the rest of the conversation. What changes would Harry like to make in his life?

9 GRAMMAR FOCUS

Wish

Use *wish* + past tense to refer to present wishes.

I **live** with my parents.
  I wish I **didn't live** with my parents.
  I wish I **had** my own apartment.
I **can't move** out.
  I wish I **could move** out.

Life **is** difficult.
  I wish it **were*** easier.
  I wish it **weren't** so difficult.
My parents **won't stop** worrying about me.
  I wish they **would stop** worrying about me.

***For the verb *be*, *were* is used with all pronouns after *wish*.**

GRAMMAR PLUS *see page 134*

A Read these other comments that Dylan makes. Then rewrite the sentences using *wish*. (More than one answer is possible.)

1. My mother doesn't like my girlfriend. *I wish she liked my girlfriend.*
2. My girlfriend is too short to be a model. *She wishes she were taller.*
3. My classes are really boring. ______
4. I'm not on vacation right now. ______
5. My family can't afford a bigger house. ______
6. The neighbors won't stop making noise. ______
7. Harry doesn't like his job. ______

B PAIR WORK Think of five things you wish you could change. Then discuss them with your partner.

A: What do you wish you could change?
B: Well, I don't have much free time. I wish I had time to . . .

10 SPEAKING Make it happen.

A If you could wish for three things, what would they be? Write down your wishes.

B GROUP WORK How can you make your wishes come true? Get suggestions from your classmates.

A: I wish I had more money.
B: Why don't you look for another job?
A: I don't have enough experience. I wish I had a diploma.
C: You can go back to school or take an online course.

11 INTERCHANGE 3 A dream come true

Find out more about your classmates' wishes. Go to Interchange 3 on page 116.

9 GRAMMAR FOCUS

Learning Objective: use *wish*

[CD 1, Track 26]

- Explain that we use *wish* when we would like reality to be different. Refer Ss to the conversation on page 19 and have Ss underline the four examples of *wish* that Dylan uses.
- Draw the chart below on the board. Write the four sentences about Dylan in the left-hand column. Ask Ss to complete the right-hand column with examples of Dylan's wishes from the dialog:

Dylan's reality	Dylan's wishes
1. I live with my parents.	I wish I had my own apartment.
2. I can't move out.	
3. My parents won't stop worrying about me.	
4. Life is so difficult.	

- Focus Ss' attention on the Grammar Focus box. Explain that if we want the present situation to change, we use the past tense form of the verb with *wish*.
- Go over the wishes in the box and ask Ss to underline the past tense verbs. (Answers: *didn't live, had, could move, were, weren't, would stop*)
- Point out that the *wish* sentence must be the opposite of the reality. For example: *I am poor. I wish I were rich.* or *I wish I weren't poor.*
- Point out that with the verb *be*, we use *were/weren't* after *wish* with all pronouns, even *it*. Some native speakers also use *was/wasn't* in informal situations (e.g., *I wish I was . . .*).
- Practice this drill with the class. Give the real situation and have Ss say a sentence using *wish*. For example:

T: I don't have a car.
S: I wish I had a car.
T: I can't fly.
S: I wish I could fly.
T: I'm tired.
S: I wish I weren't tired.
T: It won't stop raining.
S: I wish it would stop raining.

For more practice, play the ***Chain Game*** – download it from the website.
S1: I wish I could fly.
S2: S1 wishes he could fly, and I wish I were . . .
S3: S1 wishes he could fly, S2 wishes she were . . . , and I wish . . .

- Play the audio program to present the statements.

A

- Explain the task and any new vocabulary.
- Ss complete the task individually and then compare answers in pairs. Elicit Ss' responses.

Answers

1. I wish she liked my girlfriend.
2. She wishes she were taller./She wishes she weren't so short.
3. I wish my classes weren't so boring./I wish my classes were more interesting.
4. I wish I were on vacation right now.
5. We wish we could afford a bigger house./I wish my family could afford a bigger house.
6. I wish the neighbors/they would stop making noise.
7. Harry/He wishes he had another job./ Harry/He wishes he could find another job.

B *Pair work*

- Go over the instructions and give Ss' time to think of five wishes. Ask two Ss to model the example conversation. Then have Ss discuss their wishes in pairs.

10 SPEAKING

Learning Objective: discuss wishes

A

- Explain the task and remind Ss to use language from the unit. Have them write their three wishes.

B *Group work*

- Model the example with a S. Focus Ss' attention on the structure to give the suggestion (*Why don't you, You can, . . .*)
- Have Ss compare their wishes in small groups and discuss some possible ways to achieve them.

11 INTERCHANGE 3

See page T-116 for teaching notes.

12 READING

Learning Objective: skim, scan, and summarize an article about living without money

A

- Books closed. Ask: "What do we need money for? What can you do to save money? What would life be like if we had no money?"
- Books open. Explain that the article is about living without money. Ask: "Which of these sentences is true?" Have Ss skim the text quickly to find the answer. (Answer: Boyle wanted to give people the chance to live a different lifestyle.)
- ***Option:*** Point out that the answers are in the first paragraph. Explain that it's common to write the main points at the beginning of an article.
- Ask Ss what they would miss the most if they lived on a farm with no money at all. Have a brief discussion.

B

- Explain the task. Have Ss read the article and guess the meaning of the vocabulary from context. Then elicit the answers and explain any new vocabulary.

Answers

1. good at
2. spent too much
3. so he didn't have to pay rent
4. the forest
5. better

C

- Have Ss read the article again silently and at their own pace, without using their dictionaries. Ask them to underline, circle, or highlight any words they can't guess from context.

Vocabulary

damage: harm or injury
waste: a bad use of something useful
mobile home: a long, narrow home that can be moved from one place to another
park (a vehicle): to stop a vehicle temporarily in one place
grow one's own: plant one's own food crops
seed: a small object produced by a plant that a new plant can grow from

! For a new way to practice this vocabulary, try ***Vocabulary Mingle*** – download it from the website.

- Explain the task. Ss read the sentences and decide the purpose of each paragraph. Read the first sentence aloud and ask the class to which paragraph it refers. (Answer: paragraph C)
- Ss complete the task individually and then compare answers in pairs.
- Write the answers on the board and then go over them with the class.

Answers

1. C 2. D 3. A 4. B 5. E

D *Pair work*

- Have Ss discuss the question in pairs and share the answers with the class.

! For more speaking practice, play ***Just One Minute*** – download it from the website. Give Ss topics (e.g., *my ideal home, houses and apartments, common wishes, bad habits*).

End of Cycle 2

See the Supplementary Resources chart at the beginning of this unit for additional teaching materials and student activities related to this Cycle.

12 READING

A Skim the article. Which of these sentences is true?

Boyle decided that a life without money was impossible to live.

Boyle wanted to give people the chance to live a different lifestyle.

THE MAN WITH NO MONEY

A Can you imagine your life without any money? Not even a cent, a real, or a peso? One man decided to try it out.

B Mark Boyle was a successful manager of an organic food company in Ireland. He had a good life. But he worried about the damage humans were doing to the environment. He also believed people bought more things than they needed. Boyle wished we grew our own food and made our own furniture, so we wouldn't waste as much as we do today. So one day, he left his job and started an experiment – could he live for a year without buying anything?

C He sold his houseboat and moved into an old mobile home. He got it for free from a website where people give away things they don't want. It wasn't as comfortable as his old place at first, but he soon made it feel like home. He parked it on a farm near Bristol, England. Instead of paying rent, he worked on the farm. He burned wood from the forest to heat his home, so he didn't pay electricity or gas bills.

D Boyle didn't go shopping, either. He grew his own fruit and vegetables. He also looked for food in the trash cans of supermarkets and cooked it on a wood stove. He made his own toothpaste from fish bones and seeds. To wash his clothes, he used a special type of nut to make soap. Boyle even built his own toilet and used old newspapers from the farm for toilet paper.

E He began using money again after eighteen months. He says his life change made him feel healthier, happier, and closer to nature. He wrote two books about his experience and used the money to start "The Free House," a farm in Ireland where people can live without money.

B Read the article. Then circle the correct word or words.

1. Before the experiment, Mark Boyle was **good at / unhappy with** his job.
2. Boyle thought that people **spent too much / discussed money too often**.
3. Boyle worked on a farm **to earn money to pay rent / so he didn't have to pay rent**.
4. Boyle made cleaning products from things he found in **trash cans / the forest**.
5. Boyle generally felt **worse / better** after living without money.

C Match the sentences to the paragraphs they describe. Write the letter.

____ **1.** Describes a big change that happened in the person's life

____ **2.** Describes the way the person's everyday habits changed

____ **3.** Asks a question to make the reader think about the topic

____ **4.** Gives general information about the past of the main person in the story

____ **5.** Explains how the person felt about the whole experiment

D **PAIR WORK** Discuss Boyle's experience. Would you like to try it?
Do you think people today spend too much money on things they don't need?

Unit 4 Supplementary Resources Overview

	After the following SB exercises	You can use these materials in class	Your students can use these materials outside the classroom
CYCLE 1	**1 Snapshot**		
	2 Conversation		**SS** Unit 4 Speaking 1–2
	3 Pronunciation		
	4 Grammar Focus	**TSS** Unit 4 Extra Worksheet	**SB** Unit 4 Grammar Plus, Focus 1 **SS** Unit 4 Grammar 1 **GAME** Say the Word (Simple past vs. present perfect 1) **GAME** Sentence Runner (Simple past vs. present perfect 2)
	5 Listening		
	6 Speaking		
	7 Interchange 4		**WB** Unit 4 exercises 1–3
CYCLE 2	**8 Word Power**	**TSS** Unit 4 Vocabulary Worksheet	**SS** Unit 4 Vocabulary 1–2 **GAME** Name the Picture (Cooking methods)
	9 Perspectives		
	10 Grammar Focus	**TSS** Unit 4 Grammar Worksheet	**SB** Unit 4 Grammar Plus, Focus 2 **SS** Unit 4 Grammar 2 **GAME** Word Keys (Sequence adverbs)
	11 Listening	**TSS** Unit 4 Listening Worksheet	
	12 Speaking		
	13 Writing	**TSS** Unit 4 Writing Worksheet	
	14 Reading	**TSS** Unit 4 Project Worksheet **VID** Unit 4 **VRB** Unit 4	**SS** Unit 4 Reading 1–2 **SS** Unit 4 Listening 1–3 **SS** Unit 4 Video 1–3 **WB** Unit 4 exercises 4–8

With or instead of the following SB section	You can also use these materials for assessment
Units 3–4 Progress Check	**ASSESSMENT PROGRAM** Units 3–4 Oral Quiz **ASSESSMENT PROGRAM** Units 3–4 Written Quiz

Key **GAME:** Online Game **SB:** Student's Book **SS:** Online Self-study **TSS:** Teacher Support Site
VID: Video DVD **VRB:** Video Resource Book **WB:** Online Workbook/Workbook

My Plan for Unit 4

Use the space below to customize a plan that fits your needs.

With the following SB exercises	I am using these materials in class	My students are using these materials outside the classroom

With or instead of the following SB section	I am using these materials for assessment

4 Have you ever tried it?

- Describe past personal experiences
- Discuss food, recipes, and cooking methods

1 SNAPSHOT

TRADITIONAL DISHES FROM AROUND THE WORLD

Lebanon	South Korea	Singapore	Brazil

Kibbeh Labanieh	**Galbi**	**Gulai Kepala Ikan**	**Moqueca**
Lamb or beef meatballs cooked in yogurt with spices	Korean-style barbecued meat	A dish made from a fish head cooked in a rich curry sauce	Fish and shellfish stew cooked in coconut milk in a clay pot

Which dishes are made with meat? with fish?
Have you ever tried any of these dishes? Which ones would you like to try?
What traditional foods are popular in your country?

2 CONVERSATION I've never heard of that!

A Listen and practice.

Aiden: Hey, this sounds strange – frog legs with butter and garlic sauce. Have you ever eaten frog legs?

Claire: Yes, I have. I had them here just last week.

Aiden: Did you like them?

Claire: Yes, I did. They were delicious! Why don't you try some?

Aiden: No, I don't think so. I'm a little scared of them.

Server: Have you decided on an appetizer yet?

Claire: Yes. I'll have a small order of frog legs, please.

Server: And you, sir?

Aiden: I think I'll have the snails.

Claire: Snails? That's adventurous of you!

B Listen to the rest of the conversation. How did Aiden like the snails? What else did he order?

4 Have you ever tried it?

By the end of Cycle 1, students will be able to describe personal experiences using the past tense and the present perfect. By the end of Cycle 2, students will be able to describe recipes using sequence adverbs.

Cycle 1, Exercises 1–7

1 SNAPSHOT

Learning Objective: discuss food and traditional dishes

- Books closed. Ss discuss food.
  In a heterogeneous class: Ask for names of some popular or traditional dishes that people like to eat in the Ss' countries. Elicit additional information about the dishes Ss mention. Ask: "What's it made of? Do you eat it only on special occasions?"
  In a homogeneous class: Ask Ss about their favorite foods from other countries (e.g., Japanese sushi, Italian pizza, Korean kimchi, Indian curry, Mexican tacos).
- Books open. Give Ss a few minutes to look over the information in the Snapshot. Explain any unknown words or expressions.
- Go over the questions. Then have Ss discuss them in pairs or groups.
- ***Option:*** To prepare Ss for vocabulary in the unit, have the class brainstorm in groups four kinds of meat, fish, vegetables, and fruit. This could be done as a race against each other or against time.

Possible answers

Meat	Fish/seafood	Vegetables	Fruit
chicken	shrimp	(chili) pepper	banana
lamb	shellfish	onion	coconut
beef	tuna	carrot	tomato
pork	lobster	eggplant	lime

2 CONVERSATION

Learning Objective: use the simple past and present perfect in a conversation about past food experiences

A *[CD 1, Track 27]*

- Ask Ss to look at the picture. Ask: "Where are these people? What do you think they are eating? What do you think they're feeling?" Accept any reasonable answers.
- Elicit or explain any new vocabulary.

Vocabulary

garlic: a plant used in cooking to give a strong taste
appetizer: a small dish served at the beginning of a meal
(an) order: a portion of food
snails: small land animals with a hard round shell and no legs
adventurous: willing to try something new and unusual

- Books closed. Write these questions on the board:
  1. *Has the man eaten frog legs before?*
  2. *Has the woman eaten frog legs before?*
  3. *Has the woman eaten snails before?*
- Play the audio program. Ss listen for answers to the questions on the board. Elicit Ss' answers. (Answers: 1. no 2. yes 3. no)
- Books open. Play the audio program again. Have Ss listen and read silently.
- ***Option:*** Focus Ss' attention on the word *have* in the conversation. Explain that we don't stress the word *have* in *Have you ever . . .?* when it's an auxiliary verb, but we do stress *have* in *I'll have . . .* when it's the main verb. Play the audio program again, this time pausing so Ss can practice the difference in pronunciation.
- Ss practice the conversation in groups of three. Encourage them to use facial expressions and to have fun.
- ***Option:*** Books closed. Have Ss act out the conversation in front of the class. Tell them that they can substitute any food words they want.

! For another way to practice this conversation, try ***Disappearing Dialog*** – download it from the website.

B *[CD 1, Track 28]*

- Read the questions and then play the rest of the audio program. Ss listen for the answers.
- After Ss compare responses in pairs or groups, elicit answers and check them as a class.

Audio script

See page T-170.

Answers

Aiden didn't like the snails (at all). He ordered a (nice, juicy) steak, french fries, and a large soda.

3 PRONUNCIATION

Learning Objective: sound more natural when pronouncing common consonant clusters

A *[CD 1, Track 29]*

- Play the audio program. Ss listen and notice how two consonants at the beginning of a word, called consonant clusters, are pronounced.
- Play the audio program again, pausing after each word.

B *Pair work*

- Refer Ss to page 22 and have them find examples of the consonant clusters. Check answers as a class.

Possible answers

scared, strange, small, snails, frog

4 GRAMMAR FOCUS

Learning Objective: ask and answer questions using the simple past and the present perfect

[CD 1, Track 30]

Simple past and present perfect

- As a review, write these sentences on the board:
  1. *We use the ______________ for experiences at a definite time in the past.*
  2. *We use the ______________ for experiences that happened at an indefinite time in the past.*
  3. *We use the ______________ for experiences that began in the past and continue up to the present.*
  4. *We usually use the ______________ with ever and never.*
- Ask Ss to complete the sentences with either simple past or present perfect. Then elicit answers from the class. (Answers: 1. simple past 2. present perfect 3. present perfect 4. present perfect)
- Draw the following time line on the board to show how we use the present perfect to describe experiences that occur any time between birth and now.

Birth (from birth until now) Now

|————————————————————|

Have you (ever) eaten snails?

Present perfect

- Have Ss circle the past participles in the conversation on page 22. (Answers: eaten, decided) If necessary, copy and give the Ss the appendix on page T-151 so Ss can use more irregular participles.
- Play the audio program. Ss listen and repeat.

A

- Read the instructions and model the first dialog with a S. Have Ss complete the task individually. Check responses before pairs practice together.

Answers

1. A: Have you ever **eaten** sushi?
   B: Yes, I **have**. In fact, I **ate** some just last week.
2. A: Have you ever **tried** Moroccan food?
   B: No, I **haven't,** but I'd like to.
3. A: Did you **have** breakfast today?
   B: Yes, I **did**. I **ate** a huge breakfast.
4. A: Have you ever **been** to a picnic at the beach?
   B: Yes, I **have**. My family and I **had** a picnic on the beach last month. We **cooked** hamburgers.
5. A: Did you **cook** dinner last night?
   B: Yes, I **did**. I **made** spaghetti with tomato sauce.

B *Pair work*

- Explain the task. Encourage Ss to give their own information. Then model the task with a S.
  T: Have you ever been to a picnic at the beach?
  S: Yes, I have. We ate chicken and . . .
- Ss work in pairs. Go over problems when Ss finish.

5 LISTENING

Learning Objective: listen for details make inferences about ordering food in a restaurant

A *[CD 1, Track 31]*

- Set the scene. People are asking questions in a restaurant. Explain the task and the listed items.
- Play the audio program. Ss write Y or N in each item and then compare answers with their partner. Check answers as a class.

Audio script

See page T-170.

Answers

1. N	3. Y	5. N
2. N	4. Y	6. N

B *[CD 1, Track 32]*

- Ask Ss to guess what the speaker may be talking about. Encourage the students to give reasons for their guesses. Give them five minutes to write their answers then have Ss share with the class. (Possible answers: 1. soda 2. soup 5. coffee 6. the check)

3 PRONUNCIATION Consonant clusters

A Listen and practice. Notice how the two consonants at the beginning of a word are pronounced together.

/k/	/t/	/m/	/n/	/p/	/r/	/l/
scan	start	smart	snack	spare	brown	blue
skim	step	smile	snow	speak	gray	play

B **PAIR WORK** Find one more word on page 22 for each consonant cluster in part A. Then practice saying the words.

4 GRAMMAR FOCUS

Simple past vs. present perfect

Use the simple past for experiences at a definite time in the past.
Use the present perfect for experiences within a time period up to the present.

Have you ever **eaten** frog legs?
Yes, I **have**. I **tried** them last month.
Did you **like** them?
Yes, I **did**. They **were** delicious.

Have you ever **been** to a Vietnamese restaurant?
No, I **haven't**. But I **ate** at a Thai restaurant last night.
Did you **go** alone?
No, I **went** with some friends.

GRAMMAR PLUS *see page 135*

A Complete these conversations. Then practice with a partner.

1. **A:** Have you ever *eaten* (eat) sushi?
   B: Yes, I ________. In fact, I ________ (eat) some just last week.
2. **A:** Have you ever ________ (try) Moroccan food?
   B: No, I ________, but I'd like to.
3. **A:** Did you ________ (have) breakfast today?
   B: Yes, I ________. I ________ (eat) a huge breakfast.
4. **A:** Have you ever ________ (be) to a picnic at the beach?
   B: Yes, I ________. My family and I ________ (have) a picnic on the beach last month. We ________ (cook) hamburgers.
5. **A:** Did you ________ (cook) dinner last night?
   B: Yes, I ________. I ________ (make) spaghetti with tomato sauce.

B **PAIR WORK** Ask and answer the questions in part A. Give your own information.

5 LISTENING Have you tried this before?

A Listen to six people ask questions in a restaurant. Are they talking about these items? Write **Y** (yes) or **N** (no).

1. *N* plate
   juice
2. ___ the check
   ____
3. ___ cake
   ____
4. ___ meat
   ____
5. ___ water
   ____
6. ___ the menu
   ____

B Listen again. For the no (**N**) items, write what they might be talking about instead.

6 SPEAKING How did you like it?

PAIR WORK Ask your partner these questions and four more of your own. Then ask follow-up questions.

Have you ever drunk fresh sugar cane juice?
Have you ever been to a vegetarian restaurant?
Have you ever had an unusual ice cream flavor?
Have you ever eaten something you didn't like?

A: Have you ever drunk fresh sugar cane juice?
B: Yes, I have. I drank it in Egypt once.
A: How did you like it?
B: I loved it, actually.

7 INTERCHANGE 4 Oh, really?

Find out some interesting facts about your classmates. Go to Interchange 4 on page 117.

8 WORD POWER Cooking methods

A How do you cook the foods below? Check (✓) the methods that are most common.

bake

boil

fry

grill

roast

steam

Methods	Foods								
	fish	shrimp	eggs	chicken	beef	potatoes	onions	corn	bananas
bake	☐	☐	☐	☐	☐	☐	☐	☐	☐
boil	☐	☐	☐	☐	☐	☐	☐	☐	☐
fry	☐	☐	☐	☐	☐	☐	☐	☐	☐
grill	☐	☐	☐	☐	☐	☐	☐	☐	☐
roast	☐	☐	☐	☐	☐	☐	☐	☐	☐
steam	☐	☐	☐	☐	☐	☐	☐	☐	☐

B **PAIR WORK** What's your favorite way to cook or eat the foods in part A?

A: Have you ever fried bananas?
B: No, I haven't. But sometimes I grill them.

6 SPEAKING

Learning Objective: describe experiences and ask follow-up questions using the simple past and the present perfect

Pair work

- Explain the task. Ss practice asking questions using the present perfect and responding using the simple past.
- Present the questions and model the example conversation. Ss make up four more questions to ask a partner.
- Ss complete the activity in pairs. Go around the class and give help as needed.
- ***Option:*** Set this up as a competition. The pair that continues talking the longest wins!

! For more speaking practice, try the ***Onion Ring*** technique – download it from the website.

7 INTERCHANGE 4

See page T-117 for teaching notes.

End of Cycle 1

See the Supplementary Resources chart at the beginning of this unit for additional teaching materials and student activities related to this Cycle.

Cycle 2, Exercises 8–14

8 WORD POWER

Learning Objective: discuss ways to cook different types of food

A

- Focus Ss' attention on the six pictures above the chart. Say the words and have the class repeat.
- Explain the task. Then read the words in the chart and have Ss repeat. Explain any words that Ss don't know.
- Model how to check (✓) the most common cooking method(s) used for each food in the chart. Read aloud the first food: fish. Ask: "How do people cook fish in your country? Do they usually bake it, boil it, fry it, grill it, roast it, or steam it?"
- Ss work individually to check (✓) the cooking methods that are most common in their country. Go around the class and give help as needed.
- Stop the activity after a few minutes and have Ss compare their charts in pairs. Then ask a few Ss to write their ideas on the board.

Possible answers

(The answers given here generally reflect North American cooking techniques.)
fish: bake, fry, grill, steam, roast
shrimp: boil, fry, grill
eggs: boil, fry
chicken: bake, fry, grill, roast
beef: grill, roast
potatoes: bake, boil, fry, roast
onions: fry, roast
corn: boil, roast, steam
bananas: bake in bread or pies, fry, grill

B *Pair work*

- Ask two Ss to read the example conversation. Have Ss work in pairs or groups. Then use a show of hands to find out which cooking method is the favorite for each of the foods in part A.

To practice the vocabulary, play the ***Chain Game*** – download it from the website. Have Ss make sentences like this:

S1: Last night I baked bread.
S2: Last night I baked bread and boiled fish.
S3: Last night I baked bread, boiled fish, and fried some potatoes.

9 PERSPECTIVES

Learning Objective: identify sequence adverbs in context

- Books closed. Ask: "What is something you eat that makes you think of your childhood?" Write some answers on the board. Ask additional questions about ingredients and preparation.

A *[CD 1, Track 33]*

- Set the scene. Someone is describing how to make a famous American comfort food. Write these questions on the board:
  1. What foods do you need to make pasta?
  2. What are the steps to make pasta? (Answers: 1. You need pasta, water, salt, and sauce. 2. boil the pasta, make the sauce, combine both)
- Elicit answers from the class.
- Play the audio program. Then check Ss' answers to the questions on the board.
- Books open. Play the audio program again. Ss listen and read along silently. Ask: "Do you think this is a healthy dish?" (Answer: No)
- ***Option:*** Ss list the kitchen tools and appliances that a person needs to cook or eat a pasta dish (stove burner, oven, pot, pan, spoon, fork, etc.)

B *Pair work*

- Explain the task. Ss number the pictures from 1 to 5. Elicit answers.

Answers

2, 5, 3, 1, 4

- ***Option:*** Have Ss describe how to make the macaroni and cheese from memory. Don't expect Ss to use sequence adverbs at this point.
- Ask Ss: "Would you like to try the macaroni and cheese? Why or why not?" Elicit responses.

10 GRAMMAR FOCUS

Learning Objective: describe how to prepare food using sequence adverbs

[CD 1, Track 34]

- Play the audio program to present the sentences in the box. Ss listen and repeat. Explain that these sequence adverbs – *first, then, next, after that,* and *finally* – are connecting words that show the order of steps in a process or events in a story.
- Point out that *then, next,* and *after that* are interchangeable. In other words, after *first* and before *finally*, they can be used in any order.

A

- Go over the task. If necessary, use the pictures to explain new vocabulary. Then model the first part of the task by using the first picture.

  T: In the first picture, there are chopped olives, some parsley, and cheese. Look at the mixed-up sentences in the list for the one that matches it. Can anyone find it?
  S: Yes, it's the second sentence, *chop some olives, parsley, and cheese.*
  T: That's right. So write 1 in the box to the left of that sentence.

TIP
To get Ss' attention while you explain the instructions, vary your technique and position (e.g., give the instructions from the back of the classroom sometimes).

- Ss complete the first part of the task individually. Check answers before Ss begin the second part.

Answers

(Answers here are for both parts of the task.)
1. **First,** chop some olives, parsley, and cheese.
2. **Then** boil a pot of water.
3. **Next,** pour some couscous into the hot water and let it sit for 10 minutes.
4. **After that,** drain the couscous and let it cool.
5. **Finally,** toss the cooked couscous with the olives, parsley, and cheese.

- Ss complete the second part of the task. When they finish, go over answers (see above).

B *Pair work*

- Explain the task. Ss cover the recipe in part A and look only at the five pictures showing how to make couscous salad. Ss take turns explaining each step to a partner. They do not need to use exactly the same words. Remind Ss to use sequence adverbs.

For more practice with sequence adverbs, play ***Mime*** – download it from the website. Ask Ss to act out a sequence of actions, such as changing a flat tire.

9 PERSPECTIVES Comfort food

A Listen to this recipe for macaroni and cheese. Do you think this is a healthy dish?

Baked Macaroni and Cheese

1 package elbow macaroni
4 tablespoons butter
2 cups heavy cream
4 cups cheddar cheese, shredded

First, boil the macaroni in a large pot for 5 minutes.
Then melt the butter on medium heat and add the cream. Stir for about 2 minutes. Next, add the cheese. Stir until the cheese is melted. Season with salt and pepper.
After that, add the cooked macaroni and mix well. Finally, bake for 20 minutes.

B **PAIR WORK** Look at the steps in the recipe again. Number the pictures from 1 to 5. Would you like to try this traditional American dish?

10 GRAMMAR FOCUS

Sequence adverbs

First, boil the macaroni in a large pot.
Then melt the butter on medium heat.
Next, add the cheese.
After that, add the cooked macaroni.
Finally, bake for 20 minutes.

GRAMMAR PLUS *see page 135*

1

2

3

A Here's a recipe for a couscous salad. Look at the pictures and number the steps from 1 to 5. Then add a sequence adverb to each step.

- ☐ ________ drain the couscous and let it cool.
- 1 First, ________ chop some olives, parsley, and cheese.
- ☐ ________ toss the cooked couscous with the olives, parsley, and cheese.
- ☐ ________ pour some couscous into the hot water and let it sit for 10 minutes.
- ☐ ________ boil a pot of water.

4

5

B **PAIR WORK** Cover the recipe and look only at the pictures. Explain each step of the recipe to your partner.

11 LISTENING How do you make it?

A Listen to people explain how to make these snacks. Which snack are they talking about? Number the photos from 1 to 4. (There is one extra photo.)

☐ spaghetti

☐ chocolate chip cookies

☐ salsa

☐ French toast

☐ popcorn

B Listen again. Check (✓) the steps you hear for each recipe.

1.	2.	3.	4.
☑ add	☐ cut	☐ stir	☐ mix
☑ chop	☐ heat	☐ cook	☐ bake
☐ heat	☐ pour	☐ cover	☐ mash

C **PAIR WORK** Tell your partner how to make one of the snacks above. Your partner will guess which snack it is.

12 SPEAKING It's my favorite food.

GROUP WORK Discuss these questions.

What's your favorite food?
Is it easy to make?
What's in it?
How often do you eat it?
Where do you usually eat it?
How healthy is it?

"My favorite food is pizza. It's not difficult to make. First, . . ."

13 WRITING My cookbook

A Read this recipe. Is this an easy recipe to make?

Guacamole

First, chop the tomato, onion, chili pepper, and cilantro. Then scoop out the flesh of the avocados and mash it with a fork. Next, squeeze the lime and mix the juice with the avocado. Finally, combine all the ingredients, mix well, and season with salt to taste.

1 tomato
half a red onion
3 avocados
1 lime
1 fresh green chili pepper
2 tablespoons cilantro

B Now think of something you know how to make. First, write down the things you need. Then describe how to make it.

C **GROUP WORK** Read and discuss each recipe. Then choose one to share with the class. Explain why you chose it.

11 LISTENING

Learning Objective: listen for details in passages about making food

- Ask: "What are some of your favorite snacks?"
- Set the scene. Four people are describing their favorite snacks. In pairs, have Ss look at the pictures and predict some of the words they are going to hear (e.g., pasta, spread, cheese, cut, pop).

A *[CD 1, Track 35]*

- Explain the task.
- Play the audio program, pausing after each speaker. Ss listen and match the picture of each snack with the number of the speaker who described it. Then go over answers with the class.

Audio script

See page T-170.

Answers

1. salsa	3. French toast
2. popcorn	4. chocolate chip cookies

B *[CD 1, Track 36]*

- Play the audio again and have Ss check the boxes. Go over any new vocabulary.

Answers

1. add, chop	3. stir, cook
2. heat, pour	4. mix, bake

C *Pair work*

- Divide the Ss in pairs and have them explain the cooking method while the other person tries to guess the snack. Go around the class helping with vocabulary.

12 SPEAKING

Learning Objective: describe how to make food using sequence adverbs

Group work

- Model the activity by having a S ask you the questions. Tell the class how to make your favorite food.
- Give Ss time to think about their favorite food. Some Ss may need to check a dictionary or ask you for specialized vocabulary.
- Put Ss into groups. Ss take turns asking and answering questions about their favorite food. Set a time limit of about ten minutes for this. Encourage group members to ask follow-up questions. Go around the class and give help as needed.

TIP
To stop an activity, silently raise your right hand and keep it there. When Ss see your hand up, they should also put their right hand up and stop talking. Alternatively, count down from five to zero, giving Ss a chance to finish their sentences.

- ***Option:*** Have Ss describe their favorite food again but without saying the name of it. The others try to guess what it is. Or you can prepare pictures so Ss can use them to describe or guess.

TIP
It's important to give Ss feedback on their speaking. If possible, try to include both praise and correction.

13 WRITING

Learning Objective: write a recipe using cooking methods and sequence adverbs

A

- Go over the instructions and example recipe. Answer any vocabulary questions.
- Point out that recipes usually have two separate parts: a list of ingredients and a series of steps, usually written as imperatives.

B

- Ss work individually to write a first draft. Go around the class and give help as needed. Alternatively, let Ss come to you with their questions and drafts.
- When Ss are finished, have them read their drafts to check their grammar and spelling and to make sure they didn't leave out any important ingredients or directions.

C *Group work*

- Explain the task. Ss take turns discussing their recipes in groups.
- Have each group share one recipe with the class. Have Ss explain why they chose that recipe.
- ***Option:*** Post the recipes on the walls for the whole class to read. Alternatively, turn this into a project. Put Ss' favorite recipes together in a class cookbook.

14 READING

Learning Objective: scan an article for specific details and make inferences

A

- Books closed. Ask: "What foods do you think are the most common in the world? Where are they originally from?"
- Books open. Set a time limit of one to two minutes. Ss skim the article to find the answers to the questions. (Answers: Pizza comes from the city of Naples; Pizza arrived in the U.S. in the 1890s; People in Japan like squid, octopus, and seaweed on their pizzas.)
- ***Option:*** Pre-teach some vocabulary in the article by asking the Ss: "How many different pizza toppings can you find in the article?" (Answers: cheese, tomato, peanuts, banana, octopus, squid, roasted seaweed, kangaroo, crocodile, and mango. Total: 10)

B

- Ss read the article silently. Encourage Ss to guess the meaning of words they don't know before checking their dictionaries.
- Go over any new vocabulary.
- ***Option:*** Have Ss tell the class about a strange pizza topping they remember or have tried before.
- Explain the task. Ss place the correct paragraph number next to each detail sentence.

Vocabulary

knowledge: information and understanding in your mind
fit: be right for
taste: preferences in food
baker: a person that makes bread and other baked goods
at first: at the start
squid: a long, soft sea creature with eight long arms
seaweed: a type of plant that grows in the ocean
topping: a layer of food spread over a base
takeout: a meal bought at a restaurant and eaten at home
slice: a piece shaped like a triangle
standing up: upright, on one's feet

Answers

1. c
2. a
3. d
4. e
5. b

C

- Go over the questions. Then have Ss discuss the questions as a class.

End of Cycle 2

See the Supplementary Resources chart at the beginning of this unit for additional teaching materials and student activities related to this Cycle.

14 READING

A Scan the article. Which city does pizza come from? When did pizza arrive in New York? What do people in Japan like on their pizzas?

PIZZA: The World's Favorite Food?

Food, and the way we eat it, is always changing. As society develops, we learn new ways of growing, processing, and cooking food. [a] Also, when people travel to live in other countries, they take their knowledge of cooking with them. And food must fit modern lifestyles and local tastes, too. One food that has done this successfully is the pizza.

The pizza we recognize today first appeared in Italy in 1889. A famous baker from Naples made a special pizza for the Italian royal family. [b] Queen Margherita loved the dish so much, the baker named it after her. Since then, this simple meal of bread, cheese, and tomato has traveled the world, and it has adapted to local cultures.

Pizza began its journey in the 1890s, when many Italians moved to New York in search of a better life. There they continued to make pizzas, and the first pizzeria opened in 1905.

At first it was only popular with Italians, but by the late 1940s, Americans discovered a taste for it. Today, they spend an incredible $37 billion a year on pizzas. [c]

Pizza continued its travels around the world, adapting all the time. In Sweden, for example, it is not unusual to have peanuts and bananas on your pizza. [d] Japan is a nation of seafood lovers, so not surprisingly, they love octopus and squid, as well as roasted seaweed, toppings. Australians sometimes choose kangaroo or crocodile, and in the Philippines they like mango on their pizza.

The popularity of the pizza is also related to our changing lifestyles. In today's super-fast society, people often don't have the time or energy to cook. So, they order takeout – and very often, it's a pizza. [e] If you don't even have time to sit down, buy a single slice and eat it standing up!

The pizza has come a long way. From its beginnings in an Italian city, it has grown to become one of the world's favorite foods.

B Read the article. Where do these sentences belong? Write the letters a–e.

____ **1.** That's more than $100 per American!
____ **2.** What we ate 200 years ago was very different from what we eat today.
____ **3.** In Belgium, people eat chocolate pizzas with marshmallows on top.
____ **4.** Sometimes you don't even have to pick it up; it's delivered to your home.
____ **5.** He was very worried they wouldn't like it, but they did.

C How has local food changed in your country in the last 50 years? What new foods do you eat now that you didn't eat before?

Units 3–4 Progress check

SELF-ASSESSMENT

How well can you do these things? Check (✓) the boxes.

I can . . .	Very well	OK	A little
Evaluate a house or apartment (Ex. 1)	☐	☐	☐
Express opinions about houses or apartments; agree and disagree (Ex. 1)	☐	☐	☐
Discuss life changes (Ex. 2)	☐	☐	☐
Describe past personal experiences (Ex. 3)	☐	☐	☐
Describe recipes (Ex. 4)	☐	☐	☐

1 SPEAKING For rent

A **PAIR WORK** Use the topics in the box to write an ad for an apartment. Use this ad as a model. Make the apartment sound as good as possible.

> **FOR RENT**
>
> Comfortable 1-bedroom apartment
>
> Spacious, bright; located downtown; convenient to public transportation; 1 bathroom, modern kitchen; 1-car garage
>
> $1200 a month

age	windows	parking
size	bathroom(s)	cost
location	bedroom(s)	noise

B **GROUP WORK** Join another pair. Evaluate and compare the apartments. Which would you prefer to rent? Why?

A: There aren't enough bedrooms in your apartment.
B: But it's convenient.
C: Yes, but our apartment is just as convenient!

2 LISTENING Making changes

A Listen to three people talk about things they wish they could change. Check (✓) the topic each person is talking about.

1. ☐ city ☐ travel ______________________
2. ☐ school ☐ skills ______________________
3. ☐ free time ☐ money ______________________

B Listen again. Write one change each person would like to make.

C **PAIR WORK** Use the topics in part A to express your own wishes.

Units 3–4

Progress check

SELF-ASSESSMENT

Learning Objectives: reflect on one's learning; identify areas that need improvement

- Ask: "What did you learn in Units 3 and 4?" Elicit Ss' answers.
- Ss complete the Self-assessment. Explain to Ss that this is not a test; it is a way for them to evaluate what they've learned and identify areas where they need additional practice. Encourage them to be honest, and point out they will not get a bad grade if they check (✓) "A little."
- Ss move on to the Progress check exercises. You can have Ss complete them in class or for homework, using one of these techniques:
  1. Ask Ss to complete all the exercises.
  2. Ask Ss: "What do you need to practice?" Then assign exercises based on their answers.
  3. Ask Ss to choose and complete exercises based on their Self-assessment.

1 SPEAKING

Learning Objective: demonstrate one's ability to describe and express opinions about a house or apartment

A *Pair work*

- Explain the task. Ss write a short ad for an apartment. Read the example ad and the topics in the box.
- Have Ss form pairs. Remind them to make the apartment sound as good as possible. Set a time limit of about ten minutes. Go around the class and give help as needed.

B *Group work*

- Each pair joins another pair to evaluate and compare the apartments. Remind Ss that an evaluation is a statement based on an opinion (e.g., *It's very cheap.*), while a comparison measures one thing against another (e.g., *It's not as cheap as the other apartment.*). Ask three Ss to read the example conversation aloud. Point out that after making their evaluations and comparisons, Ss should say which they would prefer to rent and why.
- Ss complete the task. Go around the class, paying particular attention to Ss' use of comparisons with nouns and adjectives.
- Write a list on the board of some comparisons you heard. Include some incorrect comparisons for the class to correct.

2 LISTENING

Learning Objective: demonstrate one's ability to understand and express personal wishes

A *[CD 1, Track 37]*

- Set the scene. Three people are talking about things they wish they could change.
- Play the audio program. Ss listen and check (✓) the topic each person is talking about. Then go over answers with the class.

Audio script

See page T-171.

Answers

1. city
2. skills
3. money

B *[CD 1, Track 38]*

- Read the instructions. Then play the audio program again. Ss listen and write the changes.
- Go over answers with the class.

Possible answers

1. She wishes she could move to a big city.
2. He wishes he spoke Spanish.
3. She wishes she could find a better job.

C *Pair work*

- Ss form pairs and use the topics in part A. Each person expresses at least three wishes and the other offers suggestions on how to make the wishes come true.
- Ss take turns talking about their wishes. Go around the class and listen to Ss' use of *wish*.

3 SURVEY

Learning Objective: demonstrate one's ability to ask and answer questions about past actions and personal experiences

A

- Explain the task. First, Ss complete sentences with their own opinions and experiences. Read the five sentences aloud. Then Ss complete them individually.
- Now explain the second task. Ss use the information from the sentences they wrote to make questions. Model the first question with a few Ss:

  T: What are your first sentences, Sonia?
  S: "I've eaten octopus. I liked it."
  T: OK. Can you turn those into questions to ask someone else?
  S: "Have you ever eaten octopus? Did you like it?"
- Ss work individually to write their five questions. Go around the class to check Ss' questions, or ask Ss to read their questions aloud. Make sure Ss check their questions before moving on to part B.

B *Class activity*

- Explain the task and go over the example conversation with the class. If necessary, have two Ss model the second question in front of the class.
- Point out that Ss write a classmate's name only if they share the experience or opinion (e.g., *Student A didn't like the sloppy joe, and Student B didn't either.*). If the experience or opinion is different, Student A asks another S the same question. Remind Ss to write a classmate's name only once.
- Encourage Ss to stand up and move around the room. They continue to ask and answer questions until they complete the list of classmates' names in the Name column.
- ***Option:*** Ask a few Ss to tell the class some interesting things they found out about their classmates.
- ***Option:*** if you have only one S, have the S ask you the questions. Encourage them to ask follow-up questions.

4 ROLE PLAY

Learning Objective: demonstrate one's ability to describe recipes

Group work

- Explain the meaning of the title. Tell Ss that *Reality cooking competition* is a reference to reality TV shows about cooking.
- Divide the class into groups of four. Assign roles. In each group, two Ss are judges and two Ss are chefs.
- Tell the judges to write down three ingredients for the chefs to use. While the judges are making their lists, go over the task with the chefs. Explain that they will have to make a recipe using the three basic ingredients (from the judges) and others of their own. Use the example sentences to model how to explain the recipe.
- Tell the judges to give their lists to the chefs. Then the chefs have a few minutes to think of a recipe and name it.
- Chefs take turns telling the judges about their recipes, using sequence markers. Go around the class and listen to the descriptions without interrupting. Make a note of common errors or ways that the role plays could be improved.
- When both chefs have explained their recipes, the judges explain what they liked and didn't like about each one. Then they declare a winner (or not).
- Give feedback to the class on their performance and language. Make suggestions on how they could improve their role plays. Give examples of good communication that you heard.
- Ss change roles and perform the role play again.

WHAT'S NEXT?

Learning Objective: become more involved in one's learning

- Focus Ss' attention on the Self-assessment again. Ask: "How well can you do these things now?"
- Ask Ss to underline one thing they need to review. Ask: "What did you underline? How can you review it?"
- If needed, plan additional instruction, activities, or reviews based on Ss' answers.

3 SURVEY Memorable meals

A Complete the survey with your food opinions and experiences. Then use your information to write questions.

Me	Name
1. I've eaten ______________________. I liked it. *Have you ever eaten* ____________? *Did you like it* ____________?	
2. I've eaten ______________________. I hated it. ______________________? ______________________?	
3. I've never tried ______________________. But I want to. ____?	
4. I've been to the restaurant ______________________ I enjoyed it. ____?	
5. I've made ______________________ for my friends. They loved it. ____?	

B **CLASS ACTIVITY** Go around the class and ask your questions. Find people who have had the same experiences as you. Write a classmate's name only once.

A: Have you ever eaten a sloppy joe sandwich?
B: Yes, I have.
A: Did you like it?
B: Yes . . . but it was too messy.

4 ROLE PLAY Reality cooking competition

GROUP WORK Work in groups of four. Two students are the judges. Two students are the chefs.

Judges: Make a list of three ingredients for the chefs to use. You will decide which chef creates the best recipe.

Chefs: Think of a recipe using the three ingredients the judges give you and other basic ingredients. Name the recipe and describe how to make it. "My recipe is called . . . . To make it, first . . . . Then . . . . Next, ..."

Change roles and try the role play again.

WHAT'S NEXT?

Look at your Self-assessment again. Do you need to review anything?

Unit 5 Supplementary Resources Overview

	After the following SB exercises	You can use these materials in class	Your students can use these materials outside the classroom
CYCLE 1	1 Snapshot		
	2 Conversation		**SS** Unit 5 Speaking 1–2
	3 Grammar Focus	**TSS** Unit 5 Listening Worksheet	**SB** Unit 5 Grammar plus, Focus 1 **SS** Unit 5 Grammar 1 **GAME** Word Keys (Future *with be going to* and *will*) **GAME** Speak or Swim (Definite or possible plans)
	4 Word Power	**TSS** Unit 5 Vocabulary Worksheet	**SS** Unit 5 Vocabulary 1–2 **GAME** Name the Picture (Vocabulary for travel)
	5 Interchange 5		**WB** Unit 5 exercises 1–3
CYCLE 2	6 Perspectives		
	7 Grammar Focus	**TSS** Unit 5 Grammar Worksheet	**SB** Unit 5 Grammar plus, Focus 2 **SS** Unit 5 Grammar 2 **GAME** Say the Word (Modals for necessity and suggestion)
	8 Pronunciation		
	9 Listening		
	10 Writing	**TSS** Unit 5 Writing Worksheet	
	11 Discussion	**TSS** Unit 5 Extra Worksheet	
	12 Reading	**TSS** Unit 5 Project Worksheet **VID** Unit 5 **VRB** Unit 5	**SS** Unit 5 Reading 1–2 **SS** Unit 5 Listening 1–3 **SS** Unit 5 Video 1–3 **WB** Unit 5 exercises 4–9

Key
GAME: Online Game **SB:** Student's Book **SS:** Online Self-study **TSS:** Teacher Support Site
VID: Video DVD **VRB:** Video Resource Book **WB:** Online Workbook/Workbook

My Plan for Unit 5

Use the space below to customize a plan that fits your needs.

With the following SB exercises	I am using these materials in class	My students are using these materials outside the classroom

With or instead of the following SB section	I am using these materials for assessment

5 Hit the road!

- Discuss vacation and travel plans
- Give travel advice

1 SNAPSHOT

What do you like to do on vacation?

take a fun trip
- ☐ *visit a foreign country*
- ☐ *travel in my own country*

discover something new
- ☐ *go to a music festival*
- ☐ *take a photography course*

stay home
- ☐ *hang out with friends*
- ☐ *host a family reunion*

enjoy nature
- ☐ *go camping*
- ☐ *relax at the beach*

Which activities do you like to do on vacation? Check (✓) the activities.
Which activities would you like to do on your next vacation?
Make a list of other activities you like to do on vacation. Then compare with a partner.

2 CONVERSATION I guess I'll just stay home.

A Listen and practice.

Nora: I'm so excited! We have two weeks off! What are you going to do?
Lily: I'm not sure. I guess I'll just stay home. Maybe I'll hang out with some friends and watch my favorite series. What about you? Any plans?
Nora: Yeah, I'm going to relax at the beach with my cousin. We're going to go surfing every day. And my cousin likes to snorkel, so maybe we'll go snorkeling one day.
Lily: Sounds like fun.
Nora: Hey, why don't you come with us?
Lily: Do you mean it? I'd love to! I'll bring my surfboard!
Nora: That's great! The more the merrier!

B Listen to the rest of the conversation. Where are they going to stay? How will they get there?

5 Hit the road!

Cycle 1, Exercises 1–5

By the end of Cycle 1, students will be able to describe plans using the future with *be going to* and *will*. By the end of Cycle 2, students will be able to give travel advice using modals for necessity and suggestion.

1 SNAPSHOT

Learning Objective: discuss vacation activities

- Books closed. Brainstorm types of vacations with the class and write responses on the board. For example:

Types of Vacations

go abroad	*visit relatives*
go skiing	*travel around the world*
relax	*have fun*
go on a cruise	*take a bicycle tour*

- Books open. Ss read the Snapshot individually. Ask: "Which categories (*take a fun trip, discover something new*, etc.) describe the ideas on the board? Do we need to add any new categories?"
- Elicit or explain any new vocabulary.
- Read the discussion questions. Ss discuss the topics in small groups.

TIP
Tell Ss to make a "time-out" signal (by forming a T shape with their hands) or stand up if they want to use their first language.

- ***Option:*** Ask Ss to bring vacation images to class. Encourage them to share and explain their images.
- Use a show of hands to find out which activities are their favorites.
- ***Option:*** To review the verb *wish* from Unit 3, have Ss express some wishes about vacations (e.g., *I wish I had more vacation time. I wish I could go on a cruise.*).

2 CONVERSATION

Learning Objective: use *be going to* and *will* in a conversation about vacation plans

A *[CD 1, Track 39]*

- Focus Ss' attention on the picture. Tell them to cover the text. Ask: "Are these people friends? How old are they? What do they do? What time of year is it? How do they feel?" Ss predict the answers.
- Play the first two lines of the audio program. Ask: "Why are they so happy?" (Answer: They have two weeks off.)
- Set the scene. Two friends are talking about vacation plans.
- Write these focus questions on the board:
  1. *What is Lily going to do?*
  2. *What is Nora going to do?*
  3. *What sport is Nora going to practice?*
  4. *What does Nora invite Lily to do?*
- Point out that Nora is the first speaker and Lily is the second. Ask Ss to listen for the answers to the questions on the board. Play the audio program. Then elicit responses. (Answers: 1. She isn't sure. 2. relax at the beach 3. surfing 4. Nora invites Lily to join her at the beach.)
- With Ss now looking at the text, play the audio program again. Explain any new vocabulary. Explain the expression "The more the merrier!" (An activity is more fun when more people participate. *Merry* is an old word for *happy*. It isn't used much these days except in this expression and in "Merry Christmas.")
- Focus Ss' attention on the follow-up questions used by Lily and Nora to keep the conversation going (e.g., *What are you going to do? What about you? Any plans?*). Explain that Ss will practice this in the next few units.
- Ss practice this conversation in pairs.

! To practice this conversation several times, try ***Moving Dialog*** – download it from the website.

- ***Option:*** Discuss the situation with the class. Ask: "Have you ever been on vacation at the beach? Have you ever spent a vacation with your cousin? Have you ever invited a classmate or friend to go on vacation with you?"

B *[CD 1, Track 40]*

- Read the two questions. Then play the rest of the audio program and elicit answers from the class.

Audio script

See page T-171.

Answers

They are going to stay at a hotel near the beach.
They will get there by bus.

- ***Option:*** Ss write a conversation between Nora (or Lily) and a friend describing what happened on the vacation. Then Ss practice the conversation in pairs.

3 GRAMMAR FOCUS

Learning Objective: use *be going to* and *will* to talk about future plans

[CD 1, Track 41]

- Have Ss read the Conversation on page 30 again as you write this on the board:

  be going to   will

- Ask Ss to find examples of *be going to* and *will* in the conversation and write them in the correct column on the board. (Answers: **be going to:** What are you going to do?, I'm going to relax . . . , We're going to go surfing . . . ; **will:** I guess I'll just stay home., Maybe I'll hang out with my friends . . . , . . . so maybe we'll go snorkeling one day, I'll bring my surfboard!)
- Elicit or explain the difference between *be going to* and *will*. Ask: "Who has definite plans, Nora or Lily?" (Answer: Nora) "Does Nora use *be going to* or *will*?" (Answer: *be going to*) "Lily is not sure of her plans. What does she use?" (Answer: *will*) "What other words does Lily use to show she is not certain?" (Answer: *not sure, I guess, maybe*)

Be going to + *verb*

- Explain that we use *be going to* + verb for plans we have decided on. Nora is 100 percent sure, so she uses *be going to*.

Will + *verb* + I guess/maybe/I think/probably

- We use *will* + verb for possible plans. *Will* is often accompanied by other words to show possibility or probability (e.g., *I guess, maybe, I think, probably, I suppose, I expect*). We also use *will* for spontaneous offers and sudden decisions (e.g., *I'll bring my surfboard! I'll help you! I'll get the phone.*).
- Refer Ss to the Grammar Focus box. Point out that *be* in *be going to* is normally contracted in conversation. Ask Ss to find examples in the left-hand column (e.g., *I'm, We're*). Move to the right-hand column. Show *will* and *will not* in contracted forms (*I'll, I won't*).
- Practice *be going to* by asking questions: "What are you going to do tonight/on Friday/this weekend?" etc. Ss give real responses with *be going to* + verb. Repeat the activity with *will*: "What will you probably do this summer/next year?" etc.
- Play the audio program to present the information in the box. Have Ss listen and repeat.

A

- Go over the instructions. Model the first one or two blanks with a S. Then have Ss complete the task individually. As this is a conversation, tell Ss to use contractions where they can. Go around the class and give help as needed.
- Ss compare answers in pairs. Then elicit Ss' answers.

Answers

1. A: Have you made any vacation plans?
   B: Well, I've decided on one thing — I**'m going to** take a bike tour.
   A: That's great! For how long?
   B: I**'m going to** be away for about a week. I need to take some time off.
   A: So, when are you leaving?
   B: I'm not sure. I**'ll** probably leave around the end of next month.
   A: And where **are** you **going to** go?
   B: I haven't thought about that yet. I guess I**'ll** go down south.
   A: That sounds like fun. **Are** you **going to** buy a new bicycle?
   B: I'm not sure. Actually, I probably **won't** buy one — I don't have enough money right now. I guess I**'ll** rent one.
   A: **Are** you **going to** go with anyone?
   B: No. I need some time alone. I**'m going to** travel by myself.
2. A: What are your plans for the holiday weekend?
   B: I**'m going to** visit my parents.
   A: What **are** you **going to** do there?
   B: Nothing much. I**'m going to** hang out with some old school friends. And we**'ll** probably have a barbecue on Sunday.
   A: That sounds like fun. When **are** you **going to** leave?
   B: I'm not sure yet. I**'ll** probably leave on Friday night if I don't need to work on Saturday.
   A: **Are** you **going to** fly there?
   B: I wish I could, but it's too expensive. I guess I**'ll** take the train.
   A: **Are** you **going to** go alone?
   B: Maybe my brother **will** go, too. He hasn't decided yet.
   A: Do you know when you are coming back?
   B: I think **I'll** come back on Monday.
   A: Good. Then we can have dinner together on Monday.

! For another way to practice this conversation, try the ***Onion Ring*** technique – download it from the website.

B

- Explain the task. Then read the questions and have Ss repeat.
- Ask a few Ss to answer the first question.
- Ss work individually to complete the task on a separate piece of paper. While Ss work, go around the room and check their use of *be going to* and *will*.

C *Group work*

- Explain the task. Ss look over their notes and then talk about their vacation plans in groups. Encourage them to ask questions and give additional information.
- ***Option:*** Each group shares their most interesting or unusual vacation plans with the rest of the class.

3 GRAMMAR FOCUS

Future with *be going to* and *will*

Use *be going to* + verb for plans you've decided on.

What **are** you **going to do**?
- I**'m going to relax** at the beach.
- We**'re going to go** surfing every day.
- I**'m** not **going to do** anything special.

Use *will* + verb for possible plans before you've made a decision.

What **are you going to do**?
- I'm not sure. I **guess** I**'ll** just **stay** home.
- **Maybe** I**'ll take** a course.
- I don't know. I **think** I**'ll go** camping.
- I **probably won't go** anywhere.

GRAMMAR PLUS *see page 136*

A Complete the conversation with appropriate forms of *be going to* or *will*. Then compare with a partner.

1. **A:** Have you made any vacation plans?
B: Well, I've decided on one thing – I ________ take a bike tour.
A: That's great! For how long?
B: I ________ be away for about a week. I need to take some time off.
A: So, when are you leaving?
B: I'm not sure. I ________ probably leave around the end of next month.
A: And where ________ you ________ go?
B: I haven't thought about that yet. I guess I ________ go down south.
A: That sounds like fun. ________ you ________ buy a new bicycle?
B: I'm not sure. Actually, I probably ________ buy one – I don't have enough money right now. I guess I ________ rent one.
A: ________ you ________ go with anyone?
B: No. I need some time alone. I ________ travel by myself.

2. **A:** What are your plans for the holiday weekend?
B: I ________ visit my parents.
A: What ________ you ________ do there?
B: Nothing much. I ________ hang out with some old school friends. And we ________ probably have a barbecue on Sunday.
A: That sounds like fun. When ________ you ________ leave?
B: I'm not sure yet. I ________ probably leave on Friday night if I don't need to work on Saturday.
A: ________ you ________ fly there?
B: I wish I could, but it's too expensive. I guess I ________ take the train.
A: ________ you ________ go alone?
B: Maybe my brother ________ go, too. He hasn't decided yet.
A: Do you know when you are coming back?
B: I think I ________ come back on Monday.
A: Good. Then we can have dinner together on Monday.

B Have you thought about your next vacation? Write answers to these questions. (If you already have plans, use *be going to*. If you don't have fixed plans, use *will*.)

1. How are you going to spend your next vacation?
2. Where are you going to go?
3. When are you going to take your vacation?
4. How long are you going to be on vacation?
5. Is anyone going to travel with you?

I'm going to spend my next vacation . . .
OR I'm not sure. Maybe I'll . . .

C **GROUP WORK** Take turns telling the group about your vacation plans. Use your information from part B.

4 WORD POWER Travel preparations

A Complete the chart. Then add one more word to each category.

ATM card	cash	medication	plane ticket	swimsuit
backpack	first-aid kit	money belt	sandals	travel insurance
carry-on bag	hiking boots	passport	suitcase	vaccination

Clothing	Money	Health	Documents	Luggage

B **PAIR WORK** What are the five most important items you need for these vacations?

a beach vacation　　a rafting trip　　a trip to a foreign country

5 INTERCHANGE 5 Fun trips

Decide between two vacations. Student A, go to Interchange 5A on page 118; Student B, go to Interchange 5B on page 120.

6 PERSPECTIVES Travel advisor

A Listen to these pieces of advice from experienced travelers. What topic is each person talking about?

B **PAIR WORK** Look at the advice again. Do you think this is all good advice? Why or why not?

4 WORD POWER

Learning Objective: discuss things needed to prepare for a trip

A

- Model the pronunciation of the words in the list and the category headings in the chart. Answer any vocabulary questions.
- Ss work individually or in pairs to complete the task, using dictionaries if necessary. Remind them to add one more word to each category. Then check answers.

Answers

Clothing: hiking boots, sandals, swimsuit, *hat*
Money: ATM card, cash, money belt, *local currency*
Health: first-aid kit, medication, vaccination, *vitamins*
Documents: passport, plane ticket, travel insurance, *driver's license*
Luggage: backpack, carry-on bag, suitcase, *briefcase*
(Note: Additional examples are italicized.)

B *Pair work*

- Explain the three types of vacations. In pairs, Ss discuss the five most important things needed for each vacation. Encourage them to use words from part A.
- Elicit answers by asking Ss to use *be going to* (e.g., *We're going to take our passports to a foreign country.*).
- To review the vocabulary, play ***Bingo*** – download it from the website. Give definitions if possible.

TIP
To help Ss remember the new vocabulary, always review it during the next class. Ss forget new words quickly (80 percent is lost after 24 hours).

5 INTERCHANGE 5

See pages T-118 and T-119 for teaching notes.

End of Cycle 1

See the Supplementary Resources chart at the beginning of this unit for additional teaching materials and student activities related to this Cycle.

Cycle 2, Exercises 6–12

6 PERSPECTIVES

Learning Objectives: discuss travel advice; identify modal verbs for necessity and suggestion in context

A *[CD 1, Track 42]*

- Books closed. Ask Ss to imagine that someone is going to visit their city. Ask: "What advice would you give about the climate?" (e.g., *Bring a warm sweater.*)
- Write these sentences on the board:
  1. *It's necessary to have a valid passport when you travel.*
  2. *Travelers should try eating at stalls on the street.*
  3. *You need to keep important things in your suitcase.*
  4. *You should keep a copy of your credit card numbers.*
  5. *You must be 21 or older to drive a car.*
  6. *You should buy travel insurance.*
- Explain the task. Ss will hear six pieces of advice from travelers and decide if the statements on the board are true or false.
- Play the audio program. Then elicit answers. (Answers: 1. T 2. F 3. F 4. T 5. T 6. T)
- Books open. Play the audio program again. Have Ss listen and read along.
- In pairs, have Ss decide what topic each person is talking about. Elicit answers and ask which words helped them with each answer.

Possible answers

Documentation (passport), food (specialties, water), health (travel insurance), packing (carry-on bag, checked luggage), money (credit cards, cash), driving (driver's license)

TIP
If Ss are worried about a new structure they see in the Perspectives section, tell them that they only need to understand the *meaning*. They will learn how to form the structure in the next exercise.

B *Pair work*

- In pairs, Ss discuss the value of each piece of advice. Encourage them to use words from part A.

7 GRAMMAR FOCUS

Learning Objective: use modal verbs to express necessity and suggestion

[CD 1, Track 43]

Modals for necessity

- Focus Ss' attention on the Grammar Focus box. Point out that there are many ways to express necessity. Explain that *must, need to*, and *have to* have similar meanings and are therefore interchangeable.
- Refer Ss to the travel advice in Exercise 6. Have Ss underline the modals for necessity.

Modals for suggestion

- Point out that *had better, ought to*, and *should* have similar meanings but differ in strength. They are listed in the chart with the strongest (*had better*) first. Refer Ss to the travel advice in Exercise 6. Have Ss circle the modals for suggestion.
- Play the audio program to present the sentences in the box. Ss listen and repeat.

A

- Explain the task. Elicit or explain any new vocabulary.
- Model the first item for the class. Ss work individually to complete the task and then compare answers in pairs. Go over answers with the class.

Answers

1. shouldn't
2. must
3. ought to
4. 'd better
5. should
6. need to

B *Pair work*

- Explain the task and read the example sentence. Ss take turns giving each other the advice in pairs. Go around the class and give help as needed. Then check answers.
- Culture note: An ATM (Automated Teller Machine) card allows people to withdraw money from their bank accounts using an automated machine. In North America, ATMs can be found outside banks and inside many stores, hotels, and restaurants.

Possible answers

1. must/have to/need to/should
2. should/ought to/'d better
3. must/have to/need to
4. shouldn't
5. must/have to/need to
6. don't have to

- ***Option:*** Pairs add four more pieces of advice.

8 PRONUNCIATION

Learning Objective: sound more natural when pronouncing linked sounds with /w/ or /y/

[CD 1, Track 44]

- Explain that some words are linked together by a /w/ or /y/ sound. This happens when words end in a *w* or *y* sound and are followed by a vowel (e.g., *know about, carry a*). When a word ends with a /oo/ or /o/ sound and is followed by a word that begins with a vowel sound, the words are linked with a /w/ sound. When a word ends with an /a/, /ee/, or /i/ sound and is followed by a word beginning with a vowel sound, the words are linked with a /y/ sound.
- Play the audio program. Ss listen and notice how the words are linked. Then play the audio program again while Ss listen and repeat.

TIP

To practice linking, use the *Back Chaining* technique. Ss practice the last word, then the last two words, then the last three words, etc., until they can say the whole line.

- ***Option:*** Refer Ss to the Perspectives section on page 32. Ask them to listen again and find examples of words linked with /w/ or /y/ (e.g., *copy of your credit card numbers, when you go out*).

7 GRAMMAR FOCUS

Modals for necessity and suggestion

Describing necessity	Giving suggestions
You **must** have health insurance.	You**'d better** avoid the stalls on the street.
You **need to** be 21 or over.	You **ought to** make a copy of your passport.
You **have to** get a passport.	You **should** try some local specialties.
You **don't have to** get vaccinations.	You **shouldn't** carry a lot of cash.

GRAMMAR PLUS *see page 136*

A Choose the best advice for someone who is going on vacation. Then compare with a partner.

1. You ____________ pack too many clothes. You won't have room to bring back any gifts. (don't have to / shouldn't)
2. You ____________ carry identification with you. It's the law! (must / should)
3. You ____________ buy a money belt to carry your passport, ATM card, and cash. (have to / ought to)
4. You ____________ make hotel reservations in advance. It might be difficult to find a room after you get there. (have to / 'd better)
5. You ____________ buy a round-trip plane ticket because it's cheaper. (must / should)
6. You ____________ check out of most hotel rooms by noon if you don't want to pay for another night. (need to / ought to)

B **PAIR WORK** Imagine you're going to travel abroad. Take turns giving each other advice.

"You must take enough medication for your entire trip."

1. You . . . take enough medication for your entire trip.
2. You . . . take your ATM card with you.
3. You . . . get the necessary vaccinations.
4. You . . . forget to pack your camera.
5. You . . . have a visa to enter some foreign countries.
6. You . . . change money before you go. You can do it when you arrive.

8 PRONUNCIATION Linked sounds with /w/ and /y/

Listen and practice. Notice how some words are linked by a /w/ sound, and other words are linked by a /y/ sound.

You should know about local conditions. (/w/)

You ought to do it right away. (/w/)

You shouldn't carry a lot of cash. (/y/)

You must be at least 21 years old. (/y/)

9 LISTENING A pleasant trip

A Listen to an interview with a spokeswoman from the London Visitor Center. Number the topics she discusses in the correct order from 1 to 4.

a. ☐ money ______________________________

b. ☐ public transportation ______________________________

c. ☐ safety ______________________________

d. ☐ planning a trip ______________________________

B Listen again. Write one piece of advice that she gives for each topic.

C **GROUP WORK** Which pieces of advice for London apply to your city or town? Which don't? Why and why not?

10 WRITING Have a safe trip.

A Imagine someone is going to visit your town, city, or country. Write an email giving some suggestions for sightseeing activities.

Reply Forward

Dear Michael,

I'm so glad you're coming to visit me in Valparaiso. There are lots of things to see here, and we are going to walk a lot, so bring some comfortable shoes. Don't forget your swimsuit, because I'm planning to take you to Vina del Mar for a day at the beach. It will be warm, so you don't need to pack . . .

Valparaiso, Chile

B **PAIR WORK** Exchange emails. Is there anything else the visitor needs to know about (food, money, business hours, etc.)?

11 DISCUSSION Around the world

A **PAIR WORK** You just won a free 30-day trip around the world. Discuss the following questions.

When will you leave and return?
Which direction will you go (east, west, north, or south)?
Where will you choose to stop? Why?
How will you get from place to place?
How long will you stay in each place?

B **PAIR WORK** What do you need to do before you go? Discuss these topics.

shopping	documents	reservations
packing	money	vaccinations

A: I think we'd better buy new suitcases.
B: Good idea. And we should check the weather before we pack.

9 LISTENING

Learning Objectives: listen for the main idea and details in a dialog about travel advice; summarize key information

A *[CD 1, Track 45]*

- Books closed. Explain the situation. A woman is giving some advice to people who visit London. Ask: "What do you already know about London? Do you know any famous places to visit?" Elicit answers from the class.
- Books open. Explain the task. Play the audio program while Ss number the topics from 1–4.

Audio script

See page T-171.

- Have Ss compare answers in pairs. Then elicit Ss' responses.

Answers

a. 4 money	c. 3 safety
b. 2 public transportation	d. 1 planning a trip

B *[CD 1, Track 46]*

- Explain the task. For each topic, Ss write one piece of advice that the woman gives. Ss should write only key words and phrases to summarize each piece of advice.
- Play the audio program. Pause to give Ss a chance to take notes.
- Encourage Ss to use their notes to write complete sentences using modals. Then go over their answers. Ask the S with the best or most correct piece of advice for each topic to write it on the board.

Possible answers

a. money: If you're a student, you should bring your student ID card with you.
b. public transportation: You ought to go online and investigate. You shouldn't be afraid to ask questions.
c. safety: You should be careful. You shouldn't go off on your own, especially at night. You shouldn't carry much cash on you.
d. planning a trip: You should start planning before you get here. You ought to decide in advance which sights you most want to see.

For another way to practice modals, play ***Just One Minute*** – download it from the website.

C *Group work*

- Ss answer the question in small groups. Go around helping with vocabulary and structure. Ask one S to present their ideas to the class.

10 WRITING

Learning Objective: write a personal email using *be going to* and modals to give advice

A

- Ask Ss to read the example email. Explain any vocabulary that Ss don't understand.
- Point out features of an email to a friend (e.g., use *Dear + first name* to open the email; include an introductory sentence; close the email with a phrase like *Can't wait to see you!* and a final good-bye, such as *Best wishes, Love, All the best, Your friend,* and their own name).
- Have Ss write their first draft individually. Go around the class and give help as needed.

B *Pair work*

- Ss exchange drafts and read their partner's email to see what else the writer should include (e.g., information about money, climate, visas). Encourage Ss to focus on content rather than grammar or spelling.
- Pairs give each other feedback. Then Ss write a second draft, using correct grammar and spelling.
- ***Option:*** Have Ss send the email to a partner electronically during class or at home. Have Ss write a response and email back.

11 DISCUSSION

Learning Objective: discuss vacation plans using *be going to* and *will*, modals for necessity and suggestion

A *Pair work*

- Focus Ss' attention on the title of the exercise. Ask: "What do you think a 30-day trip means?" (Answer: a trip that lasts for 30 days)
- Explain the task. Have a S read the questions aloud, and check pronunciation. Then Ss discuss the questions in pairs.

B *Pair work*

- Go over the topics and the example conversation. With the same partner, Ss take turns discussing the things they need to do before their trip. Encourage Ss to ask follow-up questions.

12 READING

Learning Objective: summarize key information and make inferences

A

- Books closed. Write these words on the board:
  travel, adventure, danger, forest, snowshoes, survival skills
- Tell Ss the words are all related to the topic. Ask Ss to guess what the article is about.
- Books open. Have Ss read the title. Elicit the meaning of *Adventure Vacations* (answer: a vacation where you do exciting activities in remote places)
- Tell Ss to match the paragraphs to the picture.
- Remind Ss to look for the information quickly and not to worry about words they don't know. Then elicit the answers. (Answers: 1. C, 2. A, 3. B)
- Ss read the article silently. Tell the Ss to underline three new vocabulary words and then look them up in their dictionaries.
- When the class finishes reading, ask Ss to tell the class which three words they underlined. Write them on the board and go over the definitions. Look at the sentences and point out any contextual clues. These clues can sometimes help Ss guess the meaning of unfamiliar words.
- Elicit or explain any other new vocabulary.

Vocabulary
pleasant: enjoyable
danger: the possibility of suffering harm or injury
whole: all of; entire
pick (someone) up: collect someone who is waiting for you
sub-zero: below zero degrees; very cold
pick: choose

B

- Make sure Ss know why the words *nowadays, so,* and *afterward* are used in the summary (answer: nowadays: at present time; So: consequently; afterward: later)
- Explain the task. Ss read the article again and then fill in the blanks with the correct words.
- Ss work individually and then check their answers in pairs. Check answers with the class and write all answers on the board.

Answers

1. adventure
2. tent
3. snowshoes
4. reindeer
5. local guides
6. week

- ***Option:*** Ss rewrite the summary in their own words.

C

- Explain the task. Read the sentences out loud for the class and explain any vocabulary.
- Have Ss work individually and then check answers in pairs.
- ***Option:*** Have Ss write a comment about a vacation they would like to take.

Answers

1. B or C
2. A
3. B
4. C
5. A
6. C

For more speaking practice, play ***Hot Potato*** – download it from the website. The first S begins by saying something about the text from memory. Then he or she throws an object to another S, who says another fact from the text. Ss continue to throw the object and say things about the text.

D *Group work*

- In small groups, Ss take turns discussing the questions.

End of Cycle 2

See the Supplementary Resources chart at the beginning of this unit for additional teaching materials and student activities related to this Cycle.

12 READING

A Skim the article. Match paragraphs A, B, and C to the photos.

ADVENTURE VACATIONS

Home | About | Vacations | Hot spots | Discounts

A good vacation, for many people, means comfortable accommodations, a great atmosphere, and tasty food. It's a pleasant, relaxing experience. But for some, this type of vacation just isn't enough!

In today's world, many of us have safe, sometimes boring lives. We work, sleep, eat, and watch TV. So more and more people are looking for adventure. They want excitement and danger. They might even want to feel a little afraid!

___ A How about staying on a desert island in the middle of the Indian Ocean? If you want, you can spend your whole vacation completely alone. You'll sleep in a tent and go fishing for your food. Your only company will be the monkeys and lizards. But don't worry. If you get bored, just call the travel company and they'll send a boat to pick you up!

___ B Or how about spending a week in the sub-zero temperatures of the North? You will fly to the Arctic, and the local Sami people will teach you to survive in this very difficult environment. You'll learn how to keep yourself warm and make special snowshoes. You can also go ice-fishing and look after reindeer. You'll even learn how to tell when it is going to snow.

___ C But if the Arctic's too cold, you could try the heat of the jungle instead. Deep in the Amazon rain forest, you'll sleep in the open air. At first, you'll spend a week with local guides. They will train you to do many things, like find food and water or light fires with stones. They will even teach you to pick the tastiest insects for dinner! Then you'll spend a week by yourself with no tent, no extra clothes, and no cell phone. You'll be completely alone – except for the crocodiles and snakes, of course!

1

2

3

B Read the article. Then complete the summary using words from the article.

Nowadays, life can sometimes be a little boring. So, many people are searching for an exciting or dangerous **1)** ___ during their vacations. Some people like the idea of visiting a desert island. There, they spend nights in a **2)** ___ and look for fruit and other plants to eat. If they decide to go to the Arctic instead, they will walk around with unusual **3)** ___ on their feet, and they'll have the experience of taking care of **4)** ___. If they decide to choose a trip to the rain forest, they'll learn many things from **5)** ___, and afterward, they'll live for a whole **6)** ___ completely alone.

C Read the comments of people who are on one of these three trips. Which vacation are they on? Write the letter.

___ 1. "I know what the weather will be like tomorrow."
___ 2. "I haven't seen anybody since the moment I arrived."
___ 3. "My whole body is absolutely freezing!"
___ 4. "I've learned so much these first seven days."
___ 5. "I've had enough now! I'm going to call for help."
___ 6. "I haven't eaten anything like this before!"

D **GROUP WORK** Which of these three vacations would you be prepared to try? Which would you refuse to go on? Why?

Unit 6 Supplementary Resources Overview

	After the following SB exercises	You can use these materials in class	Your students can use these materials outside the classroom
CYCLE 1	1 **Snapshot**		
	2 **Conversation**		**SS** Unit 6 Speaking 1–2
	3 **Grammar Focus**		**SB** Unit 6 Grammar plus, Focus 1 **SS** Unit 6 Grammar 1
	4 **Pronunciation**		**GAME** Spell or Slime (Two-part verbs 1) **GAME** Word Keys (Two-part verbs 2)
	5 **Word Power**	**TSS** Unit 6 Vocabulary Worksheet	**SS** Unit 6 Vocabulary 1–2 **GAME** Speak or Swim (Apologizing)
	6 **Listening**		**WB** Unit 6 exercises 1–3
CYCLE 2	7 **Perspectives**		
	8 **Grammar Focus**		**SB** Unit 6 Grammar plus, Focus 2 **SS** Unit 6 Grammar 2 **GAME** Say the Word (Requests with modals and *Would you mind . . .* ?)
	9 **Speaking**	**TSS** Unit 6 Grammar Worksheet **TSS** Unit 6 Listening Worksheet **TSS** Unit 6 Extra Worksheet	
	10 **Interchange 6**		
	11 **Writing**	**TSS** Unit 6 Writing Worksheet	
	12 **Reading**	**TSS** Unit 6 Project Worksheet **VID** Unit 6 **VRB** Unit 6	**SS** Unit 6 Reading 1–2 **SS** Unit 6 Listening 1–2 **SS** Unit 6 Video 1–3 **WB** Unit 6 exercises 4–11

With or instead of the following SB section	You can also use these materials for assessment
Units 5–6 Progress Check	**ASSESSMENT PROGRAM** Units 5–6 Oral Quiz **ASSESSMENT PROGRAM** Units 5–6 Written Quiz

Key **GAME:** Online Game **SB:** Student's Book **SS:** Online Self-study **TSS:** Teacher Support Site
VID: Video DVD **VRB:** Video Resource Book **WB:** Online Workbook/Workbook

My Plan for Unit 6

Use the space below to customize a plan that fits your needs.

With the following SB exercises	I am using these materials in class	My students are using these materials outside the classroom

With or instead of the following SB section	I am using these materials for assessment

6 Sure! I'll do it.

- Discuss common complaints
- Make and respond to requests
- Apologize

1 SNAPSHOT

FAMILY COMPLAINTS

- ☐ We never have dinner together as a family.
- ☐ Everybody is always arguing about housework.
- ☐ My daughter never takes her headphones off.
- ☐ My father criticizes everything I do.
- ☐ My husband never helps around the house.
- ☐ My kids are always texting their friends.
- ☐ My mother often calls me late at night.
- ☐ My parents don't respect my privacy.
- ☐ My brother never puts his phone away.
- ☐ My wife always brings work home on weekends.

Which complaints seem reasonable? Which ones seem unreasonable? Why?
Do you have similar complaints about anyone in your family? Check (✓) the complaints.
What other complaints do people sometimes have about family members?

2 CONVERSATION I'll turn it off.

A Listen and practice.

Nolan: Please turn down the TV. I have to study.
Ken: I'm sorry. I'll turn it down.
Nolan: It's still too loud.
Ken: All right. I'll turn it off. I'll go watch this show in my room.
Nolan: Thanks.
Ken: No problem.
Nolan: This place is such a mess. Rodrigo, your clothes are all over the place.
Rodrigo: They're not mine. . . . And these books are yours, actually. Why don't you put them away?
Nolan: I'm sorry. I guess I'm kind of nervous about my exam tomorrow.
Rodrigo: That's OK. I know how you feel. Those exams drive me crazy, too.

B Listen to the rest of the conversation. What complaints do Nolan and Rodrigo have about Ken?

6 Sure! I'll do it.

Cycle 1, Exercises 1–6

By the end of Cycle 1, students will be able to use two-part verbs to make and respond to requests. By the end of Cycle 2, students will be able to make and respond to requests using modals and *Would you mind?*

1 SNAPSHOT

Learning Objective: discuss common complaints

- Books closed. Write these questions on the board and have Ss discuss them in pairs:
  1. *Do your parents, children, or siblings ever bother you?*
  2. *What do they do to bother you?*
  3. *What do you do or say about it?*
- Books open. Read the headings aloud. Have Ss skim the list of common complaints. Elicit or explain any new vocabulary.

Vocabulary
criticize: say bad things about
text: send a text message

- Read the questions aloud. Have Ss check the complaints that are true for their family and then discuss the questions in groups or pairs. Remind Ss to ask follow-up questions to keep the discussion going.
- Have Ss vote on their biggest complaint to find out which is the most common. For the last question, ask Ss to suggest some other complaints (e.g., *My parents don't let me borrow the car. My kids stay out too late. My sister spends too much time on the phone/computer.*).

2 CONVERSATION

Learning Objective: use two-part verbs and *will* in a conversation about making and responding to requests

A *[CD 1, Track 47]*

- Focus Ss' attention on the picture. Tell them to cover the text. Ask: "What are they doing? What is the problem?" Ss predict the answers.
- Books closed. Play the first six lines of the audio program (until Ken says, "No problem."). Then check answers. (Answers: Ken is watching TV while Nolan is trying to study.)
- Ask Ss to guess about the second part of the listening: "What else might Nolan complain about?"
- Play the audio program. Ask questions like: "What did Nolan complain about? Whose things are they? Why is Nolan so nervous?" Elicit answers. (Answers: the mess and clothes, Nolan's, because he has an exam)
- Books open. Play the audio program again while Ss read silently. Explain any new vocabulary words or expressions.

Vocabulary
loud: making a lot of noise
mess: something that is dirty or untidy
drive (someone) crazy: to make someone feel crazy, annoyed, or excited

- Ss practice the conversation in groups of three.

! For another way to practice this conversation, try ***Say It with Feeling!*** – download it from the website.

- ***Option:*** Ask a few Ss to act out the conversation in front of the class, using props and actions. Encourage them to use their own words.

B *[CD 1, Track 48]*

- Read the instructions and the focus question that Ss need to listen for. Tell Ss to take notes. Then play the second part of the audio program.

Audio script

See page T-171.

- After pairs compare their answers, go over them with the class.

Answers

Ken never puts his clothes away. He never does the dishes.

3 GRAMMAR FOCUS

Learning Objectives: use two-part verbs to make requests; use *will* to respond to requests

[CD 1, Track 49]

Two-part verbs

- Refer Ss to the conversation on page 36. Elicit the actions Ken and Rodrigo say and have Ss underline them. (Answers: I'll turn it down. I'll turn it off. ...put them away?)
- Explain that *turn down, turn off,* and *put away* are examples of two-part verbs. They are made up of a verb and another word called a particle, which changes the meaning of the verb.
- ***Option:*** Show Ss how to store two-part verbs in a logical way. Draw a "Ripple Diagram" on the board:

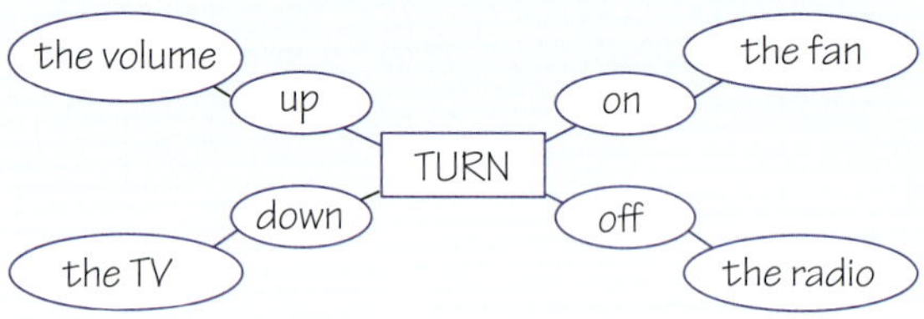

TIP
To help Ss find out how they learn best, have them try different ways to organize vocabulary in their notebooks. Then ask Ss which method(s) work best for them.

- Point out that the object noun (e.g., *TV, things*) can come before or after the particle:
  Turn *the TV* down. Put *your books* away.
  Turn down *the TV*. Put away *your books*.
- When the object of the two-part verb is a pronoun, it can only come between the verb and the particle: Turn *it* down. Put *them* away.

Making requests

- It is polite to use *please* to make a request. *Please* can go at the beginning or the end of a sentence (notice the use of a comma when *please* comes at the end): *Please* turn down the music. Turn it down, *please*.

Responding with will

- The modal *will* is used to respond to a request.
  OK. I*'ll* turn it down.
  All right. I*'ll* put them away.
- Play the audio program to present the sentences in the Grammar Focus box. Ss listen and repeat.

A

- Before Ss begin the task, focus their attention on the picture and requests below. Model the first item for the class. Then elicit suggestions for the second item. Point out that there is more than one possible answer for some of the items.
- Ss complete the task individually and then compare answers in pairs. Elicit responses.

Answers

1. Turn **the music/the TV/the lights** off, please.
2. Turn **the music/the TV/the lights** on, please.
3. Please turn **the music/the TV/the lights** down.
4. Pick up **your socks/the magazines/your jacket/your boots**, please.
5. Please put **your socks/the magazines/your jacket/your boots** away.
6. Hang **your jacket** up, please.
7. Please take **your boots/your jacket** off.
8. Clean **the yard/your boots/the room** up, please.
9. Please take **the trash** out.
10. Please let **the cat** out.

B *Pair work*

- Model the example conversation and ask one or two Ss to give their own responses. Remind Ss to use expressions like *sure, OK, no problem,* and *all right.*
- In pairs, Ss take turns making and responding to each other's requests from part A. Go around and make sure Ss use pronouns in their responses.

For more practice with two-part verbs, play ***Simon Says*** – download it from the website.

4 PRONUNCIATION

Learning Objective: sound more natural when making requests by using stress patterns in requests with two-part verbs

A *[CD 1, Track 50]*

- Play the audio program to present the sentences. Ss tap the desk or clap in time to the stress. Then they repeat.

! For another way to practice stress patterns, try ***Walking Stress*** – download it from the website.

B

- Explain and model the task by eliciting several examples and writing them on the board. Then have Ss work individually to write four more requests.
- Have Ss form pairs and take turns making their requests and giving appropriate responses.

3 GRAMMAR FOCUS

Two-part verbs; *will* for responding to requests

With nouns	With pronouns	Requests and responses
Turn down the TV.	**Turn** it **down**.	Please turn down the music.
Turn the TV **down**.	(NOT: ~~Turn down it~~.)	OK. I'**ll** turn it down.
Put away your books.	**Put** them **away**.	Put away your books, please.
Put your books **away**.	(NOT: ~~Put away them~~.)	All right. I'**ll** put them away.

GRAMMAR PLUS *see page 137*

A Complete the requests with these words. Then compare with a partner.

your boots	your socks	your jacket	the cat	the trash
the TV	✓ the lights	the magazines	the music	the yard

1. Turn *the lights* off, please.
2. Turn ______________ on, please.
3. Please turn ______________ down.
4. Pick up ______________, please.
5. Please put ______________ away.
6. Hang ______________ up, please.
7. Please take ______________ off.
8. Clean ______________ up, please.
9. Please take ______________ out.
10. Please let ______________ out.

B PAIR WORK Take turns making the requests above. Respond with pronouns.

A: Turn the lights off, please.
B: No problem. I'll turn them off.

4 PRONUNCIATION Stress in two-part verbs

A Listen and practice. Both words in a two-part verb receive equal stress.

●	●	•	●		●	•	●	●		●	•	●
Pick	up	your	things.		Pick	your	things	up.		Pick	them	up.
Turn	off	the	light.		Turn	the	light	off.		Turn	it	off.

B Write four more requests using the verbs in Exercise 3. Then practice with a partner. Pay attention to stress.

5 WORD POWER Housework

A Find a phrase that is usually paired with each two-part verb. (Some phrases go with more than one verb.) Then add one more phrase for each verb.

the garbage	**the magazines**	**the microwave**	**your coat**
the groceries	**the mess**	**the towels**	**your laptop**

clean up	______	______	take out	______	______
hang up	______	______	throw out	______	______
pick up	______	______	turn off	______	______
put away	______	______	turn on	______	______

B What requests can you make in each of these rooms? Write four requests and four excuses. Use two-part verbs.

the kitchen　　the living room
the bathroom　　the bedroom

C **PAIR WORK** Take turns making the requests you wrote in part B. Respond by giving an excuse.

A: Marabel, please pick up the wet towel you left on your bed.

B: Sorry, I can't pick it up right now. I have to put my new clothes away.

6 LISTENING Helping around the house

A Listen to the results of a survey about family life. Check (✓) the answer to each question. Sometimes more than one answer is possible.

	Men	Women	Boys	Girls
1. Who is the messiest in the house?				
2. Who does most of the work in the kitchen?				
3. Who does the general chores inside and outside the house?				
4. Who worries most about expenses?				

B Listen again. According to the survey, what specific chores do men, women, boys, and girls usually do? Take notes.

C **GROUP WORK** How does your family compare to the survey results? Who helps the most with general chores around the house? Who helps the least?

5 WORD POWER

Learning Objective: use two-part verbs to make requests about chores

A

- Explain the task. Then read the nouns and the two-part verbs while Ss repeat. Use the first two-part verb to elicit Ss' responses. Model how to complete the chart.
- Tell Ss not to use their dictionaries until they have matched all eight two-part verbs with nouns. Alternatively, have Ss work in pairs.
- Check Ss' answers. Explain any new vocabulary.

Answers

clean up	the garbage, the mess, *the kitchen*
hang up	the towels, your coat, *his shirt*
pick up	the garbage, the magazines, the mess, the towels, your coat, *the socks*
put away	the groceries, the magazines, the towels, your coat, your laptop, *your things*
take out	the garbage, your laptop, *the dog*
throw out	the garbage, the magazines, *the old food*
turn off/on	the microwave, your laptop, *the lights*

(Note: Additional phrases are italicized.)

B

- Explain the task. Ss use the words from page 37 or the chart in part A.
- Model the task by reading the example conversation in part C. Then have Ss work individually to write their requests and excuses. Encourage Ss to write creative or funny excuses. To keep an element of surprise in the next task, go around the class to check individual Ss' answers.

C *Pair work*

- Read the example conversation again. Tell Ss to listen carefully to each request so they can match it to one of their excuses.
- Ss form pairs and take turns making their requests and giving excuses. Go around the class and listen in. It's OK for responses to be silly, but if a pair's request and excuse don't match at all, help them to find a better match.

To review two-part verbs, play ***Mime*** – download it from the website.

6 LISTENING

Learning Objective: listen for the main idea and details in a conversation about chores

A *[CD 1, Track 51]*

- Ask: "Do you think men and women share housework equally? Who does more? What about boys and girls? What do they have to do?"
- Explain that Ss will listen to the results of a survey about family life. Go over the four questions and have Ss predict the answers. Explain that Ss need to check the correct answer to the question.
- Play the audio program. Ss listen and check the answers. Then go over answers with the class.

Audio script

See page T-171.

Answers

1. B 2. W 3. M and W 4. M

B *[CD 1, Track 52]*

- Read the question. Encourage Ss to take notes. Then play the audio program again, repeating if necessary.
- Ss compare answers in pairs or groups. If they disagree, play the audio program again, pausing after each section. Then elicit Ss' responses.

Answers

Men: take out the garbage, clean up the yard
Women: cook; do the dishes, clean up inside the house
Boys: put the groceries away, take out the garbage
Girls: cook, do the dishes, clean up the kitchen, put the groceries away

C *Group work*

- Explain the task. Remind Ss to ask follow-up questions and give additional information.
- In small groups, Ss use the questions from parts A and B to discuss who does these things in their family.

End of Cycle 1

See the Supplementary Resources chart at the beginning of this unit for additional teaching materials and student activities related to this Cycle.

7 PERSPECTIVES

Learning Objectives: discuss common requests; identify requests with modals and *Would you mind . . . ?* in context

A *[CD 1, Track 53]*

- Set the scene. Ss will hear five requests neighbors sometimes make.
- Explain the task. Ss read the questions and match them to the follow-up statements. Play the audio program. Ss listen and check their answers. Then elicit answers.

Answers

1. c 2. e 3. d 4. a 5. b

- Play the audio program again while Ss read silently. Explain any new vocabulary.

Vocabulary

Would you mind (doing something)?: Please (do something).
make sure: be certain that something will happen
lock: close with a key
thin: not thick or strong

- Point out that *can, could, would,* and *Would you mind . . . ?* mean the same thing. Differences in feeling will be discussed in Exercise 8.
- Pairs discuss whether or not the requests are reasonable.
- ***Option:*** Play the audio program again. Have Ss listen to the intonation of the speakers. Then Ss take turns reading the requests in pairs.

B

- Explain the task. In pairs, Ss discuss which requests they or someone else has made.
- ***Option:*** Ss share their ideas with another pair.

8 GRAMMAR FOCUS

Learning Objective: make requests with modals *can, could, would,* and *Would you mind . . . ?*

[CD 1, Track 54]

- Play the audio program to present the questions in the box. Ss listen and repeat.

***Modals* can, could, *and* would**

- Explain that it is OK to say, "please turn the music down," to people we know well. We should use a more polite request, however, for neighbors and strangers. Modals become more formal and more polite, from *can* to *could* to *would*. Tone of voice is also important.

Would you mind . . . ? + *gerund*

- Point out the structure *Would you mind . . . ?* + gerund in the Perspectives section. Explain that the verb *mind* must be followed by a gerund (verb + *-ing*). Elicit examples from Ss and write them on the board.
- Go over the negative request with *not* in the Perspectives section. Elicit other examples for the class to practice (e.g., *Would you mind* not *talking while I'm speaking? Would you mind* not *coming late to class, please?*).

A

- Explain the task. Ss work individually to match each request with a response. Then pairs compare answers. Ask the first S to finish to write the answers on the board. Check them as the S writes.

Possible answers

1. a, d	3. a	5. a, f
2. a, b	4. a, c, f	6. a, e

- Ss practice the requests and responses in pairs.

B *Pair work*

- Model the task with one or two Ss.

  T: Would you mind not using your phone in class?
  S: Sorry! It was an important call!

- In pairs, Ss take turns making the requests and giving their own responses.

! For another way to practice requests, try ***Moving Dialogue*** – download it from the website.

C *Class activity*

- Explain the task. Encourage Ss to think of unusual requests. Then Ss move around the classroom and make their requests.
- Find out who had the most unusual requests.

7 PERSPECTIVES Difficult neighbors

A Match the sentences. Then listen and check your answers. Are all the requests reasonable?

1. "Would you take your garbage out, please? ___
2. "Would you mind not parking your car in my parking space? ___
3. "Would you mind turning the music down, please? ___
4. "Could you close the door behind you and make sure it locks? ___
5. "Can you keep your cat inside, please? ___

a. We don't want strangers to enter the building."
b. It often comes into my apartment through the balcony."
c. It can attract insects."
d. The walls are really thin, so the sound goes through to my apartment."
e. I need to park mine there."

B Look at the requests again. Have you ever made similar requests? Has anyone ever asked you to do similar things?

8 GRAMMAR FOCUS

Requests with modals and *Would you mind . . . ?*

Modal + simple form of verb	***Would you mind . . .* + gerund**
Can you **keep** your cat inside, please?	**Would you mind keeping** your cat inside?
Could you **turn** the music **down**, please?	**Would you mind turning** the music **down**, please?
Would you please **park** your car in your space?	**Would you mind not parking** your car in my space?

GRAMMAR PLUS *see page 137*

A Match the requests in column A with the appropriate responses in column B. Then compare with a partner and practice them. (More than one answer may be possible.)

A

1. Would you mind not using your phone in class? ___
2. Would you mind speaking more quietly? ___
3. Would you please turn on the air conditioner? ___
4. Can you make me a sandwich? ___
5. Can you help me with my homework? ___
6. Could you lend me twenty dollars, please? ___

B

a. Sure, no problem. I'd be glad to.
b. Sorry. We didn't know we were so loud.
c. Sure. Do you want anything to drink?
d. Sorry. I had to talk to my boss.
e. I'm sorry, I can't. I don't have any cash.
f. I'm really sorry, but I'm busy.

B **PAIR WORK** Take turns making the requests in part A. Give your own responses.

C **CLASS ACTIVITY** Think of five unusual requests. Go around the class and make your requests. How many people accept? How many refuse?

A: Would you please lend me your car for the weekend?
B: Oh, I'm sorry. I'm going to wash it.

9 SPEAKING Apologies

Choose one of the situations below. Take turns making a request to your "neighbor." The "neighbor" should apologize by giving an excuse, admitting a mistake, or making an offer or a promise.

A: Would you mind not making so much noise? It's very late.
B: Oh, I'm sorry. I didn't realize it bothered you.

Different ways to apologize

give an excuse	"I'm sorry. I didn't realize . . ."
admit a mistake	"I forgot I left it there."
make an offer	"I'll take it out right now."
make a promise	"I promise I'll . . ./I'll make sure to . . ."

10 INTERCHANGE 6 I'm terribly sorry.

How good are you at apologizing? Go to Interchange 6 on page 119.

11 WRITING A public message

A Think of a problem that you could have with your neighbors. Write a message explaining the problem and making a request.

> To the person who left a big mess in the laundry room yesterday afternoon: Would you mind cleaning up after you finish your laundry? I fell down and almost broke my leg because the floor was all wet. Thank you.

B **PAIR WORK** Exchange messages with your classmates. Write a message apologizing for the problem you caused to your "neighbor."

> I'm sorry about the mess in the laundry room. My boss called me, and I had to go back to the office. I'll make sure to clean it up next time.

C **GROUP WORK** Take turns reading your messages aloud. Do you have similar problems with your neighbors? How do you solve them?

9 SPEAKING

Learning Objective: make requests and apologize

- Explain the task. Then give Ss time to think of a request to make. They can choose from one of the situations in the pictures or use their own ideas. Remind them to use the polite form of requests.
- Ask: "What reasons do students give when they come late to class? When they forget to bring their books?" Accept any reasonable answers.
- Explain that an *apology* is a statement that a person makes to show that he or she is sorry. Point out that there are different ways to apologize.
- Have Ss read the information in the chart. Explain any new vocabulary.

Vocabulary
admit a mistake: say that you did something wrong
make an offer: say you are willing to do something for someone
make a promise: say that you definitely will (or won't) do something

- Explain and model the task with a few Ss. Make requests and give direction on how Ss should apologize.

T: You're late again! Give an excuse.
S1: Oh, I'm sorry. I had to visit my aunt and . . .
T: You forgot to do your homework. Make an offer.
S2: I'm sorry. I'll do it tonight.

- In pairs, Ss take turns making requests and apologizing. Go around the class and listen.

TIP
To let Ss concentrate on what they are saying during a speaking activity, it is best not to interrupt. Listen and take note of any errors you hear. Then go over the errors at the end of the activity.

- Go over errors by writing the most common ones on the board and asking Ss to correct them. Give help as needed.

! For another way to practice complaints and apologies, try ***Question Everything*** – download it from the website. Ss put their own requests in the bag.

- ***Option:*** Discuss ways to apologize in other cultures.
  In a heterogeneous class: Ask: "How and why do people in other countries apologize? What are some differences you know about?"
  In a homogeneous class: Ask: "How and why do people in your country usually apologize?"

10 INTERCHANGE 6

See page T-120 for teaching notes.

11 WRITING

Learning Objective: write a public message using requests with modals and *Would you mind . . . ?*

A

- Ask if any Ss live in an apartment building. If so, ask: "Are there any notes around the apartment building of things that you should or shouldn't do? Who writes them?"
- Have Ss read the instructions and the example individually. Explain any new vocabulary.
- Point out the features of the message (e.g., to whom it is written, the issue, the request, what it caused).
- Ss use the situations in Exercise 9 or their own ideas.
- Ss write their own messages individually.

B *Pair work*

- Ss take turns reading their messages aloud in pairs.
- Ss discuss their problems in pairs and exchange messages.
- Have Ss write a message apologizing for the problem they caused.
- Discuss whether the apologies are *making a promise, admitting the mistake,* or *making an offer.*

C *Group work*

- Encourage Ss to ask each other questions about the problems they have at home.
- Have Ss think of suggestions to solve the problems using expressions like: "you could try to.../It's a good idea to.../Maybe you should..."
- ***Option:*** Follow up with a role play where neighbors are at a condominium meeting. In small groups, Ss read the problems they wrote and discuss the possible solutions.

12 READING

Learning Objectives: read for specific information in an article; identify meaning from context

A

- Books closed. Ask: "What kinds of strange requests do people make in a hotel? How about strange complaints?" Ss discuss the questions in small groups or as a class.
- Books open. Have Ss read the question and scan the article for the answer. (Answer: Three of the requests are about food, and one of the complaints is about food.)
- Ss read the article individually. Tell them not to use their dictionaries because guessing meaning from context is the skill practiced in part B.

B

- Explain the task. Ss work individually to complete the exercise.
- Elicit answers.

Answers

1. b 2. c 3. e 4. a 5. d

- Elicit any words that Ss still don't know. Then explain the words or have Ss check their dictionaries.

Vocabulary
look after: to take care of
almost: very close to happening
staff: people who work for an organization
gain: to get, to increase

C

- Explain the task. Point out that all the sentences are incorrect. Read the first sentence and ask Ss to find where it is incorrect. Ss correct the rest individually. Then go over answers with the class.

Answers

1. It's common for guests to request an extra-large bed.
2. One hotel guest asked to borrow an employee's suit.
3. Another guest wanted the fruit at breakfast to be the same size.
4. One person wasn't happy because he kept getting up too late.
5. Someone complained about not taking the right things to go swimming.

D *Pair work*

- Ss discuss the requests and complaints in pairs.
- Pairs share some interesting ideas that they discussed with the rest of the class.
- ***Option:*** Pairs act out one of these situations in front of the class.

For more specific practice, play ***Just One Minute*** – download it from the website.

End of Cycle 2

See the Supplementary Resources chart at the beginning of this unit for additional teaching materials and student activities related to this Cycle.

12 READING

A Scan the text. How many of the requests and complaints are about food?

HOME WORLD CULTURE TRAVEL BUSINESS SPORTS FOOD

HOTEL MADNESS: THE CRAZY THINGS PEOPLE SAY!

There are about 500,000 hotels around the world. Every day, receptionists, servers, chefs, and managers work in these hotels looking after their guests. Guests often make special requests for things like an extra-large bed or a room with a view of the water. And sometimes people complain when something is not satisfactory. In the U.S., around two-thirds of these complaints are about the noise that other guests are making. Sometimes, guests' requests and complaints can make a hotel worker's job almost impossible!

Here are some very weird requests that hotel workers have actually heard:

"Would you mind lending me your suit tomorrow? I have a job interview to go to!"

"Could one of the staff give my daughter a hand with her homework?"

"Can you please fill my bath with chocolate milk?"

"I'd like chicken for dinner, please, but only the right leg."

"Can you make sure all the strawberries in my cereal are the same size?"

Some hotel guests are also very good at finding (or imagining) problems! These are some of their crazy complaints:

At a London hotel, 40 miles from the coast: "I can't see the ocean from my room."

At a Portuguese hotel: "My bed is way too comfortable. I keep oversleeping and missing the best part of the day!"

At a hotel in Spain: "There are too many tasty dishes on the restaurant buffet. I've gained more than 5 pounds!"

To a receptionist in the middle of the night: "I haven't been able to sleep at all! My wife won't stop snoring!"

After coming back from a day trip to a water park: "Nobody told us to bring our swimsuits and towels."

So the next time you're at a hotel and the staff look tired, be patient! Maybe they've had a stressful day!

B Read the article. Find the words in *italics* in the article. Then match each word with its meaning.

1. *give (somebody) a hand* ___
2. *satisfactory* ___
3. *weird* ___
4. *snoring* ___
5. *oversleep* ___

a. to breathe in a noisy way when asleep
b. help a person do something
c. good enough
d. not wake up early enough
e. very strange

C The sentences below are false. Correct each sentence to make it true.

1. It's common for guests to request a bigger room.
2. One hotel guest asked to borrow an employee's dress.
3. Another guest wanted the fruit at breakfast to be the same color.
4. One person wasn't happy because he kept getting up too early.
5. Someone complained about not taking the right things to go sightseeing.

D **PAIR WORK** Imagine you are the managers of a hotel. How would you respond to the requests and complaints above? Try to be as polite as you can!

Units 5–6 Progress check

SELF-ASSESSMENT

How well can you do these things? Check (✓) the boxes.

I can . . .	Very well	OK	A little
Understand descriptions of people's plans (Ex. 1)	☐	☐	☐
Discuss vacation plans (Ex. 2)	☐	☐	☐
Give travel advice (Ex. 2)	☐	☐	☐
Make and respond to requests (Ex. 3, 4)	☐	☐	☐
Apologize and give excuses (Ex. 3, 4)	☐	☐	☐

1 LISTENING What are your plans?

A Listen to Lily, Tyler, and Abby describe their summer plans. What is each person going to do?

Summer plans	Reason
1. Lily ______	______
2. Tyler ______	______
3. Abby ______	______

B Listen again. What is the reason for each person's choice?

C **PAIR WORK** What did you do last summer? Listen to your partner and share with the class.

2 DISCUSSION Vacation plans

A **GROUP WORK** Imagine you are going to go on vacation. Take turns asking and answering these questions.

A: Where are you going to go on your next vacation?
B: I'm going to go to New York.
A: What are you going to do?
B: I'm going to visit the museums. Maybe I'll see a musical on Broadway.
A: Why did you choose that?
B: Well, I want to have a more cultural vacation this year.

B **GROUP WORK** What should each person do to prepare for his or her vacation? Give each other advice.

Progress check

SELF-ASSESSMENT

Learning Objectives: reflect on one's learning; identify areas that need improvement

- Ask: "What did you learn in Units 5 and 6?" Elicit Ss' answers.
- Ss complete the Self-assessment. Explain to Ss that this is not a test; it is a way for them to evaluate what they've learned and identify areas where they need additional practice. Encourage them to be honest, and point out they will not get a bad grade if they check (✓) "A little."
- Ss move on to the Progress check exercises. You can have Ss complete them in class or for homework, using one of these techniques:
  1. Ask Ss to complete all the exercises.
  2. Ask Ss: "What do you need to practice?" Then assign exercises based on their answers.
  3. Ask Ss to choose and complete exercises based on their Self-assessment.

1 LISTENING

Learning Objective: demonstrate one's ability to understand descriptions of people's plans

A *[CD 1, Track 55]*

- Set the scene. Three people are talking about their summer plans. Go over the chart and explain that Ss should complete only the first column.
- Play the audio program. Ss listen and write what each person is going to do. Check answers with the class.

Audio script

See page T-172.

Answers

1. Lily: go to the beach and go snorkeling
2. Tyler: stay home and get a job
3. Abby: work the first month and then visit her sister in Thailand

B *[CD 1, Track 56]*

- Explain the task. Ss listen for each person's reasons.
- Play the audio program again. Ss listen and complete the second column.
- Check answers with the class.

Answers

1. Lily: Last year she went white-water rafting and mountain climbing, and she was tired at the end.
2. Tyler: He needs to save money for school.
3. Abby: She wants to save some money. She wants to see what Bangkok (Thailand) is like.

C *Pair work*

- Ss discuss the question in pairs and then share answers with the class.

2 DISCUSSION

Learning Objectives: demonstrate one's ability to ask and answer questions about plans; demonstrate one's ability to give travel advice

A *Group work*

- Explain the task. Ss imagine they are going on vacation. Then Ss ask and answer questions about each other's vacation plans.
- Call on two Ss to read the example conversation. Remind Ss to add additional information and ask follow-up questions to keep the conversation going.
- Give Ss a few minutes to plan their vacation and prepare some questions to ask others in the group.
- In small groups, Ss take turns asking and answering questions about their vacations. Go around the class, paying attention to Ss' use of *be going to* and *will* and their ability to keep a conversation going.
- Give the class feedback on their discussions. What went well? What problems did you hear?

B *Group work*

- Explain the task. Then ask Ss about their vacation plans to model how to give advice.

  T: What are you going to do on your vacation?
  S1: I'm going to go skiing with my friends.
  T: I think you should take warm clothing with you.
  S2: I agree. I think you also need to take money.
- Have Ss complete the task. Go around the class, paying particular attention to their use of modals for necessity and suggestion.
- ***Option:*** Ask groups to tell the class about one vacation and how someone should prepare for it.

3 ROLE PLAY

Learning Objectives: demonstrate one's ability to make and respond to practical requests; demonstrate one's ability to apologize and give excuses

- Explain the task and focus Ss' attention on the pictures. Elicit useful vocabulary from Ss.
- Divide the class into pairs and assign roles. Student A makes a request about each picture, while Student B apologizes and either accepts or refuses the request.
- Call on two Ss to read the example conversation. Explain that here Student B agrees to the request, but Ss can also refuse the request by giving an excuse. Ask: "How could Student B politely refuse the request? What excuse could he or she make?" Elicit ideas (e.g., *I'm sorry. I forgot about them. But I can't pick them up because I have a bad back/am late for an appointment.*). Encourage Ss to be creative when they make excuses.
- Student A begins by using the picture to make a request. Student B replies with an apology and then accepts or refuses the request.
- Go around the class and listen to the role plays without interrupting. Make a note of common errors or ways in which the role plays could be better.
- Make suggestions on how Ss could improve their role plays. Give examples of good communication that you heard.
- Ss change roles and try the role play again.

4 GAME

Learning Objectives: demonstrate one's ability to make and respond to practical requests; demonstrate one's ability to apologize and give excuses

A

- Give three cards or slips of paper to each S. Explain the task. Ss write one request on each card. Read the examples and elicit more suggestions. Ask Ss to try to write one request with *Can*, one with *Could*, and one with *Would you mind . . . ?*
- Individually, Ss write one request on each card. Then tell them to write an *X* on the back of two cards.
- Collect the cards and shuffle them all together.

B *Class activity*

- Give each S three cards. Ss should make sure they did not get any of their own cards.
- Explain the task. Ss get up and move around the room, making the requests written on their cards. As they make the request, they should hold up the card so the other S can see the back of the card. If the card has an *X* on the back, the person should refuse the request. If the card does not have an *X*, the person must accept the request.
- Model the task several times with cards and different Ss.
- Ss stand up and complete the activity. Go around the class and listen to the requests and responses, paying attention to the Ss' use of modals and *will* for acceptance.

WHAT'S NEXT?

Learning Objective: become more involved in one's learning

- Focus Ss' attention on the Self-assessment again. Ask: "How well can you do these things now?"
- Ask Ss to underline one thing they need to review. Ask: "What did you underline? How can you review it?"
- If needed, plan additional activities or reviews based on Ss' answers.

3 ROLE PLAY Making excuses

Student A: Your partner was supposed to do some things, but didn't. Look at the pictures and make a request about each one.

Student B: You were supposed to do some things, but didn't. Listen to your partner's requests. Apologize and either agree to the request or give an excuse.

A: Your room is a big mess. Please clean it up.

B: I'm sorry. I forgot about it. I'll clean it up after dinner.

Change roles and try the role play again.

4 GAME Can I ask you a favor?

A Write three requests on separate cards. Put an *X* on the back of two of the cards.

Can you help me with my homework?

Could you get me a cup of coffee?

Would you mind cooking dinner tonight?

B **CLASS ACTIVITY** Shuffle all the cards together. Take three new cards.

Go around the class and take turns making requests with the cards. Hold up each card so your classmate can see the back.

When answering:

X on the back = refuse the request and give an excuse

No *X* = agree to the request

WHAT'S NEXT?

Look at your Self-assessment again. Do you need to review anything?

Unit 7 Supplementary Resources Overview

	After the following SB exercises	You can use these materials in class	Your students can use these materials outside the classroom
CYCLE 1	1 Snapshot		
	2 Perspectives		
	3 Grammar Focus		**SB** Unit 7 Grammar plus, Focus 1 **SS** Unit 7 Grammar 1 **GAME** Say the Word (Infinitives and gerunds for uses and purposes 1) **GAME** Sentence Stacker (Infinitives and gerunds for uses and purposes 2)
	4 Pronunciation		
	5 Word Power	**TSS** Unit 7 Vocabulary Worksheet	**SS** Unit 7 Vocabulary 1–2 **GAME** Spell or Slime (Vocabulary)
	6 Listening		**WB** Unit 7 exercises 1–4
CYCLE 2	7 Conversation		**SS** Unit 7 Speaking 1–2
	8 Grammar Focus	**TSS** Unit 7 Grammar Worksheet **TSS** Unit 7 Extra Worksheet	**SB** Unit 7 Grammar plus, Focus 2 **SS** Unit 7 Grammar 2 **GAME** Speak or Swim (Imperatives and infinitives for suggestions)
	9 Listening	**TSS** Unit 7 Listening Worksheet	
	10 Interchange 7		
	11 Writing	**TSS** Unit 7 Writing Worksheet	
	12 Reading	**TSS** Unit 7 Project Worksheet **VID** Unit 7 **VRB** Unit 7	**SS** Unit 7 Reading 1–2 **SS** Unit 7 Listening 1–4 **SS** Unit 7 Video 1–3 **WB** Unit 7 exercises 5–11

Key **GAME:** Online Game **SB:** Student's Book **SS:** Online Self-study **TSS:** Teacher Support Site
VID: Video DVD **VRB:** Video Resource Book **WB:** Online Workbook/Workbook

My Plan for Unit 7

Use the space below to customize a plan that fits your needs.

With the following SB exercises	I am using these materials in class	My students are using these materials outside the classroom

With or instead of the following SB section	I am using these materials for assessment

7 What do you use this for?

- Describe uses and purposes of technology
- Give suggestions

1 SNAPSHOT

Inventions We Can't Live Without

- ☐ smartphones
- ☐ digital cameras
- ☐ Internet
- ☐ e-readers
- ☐ tablet computers
- ☐ streaming TV
- ☐ robots
- ☐ 3-D printers
- ☐ driverless cars
- ☐ GPS technology
- ☐ drones
- ☐ Wi-Fi

How long have the inventions above been around in your country?
How was life different before them?
Check (✓) three inventions you couldn't live without. Compare with a partner.

2 PERSPECTIVES Smartphone usage

A How do you use your smartphone? Listen and respond to the statements.

I use my smartphone . . .	Often	Sometimes	Hardly ever	Never
to send messages	☐	☐	☐	☐
for watching videos	☐	☐	☐	☐
to take photos	☐	☐	☐	☐
to post on social media sites	☐	☐	☐	☐
for doing school assignments	☐	☐	☐	☐
to send emails	☐	☐	☐	☐
to shop online	☐	☐	☐	☐
to check the weather	☐	☐	☐	☐
to read e-books	☐	☐	☐	☐
for listening to music	☐	☐	☐	☐

B **PAIR WORK** Compare your answers. Are your answers similar or different?

7 What do you use this for?

In Unit 7, students discuss modern technology and inventions. By the end of Cycle 1, students will be able to use infinitives and gerunds to describe uses and purposes. By the end of Cycle 2, students will be able to use imperatives and infinitives to give suggestions.

Cycle 1, Exercises 1–6

1 SNAPSHOT

Learning Objective: discuss important scientific and technological inventions

- ***Option:*** Have Ss brainstorm machines and inventions they use every day (e.g., *smartphone, credit cards, TV, computer, video games*).

TIP
To help Ss get ready to speak English, start each class with a quick warm-up activity. This will also help deal with Ss who arrive late!

- Books closed. Ask questions like: "How long have you had your smartphone? Tablet? Computer? If you could buy some cool new gadget, what would it be?"
- Books open. Read all the inventions listed and explain any new vocabulary.
- Model the pronunciation of the items and have Ss repeat. Read the questions. Ss answer them in pairs or groups. Go around the class and give help as needed.
- ***Option:*** Ask Ss to describe how the inventions have changed (e.g., *Computers are much smaller now.*).

2 PERSPECTIVES

Learning Objectives: discuss technology; identify infinitives and gerunds for uses and purposes in context

A *[CD 2, Track 1]*

- Books closed. Ask Ss what they use their smartphones for (e.g., *send messages, take photos, watch videos…*). Write Ss' ideas on the board. If some Ss don't have a smartphone, ask: "How often do you use your cell phone? How do you use it? Where do you use it?" Write some common uses on the board.

TIP
To give Ss more incentive to listen to the Perspectives section, give focus questions before playing the audio program.

- Play the audio program. Ask Ss to name some of the uses they heard. Check to see if they heard any of the uses on the board.
- Books open. Explain the task. Point out that Ss can check (✓) *Often, Sometimes, Hardly ever,* or *Never*. Model the first sentence.
- Give Ss time to check (✓) the appropriate boxes.
- ***Option:*** Ss count their boxes and find out who uses the smartphone for the most purposes.
- Elicit any new vocabulary. Ask the class to give definitions or examples. Then explain any scientific or technical terms that Ss can't find in their dictionaries.

Vocabulary
post: to display in public
school assignment: project or homework

B *Pair work*

- Write these expressions on the board:

  both . . . and I . . .
  neither . . . nor I . . .
  He/She does, but I don't.

- Ss compare answers in pairs. Ask: "How different or similar are you?" Elicit responses.
- ***Option:*** Have a brief class discussion about some controversial issues concerning smartphones (e.g., ask: "What are some problems for young people on social networking sites? How often do you check your smartphone?").

3 GRAMMAR FOCUS

Learning Objective: use infinitives and gerunds to describe uses and purposes

[CD 2, Track 2]

Infinitives and gerunds

- Explain that we can describe how something is used with either an infinitive or a gerund. The meaning is the same.
- Refer Ss to the Perspectives section. Point out that the chart contains ten uses of the smartphone. The examples use both infinitives and gerunds. Elicit or explain the difference between the two forms:

  With an infinitive (*to* + verb)
  I use my cell phone **to send** messages.
  With a gerund (*for* + verb + *-ing*)
  I use my cell phone **for sending** messages
- Have Ss underline the examples of infinitives and circle the examples of gerunds.
- Play the audio program to present the statements in the Grammar Focus box. For pronunciation practice, point out that the prepositions *to* and *for* are unstressed.
- Play the audio program again. Ss listen and repeat.

A *Pair work*

- Ask Ss to skim the phrases in part A in pairs. Then elicit or explain any new vocabulary.

Vocabulary
perform: do
tasks: jobs, chores
directions: the course that must be taken in order to reach a destination
robot: a computer-controlled factory machine

- Explain the task. Point out that *You* in the second item is an impersonal pronoun. It refers to people in general.
- Model the task by eliciting three possible answers for the first item. Then have Ss complete the task in pairs. Then go over answers with both infinitives and gerunds.

Possible answers

1. Many people use tablet computers **to learn/ for learning** languages/**to get/for getting** directions/**to make/for making** video calls.
2. You can use your smartphone **to learn/ for learning** languages/**to get/for getting** directions/**to make/for making** video calls.
3. Engineers use 3D printers **to make/for making** car parts.
4. People can use the Internet **to learn/for learning** languages/**to get/for getting** directions/**to make/for making** video calls.
5. Companies sometimes use robots **to perform/ for performing** dangerous tasks.
6. The police use drones **to look/for looking** for criminals.

B *Pair work*

- In pairs, Ss brainstorm new uses.
- Encourage them to think of interesting and creative uses for each item. Ask one S in each pair to write down the pair's sentences. Go around and give help as needed.
- Call on one S from each pair to read some sentences to the class.

For more practice with infinitives and gerunds, play ***Twenty Questions*** – download it from the website. Ss guess what object someone is thinking of.

C *Group work*

- Have the Ss make groups with the pairs next to them.
- Explain that they should think of unusual uses for the items.
- Ask a S from each group to present to the rest of the class. Who has the funniest use?

4 PRONUNCIATION

Learning Objective: sound more natural by using stress in words with more than two syllables

A *[CD 2, Track 3]*

- Model how to pronounce the main stress in the words *Internet, invention,* and *engineer.* Ss tap the desk or clap in time to the stress.
- Play the audio program and have Ss pay attention to the syllable stress. Then play the audio program again. Ss listen and repeat.

B *[CD 2, Track 4]*

- Ss mark the syllable stress in the words and write them in the correct column.
- Play the audio program. Ss listen and check their answers.

Answers

● • •	driverless, media
• ● •	directions, equipment
• • ●	entertain, understand

3 GRAMMAR FOCUS

Infinitives and gerunds for uses and purposes

Infinitives	Gerunds
I use my cell phone **to send** messages.	I use my cell phone **for sending** messages.
Some people use their phones **to watch** videos.	Some people use their phones **for watching** videos.
People often use their phones **to take** photos.	People often use their phones **for taking** photos.

GRAMMAR PLUS *see page 138*

A PAIR WORK What do you know about this technology? Complete the sentences in column A with information from column B. Use infinitives and gerunds. (More than one combination is possible.)

A	B
1. Many people use tablet computers . . .	look for criminals.
2. You can use your smartphone . . .	perform dangerous tasks.
3. Engineers use 3-D printers . . .	get directions.
4. People can use the Internet . . .	make car parts.
5. Companies sometimes use robots . . .	make video calls.
6. The police use drones . . .	learn languages.

Many people use tablet computers to make video calls.
Many people use tablet computers for making video calls.

B PAIR WORK Think of one other use for the items in column A.

"Paparazzi use drones to spy on celebrities."

C GROUP WORK List some unexpected uses for these new and old items. Compare your answers with the whole class. Who came up with the most uses?

a smartphone **a paper clip** **a webcam** **a pencil** **invisible tape** **an old CD**

"You can use your smartphone for driving your car."

4 PRONUNCIATION Syllable stress

A Listen and practice. Notice which syllable has the main stress.

● • •	• ● •	• • ●
Internet	invention	engineer
messages	assignment	DVD
digital	computer	recommend
______	______	______
______	______	______

B Where is the stress in these words? Add them to the columns in part A. Then listen and check.

directions driverless entertain equipment media understand

5 WORD POWER Plugged in

A Complete the chart with words and phrases from the list. Add one more to each category. Then compare with a partner.

✓ computer whiz	hacker	check in for a flight	geek
computer crash	edit photos	download apps	software bugs
flash drive	identity theft	make international phone calls	frozen screen
smart devices	early adopter	solar-powered batteries	phone charger

Problems with technology	Gadgets and devices	People who are "into" technology	Things to do online
		computer whiz	

B **GROUP WORK** Discuss some of the positive and negative consequences of living in a connected world.

- Have you ever had any of the problems mentioned in part A? What happened? What did you do?
- Do you have any smart devices? Which ones? How do they help you? How much do you depend on them?
- Do you have any friends who never put their phone away? Is anyone in your family addicted to new technologies? Are you?
- What is one gadget you would really like to have? Why?
- Is identity theft a problem where you live? What about hackers? How do you protect against them?

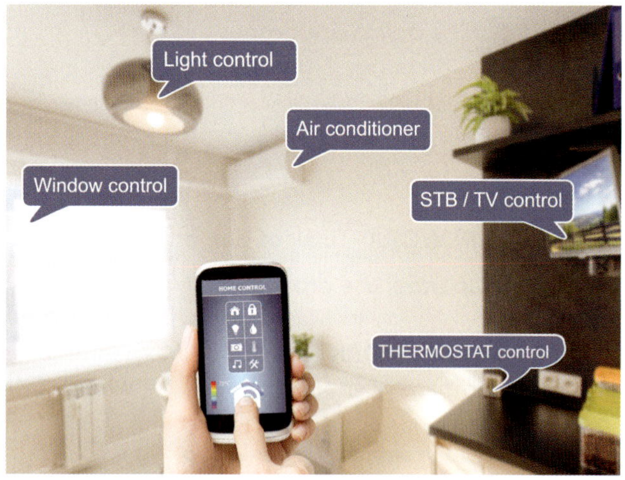

6 LISTENING They've thought of everything!

A Listen to two people talk about the best apps for travel. Check (✓) the four app categories. (There are two extra categories.)

- ☐ safety ______________________
- ☐ packing ______________________
- ☐ music ______________________
- ☐ transportation ______________________
- ☐ attractions ______________________
- ☐ hotel ______________________

B Listen again. What can you use the apps for? Write the uses next to the categories you checked above.

C **PAIR WORK** What are your favorite apps? Discuss and share with the class.

5 WORD POWER

Learning Objective: discuss computers and how they impact modern life

A

TIP
To avoid spending a long time teaching words in class, have Ss look up the vocabulary for homework before class.

- ***Option:*** Assign each S four words to look up in a dictionary. Then put Ss in groups of four and have them teach each other their words.

Vocabulary
computer whiz: a person who is an expert at computers
flash drive: a small memory storage device that plugs into a USB port on a computer
smart device: a mobile device that connects to the Internet
identity theft: the stealing of a person's private identifying information
early adopter: a person who starts using a product or technology as soon as it becomes available
geek: a person that is extremely interested in computers

- Read the instructions. Then use the example (*computer whiz*) to model the task. Remind Ss to try to add one more word to each category. Ss work individually to complete the chart.
- Draw the chart on the board. Elicit answers and write them on the board.

Answers

Problems with technology	Gadgets and devices
computer crash	flash drive
software bugs	smart devices
identity theft	phone charger
frozen screen	solar-powered batteries
People who are "into" technology	**Things to do online**
computer whiz	check in for a flight
hacker	edit photos
geek	download apps
early adopter	make international phone calls

B *Group work*

- Explain the task. Ss read the questions silently and ask any vocabulary questions. Pre-teach the words *addicted* (dependent) and *gadget* (a small mechanical or electronic device or tool).
- Ss discuss the questions in small groups. Encourage them to use the vocabulary they learned in part A. Go around the class and give help as needed.

To review this vocabulary, play ***Tic-Tac-Toe*** – download it from the website.

6 LISTENING

Learning Objective: listen for details about apps

A *[CD 2, Track 5]*

- Focus Ss' attention on part A. Ask Ss: "What do you think a good travel app should have?"
- Read the categories aloud and explain that there are two extra. Ask: "Which ones do you think are the most important?"
- Play the audio program. Ss listen to check the four app categories. Elicit answers.

Audio script

See page T-172.

Answers for parts A and B

✓ packing: to learn about the weather and pack items the app recommends
✓ music: to save new songs we like and add them to a list
✓ attractions: to look at people's pictures by country, city, or attraction and save them
✓ hotel: to find available rooms for a certain price and get a discount

B *[CD 2, Track 6]*

- Play the audio program again. Ss listen and write the uses of the apps next to the categories.
- Have Ss compare their answers in pairs.

C *Pair work*

- In small groups, Ss discuss the question. Encourage them to ask questions like: "Why is that your favorite? What do you like about it?"
- Have them share their favorite apps with the class. Which one is the most popular?

End of Cycle 1

See the Supplementary Resources chart at the beginning of this unit for additional teaching materials and student activities related to this Cycle.

7 CONVERSATION

Learning Objective: use imperatives and infinitives for giving suggestions in a conversation about technology

- ***Option:*** Introduce the topic by asking Ss what kind of problems they normally have with their smartphones. Ask them to explain how to solve one of the problems they mention. For fun and challenge, pretend you don't understand!

A *[CD 2, Track 7]*

- Books closed. Set the scene. Someone is explaining how to make a phone stop freezing. Write these questions on the board:

  1. Who has the problem?
  2. What's the first thing to do?
  3. What should he try not to do?

- Play the audio program. Then elicit Ss' answers. (Answers: 1. the man 2. install a good antivirus application 3. use public Wi-Fi networks)
- Books open. Play the audio program again as Ss look at the picture and read silently. Explain any new vocabulary.
- Write these instructions on the board:

  _____ Be sure to update it.
  _____ Don't forget to reset all your passwords.
  _____ Install a good antivirus application.
  _____ Try not to use public Wi-Fi networks.

- Have Ss put the instructions in the correct order. (Answers: 2, 3, 1, 4)
- ***Option:*** Ask Ss if they have any other suggestions.
- Ss practice the conversation in pairs.

! For another way to practice this conversation, try ***Look Up and Speak!*** – download it from the website.

B *[CD 2, Track 8]*

- Play the rest of the audio program. Ss listen to find out what else Justin wants help with. Elicit answers.

Audio script

See page T-173.

Answers

Justin needs help buying a new tablet computer. Allie suggests they go to a store together.

8 GRAMMAR FOCUS

Learning Objective: use imperatives and infinitives to give suggestions

[CD 2, Track 9]

- Play the audio program to present the sentences in the box. Have Ss listen and repeat.
- Ask Ss to look back at the previous conversation and underline some of the structures in the Grammar Focus box. (Answer: *be sure to, don't forget to*)

A

- Explain the task. Ss complete the task individually or in pairs. Go around the class and give help as needed. Then elicit answers.

Possible answers

1. a. **Make sure to/Be sure to/Remember to/Don't forget to** reset the passcode before using an electronic safe.
   b. **Make sure to/Be sure to/Remember to/Don't forget to** check if it's locked after you close it.
2. a. **Be sure not to/Try not to** get your phone wet or it might not work anymore.
   b. **Make sure to/Be sure to/Remember to/Don't forget to/Try to** back up your contacts and other important information.
3. a. **Make sure to/Be sure to/Remember to/Don't forget to** set your alarm system each time you leave home.
   b. **Be sure not to** use your birthday as a code.
4. a. **Make sure to/Be sure to/Remember to/Don't forget to/Try to** keep the lenses of your digital camera clean.
   b. **Make sure to/Be sure to/Remember to/Don't forget to/Try to** keep the lens cap on when you're not taking photos.

B *Pair work*

- Model the activity with several Ss. In pairs, have Ss take turns giving suggestions for using the four items in part A.
- ***Option:*** Play a game. Ss give advice, and the rest of the class guesses what the advice refers to.

7 CONVERSATION What do I do now?

A Listen and practice.

Justin: I can't believe my phone's frozen again.
Allie: How long have you had it?
Justin: About a year. It's not that old.
Allie: Maybe someone hacked it.
Justin: Really? You think so?
Allie: No, I'm just kidding. It's probably just a virus.
Justin: Oh. So what do I do now?
Allie: First, you'd better install a good antivirus app. And be sure to update it.
Justin: OK, I'll download one now. What else should I do?
Allie: Well, don't forget to reset all your passwords.
Justin: That's a good idea. I never remember to change my passwords.
Allie: One more thing. Try not to use public Wi-Fi networks.
Justin: You're right. I have to learn to be more careful.

B Listen to the rest of the conversation. What else does Justin want help with? What does Allie suggest?

8 GRAMMAR FOCUS

Imperatives and infinitives for giving suggestions

Be sure to update the app.
Make sure to charge your phone.
Remember to back up your files.
Don't forget to reset your passwords.
Try not to use public Wi-Fi networks.

GRAMMAR PLUS *see page 138*

A Look at the suggestions. Rewrite them using these phrases. Then compare with a partner.

Make sure to . . .	Try to . . .	Remember to . . .
Be sure not to . . .	Try not to . . .	Don't forget to . . .

1. **a.** Before using an electronic safe, you have to reset the passcode.
   b. You should check if it's locked after you close it.
2. **a.** Don't get your phone wet or it might not work anymore.
   b. It's important to back up your contacts and other important information.
3. **a.** You must set your alarm system each time you leave home.
   b. Don't use your birthday as a code.
4. **a.** You ought to keep the lenses of your digital camera clean.
   b. It's important to keep the lens cap on when you're not taking photos.

B **PAIR WORK** Take turns giving other suggestions for using the items in part A.

9 LISTENING Smart suggestions

A Listen to people give suggestions for using three of these things. Number them 1, 2, and 3. (There are two extra things.)

☐ 
portable speaker

☐ 

GPS system

☐ 
flash drive

☐ 
smartphone

☐ 
ATM card

B Listen again. Write two suggestions you hear for each thing. Then compare with a partner.

1. ______________________ ______________________
2. ______________________ ______________________
3. ______________________ ______________________

C **PAIR WORK** What do you know about the other two things in part A? Give suggestions about them.

"Be sure to buy one with lots of memory."

10 INTERCHANGE 7 Free advice

Give your classmates some advice. Go to Interchange 7 on page 121.

11 WRITING A message

A Imagine your brother is coming over for dinner, but you are going to be busy all day. Your roommate has agreed to help you. Think of three things you need help with. Then write a message with instructions.

B **GROUP WORK** Take turns reading your messages aloud. Did you ask for similar favors?

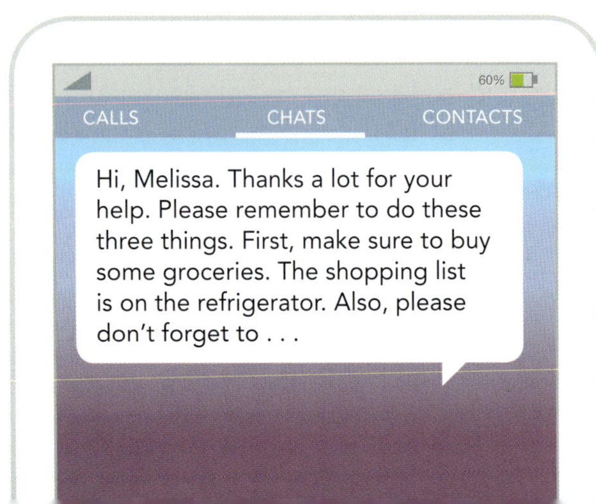

9 LISTENING

Learning Objective: listen for specific information in passages about technology

A *[CD 2, Track 10]*

- Focus Ss' attention on the pictures. Explain the task. In pairs or small groups, have Ss brainstorm the kinds of vocabulary and suggestions they expect to hear about each item.
- Play the audio program. Ss listen and number the three items in the order they are talked about. Elicit the answers.

Audio script

See page T-173.

Answers

1. smartphone 2. GPS system 3. ATM card

B *[CD 2, Track 11]*

- Play the audio program again, pausing after each speaker to give Ss time to write the suggestions. Then elicit answers.

Answers

1. Be sure to back up your photos at least once a month. Remember to put your favorite apps on the home screen.
2. Make sure to get the exact address. Be sure to watch the road.
3. Be sure to put it in correctly. Remember to press "Enter." Don't forget to count your money before you walk away from the machine.

! For grammar recognition practice, play ***Stand Up, Sit Down*** – download it from the website. Play the advice for the ATM card and GPS system. Ss listen for expressions taught in the Grammar Focus (e.g., *be sure to, remember to*).

C *Pair work*

- Explain the task. In pairs, Ss talk about the other items in part A (*portable speaker, flash drive*). Go around the class and give help as needed.
- Pairs share their best suggestions for each item with the rest of the class.
- Find out which Ss have used the things in part A. Ask: "Do you own any of these things?"

10 INTERCHANGE 7

See page T-121 for teaching notes.

11 WRITING

Learning Objective: write a personal message giving instructions using imperatives and infinitives

A

- Explain the situation. Ask Ss what they might need a roommate to do for them if they were going to be busy all day.
- Ss read the example paragraph silently. Point out that the message starts after Melissa has agreed to help. Now the writer is giving her a list of three things to do.
- Ss write a first draft. Tell them to use imperatives and infinitives where possible.
- ***Option:*** This part can also be assigned as homework.

B *Group work*

- In groups, Ss take turns reading their message aloud to the rest of the group. Ss discuss them and make suggestions for revision. Go around the class and give help as needed.
- Ss revise their drafts based on the group feedback and their own ideas.
- ***Option:*** Have Ss put their final drafts on a bulletin board or wall, exchange them with other Ss, or give them to you to read.

TIP

To increase Ss' self-confidence and create an English-speaking atmosphere in the classroom, display Ss' work on the classroom walls if possible.

12 READING

Learning Objectives: skim an article about the sharing economy; read for details

A

- Books closed. Ask Ss if they know what *sharing economy* means. Ask them if they would enjoy sharing a home or a car.
- Books open. Focus Ss' attention on the title of the article. Explain that they are going to find out about the effects of the sharing trend in our economy.
- Explain the task. Tell Ss to scan the article quickly looking for the answers to the questions. To encourage them to read quickly and not to worry about words they don't know, assign a time limit of one minute.
- Elicit the answers.

Answers

In the sharing economy, people use websites and apps to rent things and services to other people. The three examples given in the article are renting rooms, sharing cars, and sharing food.

B

- Ss read the article silently.
- Elicit or explain any new vocabulary. Encourage other Ss to explain the words using different words, pictures, or mime.

Vocabulary

rent: pay money to use something for a short time
employee: a person who is paid to work for a company
(get a) ride: a journey in a car to a place where you want to go
fee: an amount of money that you pay to do something, to use something, or to get a service
strict: must be obeyed
doubt: the feeling of not being certain about something
worth: to have a particular value

- Explain the task. Tell Ss to read the text again and circle the answer for each word. Explain that they cannot use their dictionary at this time. They should guess the meaning from context.
- Check the answers with the class.

Answers

1. makes
2. give to
3. dangerous
4. rules
5. equal

C

- Have students answer the questions individually and then check the answers in pairs.
- Check the answers with the class.

Answers

1. It's worth $20 billion a year.
2. You pay less.
3. Because there are fewer cars on the road.
4. When people use public transportation.
5. They don't have to follow safety regulations.

D

- Ss take turns answering the questions. Give suggestions or ask additional questions, if necessary.

End of Cycle 2

See the Supplementary Resources chart at the beginning of this unit for additional teaching materials and student activities related to this Cycle.

A Skim the article. What is the sharing economy? What three examples does the article give?

THE SHARING ECONOMY – GOOD FOR EVERYBODY?

Modern technology has made it easier for ordinary people to rent things or services to others. With the click of an app, we can find almost anything. It could be a new dress to wear on the weekend, or someone to clean your house. This is the sharing economy, and it is now a profitable $20 billion-a-year business. But some people are now asking: Just how good is it for society in general?

Not long ago, when people went on vacation, they usually stayed in a hotel. Today they have the choice of staying in someone's private house. They pay less, but what effect does this have on the hotel industry and the wider economy? Hotels receive fewer guests, but they still have to pay salaries to their employees and taxes to the government. Many people who rent out rooms do not. So the government gets less money, and some hotels might even close down.

Then there are car-sharing sites. Instead of using your own car for a long trip you can get a ride with someone for a small fee. Some people argue this is better for the environment, since fewer cars on the roads means less pollution. But how many people choose to use these sites rather than taking the bus or the train? Public transportation is, after all, much kinder to the environment than cars.

Many sites offer cooking services. Instead of going to a restaurant, you can use an app to order dishes from people in your neighborhood.

There is even a site where you can buy leftover food that people haven't eaten! This is sure to save you time and money. But is it risky? Can you trust the people cooking your food? Restaurants have to follow strict regulations to make sure their food is safe to eat.

There is no doubt that the sharing economy is growing. Some economists think it will be worth $335 billion by 2025. As new technology makes sharing food, accommodation, and transportation easier all the time, the question of "Is it fair?" will remain.

B Read the article. Find the words in *italics* below. Then circle the meaning of each word.

1. When a business is *profitable*, it **makes / loses** money.
2. *Taxes* are money that people **give to / receive from** the government.
3. If something is *risky*, it's **dangerous / safe**.
4. *Regulations* are **rules / people** that control how we do things.
5. When something is *fair*, everybody has **equal / different** opportunities.

C Answer the questions.

1. How much is the sharing economy worth nowadays?
2. What is the advantage of staying in a private house instead of a hotel?
3. Why is car sharing less damaging to the environment?
4. What is better for the environment than car sharing?
5. How can buying food from non-professionals be risky?

D Do you use any of these sharing-economy services? Are they ever risky? Do you think they are fair?

Unit 8 Supplementary Resources Overview

	After the following SB exercises	You can use these materials in class	Your students can use these materials outside the classroom
CYCLE 1	**1 Snapshot**		
	2 Word Power		**SS** Unit 8 Vocabulary 1–2 **GAME** Say the Word (Verb and noun collocations)
	3 Perspectives		
	4 Grammar Focus		**SB** Unit 8 Grammar plus, Focus 1 **SS** Unit 8 Grammar 1 **GAME** Word Keys (Relative clauses of time)
	5 Listening		
	6 Speaking	**TSS** Unit 8 Vocabulary Worksheet	
	7 Writing		**WB** Unit 8 exercises 1–4
CYCLE 2	**8 Conversation**		**SS** Unit 8 Speaking 1–2
	9 Pronunciation		
	10 Grammar Focus	**TSS** Unit 8 Grammar Worksheet **TSS** Unit 8 Listening Worksheet **TSS** Unit 8 Writing Worksheet	**SB** Unit 8 Grammar plus, Focus 2 **SS** Unit 8 Grammar 2 **GAME** Sentence Stacker (Adverbial clauses of time) **GAME** Sentence Runner (Relative and adverbial clauses of time)
	11 Interchange 8		
	12 Speaking		
	13 Reading	**TSS** Unit 8 Extra Worksheet **TSS** Unit 8 Project Worksheet **VID** Unit 8 **VRB** Unit 8	**SS** Unit 8 Reading 1–2 **SS** Unit 8 Listening 1–3 **SS** Unit 8 Video 1–3 **WB** Unit 8 exercises 5–10

With or instead of the following SB section	You can also use these materials for assessment
Units 7–8 Progress Check	**ASSESSMENT PROGRAM** Units 7–8 Oral Quiz **ASSESSMENT PROGRAM** Units 7–8 Written Quiz **ASSESSMENT PROGRAM** Units 1–8 Test

Key **GAME:** Online Game **SB:** Student's Book **SS:** Online Self-study **TSS:** Teacher Support Site
VID: Video DVD **VRB:** Video Resource Book **WB:** Online Workbook/Workbook

My Plan for Unit 8

Use the space below to customize a plan that fits your needs.

With the following SB exercises	I am using these materials in class	My students are using these materials outside the classroom

With or instead of the following SB section	I am using these materials for assessment

8 Time to celebrate!

- Discuss holidays and special occasions
- Describe celebrations, annual events, and customs

1 SNAPSHOT

HOLIDAYS AND FESTIVALS

Saint Patrick's Day
March 17th
People of Irish background wear green to celebrate their culture with parades, dancing, parties, and special foods.

Day of the Dead
November 2nd
Mexicans make playful skeleton sculptures and bake *pan de muerto* – bread of the dead.

Chinese New Year
January or February
Chinese people celebrate the lunar new year with fireworks and dragon dances.

Thanksgiving
November
In the United States, families get together, have a traditional meal, and give thanks for life and health.

Do you celebrate these or similar holidays in your country?
What other special days do you have?
What's your favorite holiday or festival?

2 WORD POWER Ways to celebrate

A Which word or phrase is not usually paired with each verb? Put a line through it. Then compare with a partner.

1. eat	candy	sweets	~~a mask~~
2. give	presents	a celebration	money
3. go to	decorations	a wedding	a party
4. have a	picnic	beach	meal
5. play	games	candles	music
6. send	cards	flowers	a barbecue
7. visit	relatives	food	close friends
8. watch	a birthday	a parade	fireworks
9. wear	costumes	invitations	traditional clothes

B **PAIR WORK** Do you do any of the things in part A as part of a cultural or family celebration? When? Tell your partner.

8 Time to celebrate!

Cycle 1, Exercises 1–7

In Unit 8, students discuss holidays and special occasions. By the end of Cycle 1, students will be able to describe celebrations and annual events using relative clauses of time. By the end of Cycle 2, students will be able to describe customs using adverbial clauses of time.

1 SNAPSHOT

Learning Objective: discuss holidays and festivals

- Books closed. Introduce the topic of special days by asking Ss to brainstorm public holidays in their country/countries.
- If necessary, review dates with Ss. Point out that the preposition *in* is used with months (*in December*) and the preposition *on* is used with days and dates (*on Monday, on December 25th*). Remind Ss how to say dates (e.g., *December twenty-fifth*).

For more practice with dates, play ***Line Up!*** – download it from the website. Each S chooses a holiday and lines up in order of its date. Alternatively, Ss line up in order of their birthdays.

- Books open. Ask Ss to read the information in the Snapshot, using their dictionaries if necessary. Elicit or explain any vocabulary.

Vocabulary

parade: a line of people or vehicles that moves through a public place to celebrate an occasion
skeleton: the frame of bones supporting a body
fireworks: small objects that explode to produce a loud noise and bright colors and are often used to celebrate special events

- Read the questions and have Ss discuss them in groups. Encourage Ss to ask follow-up questions. For example, after the last question, Ss could ask: "Why is it your favorite holiday? What makes it so special for you? What do you do on that day?"

2 WORD POWER

Learning Objective: use verb-noun collocations to discuss celebrations

A

- Explain the task and go over the example. Then have Ss complete the activity individually.

Answers

1. a mask	4. beach	7. food
2. a celebration	5. candles	8. a birthday
3. decorations	6. a barbecue	9. invitations

B Pair work

- Model the correct pronunciation of the words in part A that were not crossed out. If necessary, explain any unfamiliar words.
- Have Ss take turns telling a partner about the things they do during cultural or family celebrations and when they do them.
- ***Option:*** To review the new vocabulary, play ***Scrambled Letters***. Write these words on the board and have Ss unscramble them:

1. aedpar — p _ _ _ _ _ (parade)
2. lfwores — f _ _ _ _ _ _ (flowers)
3. ceodtasinro — d _ _ _ _ _ _ _ _ _ _ (decorations)
4. degnidw — w _ _ _ _ _ _ (wedding)
5. nestresp — p _ _ _ _ _ _ _ (presents)
6. rekwrfosi — f _ _ _ _ _ _ _ _ (fireworks)
7. ltevsiear — r _ _ _ _ _ _ _ _ (relatives)
8. rihyatdb — b _ _ _ _ _ _ _ (birthday)
9. lesbnarcteoi — c _ _ _ _ _ _ _ _ _ (celebration)
10. alrdatoinit — t _ _ _ _ _ _ _ _ _ _ (traditional)

When Ss have finished, have them tell you the meaning of each word.

3 PERSPECTIVES

Learning Objectives: discuss favorite holidays; identify relative clauses in context

A *[CD 2, Track 12]*

- Books closed. Explain that Ss will hear three people discuss their favorite day of the year.
- Play the audio program. Ss take notes on which holiday each speaker mentions and one thing he or she does on that day. Elicit Ss' answers.

Answers/Possible answers

1. Mother's Day – have breakfast in bed
2. Valentine's Day – give cards and presents
3. New Year's Eve – have a big party

- Write this on the board:
  - Mother's Day: It's a day when ____________
  - February 14: It's the day when ____________
  - New Year's Eve: It's a night when ____________
- Play the audio program again. Ss listen and complete the sentences. Elicit answers.
- Books open. Have Ss check their answers by reading the information and match the pictures to the descriptions. Elicit or explain any new vocabulary.

Vocabulary

look forward to: anticipate with positive feelings

Answers

1. b
2. c
3. a

- Play the audio program again while Ss listen and read along silently. Ask them to pay special attention to the emotions expressed by the speakers.

! To practice speaking and pronunciation, try ***Say It with Feeling***! – download it from the website.

B Pair work

- Ss discuss the question in pairs. Encourage them to ask follow-up questions.
- ***Option:*** Ask Ss what they know about the origins of these three holidays. Alternatively, have Ss find out about the holidays for homework and report to the class.

4 GRAMMAR FOCUS

Learning Objective: use relative clauses of time

[CD 2, Track 13]

- Ask Ss to complete these sentences from memory: *Mother's day is a day when . . . / February 14th is the day when . . . / New Year's Eve is a night when . . .* Then write the full sentences on the board.
- Point out that a relative clause of time is formed with *when*, which refers to the noun phrase (e.g., *the days, the month, the season, the time*) that comes before it. Underline the word *when* in the example sentences. Then elicit some more examples from Ss.
- Play the audio program to present the sentences in the box. Ss listen and repeat.

A

- This exercise requires Ss to use real-world knowledge. Most Ss will know enough to match some of the phrases, so they can probably complete the task by process of elimination.
- Read the question and the instructions. Then ask for Ss' suggestions for the first item. Have them complete the task individually. Check Ss' answers.

Answers

1. b 2. f 3. a 4. e 5. d 6. c

B

- Model how to complete the first sentence with the class (e.g., *Winter is the season when it snows/when it's cold/when people go skiing.*). Then Ss write their own sentences with relative clauses. Go around the class and give help as needed.
- After Ss compare answers with a partner, go over answers with the class. Accept any sentences that are logical and grammatically correct.

Possible answers

Winter is the season **when it's cold and snowy**.
Birthdays are days **when we give presents**.
Spring is the time of year **when flowers bloom**.
Children's Day is a day **when people honor their children**.
July and August are the months **when many people go to the beach**.
A wedding anniversary is a time **when couples celebrate their marriage**.

3 PERSPECTIVES Favorite celebrations

A Listen to these comments about special days of the year. Match them to the correct pictures.

___ **1.** "My favorite celebration is Mother's Day. It's a day when my husband and my kids make pancakes for me – just like I used to make for my mom – and I get to have breakfast in bed."

___ **2.** "February 14th is the day when people give cards and presents to the ones they love. I'm really looking forward to Valentine's Day! I already have a gift for my boyfriend."

___ **3.** "New Year's Eve is a night when I have fun with my friends. We usually have a big party. We stay up all night and then go out for breakfast in the morning."

a

b

c

B **PAIR WORK** What do you like about each celebration in part A?

4 GRAMMAR FOCUS

Relative clauses of time

Mother's Day is **a day**	**when** my kids make pancakes for me.
February 14th is **the day**	**when** people give cards to the ones they love.
New Year's Eve is **a night**	**when** I have fun with my friends.

GRAMMAR PLUS *see page 139*

A How much do you know about these times? Complete the sentences in column A with information from column B. Then compare with a partner.

A	B
1. Mother's Day is a day when ________	**a.** people sometimes play tricks on friends.
2. New Year's Eve is a night when ________	**b.** people celebrate their mothers.
3. April Fools' Day is a day when ________	**c.** many people like to go to the beach.
4. Valentine's Day is a day when ________	**d.** people in many countries honor workers.
5. Labor Day is a day when ________	**e.** people express their love to someone.
6. Summer is a time when ________	**f.** people have parties with family and friends.

B Complete these sentences with your own information. Then compare with a partner.

Winter is the season . . .
Birthdays are days . . .
Spring is the time of year . . .
Children's Day is a day . . .
July and August are the months . . .
A wedding anniversary is a time . . .

5 LISTENING Time for Carnival!

Carnival in Brazil

A Listen to Vanessa talk about her trip to Carnival in Brazil. Write three facts about Carnival that she mentions.

B Listen again and answer these questions about Vanessa's experience.

Why did she have to book her hotel six months early?
What happened when Vanessa got lost?
What was her favorite thing about Carnival? Why?

C **PAIR WORK** Think of another famous celebration that is similar to Carnival. Describe it to the class. They will try to guess the celebration.

6 SPEAKING Favorite holidays

A **PAIR WORK** Choose your three favorite holidays. Tell your partner why you like each one.

A: I really like Independence Day.
B: What do you like about it?
A: It's a day when we watch parades and fireworks.
B: Do you do anything special?
A: We usually have a barbecue. My father makes burgers, and my mother makes her special potato salad.

B **CLASS ACTIVITY** Take a class vote. What are the most popular holidays in your class?

7 WRITING An online entry

A Write an entry for a travel website about a festival or celebration where you live. When is it? How do people celebrate it? What should a visitor see and do?

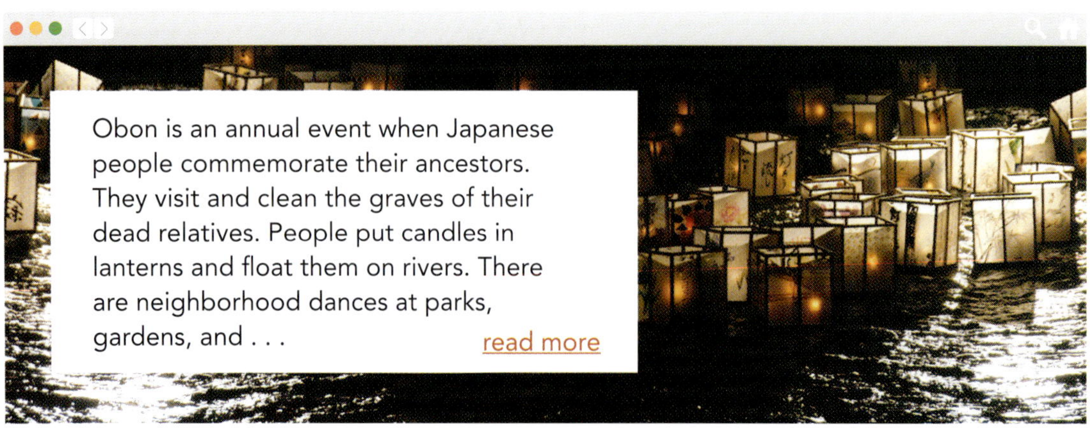

B **PAIR WORK** Read your partner's entry. What do you like about it? Can you suggest anything to improve it?

5 LISTENING

Learning Objective: listen for specific information in a passage about an international celebration

A *[CD 2, Track 14]*

- Books closed. Find out what the class knows about Carnival in Brazil. Write their ideas on the board.
- Set the scene. A woman went to Brazil and is talking about her experiences there. Play the audio program. Ss listen to find out three facts that she mentions.

Audio script

See page T-173.

Possible Answers

Carnival is a big party or celebration in Brazil in late February or early March.
Carnival lasts for four days.
People celebrate Carnival all over Brazil, but the most famous party is in Rio de Janeiro.
Hotels fill up really quickly.
There are colorful decorations all over the city.
For the parade, people work on the costumes and practice the samba dances for months as part of a competition.

B *[CD 2, Track 15]*

- Books open. Focus Ss' attention on the picture and questions. Ss listen for the answers and take notes. They should write only key words and phrases.
- Play the audio program again. Ss listen, take notes, and compare answers with a partner.

Answers

She had to book her hotel six months early because hotels fill up really quickly.
When Vanessa got lost, she didn't even have to ask for directions. People came up and offered to help her.
Her favorite thing about Carnival was the parade because the costumes and the dancing were amazing. There were people dancing everywhere.

Option: Ask Ss to share other information about Carnival with the class.

C Pair work

- Have Ss think of another celebration in pairs and write down some information to tell the class. Give pairs five minutes to think of the information.

6 SPEAKING

Learning Objectives: discuss holidays using relative clauses of time; ask follow-up questions

A Pair work

- Write these discussion topics on the board:

  date origin activities place
  special food and drink things we give/receive
  what you like about it what else people do

- Elicit questions (e.g., *What's the food like?*).
- As Ss work, go around the class and write down errors. Then go over them at the end of the activity.
- ***Option:*** Have each S prepare a short presentation. When each S finishes, encourage the rest of the class to ask follow-up questions. In large classes, Ss can give their presentations in groups.

To practice questions and answers about holidays, play ***Ask the Right Question*** – download it from the website. Prepare different statements about holidays and celebrations (e.g., *Valentine's Day is on February 14. Halloween is a day when children wear costumes.*).

B Class activity

- Have Ss write a holiday that they discussed on the board. If it is already there, don't write it again.
- Explain the task. In pairs or groups, Ss rate each holiday on the list and award points out of three (1 = not interesting, 2 = OK, 3 = excellent).
- Read the holidays on the board and ask each pair or group to tell you how many points they gave the holiday. Have a S write the points on the board and then count the totals at the end of the activity. Which holiday was most popular? Elicit reasons.

7 WRITING

Learning Objective: write a paragraph for a travel website using relative clauses of time

A

- Explain the task. Then read the example paragraph. Point out that Ss should use the discussion topics from Exercise 6 to get ideas.
- Ss use their notes to write a first draft. Go around the class and give help as needed.

B Pair work

- Ss exchange paragraphs with a partner and ask follow-up questions. Then they work individually to revise their drafts.

End of Cycle 1

See the Supplementary Resources chart at the beginning of this unit for additional teaching materials and student activities related to this Cycle.

8 CONVERSATION

Learning Objective: use adverbial clauses of time in a conversation about wedding customs

A *[CD 2, Track 16]*

- Books closed. Ask these questions about weddings: "In your country, where do weddings normally take place? Is there a ceremony and a reception? How are they different? Do the bride and groom wear special clothes? Who gives gifts? Do guests give speeches at the reception?"
- Books open. Focus Ss' attention on the photo. Ask: "What is the bride wearing?"
- Books closed. Play the audio program. Ss listen to find out about traditional Indian weddings. Elicit some information Ss heard.

TIP
Be sure to point out useful language features in the conversations. If Ss are aware of these features, they will be more likely to use them during speaking activities.

- Explain that to keep a conversation going, it is important to (1) add follow-up information, (2) ask for more information, and (3) show interest.
- Now point out these conversational features. Play the first few lines of the audio program, pausing after *Yes. We had the ceremony in India.* Ask: "How did Anusha keep the conversation going?" (Answer: She gave extra information.)
- Play the next line (*And was this your wedding dress?*). Ask: "How did Julia keep the conversation going?" (Answer: She asked a follow-up question.)
- Play the next line (*Yes. It's a sari, actually.*). Point out that Anusha not only gave the answer, but she also added some more information. Ask: "What did she say?" Play the next line and elicit the answer. (Answer: *In India, when women get married. . .*)
- Play the next line. Ask: "How did Julia show interest?" (Answer: She said, *It's beautiful* and asked a follow-up question.)
- Books open. Ss read the conversation and underline the places where someone gives extra information. Then ask Ss to circle the places where someone asks a follow-up question or shows interest.
- Ss practice the conversation in pairs.

B *[CD 2, Track 17]*

- Play the rest of the audio program. Ss listen and find out what Anusha said about her wedding reception. Then check answers.

Audio script

See page T-173.

Answer

There were two receptions. One was right after the wedding ceremony, which was organized by the bride's family. The other party took place the day after the wedding and was organized by the groom's family who hired a band and dance performers.

9 PRONUNCIATION

Learning Objective: sound more natural by using stress and rhythm in sentences

A *[CD 2, Track 18]*

- Explain that in English, stressed words or syllables occur with a more or less regular rhythm or beat, called *stress-timed rhythm*. The other words or syllables in the sentence are reduced to maintain the regular rhythm of the stressed words or syllables.
- Play the audio program and focus Ss' attention on the stressed words and syllables. Point out that the most important words, including main verbs, nouns, adjectives, and adverbs, are usually stressed. Auxiliary or modal verbs, articles, pronouns, and prepositions are usually not stressed.
- Ss listen to the sentence again and repeat.

B *[CD 2, Track 19]*

- Explain the task. Ss listen to three sentences and mark where they hear the stress. Play the audio program. Then go over answers with the class.

Answers

(stressed syllables in bold)
1. **Af**ter the **groom** ar**rives**, the **bride** and **groom** ex**change gar**lands of **flow**ers.
2. Be**fore** the **wed**ding, the **bride's fe**male **rel**atives **us**ually have a **par**ty to **cel**ebrate.
3. When the **groom** takes **off** his **shoes**, the **bride's sis**ters **steal** them.

- Ss practice the sentences.

! For another way to practice stress and rhythm, try ***Walking Stress*** – download it from the website.

8 CONVERSATION A traditional wedding

A Listen and practice.

JULIA Is this a picture from your wedding, Anusha?

ANUSHA Yes. We had the ceremony in India.

JULIA And was this your wedding dress?

ANUSHA Yes. It's a sari, actually. In India, when women get married, they usually wear a brightly colored sari, not a white dress.

JULIA It's beautiful! So, what are weddings like in India?

ANUSHA Well, in some traditions, after the groom arrives, the bride and groom exchange garlands of flowers. We did that. But we didn't do some other traditional things.

JULIA Oh? Like what?

ANUSHA Well, before the wedding, the bride's female relatives usually have a party to celebrate. But I'm an only child, and I don't have any female cousins, so we skipped that.

JULIA That makes sense. You know, I have heard about this one tradition . . . When the groom takes off his shoes, the bride's sisters steal them! I guess you didn't do that, either?

ANUSHA Oh, no, we did that part. My mom stole them!

B Listen to the rest of the conversation.
What does Anusha say about her wedding reception?

9 PRONUNCIATION Stress and rhythm

A Listen and practice. Notice how stressed words and syllables occur with a regular rhythm.

When women get married, they usually wear a brightly colored sari.

B Listen to the stress and rhythm in these sentences. Then practice them.

1. After the groom arrives, the bride and groom exchange garlands of flowers.
2. Before the wedding, the bride's female relatives usually have a party to celebrate.
3. When the groom takes off his shoes, the bride's sisters steal them.

10 GRAMMAR FOCUS

Adverbial clauses of time

When women get married,	they usually wear a brightly colored sari.
After the groom arrives,	the bride and groom exchange garlands of flowers.
Before the wedding,	the bride's female relatives usually have a party to celebrate.

GRAMMAR PLUS *see page 139*

A What do you know about wedding customs in North America? Complete these sentences with the information below.

1. Before a man and woman get married, they usually ___
2. When a couple gets engaged, the man often ___
3. Right after a couple gets engaged, they usually ___
4. When a woman gets married, she usually ___
5. When guests go to a wedding, they almost always ___
6. Right after a couple gets married, they usually ___

a. wears a long white dress and a veil.
b. go on a short trip called a "honeymoon."
c. give the bride and groom gifts or some money.
d. gives the woman an engagement ring.
e. begin to plan the wedding.
f. date each other for a year or more.

B **PAIR WORK** What happens when people get married in your country? Tell your partner by completing the statements in part A with your own information. Pay attention to stress and rhythm.

11 INTERCHANGE 8 It's worth celebrating.

How do your classmates celebrate special occasions? Go to Interchange 8 on page 122.

12 SPEAKING My personal traditions

A **GROUP WORK** How do you usually celebrate the dates below? Share your personal traditions with your classmates.

your birthday New Year's Eve your country's national day your favorite holiday

A: On my birthday, I always wear new clothes, and I often have a party. What about you?
B: I usually celebrate my birthday with my family. We have a special meal and some relatives come over.
C: I used to celebrate my birthday at home, but now I usually go out with friends.

B **CLASS ACTIVITY** Tell the class the most interesting traditions you talked about in your group. Do you share any common traditions? Did you use to celebrate those dates the same way when you were younger?

10 GRAMMAR FOCUS

Learning Objective: use adverbial clauses of time

[CD 2, Track 20]

Adverbial clauses with before, when, *and* after

- Write the words *before, when,* and *after* on the board. Model how we use them as adverbs before a noun (e.g., *When women get married, they usually wear a brightly colored sari.*).
- Now write this sentence on the board: *Before two people get married, they plan the wedding.* Point out that:
  1. The first half of the sentence is an adverbial clause (adverb + subject + verb).
  2. An adverbial clause is subordinate. It cannot occur on its own and is always attached to a main clause. *Before two people get married,* (= the subordinate clause) *they plan the wedding.* (= the main clause)
  3. Adverbial clauses of time can appear either before or after the main clause. We use a comma if the adverbial clause comes first.

  Before they marry, couples send invitations.
  Couples send invitations before they marry.
- Refer Ss to the Conversation on page 53. Tell them to look for examples of adverbial clauses with *before, when,* or *after.* (Answers: 1. when women get married 2. after the groom arrives 3. before the wedding 4. When the groom takes off his shoes)
- ***Option:*** Ask Ss to change the order of the four sentences so that the adverbial clause follows the main clause.
- Play the audio program to present the sentences in the box. Have Ss listen and read silently.

A

- Read the instructions. Elicit or explain any new vocabulary.

Vocabulary
get engaged: formally agree to get married
right (before/after): immediately (before/after)
honeymoon: the vacation a bride and groom take after their wedding
date: have a romantic relationship

- Model the first item. Have Ss complete the task individually and then compare answers in pairs. Elicit answers.

Answers

1. f 2. d 3. e 4. a 5. c 6. b

B Pair work

- Explain the task. Ss complete the phrases in part A with information about marriage customs in their country.
- Pairs write sentences with their own information. Remind Ss to use the stress and rhythm patterns they practiced in Exercise 9 when they read their sentences aloud.

11 INTERCHANGE 8

See page T-122 for teaching notes.

12 SPEAKING

Learning Objective: describe customs using adverbial clauses of time

A Group work

- Write these topics on the board:
  food   location   colors   music   traditions
- Explain the activity and model the conversation with Ss. Give Ss time to think how they celebrate these special occasions.
- Ss discuss in groups. Encourage them to ask follow-up questions, give extra information, and show interest.

B Class activity

- Groups share interesting information with the class.

To practice talking about traditions, play ***True or False?*** – download it from the website.

13 READING

Learning Objectives: skim an article about customs in different countries; identify reference words

A

- Books closed. Ask Ss if they know about any New Year's Eve traditions from around the world.

Vocabulary

strike: ring a bell in a clock to show what the time is
loaf of bread: bread that has been baked in one large piece
messy: untidy
dress: put clothes on yourself or on others
doll: a child's toy that looks like a small person

- Books open. Focus on the title *Out with the Old, In with the New*. Ask Ss what they think that means and when is it used. (Answer: It means to let go of the past and think of the future).
- Have Ss answer the question by skimming the article. They shouldn't focus on vocabulary at this point. (Answer: New Year's traditions around the world)

B

- Explain the task and have Ss work individually to complete the rest of the task. Go around the class and give help as needed.
- ***Option:*** Ss compare answers in groups.
- Elicit Ss' responses to check answers.

Answers

True	False		
	✓	1. In Ireland, people eat loaves of bread for good luck.	People hit walls with food (bread) for good luck.
	✓	2. They eat apples for good luck in Spain.	People eat grapes for good luck in Spain.
✓		3. In China, people change the color of their doors.	___________
✓		4. In Colombia, they burn a doll with old things inside.	___________
✓		5. In Germany, people watch *Dinner for One* because it's about New Year's Eve.	___________

C

- Explain the task and model the first item. Ss complete the task individually and then compare answers in pairs.

Answers

1. things
2. hitting the walls and doors of their houses with loaves of bread
3. grape
4. people in Ecuador and Colombia
5. some customs

D

- Read the questions. Ask Ss to write any other New Year's customs on the board. Ask the class who does each of the things mentioned. Ask Ss to give reasons for doing this, if they know.
- Ask Ss what their favorite New Year's traditions are. Write on the board and discuss as a class.

End of Cycle 2

See the Supplementary Resources chart at the beginning of this unit for additional teaching materials and student activities related to this Cycle.

13 READING

A Skim the article. Which of these phrases could be a title for this article?

The best New Year's resolutions
New Year's traditions around the world
How to host a New Year's Eve party

Out with the Old, In with THE NEW

It's midnight on New Year's Eve. Clocks are striking twelve as people welcome in the coming year and say goodbye to the old. It's a time when people wish for good luck in the future and forget bad things in the past. Around the world, people do different things to help their wishes come true. Some of them might surprise you.

Food is often central to New Year's customs. In Ireland, they hit the walls and doors of their houses with loaves of bread. They hope this will make good luck enter the house and bad luck leave it. The Spanish and the Mexicans eat twelve grapes in twelve seconds – one for luck in each of the coming months. Eating grapes so fast isn't easy, but it's fun and often messy!

Colors are important, too. Brazilians, for example, choose their clothes very carefully – for peace they wear white, yellow might bring success, and red means love is in the air! The Chinese believe red brings good luck, so they like to dress in this color, too. They also give family members and friends red envelopes containing money.

Some people destroy things on New Year's Eve because they want to forget the past. In Ecuador and Colombia, people make a dummy and fill it with sawdust, newspaper, or old clothes. They dress it, put a mask on it, and name it after someone famous or a friend or family member. Then they burn it.

And some customs have no reason at all; they just develop over time. On New Year's Eve in Germany, several TV stations show a short black-and-white movie called *Dinner for One*. It's a comedy in English, starring English actors. Nobody knows why they do this, not even the Germans!

B Read the article. Check (✓) True or False for each statement about New Year's customs. Then correct each false statement.

	True	False	
1. In Ireland, people eat loaves of bread for good luck.	☐	☐	
2. They eat apples for good luck in Spain.	☐	☐	
3. In China, people change the color of their doors.	☐	☐	
4. In Colombia, they burn a doll with old things inside.	☐	☐	
5. In Germany, people watch *Dinner for One* because it's about New Year's Eve.	☐	☐	

C What do the underlined words in the article refer to? Write the correct word.

1. them ____________
2. this ____________
3. one ____________
4. They ____________
5. they ____________

D What do people in your country do for the New Year? What is your favorite New Year's tradition?

Units 7–8 Progress check

SELF-ASSESSMENT

How well can you do these things? Check (✓) the boxes.

I can . . .	Very well	OK	A little
Describe uses and purposes of objects (Ex. 1)	☐	☐	☐
Give instructions and suggestions (Ex. 2)	☐	☐	☐
Describe holidays and special occasions (Ex. 3, 5)	☐	☐	☐
Understand descriptions of customs (Ex. 4, 5)	☐	☐	☐
Ask and answer questions about celebrations and customs (Ex. 5)	☐	☐	☐

1 GAME Guess my object.

A **PAIR WORK** Think of five familiar objects. Write a short description of each object's use and purpose. Don't write the name of the objects.

It's electronic. It's small. It connects to the Internet.
You wear it. It communicates with your phone.

B **GROUP WORK** Take turns reading your descriptions and guessing the objects. Keep score. Who guessed the most items correctly? Who wrote the best descriptions?

2 ROLE PLAY It's all under control.

Student A: Choose one situation below. Decide on the details and answer Student B's questions. Then get some suggestions.

Start like this: *I'm really nervous. I'm . . .*

giving a speech
What is it about?
Where is it?
How many people will be there?

going on a job interview
What's the job?
What are the responsibilities?
Who is interviewing you?

taking my driving test
When is it?
How long is it?
Have you prepared?

Student B: Student A is telling you about a situation. Ask the appropriate questions above. Then give some suggestions.

Change roles and try the role play again.

useful expressions

Try to . . .	Try not to . . .
Remember to . . .	Be sure to . . .
Don't forget to . . .	Make sure to . . .

Units 7–8

Progress check

SELF-ASSESSMENT

Learning Objectives: reflect on one's learning; identify areas that need improvement

- Ask: "What did you learn in Units 7 and 8?" Elicit Ss' answers.
- Ss complete the Self-assessment. Explain to Ss that this is not a test; it is a way for them to evaluate what they've learned and identify areas where they need additional practice. Encourage them to be honest, and point out they will not get a bad grade if they check (✓) "A little."
- Ss move on to the Progress check exercises. You can have Ss complete them in class or for homework, using one of these techniques:
  1. Ask Ss to complete all the exercises.
  2. Ask Ss: "What do you need to practice?" Then assign exercises based on their answers.
  3. Ask Ss to choose and complete exercises based on their Self-assessment.

1 GAME

Learning Objective: demonstrate one's ability to describe uses and purposes of everyday objects

A *Pair work*

- Explain the task. Ss write descriptions of objects without saying what they are. Then Ss read their descriptions and classmates guess what the object is. Read the example and remind Ss to use expressions like *It's used to . . ./for . . .* in their descriptions.
- In pairs, Ss think of five well-known objects and write a short description of each one, without naming it. Give Ss a time limit.

B *Group work*

- Each pair joins another pair. Ss take turns reading their descriptions aloud and guessing the objects. Ss win a point for every object they guess correctly.
- ***Option:*** Ss win three points for every correct first guess. If they ask a question to get more information, they win only two points for the second guess. If they are correct on the third guess, they win only one point. The maximum that a team can win is 15 points.
- Pairs keep track of their scores throughout the game. The pair with the most points wins.

2 ROLE PLAY

Learning Objective: demonstrate one's ability to give instructions and advice

- Explain the roles. Student A is going to face some stressful situations soon and is very nervous. Student B is a friend who offers advice.
- Read the three stressful situations and the *useful expressions*. Then have Ss form pairs. Each Student A chooses one of the situations and tells his or her partner which one was chosen.
- Give Student A a few minutes to think about the details. Ask Student B to use the useful expressions to prepare some advice.
- Model the role play with a S, like this:

  T: What's your stressful situation?
  S: I'm really nervous. I'm taking my driving test.
  T: Well, try not to be nervous. It'll be fine. When is it?
  S: It's at 4:00.
  T: You've got a couple of hours. How long is it?
  S: About half an hour, I think.
  T: Make sure to get there early so you're not so stressed out. And remember to bring your permit and your insurance information.
- Student A begins by telling Student B about the situation. Student B asks questions and offers at least two pieces of advice.
- During the role play, go around the class and listen. Take note of common errors.
- Suggest ways the role plays could be improved. Give examples of good communication that you heard.
- Ss change roles and do the role play again.

3 SPEAKING

Learning Objective: demonstrate one's ability to describe special days and customs

A *Pair work*

- Explain the task. Ss choose one of the imaginary holidays listed (or create their own) and describe it. Read the example and the questions while Ss look at the pictures.
- In pairs, Ss use the questions provided to write a short description of the holiday. Set a time limit. Go around the class and give help as needed.
- Give Ss a few minutes to revise their draft for errors. Encourage them to add more details, if necessary.

B *Group work*

- Explain and model the task with several Ss. Read the example again and have Ss ask you for more information (e.g., *Do people eat anything special on World Smile Day?*).
- Ss complete the task in groups. Set a time limit. When time is up, ask each group to vote. What is their favorite new holiday? Why?
- ***Option:*** Ask groups to tell the class about the holiday they liked most.

4 LISTENING

Learning Objective: demonstrate one's ability to understand descriptions of customs

A *[CD 2, Track 21]*

- Read the instructions and the information in the chart. Then explain the task.
- Play the audio program, pausing after each custom. Ss listen and match. Then go over answers with the class.

Answers

1. c   2. d   3. a   4. b

B *[CD 2, Track 22]*

- Read the sentences before you play the audio program and check any new vocabulary. Play the audio program and elicit answers.

Audio script

See page T-174.

Answers

1. When the groom leaves the table, the male wedding guests take turns kissing the bride.
2. One month before the wedding, the bride starts crying every day.
3. When they want to marry the same man, the women have a boxing match.
4. After the guests bring the dishes to the couple, they break all of them.

C *Pair work*

- Have Ss discuss the questions in pairs. Encourage them to ask follow-up questions.

5 DISCUSSION

Learning Objective: demonstrate one's ability to ask and answer questions about special days and customs

Group work

- Explain the task. Point out that Ss should try to continue the conversation for as long as possible by adding additional information and asking follow-up questions. Have Ss read the questions silently.
- In small groups, Ss discuss the questions and others of their own. Go around the class and listen. Take notes on errors you hear. Pay attention to Ss' ability to keep a conversation going.
- Go over the errors you heard. Give examples of good communication that you heard.

WHAT'S NEXT?

Learning Objective: become more involved in one's learning

- Focus Ss' attention on the Self-assessment again. Ask: "How well can you do these things now?"
- Ask Ss to underline one thing they need to review. Ask: "What did you underline? How can you review it?"
- If needed, plan additional activities or reviews based on Ss' answers.

3 SPEAKING Unofficial holidays

A **PAIR WORK** Choose one of these holidays or create your own. Then write a description of the holiday. Answer the questions below.

Buy Nothing Day

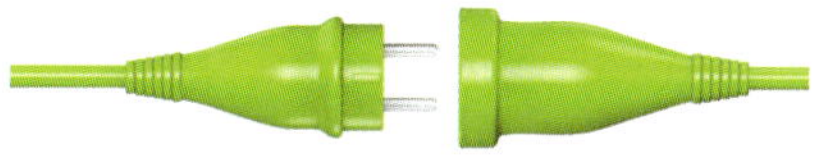

National Day of Unplugging

World Smile Day

What is the name of the holiday? When is it?
How do you celebrate it?

Buy Nothing Day is a day when you can't buy anything. It's a day to think about what we consume, what we really need, and how much money we waste.

B **GROUP WORK** Read your description to the group. Then vote on the best holiday.

4 LISTENING Marriage customs around the world

A Listen to two people discuss a book about marriage customs. Match each country to the title that describes its marriage custom.

1. Sweden ___
2. China ___
3. Paraguay ___
4. Germany ___

a. *Fighting for Love*
b. *Dishes for Good Luck*
c. *Kisses for Guests*
d. *Tears of Happiness*

B Listen again. Complete the sentences to describe the custom.

1. When the groom leaves the table, ______________________.
2. One month before the wedding, ______________________.
3. When they want to marry the same man, ______________________.
4. After the guests bring the dishes to the couple, ______________________.

C **PAIR WORK** Think of some marriage customs from your country. How are they similar to these customs? How are they different?

5 DISCUSSION Just married

GROUP WORK Talk about marriage in your country. Ask these questions and others of your own.

How old are people when they get married?
What happens after a couple gets engaged?
What happens during the ceremony?
What do the bride and groom wear?
What kinds of food is served at the reception?
What kinds of gifts do people usually give?

WHAT'S NEXT?

Look at your Self-assessment again. Do you need to review anything?

Unit 9 Supplementary Resources Overview

	After the following SB exercises	You can use these materials in class	Your students can use these materials outside the classroom
CYCLE 1	1 **Snapshot**		
	2 **Conversation**		**SS** Unit 9 Speaking 1–2
	3 **Grammar Focus**		**SB** Unit 9 Grammar plus, Focus 1 **SS** Unit 9 Grammar 1 **GAME** Say the Word (Time contrasts)
	4 **Pronunciation**		
	5 **Listening**		
	6 **Speaking**		
	7 **Writing**		**WB** Unit 9 exercises 1–4
CYCLE 2	8 **Perspectives**		
	9 **Grammar Focus**	**TSS** Unit 9 Grammar Worksheet	**SB** Unit 9 Grammar plus, Focus 2 **SS** Unit 9 Grammar 2 **GAME** Sentence Runner (Conditional sentences with *if* clauses 1) **GAME** Sentence Stacker (Conditional sentences with *if* clauses 2)
	10 **Word Power**	**TSS** Unit 9 Vocabulary Worksheet **TSS** Unit 9 Listening Worksheet	**SS** Unit 9 Vocabulary 1–2 **GAME** Name the Picture (Collocations)
	11 **Speaking**	**TSS** Unit 9 Writing Worksheet	
	12 **Interchange 9**	**TSS** Unit 9 Extra Worksheet	
	13 **Reading**	**TSS** Unit 9 Project Worksheet **VID** Unit 9 **VRB** Unit 9	**SS** Unit 9 Reading 1–2 **SS** Unit 9 Listening 1–3 **SS** Unit 9 Video 1–3 **WB** Unit 9 exercises 5–10

Key **GAME:** Online Game **SB:** Student's Book **SS:** Online Self-study **TSS:** Teacher Support Site
VID: Video DVD **VRB:** Video Resource Book **WB:** Online Workbook/Workbook

My Plan for Unit 9

Use the space below to customize a plan that fits your needs.

With the following SB exercises	I am using these materials in class	My students are using these materials outside the classroom

With or instead of the following SB section	I am using these materials for assessment

9 Only time will tell.

- Discuss life in different times
- Discuss consequences

1 SNAPSHOT

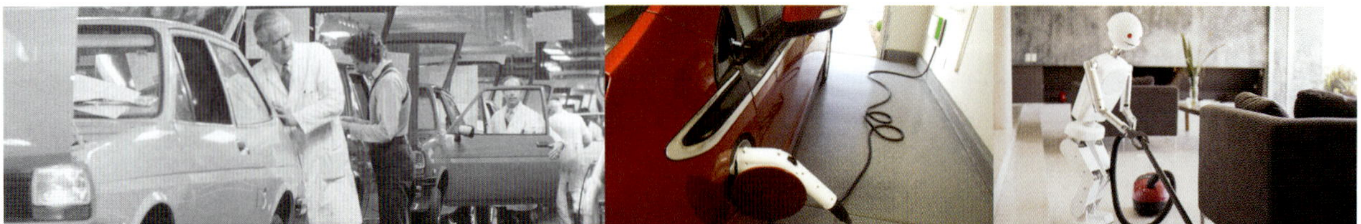

	PAST	PRESENT	FUTURE
EDUCATION	• printed books • blackboard	• e-books • digital content	• virtual classrooms • learning pills
WORK	• time clocks • assembly line	• frequent career changes • multiple workplaces	• intelligent robots • 2-hour work day
TRANSPORTATION	• steam trains • ocean liners	• non-polluting vehicles • shared cars	• driverless cars • teleportation

Which of these changes are the most important? How have they affected the way we live?
Do you think any of the future developments could happen in your lifetime?
Can you think of two other developments that could happen in the future?

2 CONVERSATION That's a thing of the past!

A Listen and practice.

Tom: I hardly recognize our old neighborhood. A few years ago, there were just houses around here.

Mia: I know. They're building a lot of new apartments. The whole neighborhood's different.

Tom: Remember the little burger restaurant we used to go to after school, Hamburger Heaven?

Mia: Of course . . . Now it's another office tower. And I hear they're tearing down our high school. They're going to build a shopping mall.

Tom: That's such a shame. Pretty soon the neighborhood will just be a bunch of malls. And maybe there won't be any schools anymore.

Mia: Probably not. Kids will study from their computers anywhere they want.

Tom: So they won't hang out with their friends after school? That's too bad. I enjoyed meeting our friends at that burger place after class.

Mia: Seriously? That's a thing of the past! Nowadays, kids only meet online.

B Listen to the rest of the conversation. What else has changed in their neighborhood?

9 Only time will tell.

Cycle 1, Exercises 1–7

In Unit 9, students discuss life in different times and consequences. By the end of Cycle 1, students will be able to use the past, present, and future tenses. By the end of Cycle 2, students will be able to discuss consequences using conditional sentences with *if* clauses.

1 SNAPSHOT

Learning Objective: discuss developments of the past, present, and future

- Books closed. Write these categories on the board:

  Education *Work* *Transportation*

- Ask: "Can you think of some ways life 100 years ago was different from life today in these categories? How do you think it will be different in the next 50 years?"
- Books open. Ss read the Snapshot.
- Check comprehension by using the pictures and asking one or two questions (e.g., ask: "How did people use to read?").
- Elicit or explain any new vocabulary.

Vocabulary

time clock: a clock used by employees to record the time when they arrive at and leave work
assembly line: a line of machines and workers in a factory
ocean liner: a large passenger ship that crosses the ocean
shared car: a model of car rental where people rent cars for short periods of time, often by the hour
driverless car: a car that does not have a driver
teleportation: transportation across a distance instantly

- Ss discuss the questions in small groups.

2 CONVERSATION

Learning Objective: use the past, present, and future tenses in a conversation about neighborhood changes

A *[CD 2, Track 23]*

- Ss cover the text and look at the picture. Ask: "What building can you see? How old are the people? Why do you think they look surprised?"
- Books closed. Set the scene. Tom and Mia are discussing how things have changed in the neighborhood where they grew up.
- Write these questions on the board:

  1. *Have things changed a little or a lot?*
  2. *Have things changed for the better or for the worse?*

- Play the audio program. Encourage Ss to listen and take notes. Then elicit answers and examples. [Answers: 1. a lot 2. for the worse (based on expressions such as *such a shame* and *that's too bad*)]
- Write this on the board:

In the past	Now
1. There were houses.	They're . . .
2. There was a burger restaurant.	It's an . . .
3. There was a high school.	They're . . .
4. People hung out with friends after school.	They . . .

- Play the audio program again. Have Ss listen and complete the sentences. (Answers: 1. new apartments 2. office tower 3. tearing it down; going to build a shopping mall 4. don't go to school, study from computers and meet online)
- Books open. Play the audio program again while Ss read along silently. Elicit or explain any new words or expressions.
- Ss practice the conversation in pairs.

TIP

To prevent Ss from reading the conversation to each other, have them stand up and face each other. They will find it more natural to look at each other and will enjoy the chance to stand.

! To practice this conversation in different situations, try ***Substitution Dialog*** – download it from the website. Ss create their own substitutions or replace the underlined words with these:

1. <u>neighborhood</u>: city/village/. . .
2. <u>a few years ago</u>: 10 years ago/5 years ago/. . .
3. <u>shopping mall</u>: computer store/hotel/. . .

B *[CD 2, Track 24]*

- Read the question. Then play the rest of the audio program and check answers.

Audio script

See page T-174.

Answer

The bookstore is now a cell phone repair store.

3 GRAMMAR FOCUS

Learning Objective: use time contrasts between past, present, and future to describe events

[CD 2, Track 25]

- Play the audio program to present the sentences in the box. Ss listen and repeat.
- Elicit the types of tenses used for referring to the three different time periods presented here (e.g., *past, present, future*). Point out the modal *might*, and explain that it indicates possibility.
- Elicit time expressions that we use with each tense and write them on the board:

Past	Present	Future
A few years ago	These days	In the future
In the past	Nowadays	Soon
We used to	Today	In a few years

- Refer Ss to the previous conversation. How many examples can they find of past, present, and future tenses? (Answer: past, three; present, five; future, five) Elicit more examples of each tense.

TIP
To prevent some Ss from dominating the lesson, divide your class into rows or sections. Explain that you will accept an answer from one group at a time.

! To practice recognizing different tenses in the conversation, try ***Stand Up, Sit Down*** – download it from the website. Play the audio program and have Ss listen for examples of past, present, or future tense verbs.

A

- Go over the phrases in column A and then the information in column B. Explain any new vocabulary.
- Ss complete the task individually and compare answers with a partner. Then elicit Ss' responses.

Answers

1. d	3. e	5. b	7. c
2. h	4. f	6. a	8. g

B

- Explain the task. Ss work individually to complete the phrases in part A with appropriate information. Go around the class and monitor Ss' use of tenses.
- If Ss have problems with particular tenses, they should review them on their own. For the past tenses, have Ss study Unit 1; for the future tenses, refer Ss to Unit 5.
- Ss form pairs and compare their sentences.

For more practice with time expressions and tenses, play ***Tic-Tac-Toe*** – download it from the website. Write time expressions (e.g., *these days, in the past, soon*) in the boxes. Ss use the expressions in a sentence with the correct verb tense (e.g., *Soon, there will be another presidential election.*).

4 PRONUNCIATION

Learning Objective: sound more natural when using statements beginning with time phrases

A *[CD 2, Track 26]*

- Play the audio program. Have Ss look at the arrows while listening to the intonation patterns.
- Play the audio program again, pausing for Ss to repeat each statement. Then check a few Ss' intonation.

TIP
To help Ss feel the intonation, have them stand up when they repeat the sentences. Ask them to stand on their toes for rising intonation and to slouch for falling intonation.

B *Pair work*

- Explain the task. Ss complete each statement with appropriate information about themselves. Point out that Ss can either use a different topic (e.g., *As a child, I used to ride my bike everywhere. Five years ago, I lived and worked in South Korea.*) or one topic to contrast three time periods (e.g., *As a child, I used to read books a lot. Nowadays, I read online. In ten years, I might write a novel.*).
- Ss complete the statements individually. Set a time limit of about five minutes. Go around the class and give help as needed.
- In pairs, Ss take turns reading their sentences aloud. Go around the class and listen to their intonation.

3 GRAMMAR FOCUS

Time contrasts

Past	Present	Future
A few years ago, there **were** just houses here.	These days, they**'re building** lots of apartments.	Soon, there **will be** apartment blocks everywhere.
We **used to go** to a burger place after class every day.	Today, people **order** food from their phones.	In the future, restaurants **might not exist**.
In the past, kids **used to hang out** with friends after school.	Nowadays, kids only **meet** online.	In a few years, we **are going to have** virtual friends.

GRAMMAR PLUS *see page 140*

A Complete the sentences in column A with the appropriate information from column B. Then compare with a partner.

A

1. In the early 1990s, ___
2. Before the airplane, ___
3. Before there were supermarkets, ___
4. In many companies these days, ___
5. In most big cities nowadays, ___
6. In many schools today, ___
7. In the next 100 years, ___
8. Sometime in the near future, ___

B

a. students have their own tablets.
b. pollution is becoming a serious problem.
c. there will probably be cities in space.
d. few people had cell phones.
e. people used to shop at small grocery stores.
f. women still receive lower salaries than men.
g. doctors might find a cure for the common cold.
h. ocean liners were the only way to travel across the Atlantic.

B Complete four of the phrases in part A, column A, with your own ideas. Then compare with a partner.

4 PRONUNCIATION Intonation in statements with time phrases

A Listen and practice. Notice the intonation in these statements beginning with a time phrase.

In the past, few women went to college.

Today, there are more women than men in college in the United States.

In the future, women all over the world will go to college.

B **PAIR WORK** Complete these statements with your own information. Then read your statements to a partner. Pay attention to intonation.

As a child, I used to . . .
Five years ago, I . . .
Nowadays, I . . .
These days, . . .
In five years, I'll . . .
In ten years, I might . . .

5 LISTENING On the other side of the world

A Listen to Katie talk to her grandfather about an upcoming trip. Check (✓) the three concerns her grandfather has about the trip.

Concern			Katie's response
1.	☐ language	☐ transportation	____________
2.	☐ meeting people	☐ money	____________
3.	☐ communication	☐ food	____________

B Listen again. Write what Katie says in response to these concerns.

C **PAIR WORK** What other problems might someone experience when they travel to another country? How might these problems change in the future?

6 SPEAKING Not anymore.

GROUP WORK How have things changed? How will things be different in the future? Choose four of these topics. Then discuss the questions below.

communications	education	housing
entertainment	fashion	shopping
environment	food	traveling
health		

What was it like in the past?
What is it like today?
What will it be like in the future?

A: In the past, people cooked all their meals at home.
B: Not anymore. Nowadays, we eat takeout food all the time.
C: In the future, . . .

7 WRITING He's changed a lot.

A **PAIR WORK** Interview your partner about his or her past, present, and hopes for the future.

B Write a paragraph describing how your partner has changed. Make some predictions about the future. Don't write your partner's name.

> *This person came to our school about two years ago. He used to be a little shy in class, and he didn't have many friends. Now, he's on the basketball team and he is very popular. He's a very talented player and, someday, he'll play on the national team. He'll be famous and very rich. I think he'll . . .*

C **CLASS ACTIVITY** Read your paragraph to the class. Can they guess who it is about?

5 LISTENING

Learning Objective: listen for the main idea and make inferences about conversations about changes in neighborhoods

A *[CD 2, Track 27]*

- Focus Ss' attention on the left side of the chart. Explain that Ss will listen for and check (✓) the topic of each conversation. Play the audio program. Have Ss listen and complete the task.
- Go over answers with the class. Ask Ss which words helped them choose the answer (e.g., *flying*).

Audio script

See page T-174.

Answers

1. transportation
2. meeting people
3. communication

B *[CD 2, Track 28]*

- Explain the task. Ss listen and take note of Katie's response to her grandpa.
- Play the audio program again. Ss write Katie's responses.
- Ss compare answers in small groups. If Ss want to listen again, play the audio program again. Then elicit answers from the class.

Answers

1. transportation: flying to other countries is common now and not as expensive as it used to be
2. meeting people: big international cities have people from all over the world; she found groups of people from the U.S. online who meet at different places in the city
3. communication: They can plan a trip for her grandpa and grandma to visit through video calls.

C *Pair work*

- Ss work in pairs to discuss other problems someone might experience when they travel to another country and how these problems might change in the future.
- Elicit ideas of other problems someone might experience with transportation. (Answers: delays, overbooked planes, etc)
- Ss work in pairs and discuss the questions.
- Go around the class and help if necessary. Have Ss share their answers with the class.

6 SPEAKING

Learning Objective: discuss changes using time contrasts between the past, present, and future

Group work

- Explain the task. Go over the list of topics and the questions. Groups choose four topics to discuss.
- Use the questions and the example conversation to model the activity with several Ss.
- Ss form groups and complete the task. Set a time limit of about ten minutes. If possible, mix older Ss with younger ones. Go around the class and note common errors. Then go over the errors as a class after the activity.

TIP
To increase Ss' speaking time, ask them to try the activity again. Be sure to give Ss a new challenge (e.g., *focusing on intonation, working with a new group*, or *adding more details*).

7 WRITING

Learning Objective: write a paragraph using time contrasts to describe someone

A *Pair work*

- Explain the task. Ss interview each other about their past, present, and hopes for the future. Encourage Ss to be imaginative during their interviews.
- Conduct a quick brainstorming activity with the class to help pairs with their interviews. Elicit possible interview questions (e.g., *What did you use to be like? What are you doing nowadays? What are you going to do in the next five years?*).
- In pairs, Ss take turns interviewing each other using the questions and others of their own.

B

- Present the example paragraph. Then Ss write a paragraph about how their partner has changed. Remind Ss that they shouldn't write their partner's name anywhere in their description.

C *Class activity*

- Collect and shuffle the papers. Give one to each S to read. Ss try to guess who the description is about.

End of Cycle 1

See the Supplementary Resources chart at the beginning of this unit for additional teaching materials and student activities related to this Cycle.

8 PERSPECTIVES

Learning Objectives: discuss consequences; identify conditional sentences with *if* clauses in context

- Books closed. Explains that "bucks" is U.S. slang for dollars and "making the big bucks" is a slang term for earning a lot of money. Draw this mind map on the board:

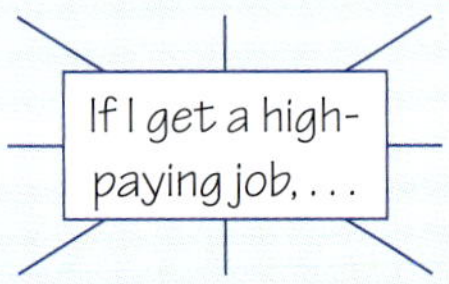

- Lead a class discussion. Ask: "Who wants to make a lot of money? Why? If you get a high-paying job, how will your life change for the better? for the worse?"
- Elicit answers from the class. Answers should be realistic, not fanciful. Ask a S to write the ideas on the board. Don't worry about Ss' grammar at this point; simply help generate ideas and get Ss interested in the topic.

A *[CD 2, Track 29]*

- Books open. Have Ss read the statements silently and compare them with the mind map. Which of the consequences did Ss mention in their discussion?
- Go over each statement and explain any new vocabulary. Then play the audio program while Ss listen and read silently. Point out the pronunciation of contractions with *will*.
- Ss practice reading the statements in pairs.

B *Pair work*

- Explain the task. In pairs, Ss go over each statement and discuss whether the consequences are advantages or disadvantages.

9 GRAMMAR FOCUS

Learning Objective: use conditional sentences with *if* clauses

[CD 2, Track 30]

- Write this example from the Perspectives section on the board:

  Possible situation — Consequence
  If you get a high-paying job, your friends might ask you for a loan.

- Explain that *If you get a high-paying job* is a possible situation, i.e., it may happen one day. The rest of the sentence is a consequence of getting a high-paying job.
- Point out that we can say these in a different order: *Your friends might ask you for a loan if you get a high-paying job.*
- Elicit or explain the rules:
  1. *If* + simple present, subject + *will/won't*
     If you eat candy, you'll gain weight.
     This is the most typical structure used with possible future situations and consequences.
  2. *If* + simple present, subject + *may/might*
     If you eat candy, you might gain weight.
     We can also use *may and might* as consequences, to show that the consequence is less likely.
  3. *will + be able to/will + have to*
     If you save some money, you'll be able to travel. (possibility)
     If you travel abroad, you'll have to get a visa. (necessity)
     We cannot say *will can* or *will must.* Instead, we say "will be able to" and "will have to."
- Refer Ss to the Perspectives section and have them find two examples of each pattern.
- Play the audio program to present the sentences in the box. Then use another situation (e.g., *If you study English, . . .*) and encourage Ss to think of new consequences.

For more practice, play the ***Chain Game*** – download it from the website. Ss begin with a clause like *If I finish my homework early, . . .* and add consequences.

A

- Ask Ss to read the *if* clauses in column A and the consequences in column B.
- Ss complete the task and compare answers in pairs. Then go over answers.

Answers

1. b 2. c 3. e 4. f 5. a 6. d

B

- Model the task by asking for suggestions to complete the first *if* clause in part A. Then have Ss complete the task individually before practicing with a partner.

8 PERSPECTIVES Making the big bucks

A Listen to some possible consequences of getting a high-paying job. Check (✓) the statements you agree with.

If you get a high-paying job, . . .

- ☐ your friends might ask you for a loan.
- ☐ you'll have a lot of money to spend.
- ☐ more people may want to be your friend.
- ☐ you won't have much time for your family.
- ☐ you'll be able to buy anything you want.
- ☐ you won't be able to take long vacations.
- ☐ you'll have to pay higher taxes.
- ☐ you won't have to worry about the future.

B **PAIR WORK** Look at the statements again. Which are advantages of getting a high-paying job? Which are disadvantages?

"The first one is a disadvantage. I'd like to help my friends, but I wouldn't like to lend them money."

9 GRAMMAR FOCUS

Conditional sentences with *if* clauses

Possible situation (present)	Consequence (future with *will, may,* or *might*)
If you **get** a high-paying job,	you**'ll have** more cash to spend.
If you **have** more cash to spend,	you**'ll be able to buy** anything you want.
If you **can buy** anything you want,	you **won't save** your money.
If you **don't save** your money,	you **may have to get** a weekend job.
If you **have to get** a weekend job,	you **might not have** any free time.

GRAMMAR PLUS *see page 140*

A Match the *if* clauses in column A with the appropriate consequences from column B. Then compare with a partner.

A

1. If you eat less fast food, ___
2. If you walk to work every day, ___
3. If you don't get enough sleep, ___
4. If you change jobs, ___
5. If you don't study regularly, ___
6. If you travel abroad, ___

B

a. you may not learn to speak fluently.
b. you might feel a lot healthier.
c. you'll stay in shape without joining a gym.
d. you'll be able to experience a new culture.
e. you won't be able to stay awake in class.
f. you may not like it better than your old one.

B Add your own consequences to the *if* clauses in column A. Then practice with a partner.

"If you eat less fast food, you will probably live longer."

10 WORD POWER Collocations

A **PAIR WORK** Find phrases from the list that usually go with each verb. (Sometimes more than one answer is possible.)

a club	a gym	in shape	money	tired
✓ a degree	a living	into college	stressed	work experience
a group	energy	jealous	time	your own money

earn *a degree* ______ ______
get ______ ______ ______
join ______ ______ ______
spend ______ ______ ______
feel ______ ______ ______

B **GROUP WORK** Share your answers with the group. Can you add one more phrase to each verb?

11 SPEAKING Who knows what will happen?

A **GROUP WORK** Choose three possible events from below. One student completes an event with a consequence. The next student adds a consequence. Suggest at least five consequences.

fall in love
join a gym
study very hard
get a part-time job
move to a foreign country

If you fall in love, you'll probably want to get married.

If you get married, you'll have to earn your own money.

If you want to earn your own money, you'll need to get a job.

If you get a job, you may spend less time at the gym.

If you spend less time at the gym, you won't keep in shape.

B **CLASS ACTIVITY** Who has the most interesting consequences for each event?

12 INTERCHANGE 9 Cause and effect

Give your opinion about some issues. Go to Interchange 9 on page 123.

10 WORD POWER

Learning Objective: use collocations to discuss possible situations and consequences

A *Pair work*

- Explain the task. Have Ss read the phrases in the list and the possible verbs in the chart. Then elicit or explain any new words or expressions.

Vocabulary
earn a living: get money for doing work
get in shape: get healthy and physically strong

- Ss form pairs and complete the chart. Go around the class and give help as needed.

B *Group work*

- Ss discuss the question in small groups. Set a time limit of about five minutes. Then invite groups to write their phrases on the board.

Answers, parts A and B

earn: a degree, money, your own money, a living, *respect*
get: in shape, into college, work experience, tired, stressed, *sick*
join: a club, a group, a gym, *a company*
spend: money, energy, time, *my vacation*
feel: jealous, stressed, tired , *embarrassed*
(Note: Additional consequences are *italicized*.)

For more practice with this vocabulary, play ***Split Sentences*** – download it from the website. Prepare cards using new words and phrases from the unit.

11 SPEAKING

Learning Objective: discuss consequences using conditional sentences with *if* clauses

A *Group work*

- Read the instructions. Then model the activity by reading the example conversation with a few Ss.
- Ss form groups and choose three possible events from the list. Then they describe a chain of events with at least five realistic consequences. Set a time limit of about ten minutes for this activity.
- ***Option:*** Have the groups write down their sentences and present them to the class.

B *Class activity*

- Ask groups to share their most interesting chain of events with the class. Then vote on the most interesting consequence for each situation.
- ***Option:*** Do the activity again as a class. If possible, have the class sit in a circle. Explain that each S thinks of a possible situation with one consequence and writes it at the top of a piece of paper. Ss pass their paper to the left, read the previous sentence, and write another one. For example:
  1. If you move into your own apartment, you'll need to pay rent.
  2. If you need to pay rent, you'll have to get a job.

  The activity continues until the paper returns to the original writer.
- ***Option:*** In pairs, Ss play ***Optimist, Pessimist.*** Student A is the optimist, and Student B is the pessimist. Student A begins with a plan, and Student B finds a reason why it's not a good idea.

  For example:

  A: Tomorrow I'm going to play tennis.
  B: But what will you do if it rains?
  A: If it rains, then I'll go to the movies.
  B: But what will you do if the movie theater is closed?

  The S who keeps the conversation going longest wins.

12 INTERCHANGE 9

See page T-123 for teaching notes.

13 READING

Learning Objectives: read an article about a changing town; scan for information

A

- ***Option:*** Books closed. Play a quick warm-up game to introduce the topic:

  What would you do if you were the mayor of a town that needed to attract more people to it?

  1. Divide the class in groups and have them think of possible marketing solutions for the town.
  2. Encourage Ss to think of two or three ideas.
  3. Set a time limit. When Ss finish, tell them who got it right.
- Have Ss look up these words before they read the article, or go over the meanings in class.

Vocabulary

move away: leave your home in order to live in a new one
falling down: (about a building) in very bad condition with a risk of breaking apart
advertisement: a picture, short film, etc. that persuades people to buy a product
health care: services provided by a country or an organization for people who are sick
improve: get better
repair: fix something that is broken or damaged
miss: feel sad about someone that you do not see now
look after: take care of someone or something

! For another way to teach this vocabulary, try ***Vocabulary Mingle*** – download it from the website.

- Read the question and briefly discuss it as a class. (Answers: Aguaviva is in the north of Spain. Luis Bricio is Aguaviva's mayor.)

B

- Read the questions aloud and explain any new vocabulary. Ss read the text silently and answer the questions. Tell them they don't need to understand every word. Elicit answers from the class.

Answers

1. Young people started leaving Aguaviva because they wanted more opportunities.
2. Bricio attracted people to Aguaviva by offering a home, a job, free health care, and education for at least five years to families with two children under the age of 12.
3. The village school went from having 37 students to more than 80 in three years.
4. Aguaviva had new jobs for builders repairing old houses and factory workers making car parts.
5. Families from Argentina had to get used to living in a small village with little public transportation. Families from Romania had to learn a new language. They all missed their families and friends back home.

C

- Explain the task. Tell Ss to read the article again and underline the parts that can help them decide who would make the comments. Go around the class and give help as needed. Check the answers with the class and ask for the reasons for their choices.

Answers

1. New immigrants
2. Young people from Aguaviva
3. Luis Bricio
4. Elderly people from Aguaviva

D

- Ss discuss the questions as a class. Ask questions like "Why do you think it was a good idea? What would you have done differently?"

End of Cycle 2

See the Supplementary Resources chart at the beginning of this unit for additional teaching materials and student activities related to this Cycle.

A Scan the article. Where is Aguaviva? Who is Luis Bricio?

AGUAVIVA: FIGHTING FOR A FUTURE

Twenty years ago, Aguaviva, a small village in the north of Spain, was dying. Young people wanted more opportunities, so they moved away to the cities. By 1991, there were only 618 people left, and most of them were old. Many of the houses were empty and falling down, and the local school had very few children. Aguaviva's future looked dark.

In 2000, the mayor, Luis Bricio, decided something had to change. He wondered, "How can I bring this place back to life?" He knew the village needed people, but from where? Then he had a brilliant idea. He flew 6,300 miles to Buenos Aires and started telling everyone about Aguaviva. He spoke on the radio and put advertisements in newspapers. The ads said, "If you are married with two children under the age of 12, we'll offer you a home, a job, free health care and education for at least five years." The following year, he did the same thing in Romania.

Many families accepted the offer and Aguaviva began to change. The village school went from having 37 students to more than 80 in three years. The sound of children shouting and playing has made the local people feel so much younger. The economy began to improve, too. There was work for builders repairing the old houses, and a factory making electrical parts for cars opened.

Of course, not everything was easy. The people from Buenos Aires were used to a big city, so living in a small village with little public transportation was difficult at first. The Romanians had to learn a new language. And they all missed their family and friends back home. But everybody had new opportunities, too. Before, many of the parents had worried about finding a job and having enough money to look after their children. After moving to Spain, their future looked brighter. Many of them thought, "We're going to stay here for many years – this place will be our home."

B Read the article. Then answer the questions.

1. Why did young people start leaving Aguaviva?
2. How did Luis Bricio try to attract people to Aguaviva?
3. How did the school change after the year 2000?
4. What kinds of new jobs were there in Aguaviva?
5. What problems did the families from Argentina and Romania have?

C Who would make the following comments? Choose the correct words from the box.

Luis Bricio	young people from Aguaviva
elderly people from Aguaviva	new immigrants

1. "I'm not going back home because life is better here." ______________
2. "I can't stay here. There are no jobs for people of my age." ______________
3. "I'm going to make this village a better place." ______________
4. "I love having all these kids around me – I don't feel so old." ______________

D Do you think Luis Bricio had a good idea? Would you move to a place like this? What would you miss most about home?

10 I like working with people.

- Discuss job skills
- Discuss kinds of jobs

1 SNAPSHOT

21ST CENTURY SKILLS

- ☐ Can you use technology to find the information you need?
- ☐ Can you evaluate the information you find?
- ☐ Do you work well with different kinds of people?
- ☐ Can you communicate with people from different cultures?
- ☐ Are you good at analyzing and solving problems?
- ☐ Can you develop new ideas?
- ☐ Do you enjoy learning new things?
- ☐ Can you teach others how to do things?

Which of these skills do you think are most important for work? in life? Why?
Check (✓) the skills that you think you have.
Look at the skills you checked. What jobs do you think you might be good at?

2 CONVERSATION I love playing video games.

A Listen and practice.

Mai: What are you doing this summer?
Jeff: Nothing much. I'm broke. I need to find a job!
Mai: So do I. Have you seen anything interesting?
Jeff: No, not yet.
Mai: Why don't you get a job at your uncle's restaurant?
Jeff: No way. They're open evenings and weekends, and I hate working on weekends.
Mai: Well, I don't mind working on weekends. Besides, I really enjoy working with people. Do you think he would give me a job?
Jeff: Why don't you go over this weekend and talk to him?
Mai: Yeah. I'll do that. Oh, I found one for you: video game tester.
Jeff: That sounds like fun. I love playing video games. I'll check that one out.

B Listen to the rest of the conversation. What is one problem with the job? What does Jeff decide to do?

10 I like working with people.

Cycle 1, Exercises 1–7

In Unit 10, students discuss jobs, abilities, and personality traits. By the end of Cycle 1, students will be able to discuss job skills using gerunds and short responses. By the end of Cycle 2, students will be able to discuss the kinds of jobs they want and don't want using clauses with *because*.

1 SNAPSHOT

Learning Objective: discuss job skills that are most important to employers

- Books closed. As a class, Ss brainstorm a list of skills needed in the 21st century. Ask: "Which skills do you think are important today?" (e.g., *People should be good at/know how to . . .*) Set a time limit.
- Books open. Ss read the information in the Snapshot.
- Read the first discussion question aloud. Then Ss discuss it in pairs. When Ss finish, have them form groups to discuss which skills are most important and why.

! For more practice ranking, try ***Vocabulary Steps*** – download it from the website. Ss draw eight steps and put the most important skill at the top of the staircase.

- Ss work individually to check (✓) which skills they think they have. Then have them compare in small groups. Alternatively, Ss take turns interviewing each other in pairs.
- Groups answer and discuss the third question.

2 CONVERSATION

Learning Objective: use gerunds and short responses in a conversation about jobs and job requirements

A *[CD 2, Track 31]*

- Focus Ss' attention on the picture. Ask: "Where are they? What are they doing? Why?" Accept any reasonable responses.
- Play the first two lines of the audio program and elicit Ss' answers.
- Books closed. Write this question on the board:

  Which two jobs do they talk about?
- Play the audio program and have Ss listen. Then check Ss' answers to the question. (Answers: working in a restaurant; video game tester)
- Write this question on the board:

  Why is Mai interested in working in a restaurant?
- Play the audio program and have Ss listen. Then elicit answers. (She doesn't mind working weekends and enjoys working with people.)
- Books open. Elicit or explain any unfamiliar words or expressions.

Vocabulary

broke: without money; poor
I don't mind: It doesn't bother me.
check something out: look into; get more information

- Play the audio program again. Tell Ss to listen and read silently.
- Ss practice the conversation in pairs.

! To practice this Conversation with various partners, try the ***Onion Ring*** technique – download it from the website.

B *[CD 2, Track 32]*

- Explain the task. Then play the second part of the audio program.

Vocabulary

bug: an error in a computer program or system
overtime: time in addition to what is normally worked

Audio script

See page T-175.

- Have Ss compare responses in pairs. Then elicit answers from the class.

Answers

Jeff may need to work overtime and on weekends sometimes. Jeff decides to apply for the job anyway.

3 GRAMMAR FOCUS

Learning Objectives: use gerunds to make statements; give short responses

[CD 2, Track 33]

Gerunds (verb + -ing)

- Refer Ss to the previous conversation. Ask them to complete Sam's sentences:
  1. *I don't mind* _______________.
  2. *I really enjoy* _______________.
- Elicit answers. (Answers: 1. working weekends 2. working with people) Explain that *working* is a gerund. It is made up of a base verb and *-ing*. Gerunds can function as nouns.
- Focus Ss' attention on the left column of the Grammar Focus box. Point out some verbs or phrases (e.g., *I love, I hate, I'm good at*) that are followed by a gerund. Elicit other examples from the box (e.g., *I don't mind, I'm not good at, I can't stand*). Then point out the examples in the far right column.

Short responses to show agreement/ disagreement

- Refer Ss to the conversation again. Ask Ss: "Who says the phrase *So do I*? Is he agreeing or disagreeing?" (Answers: Sam; He's agreeing. He also needs a job.)
- Explain that short responses with *so* and *neither* are ways of agreeing. For example, we use:
  1. *So* to agree with an affirmative statement.
     A: I need to find a job.
     B: So do I.
  2. *Neither* to agree with a negative statement.
     A: I don't like working long hours.
     B: Neither do I.
- With both *so* and *neither*, we use the verb from the original statement. The subject (noun or pronoun) comes *after* the verb.
- Do a quick drill with the class, like this:
  1. Responses with so
     T: I'm good at singing.
     S1: So am I. (= I'm good at it, too.)
     If there is no auxiliary or modal, we use *do* or *did*.
     T: I hate working overtime.
     S2: So do I. (= I hate it, too.)
     T: We used to live in New York.
     S3: So did we. (= We lived there, too.)
- Repeat the drill with *neither*:
  2. Responses with *neither*
     T: I'm not good at skiing.
     S4: Neither am I. (= I'm not good at it either.)
- Point out the six ways to disagree. Then play the audio program to present the language in the box.

For more practice with gerunds, play ***True or False?*** – download it from the website. Ss make up sentences about themselves.

A *Pair work*

- Explain the task. Ss match the phrases in columns A and B to make statements about themselves.
- Make sure Ss understand the vocabulary in column B. Then Ss work individually to complete the task.
- Model the example conversation. Then ask Ss to read their statements to each other and give short responses.
- Go around the class and give help as needed. Take note of common problems and go over them with the whole class after the activity.
- ***Option:*** Ss repeat the activity with a new partner.

B *Group work*

- Explain the task. Model an example conversation with a S:
  T: I'm really interested in working abroad.
  S: Really? Where would you like to work?
  T: Maybe in Mexico or in Chile.
- Refer Ss to the conversation on page 64. Remind them how Sam and Pat showed interest by asking follow-up questions and giving additional information.
- Ss work individually to complete the phrases in part A with their own information. Then Ss take turns reading their statements in groups. Other Ss ask questions to get more information.

4 PRONUNCIATION

Learning Objectives: differentiate between unreleased and released /t/ and /d/ sounds; sound more natural when pronouncing words ending in /t/ or /d/

A *[CD 2, Track 34]*

- Explain that at the end of a word, the sounds /t/ and /d/ are not released, i.e., they are not fully articulated, when they are followed by a consonant sound. Play the audio program. Point out how the sound is hardly heard.
- Repeat the previous steps for released sounds. Point out that the /t/ and /d/ sounds are released when they are followed by a vowel sound.

B *Pair work*

- Explain the task. Ss write their sentences individually and then practice them in pairs.

3 GRAMMAR FOCUS

Gerunds; short responses

Affirmative statements with gerunds	Agree	Disagree
I love playing video games.	So do I.	I don't.
I hate working on weekends.	So do I.	Really? I like it.
I'm good at solving problems.	So am I.	Oh, I'm not.
Negative statements with gerunds		
I don't mind working evenings.	Neither do I.	I do.
I'm not good at selling.	Neither am I.	Well, I am.
I can't stand commuting.	Neither can I.	Oh, I don't mind it.

Other verbs or phrases followed by gerunds

like
enjoy
be interested in

GRAMMAR PLUS *see page 141*

A PAIR WORK Match the phrases in columns A and B to make statements about yourself. Then take turns reading your sentences and giving short responses.

A	B
1. I can't stand ___	**a.** working the night shift.
2. I'm not very good at ___	**b.** solving other people's problems.
3. I'm good at ___	**c.** working alone.
4. I don't like ___	**d.** sitting in long meetings.
5. I hate ___	**e.** working on weekends.
6. I'm interested in ___	**f.** speaking in public.
7. I don't mind ___	**g.** managing my time.
8. I enjoy ___	**h.** learning foreign languages.

A: I can't stand sitting in long meetings.
B: Neither can I.

B GROUP WORK Complete the phrases in column A with your own information. Then take turns reading your statements. Ask questions to get more information.

4 PRONUNCIATION Unreleased and released /t/ and /d/

A Listen and practice. Notice that when the sound /t/ or /d/ at the end of a word is followed by a consonant, it's unreleased. When it is followed by a vowel sound, it's released.

Unreleased	Released
She's not good at dealing with stress.	He's not a good artist.
I hate working on Sundays.	They really hate it!
You need to manage money well.	I need a cup of coffee.

B PAIR WORK Write three sentences starting with *I'm not very good at* and *I don't mind*. Then practice the sentences. Pay attention to the unreleased and released sounds /t/ and /d/.

5 SPEAKING Do what you love.

A **PAIR WORK** How does your partner feel about doing these things? Interview your partner. Check (✓) his or her answers.

How do you feel about . . . ?	I enjoy it.	I don't mind it.	I hate it.
dealing with the public	☐	☐	☐
working alone	☐	☐	☐
being part of a team	☐	☐	☐
meeting deadlines	☐	☐	☐
leading a team	☐	☐	☐
working on weekends	☐	☐	☐
learning new skills	☐	☐	☐
doing the same thing every day	☐	☐	☐
traveling	☐	☐	☐
making decisions	☐	☐	☐
helping people	☐	☐	☐
solving problems	☐	☐	☐

B **PAIR WORK** Look back at the information in part A. Suggest a job for your partner.

A: You enjoy dealing with the public, and you hate working alone. You'd be a good salesperson.
B: But I hate working on weekends.
A: Maybe you could . . .

6 LISTENING My ideal career

A Listen to people talk about the kind of work they are looking for. Then check (✓) each person's ideal job.

1. Alex
- ☐ architect
- ☐ accountant
- ☐ teacher

2. Evelyn
- ☐ banker
- ☐ doctor
- ☐ lawyer

3. Edward
- ☐ marine biologist
- ☐ songwriter
- ☐ flight attendant

B Listen again. Write two reasons each person gives for his or her ideal job.

1. Alex ______________________ ______________________
2. Evelyn ______________________ ______________________
3. Edward ______________________ ______________________

7 INTERCHANGE 10 You're hired.

Choose the right person for the job. Go to Interchange 10 on page 124.

5 SPEAKING

Learning Objective: discuss work activities using gerunds and short responses

A *Pair work*

- Have Ss read the list of activities silently. Elicit and explain any unfamiliar vocabulary. Then explain the task.
- Remind Ss about pronunciation. Point out that *How do you feel about . . . ?* ends in the sound /t/. If the next word begins with a consonant (e.g., *working*), Ss should not release the /t/. If the next word begins with a vowel (e.g., *asking*), Ss need to release the /t/.
- ***Option:*** Read the questions aloud. Ss repeat the correct pronunciation and intonation.
- Ss form pairs and take turns interviewing each other. They should check (✓) their partner's answers.

B *Pair work*

- Explain the task. In pairs, Ss look at each other's answers in part A and make suggestions. Elicit jobs that Ss might suggest based on their partner's answers. Ask: "What jobs are good for someone who likes leading a team? Traveling? Solving problems?" (Possible answers: project manager, salesperson, accountant)
- Remind Ss to use the structures *You don't mind* and *You enjoy.*

TIP

To check that Ss understand the instructions, use concept questions. For example, ask Ss: "Are you going to work in pairs or groups? What suggestions are you going to make?"

- Ss form pairs and make job recommendations. Go around the class and give help as needed.

6 LISTENING

Learning Objective: listen for the main idea and make inferences about some conversations about jobs

A *[CD 2, Track 35]*

- Ask Ss what they think their ideal career is. Ask if anyone knows what their ideal job would be/is, and put them in the "hot seat." Have the rest of the class ask them questions.
- Explain the situation. Three people are being asked about the kind of work they are looking for. Note that the speakers don't say exactly which job they are looking for. Ss need to listen and make inferences.
- Play the first item in the audio program. Have Ss tell you which job would be best for Alex. Ask how they chose the answer. (Answers: architect; He likes to draw houses.)
- Play the rest of the audio program, pausing after each speaker. Then check answers. Again, ask Ss why they chose the answers.

Audio script

See page T-175.

Answers

1. Alex: architect
2. Evelyn: doctor
3. Edward: flight attendant

B *[CD 2, Track 36]*

- Read the questions and play the audio program again, pausing after each speaker. Ss listen and answer the questions. Have Ss compare answers in pairs. Then go over answers with the class.

Possible Answers

1. he doesn't want a regular nine-to-five job; he'd like to work for himself; he's good at drawing and thinks it would be fun to design people's homes and businesses; he's done some drawings recently of his dream house
2. she'd like to have a job where she helps people; she'd love working in a children's hospital in a developing country; she has plans to get into medical school
3. he enjoys working with people; he loves traveling; he doesn't want a job where he's stuck in an office all day; he's not really interested in making a lot of money at this point in his life; he wants to get out and see the world

7 INTERCHANGE 10

See page T-124 for teaching notes.

End of Cycle 1

See the Supplementary Resources chart at the beginning of this unit for additional teaching materials and student activities related to this Cycle.

8 WORD POWER

Learning Objective: use adjectives for describing personality traits

A

- Focus Ss' attention on the pictures. Explain the subtitle *Personality traits*.
- Read the instructions and explain the difference between positive (good) and negative (bad). Point out that the first adjective (*creative*) in the chart is positive, so the letter *P* is written in the blank. Ask Ss to find a negative adjective and to write *N* next to it.
- Ss complete the task individually without using a dictionary. Go around the class and give help as needed.

TIP
To monitor Ss equally, vary your routine. For example, if you always start at the front of the class, start from the back sometimes.

- Elicit answers from the class. Model the pronunciation of adjectives that Ss have problems with.

Answers

P: creative, efficient, generous, hardworking, level-headed, punctual, reliable
N: critical, disorganized, forgetful, impatient, moody, short-tempered, strict

B *Pair work*

- Write these words on the board:
  neighbor, parents, children, friend, classmate, teacher, brother, sister, co-worker, boss
- Read the instructions and the example sentence. Encourage Ss to make similar statements using adjectives from the list and people from the board.
- Ss form pairs and talk about people they know with these personality traits. Remind Ss to give additional information and ask follow-up questions.

To review the vocabulary in the next class, play ***Mime*** – download it from the website.

C *[CD 2, Track 37]*

- Explain the task and play the audio program. Ss listen and check (✓) the adjectives. Then go over answers.

Audio script

See page T-175.

Answers

1. serious	3. moody
2. generous	4. short-tempered

9 PERSPECTIVES

Learning Objectives: discuss job profiles; identify clauses with *because* in context

A *[CD 2, Track 38]*

- Books closed. Write these questions on the board:
  What kind of work would you like to do?
  What kind of job would you be good at? Why?
- Ss work in pairs or groups to answer the questions. Alternatively, have a class discussion.
- Set the scene. Three people are answering the question *What kind of work would you like to do?* Play the audio program. Tell Ss to listen to find out what job each person talks about. (Answers: journalist, stockbroker, teacher)
- Elicit or explain any new vocabulary.

Vocabulary
journalist: someone who writes for a news source
stockbroker: someone who buys and sells stock (part ownership of a company)

- Write these questions on the board:
  Which speaker . . .
  can't make decisions quickly?
  is creative but impatient?
  used to work as a reporter?
  doesn't mind working hard?
- Play the audio program again. Ss listen and answer the questions. Elicit answers. (Answers: 2, 3, 1, 2)
- Books open. Play the audio program again. Ss listen and read silently.

B *Pair work*

- In pairs, Ss discuss which person they resemble most. Encourage them to think about personality traits and attitudes, not just skills. Elicit answers from the class.

8 WORD POWER Personality traits

A Which of these adjectives are positive (**P**)? Which are negative (**N**)?

creative	P	impatient	
critical		level-headed	
disorganized		moody	
efficient		punctual	
forgetful		reliable	
generous		short-tempered	
hardworking		strict	

disorganized

hardworking

B **PAIR WORK** Tell your partner about people you know with these personality traits.

"My boss is very short-tempered. She often shouts at people . . ."

C Listen to four conversations. Then check (✓) the adjective that best describes each person.

1. a boss
- ☐ creative
- ☐ forgetful
- ☐ serious

2. a co-worker
- ☐ unfriendly
- ☐ generous
- ☐ strange

3. a teacher
- ☐ moody
- ☐ patient
- ☐ hardworking

4. a relative
- ☐ short-tempered
- ☐ disorganized
- ☐ reliable

9 PERSPECTIVES Making the right choice

A Listen to these people answer the question, "What kind of work would you like to do?" What job does each person talk about? Do they want that job?

Paula

"Well, I think I'd make a good journalist because I'm good at writing. When I was in high school, I worked as a reporter for the school website. I really enjoyed writing different kinds of articles."

Shawn

"I know what I *don't* want to do! A lot of my friends work in the stock market, but I could never be a stockbroker because I can't make decisions quickly. I don't mind working hard, but I'm terrible under pressure!"

Dalia

"I'm still in school. My parents want me to be a teacher, but I'm not sure yet. I guess I could be a teacher because I'm very creative. I'm also very impatient, so maybe I shouldn't work with kids."

B **PAIR WORK** Look at the interviews again. Who are you most like? least like? Why?

10 GRAMMAR FOCUS

Clauses with *because*

The word *because* introduces a cause or reason.

I'd make a good journalist **because I'm good at writing**.

I could be a teacher **because I'm very creative**.

I wouldn't want to be a teacher **because I'm very impatient**.

I could never be a stockbroker **because I can't make decisions quickly**.

GRAMMAR PLUS *see page 141*

A Complete the sentences in column A with appropriate information from column B. Then compare with a partner.

A	B
1. I'd like to be a physical therapist ___	**a.** because I'm very disorganized.
2. I would make a bad librarian ___	**b.** because I love animals.
3. I couldn't be a diplomat ___	**c.** because I enjoy helping people.
4. I wouldn't mind working as a veterinarian ___	**d.** because I'm not good at managing money.
5. I could be a flight attendant ___	**e.** because I'm short-tempered.
6. I could never be a financial advisor ___	**f.** because I really enjoy traveling.

B **GROUP WORK** Think about your personal qualities and skills. Then complete these statements. Take turns discussing them with your group.

I could never be a . . . because . . .

I wouldn't mind working as a . . . because . . .

I'd make a good . . . because . . .

The best job for me is . . . because . . .

11 WRITING An online cover letter for a job application

A Imagine you are applying for one of the jobs in this unit. Write a short cover letter for a job application.

Reply Forward

To: Catherine West

Subject: News reporter position – ref. 04532

Dear Ms. West,

I was excited to see your opening for a news reporter, and I hope to be invited for an interview. I think I could make a great addition to your team because I'm very hardworking, and I really enjoy writing.

As you can see from my résumé, I've had a lot of experience writing for my high school newspaper and for my college website. I also worked . . .

B **PAIR WORK** Exchange papers. If you received this cover letter, would you invite the applicant for a job interview? Why or why not?

10 GRAMMAR FOCUS

Learning Objective: use clauses with *because*

[CD 2, Track 39]

- Write these statements on the board:

I'd make a good journalist because . . .	*I'm terrible under pressure.*
I could be a teacher because . . .	*I'm good at writing.*
I could never be a stockbroker because . . .	*I'm very creative.*

Because

- Ask Ss to look back at the Perspectives section and match the phrases on the board.
- Explain that the conjunction *because* can connect two independent clauses into one sentence. *Because* answers the question "Why?"
- Point out that the clauses starting with *because* can come either before or after the main clause (e.g., *Because I'm good at writing, I'd make a good journalist./I'd make a good journalist because I'm good at writing.*). Point out the comma in the first example. No comma is used, however, when *because* is in the middle of the sentence.

Could/would

- Explain that *could* and *would* are used to talk about hypothetical situations. Point out that *would* is reduced to *'d* when speaking.
- Play the audio program to present the sentences in the box.
- ***Option:*** Play this game to practice the new structure and vocabulary:
  1. Write one sentence on the board, e.g., *I'd make a good journalist because I'm attentive.*
  2. Invite a S to come to the board and change or add one word only, e.g., *I'd make a good journalist because I'm organized.*
  3. The next S changes another word in the sentence, e.g., *I'd make a good teacher because I'm organized.*

  Ss can play this in teams on the board. The team that makes the most changes wins.

A

- Explain the task. Ss complete the task individually and then compare answers in pairs. Check Ss' answers.

Answers

1. c 2. a 3. e 4. b 5. f 6. d

B *Group work*

- Write these expressions on the board:

  Really? Why is that?
  Do you think so? I think . . .
  I don't agree. In my opinion, . . .
  But maybe you have other skills, like . . .
- Explain the task. Then model how to complete the statements using examples from several Ss. Give them a few minutes to do the first part of the task.
- Have Ss form groups and take turns reading their statements aloud. Remind them to ask questions to get more information, especially reasons and explanations.

TIP

To make sure that all Ss ask follow-up questions, have them put three small coins (or paper clips) in front of them on the desk. Each time they ask a follow-up question, they can take a coin back from the pile.

- ***Option:*** Groups take turns sharing some of the interesting statements from part B with the class.

11 WRITING

Learning Objective: write a cover letter for a job application using gerunds and clauses with *because*

A

- ***Option:*** Ss quickly review the unit and list all the jobs they can find.
- Explain the task. Read the example paragraph, choose a S to read it, or give Ss time to read it silently.
- Encourage Ss to brainstorm the type of job they want to write about – one they would be interested in applying for. Tell Ss to write down their ideas in the form of words, mind maps, or notes, and to include examples, reasons, and explanations. Go around the class and give help as needed.
- Ss use their notes to write a cover letter.
- ***Option:*** This part of the task could be done for homework on a computer.

B *Pair work*

- Ss form pairs and read each other's letters. Then they decide if they would invite their partner for a job interview. They should explain why or why not and give feedback to their partner.

12 READING

Learning Objectives: skim an advertisement about jobs and make inferences; distinguish between main ideas and supporting ideas

A

- Books closed. Brainstorm with the class. Ask: "What are cross-cultural problems?" Then elicit examples and write suggestions on the board. For example:
  Common cross-cultural problems at work:
  - how to treat your co-workers
  - punctuality
  - agreement
  - communication

! For an alternative way to present this topic, try ***Running Dictation*** – download it from the website. Use the first two paragraphs of the article.

- Books open. Read the title and the question. Elicit the answer. (Answer: The three cross-cultural problems that are mentioned are ideas of work time, contracts aren't used in the same way in different countries, and some cultures are more direct in the way they communicate than others.)
- Have Ss read the article without using their dictionaries. Tell them to circle, underline, or highlight any words or expressions whose meanings they can't guess from context.
- ***Option:*** Ss work in pairs or small groups to help each other understand any words they weren't able to guess.
- Elicit or explain any new words.

Vocabulary

cross-cultural: involving two or more different cultures and their ideas and customs
abroad: in or to a foreign country
punctuality: arriving at the right time and not too late
timetable: a list of times when buses, trains, etc. arrive and leave
realize: notice or understand something that you did not notice or understand before
chat: talk with someone in a friendly and informal way
agreement: a promise or decision made between two or more people
straight talk: honesty and directness in speech or writing

B

- Elicit the difference between a main idea (the most important and general idea in a paragraph) and a supporting idea (an idea that gives an example, explains, or adds information about the main idea). Explain that Ss need to correct the three sentences so they show the main ideas in the advertisement. Ask a S to correct the first sentence.
- Ss complete the task individually and then check their answers in pairs. Then go over answers with the class.

Answers

1. Ideas about work time are different in Africa and the U.S.A.
2. Written contracts are less important in China than in the U.S.A.
3. American and Asian workers have different ways of communicating.

C

- Explain the task and remind Ss to fill in the blanks with words from the text, not their own.
- Ss complete the task individually. Discuss answers as a class. Ask: "Do these sentences show the main ideas in the advertisement or supporting ideas?" (Answer: supporting ideas)

Answers

1. punctual, on time
2. relationships
3. handshake
4. disagree
5. avoid

D

- Ss take turns asking and answering the questions. Encourage Ss to give examples and reasons and to ask follow-up questions.
- ***Option:*** Ss form small groups. Each group chooses a topic to discuss, e.g., punctuality. Then have them think of advice on how to deal with this issue in their country, e.g., *In Brazil, people are always a little late, so they don't worry as much about punctuality. Also . . .* After all the groups have discussed, have one S from each group write one piece of advice on the board.

End of Cycle 2

See the Supplementary Resources chart at the beginning of this unit for additional teaching materials and student activities related to this Cycle.

12 READING

A Skim the advertisement. Which three cross-cultural problems does it mention?

GLOBAL WORK SOLUTIONS

At GW Solutions, we recognize the importance of cross-cultural training for U.S. employees working abroad. Lack of cultural understanding results in lost contracts and less business. Here are some examples of what our courses can teach you.

In the U.S.A., we say that time is money. For American workers, punctuality and timetables are always important. At work, people concentrate on the task they are doing. They usually do not spend a lot of time on small talk. However, it's important to realize that not all cultures see time in this way. In many African countries, for example, getting work done isn't the only valuable use of time. Spending time at work to build close relationships with colleagues is equally important. It's important to ask about your colleague's personal life. Understanding these cultural differences is essential for working in a global team. If an American doesn't realize this, he or she might think that an African colleague who spends a lot of time chatting with co-workers is being lazy or avoiding doing his or her work. And an African worker might think their American colleague is the rudest person they've ever met!

In the U.S.A., written agreements are essential. Business deals are always agreed through a contract and once it has been signed, we consider it to be final. The conditions of the agreement don't usually change without the signing of another contract. But you may do business in places where this is not the case. In China, for example, people generally place more trust in a person's word than in a signed contract. Once a good relationship exists, a simple handshake might be enough to reach a business deal.

In the U.S.A., workers generally speak directly, and they openly disagree with colleagues. This kind of "straight talk" is seen as a mark of honesty. But where we see honesty, others may see rudeness. In some parts of Asia, open disagreement with colleagues may not be acceptable because it makes people feel embarrassed. Instead, you should stop and think for a while. Afterward you could say, "I agree in general, but could a different idea work in this situation?" And your body language is important, too. In the West, direct eye contact is good because it's a sign of honesty. In some Asian cultures, it's polite to avoid looking directly at your colleagues in order to show respect.

Did you learn something new? Need to know more? Sign up for one of our training courses and learn how to do business wherever you go.

B Read the advertisement. Then correct the sentences.

1. Ideas about work time are the same in Africa and the U.S.A.
2. Written contracts are more important in China than in the U.S.A.
3. American and Asian workers have similar ways of communicating.

C Complete these sentences with words from the advertisement.

1. In the U.S.A., being ______________ is very important at work.
2. African workers like to have strong ______________ with their co-workers.
3. In China, people might agree to a business deal with a ______________.
4. For Americans, it's normal to ______________ openly when they have a different opinion.
5. Some workers ______________ making eye contact when talking to others.

D Look at the sentences in part C. Are they true for your country? What advice would you give to a foreigner coming to work in your country?

Units 9–10 Progress check

SELF-ASSESSMENT

How well can you do these things? Check (✓) the boxes.

I can . . .	Very well	OK	A little
Describe people and things in the past, present, and future (Ex. 1)	☐	☐	☐
Discuss possible consequences of actions (Ex. 2)	☐	☐	☐
Understand descriptions of skills and personality traits (Ex. 3, 4)	☐	☐	☐
Discuss job skills (Ex. 4)	☐	☐	☐
Give reasons for my opinions (Ex. 4)	☐	☐	☐

1 SPEAKING Things have changed.

A **PAIR WORK** Think of one more question for each category. Then interview a partner.

Free time How did you spend your free time as a child? What do you like to do these days? How are you going to spend your free time next year?

Friends Who used to be your friends when you were a kid? How do you meet new people nowadays? How do you think people will meet in the future?

B **GROUP WORK** Share one interesting thing about your partner.

2 GAME Share the consequences

A Add two situations and two consequences to the lists below.

Situation	Consequences
☐ you spend too much time online	☐ learn about a different culture
☐ you get a well-paid job	☐ get good grades
☐ you move to a foreign country	☐ buy an expensive car
☐ it's sunny tomorrow	☐ feel jealous sometimes
☐ you don't study hard	☐ go to the beach
☐ you fall in love	☐ have time for your family and friends
☐ ______________________	☐ ______________________
☐ ______________________	☐ ______________________

B **CLASS ACTIVITY** Go around the class and make sentences. Check (✓) each *if* clause after you use it. The student who uses the most clauses correctly wins.

"If you spend too much time online, you won't . . ."

Units 9–10

Progress check

SELF-ASSESSMENT

Learning Objectives: reflect on one's learning; identify areas that need improvement

- Ask: "What did you learn in Units 9 and 10?" Elicit Ss' answers.
- Ss complete the Self-assessment. Explain to Ss that this is not a test; it is a way for them to evaluate what they've learned and identify areas where they need additional practice. Encourage them to be honest, and point out they will not get a bad grade if they check (✓) "A little."
- Direct Ss to move on to the Progress check exercises. You can have Ss complete them in class or for homework, using one of these techniques:
  1. Ask Ss to complete all the exercises.
  2. Ask Ss: "What do you need to practice?" Then assign exercises based on their answers.
  3. Ask Ss to choose and complete exercises based on their Self-assessment.

1 SPEAKING

Learning Objective: demonstrate one's ability to describe people and things in the past, present, and future

A *Pair work*

- Explain the task. Ss will talk about two categories (free time and friends) using past, present, and future tenses. If helpful, make a list on the board of tenses that Ss might use during their conversation (simple past, *used to*, simple present, present continuous, future with *will*, *might*, and *be going to*).
- Have Ss read the questions silently. Then have them add one more question to each category.
- Ss form pairs and use their questions to interview each other. Remind Ss to give additional information and ask follow-up questions.

B *Group work*

- Have each pair join another pair. Ask them to share at least one interesting thing about their partners. Again, encourage Ss to ask follow-up questions.
- ***Option:*** Ss earn one point for every follow-up question they ask.
- As Ss discuss in groups, go around the class and write down any errors you hear. Pay attention to Ss' ability to keep a conversation going and to use different tenses.
- Go over any errors you noticed with the class. Be sure to praise examples of good communication.

2 GAME

Learning Objective: demonstrate one's ability to describe possible consequences of actions

A

- Briefly review how to make conditional sentences using *may*, *might*, or *will*. Write a situation on the board and elicit some possible consequences from Ss. For example:

Situation:	Consequence:
If you join a gym, . . .	you may lose weight.
	you might make new friends.

- Ask Ss to read the lists of situations and consequences. Elicit or explain any unfamiliar vocabulary. Then tell Ss to work individually to add two situations and two consequences to the lists in the chart. Remind Ss that the situation and consequence must match each other.

B *Class activity*

- Explain and model the task with a few Ss. Read one situation (e.g., *If you move to a foreign country, . . .*) and ask a S to complete the sentence with a consequence (e.g., *you'll learn to communicate in a new language*). Check (✓) the *if* clause you used and allow the S to read another situation. Then repeat the activity with another S, using a different clause.
- Ss get up and move around the class, making sentences together and checking (✓) the *if* clauses they use. The first person to use all the clauses correctly wins.

3 LISTENING

Learning Objective: demonstrate one's ability to listen to and understand descriptions of abilities and personalities

A *[CD 2, Track 40]*

- Read the instructions aloud and focus Ss' attention on the left side of the chart. Explain the task. Ss listen to find out what jobs Michelle and Robbie are talking about.
- Play the audio program, pausing after each discussion. Ss listen and complete the left side of the chart only. Then elicit Ss' responses.

Audio script

See page T-176.

Answers

1. Michelle	politician	bad
	computer engineer	good
2. Robbie	restaurant manager	bad
	teacher	good

B *[CD 2, Track 41]*

- Explain that now Ss will listen for the reasons that Michelle and Robbie give.
- Play the audio program again. Ss listen and complete the rest of the chart. Then go over answers with the class.

Answers

1. Michelle
   not good at working with other people; too moody; has always helped with computer problems; loves solving problems and making new things; likes working alone
2. Robbie
   would be terrible at managing other people; too disorganized; likes working with kids; pretty patient; very hardworking

C *Pair work*

- Tell Ss to ask their partner questions like "What job do you prefer? Why? Which do you think you would be good at?" or "Does anyone in your family do any of these jobs? Do they like it? Why?"
- Ask Ss to share their answers with the class.

4 DISCUSSION

Learning Objectives: demonstrate one's ability to ask and answer questions about preferences and skills; demonstrate one's ability to give reasons for opinions

A

- Focus Ss' attention on the photos and read the questions below. Explain any new vocabulary.
- Explain the first task. Ss use the questions to help them write their own job profile. Tell them to write the profile on a separate piece of paper.
- Ask a S to help you prepare a sample job profile on the board, like this:

  Personal Job Profile for . . . (name of S)

  Skills
  - can type 45 words a minute
  - speaks Spanish, Portuguese, and English
  - knows how to use accounting software programs
  - is good with numbers

  Job Preferences
  likes working 9 to 5
  prefers having an office job
  doesn't mind wearing a suit to work

- Give Ss a few minutes to complete the task. Go around the class and give help as needed.
- Ask two Ss to read the example conversation.
- Ss work in pairs to compare their profiles. Go around the class and give help as needed.

B *Group work*

- Explain the task. S1 reads his or her job profile. The group discusses the profile and suggests suitable jobs. Remind Ss that they should give reasons for their suggestions. Allow the S to respond before the group continues with the next profile.
- Ask two Ss to read the example conversation.
- Ss form groups and take turns discussing job profiles and possible jobs. Go around the class and take note of any errors you hear.

WHAT'S NEXT?

Learning Objective: become more involved in one's learning

- Focus Ss' attention on the Self-assessment again. Ask: "How well can you do these things now?"
- Ask Ss to underline one thing they need to review. Ask: "What did you underline? How can you review it?"
- If needed, plan additional instruction, activities, or reviews based on Ss' answers.

3 LISTENING What do you want to do?

A Listen to Michelle and Robbie discuss four jobs. Write down the jobs and check (✓) if they would be good or bad at them.

	Job	Good	Bad	Reason
1. Michelle	______	☐	☐	______
	______	☐	☐	______
2. Robbie	______	☐	☐	______
	______	☐	☐	______

B Listen again. Write down the reasons they give.

C **PAIR WORK** Look at the jobs from part A. Which ones would you be good at? Why?

4 DISCUSSION Job profile

A Prepare a personal job profile. Write your name, skills, and job preferences. Think about the questions below. Then compare with a partner.

Do you . . . ?
enjoy helping people
have any special skills
have any experience
have a good memory

Are you good at . . . ?
communicating with people
solving problems
making decisions quickly
learning foreign languages

Do you mind . . . ?
wearing a uniform
traveling frequently
working with a team
working long hours

A: Do you enjoy helping people?
B: Sure. I often do volunteer work.
A: So do I. I help at our local . . .

B **GROUP WORK** Make suggestions for possible jobs based on your classmates' job profiles. Give reasons for your opinions. What do you think of their suggestions for you?

A: Victor would be a good psychologist because he's good at communicating with people.
B: No way! I could never be a psychologist. I'm very moody and short-tempered!

WHAT'S NEXT?

Look at your Self-assessment again. Do you need to review anything?

Unit 11 Supplementary Resources Overview

	After the following SB exercises	You can use these materials in class	Your students can use these materials outside the classroom
CYCLE 1	1 Snapshot		
	2 Perspectives		
	3 Grammar Focus		**SB** Unit 11 Grammar plus, Focus 1 **SS** Unit 11 Grammar 1 **GAME** Sentence Runner (Passive with *by* – simple past) **GAME** Sentence Stacker (Passive with *by* – simple past)
	4 Interchange 11		
	5 Pronunciation		
	6 Listening		**WB** Unit 11 exercises 1–3
CYCLE 2	7 Word Power	**TSS** Unit 11 Vocabulary Worksheet	**SS** Unit 11 Vocabulary 1–2
	8 Conversation		**SS** Unit 11 Speaking 1
	9 Grammar Focus	**TSS** Unit 11 Listening Worksheet **TSS** Unit 11 Grammar Worksheet	**SB** Unit 11 Grammar plus, Focus 2 **SS** Unit 11 Grammar 2 **GAME** Speak or Swim (Passive without *by* – simple present) **GAME** Say the Word (Passive with and without *by* – simple present)
	10 Listening		
	11 Speaking	**TSS** Unit 11 Extra Worksheet	
	12 Writing	**TSS** Unit 11 Writing Worksheet	
	13 Reading	**TSS** Unit 11 Project Worksheet **VID** Unit 11 **VRB** Unit 11	**SS** Unit 11 Reading 1–2 **SS** Unit 11 Listening 1–3 **SS** Unit 11 Video 1–3 **WB** Unit 11 exercises 4–10

Key **GAME:** Online Game **SB:** Student's Book **SS:** Online Self-study **TSS:** Teacher Support Site
VID: Video DVD **VRB:** Video Resource Book **WB:** Online Workbook/Workbook

My Plan for Unit 11

Use the space below to customize a plan that fits your needs.

With the following SB exercises	I am using these materials in class	My students are using these materials outside the classroom

With or instead of the following SB section	I am using these materials for assessment

11 It's really worth seeing!

- Discuss famous landmarks, monuments, and works of art
- Discuss countries around the world

1 SNAPSHOT

AMAZING FACTS ABOUT AMAZING LANDMARKS

The Eiffel Tower – When it was opened in 1889, the tower was red. After a decade, it was painted yellow, and later, it was covered in different shades of brown.

Machu Picchu – It is located 2,430 m (7,972 ft) above sea level, and it has resisted several earthquakes. When there is an earthquake, the stones "dance" and fall back into place.

The Neuschwanstein Castle – This beautiful castle in Germany was the inspiration for the Walt Disney Magic Kingdom Sleeping Beauty Castle.

Mount Fuji – The highest mountain in Japan is made up of a few volcanoes. The last recorded eruption started in 1707.

The Statue of Liberty – The 350 pieces were made in France and then shipped to the United States.

Big Ben – The tower is named Elizabeth Tower. Big Ben is the name of the bell inside it.

Did you know these facts about the landmarks above? What else do you know about them?
Have you ever visited any of them? Which would you like to visit? Why?
Do you know any interesting facts about landmarks in your country?

2 PERSPECTIVES Where dreams come true

A How much do you know about the Walt Disney Company and theme parks? Find three mistakes in the statements below. Then listen and check your answers.

1. The Walt Disney Company was founded in 1923 in California by Walt Disney and his brother Roy.
2. Their most famous character, Donald Duck, first appeared in a movie in 1928.
3. The first Disney theme park, Disneyland, was opened in 1955 in New York and soon became an international attraction.
4. The official opening was broadcast live by the ABC television network.
5. In 1971, the company opened their second park, Disney World.
6. Some of their most popular parks in Florida include Magic Kingdom, Animal Kingdom, and Epcot Center.
7. In 1983, the company opened their first foreign park, London Disneyland. Later, theme parks were also opened in Paris, Hong Kong, and Shanghai.

B **GROUP WORK** Have you been to a Disney park? Which one? How did you like it? Which one would you like to go to? Why?

11 It's really worth seeing!

Cycle 1, Exercises 1–6

In Unit 11, students discuss remarkable places in the world. By the end of Cycle 1, students will be able to discuss famous landmarks, monuments, and works of art using the passive with *by* (simple past). By the end of Cycle 2, students will be able to discuss key features of countries around the world using the passive without *by* (simple present).

1 SNAPSHOT

Learning Objective: discuss famous landmarks

TIP
To create interest in the topic, bring (or ask Ss to bring) related items to class. A large world map, photos, postcards, or information from the Internet about cities and countries around the world would be helpful.

- ***Option:*** Explain that this unit is about famous places in the world. As a warm-up, have Ss skim the unit to find all the countries listed.
- Books closed. Elicit the meaning of *landmark* (an easily recognized object). To prepare Ss for the topic, tell them they're going to read about some amazing landmarks – famous places to visit in different countries. Ask them to guess what places they might read about.
- Books open. Ss read the Snapshot and discuss the questions.
- Elicit or explain any unfamiliar vocabulary.

Vocabulary
shade: how light or dark a color is
earthquake: sudden movement of Earth's surface, often causing damage
Sleeping Beauty: a fairy-tale princess who slept for a hundred years until woken by the kiss of a prince
make up: to form the whole of an amount
bell: a hollow, metal object that makes a sound when hit

- Ss discuss the questions in pairs or small groups. Then elicit Ss' answers.

Possible answers

The Eiffel Tower: It was only intended to stand temporarily. The city of Paris almost tore it down in 1909.
Machu Picchu: When the Spanish arrived in the 16th century, the city, which had been built by the Incas in 1450, was abandoned.
The Neuschwanstein Castle: It is very popular with tourists, receiving around 1.4 million visitors a year.
Mount Fuji: It can be seen from Tokyo, as it is only about 60 miles (100 km) from the capital.
The Statue of Liberty: Most people recognize it as a symbol of freedom and democracy. Also, it was a gift from France to the United States.
Big Ben: The origin of the name has a few theories, but the most accepted is that it was named after Sir Benjamin Hall, a large man known as "Big Ben."

2 PERSPECTIVES

Learning Objectives: discuss a famous place; identify the passive with *by* (simple past) in context

A *[CD 2, Track 42]*

- Books closed. Ask Ss what they know about the Walt Disney Company. Where are its theme parks located?
- Books open. Ss read the information and identify the three incorrect statements.

Audio script

See page T-176.

- Play the audio program. Ss listen and check their answers.

Answers

2. Their most famous character, ~~Donald Duck~~ *Mickey Mouse*, first appeared in a movie in 1928.
3. The first Disney theme park, Disneyland, was opened in 1955 in ~~New York~~ *California* . . .
8. In 1983, the company opened their first foreign park, ~~London~~ *Tokyo* Disneyland. Later, theme parks were also opened in Paris, Hong Kong, and Shanghai.

B *Group work*

- Have Ss form groups to discuss the questions.
- As a class, discuss which facts about Disney are the most surprising.

3 GRAMMAR FOCUS

Learning Objective: use the passive with *by*

[CD 2, Track 43]
Passive (simple past)

- Prepare six cards and write these words and phrases on them:

  Card 1: the Disney brothers — Card 4: in 1923
  Card 2: founded — Card 5: was
  Card 3: the company — Card 6: by

- Ask four Ss to stand in a row and hold up the first four cards:

  S1 S2 S3 S4
  the Disney brothers ***founded*** *the company in 1923*

- Now explain that in English we can say the same thing in another way. Ask two more Ss to take the last two cards. Ss should hold up the cards in this order:

  S3 S5 S2 S6 S1
  the company ***was founded by*** *the Disney brothers*
  S4
  in 1923

- Elicit or explain the following rules:

  Active
  The Disney brothers ***founded*** *the company.*
  Subject + verb + object

  Here, the emphasis is on **the Disney brothers**. It wasn't John Smith who founded the company. It was **the Disney brothers**.

  Passive
  The company ***was founded*** *(by the Disney brothers)*
  Object + *was/were* +past participle + (by + subject)

  Here, the emphasis is on **the company**. The most important fact is that the **company was founded.**

- The passive is the best way to express an idea when:
  1. We don't know who did the action, e.g., ***My house was broken into*** *on Friday.*
  2. There is no "doer" of the action, e.g., ***He was killed*** *in an earthquake.*
  3. The fact is more important than the "doer" of the action, e.g., ***My dog was run over*** *by a car.*
- Remind Ss that the past passive verb is made up of *was/were* + past participle. We don't always use *by* to show "who" or "what" did the action.
- Have Ss look at the Snapshot and Perspectives sections on the previous page to find examples of the passive in the simple past tense. (Answers: There are nine examples in total; two contain the word *by*.)
- Play the audio program to present the sentences. Tell Ss to pay attention to the pronunciation of *was*. Point out that it is usually unstressed in passive sentences.

A

- Focus Ss' attention on the picture and elicit information about it.
- Do the first example with the class.
- Have Ss complete the task individually. Then go over answers with the class.

Answers

1. *Mont Sainte-Victoire* **was painted** by the French artist Paul Cézanne.
2. The first Star Wars film **was written** and **directed** by George Lucas.
3. The Statue of Liberty **was designed** by the French sculptor Frédéric Auguste Bartholdi.
4. The 2014 World Cup final **was won** by Germany. The final match **was seen** by almost 1 billion people all over the world.
5. The songs *Revolution* and *Hey Jude* **were recorded** by the Beatles in 1968.
6. In the 2007 film *I'm Not There*, the American musician Bob Dylan **was played** by six different people, including Australian actress Cate Blanchett.
7. The 2016 Oscar for Best Actress **was given** to Brie Larson for her role in the movie *Room*.
8. The first iPad **was released** in 2010.

B *Pair work*

- Explain the following words and expressions:

Vocabulary
HDTV: high-definition television, a special television system that shows sharp, clear images
manual typewriter: a non-electric typewriter

- Explain the task. Point out that a date or year can appear in several places in a passive sentence – at the beginning, in the middle, or at the end.
- As Ss complete the task individually, go around the class and give help as needed. Then Ss take turns reading their sentences in pairs. Elicit Ss' answers.

Possible Answers

1. Stephen Hawking was played by Eddie Redmayne in the 2014 film *The Theory of Everything*.
2. *100 Years of Solitude* was written by Gabriel García Márquez in 1967.
3. The Empire State Building was designed by the American architect William Lamb.
4. The first digital HDTV was produced by Woo Paik in 1991.
5. The first Harry Potter book was written on an old manual typewriter by J. K. Rowling.
6. Indiana Jones was chosen as the greatest movie character of all time by *Empire* magazine readers.

4 INTERCHANGE 11

See page T-125 for teaching notes.

3 GRAMMAR FOCUS

Passive with *by* (simple past)

The passive changes the focus of a sentence.
For the simple past, use the past of *be* + past participle.

Active	Passive
The Disney brothers **founded** the company in 1923.	It **was founded by** the Disney brothers in 1923.
Walt Disney **opened** Disneyland in 1955.	Disneyland **was opened by** Walt Disney in 1955.
The ABC network **broadcast** the opening of the park.	The opening **was broadcast by** ABC.

GRAMMAR PLUS *see page 142*

A Complete the sentences with the simple past passive form of the verbs. Then compare with a partner.

1. *Mont Sainte-Victoire* ______________ (paint) by the French artist Paul Cézanne.
2. The first Star Wars film ______________ (write) and ______________ (direct) by George Lucas.
3. The Statue of Liberty ______________ (design) by the French sculptor Frédéric Auguste Bartholdi.
4. The 2014 World Cup final ______________ (win) by Germany. The final match ______________ (see) by almost 1 billion people all over the world.
5. The songs *Revolution* and *Hey Jude* ______________ (record) by the Beatles in 1968.
6. In the 2007 film *I'm Not There*, the American musician Bob Dylan ______________ (play) by six different people, including Australian actress Cate Blanchett.
7. The 2016 Oscar for Best Actress ______________ (give) to Brie Larson for her role in the movie *Room*.
8. The first iPad ______________ (release) in 2010.

B **PAIR WORK** Change these sentences into passive sentences with *by*. Then take turns reading them aloud.

1. Eddie Redmayne played Stephen Hawking in the 2014 film *The Theory of Everything*.
   ____
2. Gabriel García Márquez wrote the novel *One Hundred Years of Solitude* in 1967.
   ____
3. The American architect William Lamb designed the Empire State Building.
   ____
4. Woo Paik produced the first digital HDTV in 1991.
   ____
5. J. K. Rowling wrote the first Harry Potter book on an old manual typewriter.
   ____
6. *Empire* magazine readers chose Indiana Jones as the greatest movie character of all time.
   ____

4 INTERCHANGE 11 True or false?

Who created these well-known works? Go to Interchange 11 on page 125.

5 PRONUNCIATION The letter *o*

A Listen and practice. Notice how the letter *o* is pronounced in the following words.

/a/	/ou/	/u/	/ʌ/
not	no	do	one
top	don't	food	love
________	________	________	________
________	________	________	________

B How is the letter *o* pronounced in these words? Write them in the correct column in part A. Then listen and check your answers.

come done lock own shot soon who wrote

6 LISTENING Man-made wonders of the world

A Listen to three tour guides describe some famous monuments. Take notes to answer the questions below. Then compare with a partner.

1. Taj Mahal
Why was it built?
What do the changing colors of the building represent?

2. Palace of Versailles
What did King Louis XIV want the Hall of Mirrors to show?
What problem did the candles cause? How did the mirrors help?

3. La Sagrada Familia
What did the architect think about man-made structures versus nature?
Why are no straight lines used?

B **PAIR WORK** Think of another famous monument. Describe it to the rest of the class. They will try to guess the monument.

7 WORD POWER Country fast facts

A Complete the sentences with words from the list.

✓ cattle	dialects	electronics	handicrafts	languages
sheep	souvenirs	✓ soybeans	textiles	wheat

1. The United States **grows** ___soybeans___ and ________.
2. Australia **raises** ___cattle___ and ________.
3. China **manufactures** ________ and ________.
4. In India, people **speak** many different ________ and ________.
5. You can **find** ________ and ________ at different shops in Brazil.

B **PAIR WORK** Talk about your country. Use the sentences in part A with your own information.

"We raise cattle and chickens. We grow corn and oats. You can find . . . "

5 PRONUNCIATION

Learning Objectives: differentiate between the different ways the letter *o* is pronounced; sound more natural when pronouncing it

A *[CD 2, Track 44]*

- Books closed. Write these words on the board and read them aloud. Ask: "What is different about the letter *o* in each word?"

  not no do one

- Books open. Point out that the letter *o* is pronounced in different ways in English. Play the audio program. Ss listen to how the letter *o* is pronounced.
- Play the audio program again. Ask individual Ss to repeat to check their pronunciation.

B *[CD 2, Track 45]*

- Explain the task. Ss read the words and write them in a column in part A.

  Then play the rest of the audio program. Ss check their answers.

Answers

/a/ = lock, shot
/ou/ = own, wrote
/u:/ = soon, who
/ʌ/ = come, done

For more practice, play ***Run for It!*** – download it from the website. Assign each wall an *o* sound and then say words containing the letter *o*. For more of a challenge, write them on the board.

6 LISTENING

Learning Objective: listen for the main idea and specific information in passages about old monuments

A *[CD 2, Track 46]*

- Give Ss time to look at the pictures and questions. Then ask Ss to predict the answers and tell a partner what else they would like to know about these places.
- Explain the task. Ss will hear three tour guides talk about these places. Ss listen for the answers.
- Play the audio program. Ss listen to check their predictions and take notes. Have Ss compare answers in pairs. Then go over answers with the class.

Audio script

See page T-176.

Answers

1. Taj Mahal: built for the Emperor Shah Jahan's wife when she died; the changing colors of the building represent the different moods of women
2. Palace of Versailles: Hall of Mirrors shows all the riches and power of France; the candles caused smoke; the mirrors reflected the light of the candles, so fewer candles were used (causing less smoke damage to the room)
3. La Sagrada Familia: Gaudí thought man-made structures should reflect nature; no straight lines were used because straight lines don't exist in nature

B *Pair work*

- Ask Ss to suggest famous monuments they know (e.g., St. Basil's Cathedral in Moscow, the Pyramids in Egypt, Christ the Redeemer in Rio de Janeiro).
- Have a S from each pair write one or two suggestions on the board. Once a place is written on the board, make sure students do not repeat it.

End of Cycle 1

See the Supplementary Resources chart at the beginning of this unit for additional teaching materials and student activities related to this Cycle.

Cycle 2, Exercises 7–13

7 WORD POWER

Learning Objective: discuss products from different countries

A

- Elicit or explain any new vocabulary.
- Ss complete the sentences with the words given. Check the answers as a class.

Answers

1. The United States **grows** soybeans and wheat.
2. Australia **raises** cattle and sheep.
3. China **manufactures** electronics and textiles.
4. In India, people **speak** many different languages and dialects.
5. You can **find** souvenirs and handicrafts at different shops in Brazil.

B *Pair work*

- Ss work in pairs to make as many sentences as they can. Then Ss share sentences with the class.

8 CONVERSATION

Learning Objective: use the passive without *by* (simple present) in a conversation about asking for and giving information

A *[CD 2, Track 47]*

- Books closed. Set the scene. A girl is asking a friend for information about the Netherlands (a country in western Europe). Write these questions on the board:

  1. *What is she going to do there?*
  2. *What currency is used in the Netherlands?*
  3. *What should she buy there?*

- Play the audio program. Ss listen. Then elicit answers to the questions. (Answers: 1. She's going to a conference 2. the euro 3. cheese)
- ***Option:*** Ask the class: "What else do you know about the Netherlands?"
- Write this comprehension question on the board:

  What other things does Lisa ask about the Netherlands?

- Play the audio program again and check answers. (Answers: does she need to take euros, where can she buy cheese)
- Books open. Play the audio program again while Ss look at the picture and read silently.
- Explain that dairy cows are cows bred to produce large quantities of milk.
- Ss practice the conversation in pairs.

! To improve pronunciation and have fun with this conversation, try ***Say It with Feeling!*** – download it from the website. Encourage Ss to use actions, too.

B *[CD 2, Track 48]*

- Have Ss try to guess what other suggestion Erik gives Lisa (e.g. *places to visit, what to eat, what not to do . . .*).
- Play the audio program and have Ss check their answers.

Answer

Erik suggests that Lisa visit the tulip gardens.

Audio script

See page T-177.

9 GRAMMAR FOCUS

Learning Objective: use the passive without *by* (simple present)

[CD 2, Track 49]

- Explain that, as Ss saw with the simple past passive, we change the emphasis when we use the simple present passive. Instead of saying: "**They** use the euro in most of Europe," we can say "**The euro** is used in most of Europe." The focus changes from "they" (which is not clear) to "the euro" (which is what we're interested in). Play the audio program to present the sentences in the box.
- Write these passive sentences on the board to demonstrate how the *by* phrase is omitted here:

  The euro is used in most of Europe (by people).
  Cars are manufactured in Europe (by manufacturers).

- Explain that the "doer" of the action in each of these sentences is obvious or not important, so the *by* phrase can be omitted.
- Refer Ss to the previous conversation and ask them to underline the examples of the simple present passive. (There are three questions and one statement.)

A

- Explain the task and read the verbs in parentheses. Have Ss check any new words in their dictionaries.
- Ss complete the passage individually. If necessary, you can also copy and give the Ss the appendix on page T-151 so Ss can use more irregular past participles. Then go over answers.

Answers

1. are spoken	3. are manufactured	5. are sold
2. is grown	4. is used	6. are raised

B

- Explain and model the task by eliciting the answer to the first blank.
- Ss work individually. Then go over answers.

Answers

Many crops **are grown** in Taiwan. Some crops **are consumed** locally, but others **are exported**. Tea **is grown** in cooler parts of the island, and rice **is cultivated** in warmer parts. Fishing is also an important industry. A wide variety of seafood **is caught** and **shipped** all over the world. Many people **are employed** in the food-processing industry.

C *Pair work*

- Ss use the passive of the verbs in part A to talk about their country (and other countries they know).
- ***Option:*** Ss share their ideas with the class.

8 CONVERSATION What do you want to know?

A Listen and practice.

Lisa: Erik, you're from Amsterdam, aren't you?
Erik: Yeah . . . Why?
Lisa: I'm going there for a conference, and I'd like some information.
Erik: Sure. What do you want to know?
Lisa: Do you use the euro in the Netherlands?
Erik: Yes. The euro is used in most of Europe, you know.
Lisa: And do I need to take euros with me?
Erik: Not really. International credit cards are accepted everywhere, and they're much safer.
Lisa: Of course. And what should I buy there?
Erik: Cheese, definitely. We raise dairy cows, and some really excellent cheese is made from their milk.
Lisa: Good. I love cheese. Where is it sold?
Erik: You can find it at cheese shops all around the city. And don't forget to bring me a piece.

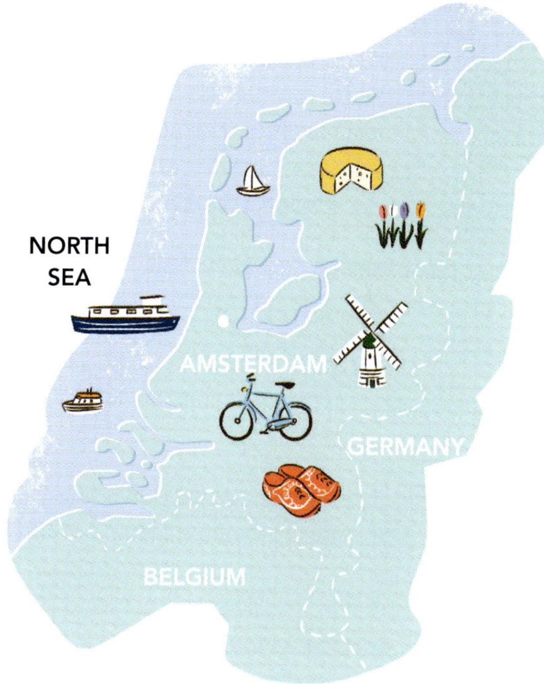

B Listen to the rest of the conversation. What other suggestion does Erik give Lisa?

9 GRAMMAR FOCUS

Passive without *by* (simple present)

For the simple present, use the present of *be* + past participle.

Active	Passive
They **use** the euro in most of Europe.	The euro **is used** in most of Europe.
Most places **accept** credit cards.	Credit cards **are accepted** at most places.
We **raise** dairy cattle in the Netherlands.	Dairy cattle **are raised** in the Netherlands.

GRAMMAR PLUS *see page 142*

A Complete the sentences. Use the passive of these verbs.

grow manufacture raise speak sell use

1. French and Flemish __________ in Belgium.
2. Rice __________ in many Asian countries.
3. Cars and electronics __________ in Japan.
4. Sheep's milk __________ for making feta cheese.
5. Handicrafts __________ in the streets in Thailand.
6. A lot of cattle __________ in Australia.

B Complete this passage using the simple present passive form.

Many crops ____________ (grow) in Taiwan. Some crops ____________ (consume) locally, but others ____________ (export). Tea ____________ (grow) in cooler parts of the island, and rice ____________ (cultivate) in warmer parts. Fishing is also an important industry. A wide variety of seafood ____________ (catch) and ____________ (ship) all over the world. Many people ____________ (employ) in the food-processing industry.

C **PAIR WORK** Use the passive of the verbs in part A to talk about your country and other countries you know.

10 LISTENING Is all tourism good?

A Listen to a news report about tourism in Costa Rica. Select the six effects of mass tourism that are mentioned. (There are two extra effects.) Indicate if they are positive (**P**) or negative (**N**).

P English is spoken.	The ocean is polluted.
Tourism jobs are available all over the country.	High-rise hotels are built.
More foreigners are investing there.	Fish and lobster are hunted.
Acres of jungle are cut down.	The government becomes corrupt.

B Listen again. Write down three criteria the hotel fulfills in order to be an ecotourism business in Costa Rica.

______________ ______________ ______________

C **GROUP WORK** What is tourism like in your country? Talk about some positive and negative aspects.

Costa Rica

11 SPEAKING Give me a clue.

A **PAIR WORK** Choose a country. Then answer these questions.

Where is it located?
What traditional dishes are eaten there?
What languages are spoken?
What currency is used?
What famous tourist attraction is found there?
What souvenirs are found there?

B **CLASS ACTIVITY** Give a short talk about the country you chose. Don't say the country's name. Can the class guess the country?

12 WRITING A city guide

A Choose a city or area in your country and write the introduction for an online city guide. Include the location, size, population, main attractions, shopping and travel tips, etc.

Bruges is located in the northwest of Belgium, and it has a population of about 120,000 people. It is known for its canals and medieval buildings. In 2000, it was declared a World Heritage City by UNESCO. Bruges is also a good place to buy Belgium chocolate. It is sold . . .

B **GROUP WORK** Exchange papers. Do you think the introduction gives a good idea of the place? Would it attract tourists or businesses to the place? What other information should be included?

Bruges, Belgium

10 LISTENING

Learning Objective: listen for specific information in a passage about a country

A *[CD 2, Track 50]*

- Present the topic and pictures. Ask questions like "Is tourism always good for a country? When is it bad? Can you think of some examples?"

To help Ss make predictions before listening, play ***Prediction Bingo*** – download it from the website.

- Tell Ss to listen and take notes to complete the chart with *P* for positive effects and *N* for negative effects. Then play the audio program.

Audio script

See page T-177.

Answers

P = English is spoken more than ever; more foreigners are investing there; tourism jobs are available all over the country
N = fish and lobster are hunted; acres of jungle are cut down; seventy-five percent of the land is unprotected

B *[CD 2, Track 51]*

- Play the audio program again. This time, have Ss listen and write the three criteria in order to be an ecotourism business. Have Ss compare answers in pairs. Then elicit answers from the class.

Answers

local Costa Ricans are employed; waste is recycled; energy-saving devices are used; visitors are educated about the culture and environment

For more practice using the passive voice, play ***Ask the Right Question*** – download it from the website.

C *Group work*

- Divide the class into small groups and have Ss discuss the question. Encourage them to ask follow-up questions and make a list of some positive and negative aspects.
- Elicit ideas from each group and write them under *Positive* and *Negative* heads on the board.

11 SPEAKING

Learning Objective: discuss a country using the simple present passive

A *Pair work*

- Explain the task. In pairs, Ss choose a country and write answers to the questions. Set a time limit of about five minutes. If Ss want to research a country, this part could be assigned as homework.
- Help Ss brainstorm other information they could include (e.g., geographical features, religion, capital city). For more ideas, refer Ss to Exercises 7A and 10A.
- Remind Ss not to include the name of the country in their talk.

B *Class activity*

- Ss take turns giving a short talk about the country they chose. Encourage Ss to present the information without simply reading their notes from part A. The class listens and guesses the country's name.

12 WRITING

Learning Objective: write a descriptive passage about a country using the simple present passive and vocabulary for discussing products

A

- Explain the task and read the example paragraph. Point out the passive sentences used in the example.
- Ask Ss to choose a country to write about. They can choose one that they already know about or research another country. If Ss research a country, this part could be assigned as homework.
- Ss gather information and make a chart. Then they use their notes to write a draft of their introduction.

! To help Ss organize their writing, try ***Mind Mapping*** – download it from the website.

B *Group work*

- In groups, Ss exchange papers and take turns reading them aloud. Encourage Ss to ask for more information.

13 READING

Learning Objectives: scan an article about unusual tourist attractions; identify meaning from context; organize key parts of the text

A

- Books closed. Write the word *Museums* in a box in the middle of the board and ask Ss what kinds of museums are in their city, town, or country. Elicit ideas and write them on the board as a mind map:

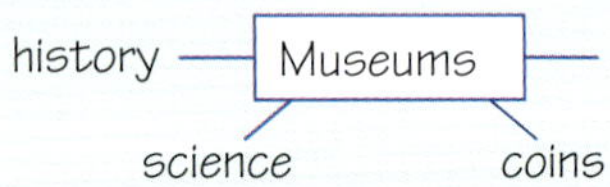

- Ask Ss if they have ever been to or heard about any unusual museums.
- Books open. Ask Ss what they see in the pictures. Explain the task and tell Ss to scan the article as quickly as possible for the answers. Then elicit answers. (Answers: you can see nearly 300 types of toilets; the underwater sculptures were designed in 2009; the world's smallest book is 0.6 millimeters in size.)

TIP

To help Ss scan quickly and focus on key words only, have Ss who finish raise their hands and leave them up. This will encourage those who haven't finished to work more quickly.

B

- Explain to Ss that they are going to guess the meanings of some new words and expressions from context. As an example, read the first paragraph aloud and ask Ss to guess the meaning of *Ever wondered about . . .*
- Ss complete the exercise individually. Then go over answers with the class. Ask Ss how they guessed the correct answers.

Answers

1. interested	4. all the time
2. best	5. on show
3. different from	6. sewing

- Elicit other new words in the text. Tell Ss to use their dictionaries or work in pairs to guess the meaning from context.

Vocabulary

wonder: feel curious
B.C.E: before the Common Era (before the Christian era)
drawing: a picture made with a pencil, pen, or crayon
seabed: the floor of the ocean
life-size: not a miniature; the real size of the object or person
tiny: very small
chess set: a chessboard and its chess pieces
pin: a thin piece of metal with a sharp point at one end and a round head at the other
needle: a very fine and thin piece of metal with a point at one end and a hole at the other, used in sewing

C

- Explain the task. Tell Ss that they need to guess the paragraph, but not the exact place in the paragraph where each sentence could go. Model the task with the first sentence. Then ask Ss how they guessed the correct answer.
- Ss complete the task individually. Then go over answers with the class. Ask Ss how they guessed the answers.

Answers

1. C 2. A 3. B

D

- Have Ss think about the questions. Elicit responses. Encourage Ss to give reasons for their responses.
- ***Option:*** As a follow-up, Ss write a paragraph about a museum in their city, town, or country. These can be displayed in the classroom or given to you to check.

To review vocabulary from this reading, play ***Tic-Tac-Toe*** – download it from the website.

End of Cycle 2

See the Supplementary Resources chart at the beginning of this unit for additional teaching materials and student exercises related to this Cycle.

13 READING

A Scan the advertisements. How many types of toilets can you see at the museum? When were the underwater sculptures designed? How big is the world's smallest book?

A SULABH INTERNATIONAL MUSEUM OF TOILETS, NEW DELHI, INDIA

Ever wondered about the history of toilets? Probably not! But visit the fascinating Sulabh Museum and see just how interesting they can be. Admire nearly 300 different toilets dating back to 2500 B.C.E. Some are beautifully decorated, one is made of solid gold, and there is an electric toilet that works without water. The star of the collection is a copy of a 16th century toilet. It was used by King Louis XIV of France – sometimes while speaking to his government. See drawings, photographs, and poems about toilets, too. One photo shows a toilet that was used by an elephant!

B UNDERWATER MUSEUM, CANCUN, MEXICO

Join one of our unique tours and discover an amazing underwater world 27 feet below the sea. Designed by Jason deCaires Taylor in 2009, it has over 450 sculptures. They are made from natural materials and show art and nature existing side by side. The *Silent Evolution* shows men, women, and children standing together on the seabed. They look so real that you'll want to talk to them. There are also sculptures of a house and a life-size Beetle car. The sculptures are covered in beautiful corals, and their appearances are constantly changing. Watch as an incredible variety of fish swim in and out of them.

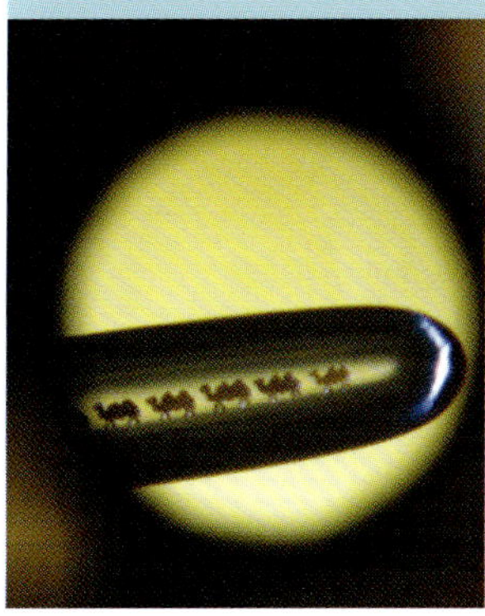

C MICROMINIATURE MUSEUM, KIEV, UKRAINE

Small really is beautiful in this museum of art with a difference. The exhibits, created by artist Nikolai Syadristy, are so tiny they can only be seen clearly with a microscope. Read the world's smallest book – it is only 0.6 millimeters in size, but contains twelve pages of poems and drawings. There is a chess set on the head of a pin and the world's smallest electric motor. It is 20 times smaller than a piece of sand. Look closely at the eye of a needle and discover the seven camels inside. Read the words "Long Live Peace" not on paper, but written on a human hair!

B Read the advertisements. Find the words in *italics* below. Then circle the meaning of each word.

1. Something *fascinating* makes you feel very **interested / angry**.
2. The *star* of a collection is the **worst / best** part.
3. A *unique* thing is **different from / the same as** all others.
4. If something is changing *constantly*, it's changing **very little / all the time**.
5. An *exhibit* is an object that is **on show / for sale**.
6. A *needle* is a metal object that is used for **cutting / sewing**.

C Read the comments of three visitors to the museums. Write the letter (A, B, or C) of the museum you think they visited.

_____ **1.** "I just don't know how he made such little things."
_____ **2.** "I can't believe that an animal would use something like that."
_____ **3.** "I felt a little afraid about going down, but it was a great experience in the end."

D Which museum would you most like to visit? Why?

Unit 12 Supplementary Resources Overview

	After the following SB exercises	You can use these materials in class	Your students can use these materials outside the classroom
CYCLE 1	1 **Snapshot**		
	2 **Perspectives**		
	3 **Grammar Focus**		**SB** Unit 12 Grammar plus, Focus 1 **SS** Unit 12 Grammar 1 **GAME** Sentence Runner (Past continuous vs. simple past)
	4 **Listening**	**TSS** Unit 12 Listening Worksheet **TSS** Unit 12 Extra Worksheet	
	5 **Word Power**		**SS** Unit 12 Vocabulary 1–2 **GAME** Spell or Slime (Adverbs)
	6 **Writing**		**WB** Unit 12 exercises 1–5
CYCLE 2	7 **Conversation**		**SS** Unit 12 Speaking 1–2
	8 **Grammar Focus**	**TSS** Unit 12 Vocabulary Worksheet **TSS** Unit 12 Writing Worksheet	**SB** Unit 12 Grammar plus, Focus 2 **SS** Unit 12 Grammar 2 **GAME** Say the Word (Present perfect continuous 1) **GAME** Speak or Swim (Present perfect continuous 2)
	9 **Pronunciation**	**TSS** Unit 12 Grammar Worksheet	
	10 **Speaking**		
	11 **Interchange 12**		
	12 **Reading**	**TSS** Unit 12 Project Worksheet **VID** Unit 12 **VRB** Unit 12	**SS** Unit 12 Reading 1–2 **SS** Unit 12 Listening 1–3 **SS** Unit 12 Video 1–3 **WB** Unit 12 exercises 6–10

With or instead of the following SB section	You can also use these materials for assessment
Units 11–12 Progress Check	**ASSESSMENT PROGRAM** Units 11–12 Oral Quiz **ASSESSMENT PROGRAM** Units 11–12 Written Quiz

Key **GAME:** Online Game **SB:** Student's Book **SS:** Online Self-study **TSS:** Teacher Support Site
VID: Video DVD **VRB:** Video Resource Book **WB:** Online Workbook/Workbook

My Plan for Unit 12

Use the space below to customize a plan that fits your needs.

With the following SB exercises	I am using these materials in class	My students are using these materials outside the classroom

With or instead of the following SB section	I am using these materials for assessment

12 It's a long story.

- Tell stories
- Discuss recent activities

1 SNAPSHOT

True Stories of Incredible Coincidences

One day, the American novelist Anne Parrish was in a bookstore in Paris and she saw an old, used copy of one of her favorite childhood books. When she opened it, she saw on the first page: "Anne Parrish, 209 N. Weber Street, Colorado Springs." It was Anne's own book.

A 10-year-old girl named Laura Buxton released a bunch of balloons into the air. She attached a note to the balloons that asked the person who found it to write back to her. A couple of weeks later, she received a reply. It was from another 10-year-old girl also named Laura Buxton who lived 150 miles away.

Which of these stories do you think is more amazing? more difficult to believe?
Have you ever had an experience that is hard to believe?
Do you know of anyone who has? What happened?

2 PERSPECTIVES What next?

A Listen to what happened to these people. Check (✓) the things that have happened to you.

- ☐ "I was having lunch when I spilled a cup of coffee on my clothes."
- ☐ "I was driving to the airport to pick up a friend, but I got a flat tire."
- ☐ "I was studying for an important test when the lights went out."
- ☐ "While I was walking down the street, I found a wallet with lots of money."
- ☐ "I was traveling in another country when I met an old school friend."
- ☐ "I was getting off a bus when I slipped and fell on the sidewalk."
- ☐ "While I was shopping one day, a celebrity walked into the store."

B Choose one statement that you checked. What happened next?

"I tried to clean it, but I couldn't. So I had to wear a jacket for the rest of the day."

12 It's a long story.

Cycle 1, Exercises 1–6

In Unit 12, students discuss recent activities and tell stories. By the end of Cycle 1, students will be able to discuss events, accidents, and accomplishments in their lives using the past continuous and the simple past. By the end of Cycle 2, students will be able to discuss events using the present perfect continuous.

1 SNAPSHOT

Learning Objective: discuss stories

- Books closed. Ask Ss: "Do you believe in coincidences?" Then write these questions on the board and have Ss brainstorm ideas:

  What coincidences could happen . . .
  . . . at a used book store?
  . . . by releasing balloons in the air?

- Ask Ss to read the two stories, underlining any words they don't know.
- Explain new words by giving definitions or examples, e.g., *novelist* = someone who writes novels (stories about imaginary people and events); *release* = stop holding someone or something; *bunch* = a number of things of the same type that are joined or held together.

Alternatively, tell Ss to ask their classmates for definitions or examples of any words they can't understand from context. Then Ss discuss the questions in small groups. Go around the class and give help as needed.

! For another way to teach this Snapshot, try ***Jigsaw Learning*** – download it from the website. In groups of three, each S reads about one invention and then shares the information with the others.

- Elicit feedback from Ss about which story the group felt is the most amazing and any other incredible coincidences they know of.

2 PERSPECTIVES

Learning Objectives: discuss fortunate and unfortunate events; identify the past continuous in context

A *[CD 2, Track 52]*

- Books closed. Ask the class: "Have you ever met or seen a famous person?" Elicit some experiences.
- Explain the task. Ss listen to people talk about things that have happened to them. As Ss listen, they write down what each person says. Play the audio program, pausing after each speaker to give Ss time to write.
- Books open. Ss read the statements and correct their notes.
- Play the audio program again. This time, Ss read and check (✓) the things that have happened to them. Point out that it does not have to be exactly the same event but can be something similar.
- In groups, ask Ss to discuss which things have happened to them. What happened? When? What did the S do? Encourage the rest of the group to ask for more information.

TIP
To prevent Ss from using their first language when working in groups, explain that they must ask for "time out" when they want to use their L1. If necessary, place a limit on the number of "time outs."

B

- Explain the task and read the example sentence. Remind Ss to ask follow-up questions (e.g., *Was your friend upset?*).
- In groups, Ss take turns talking about what happened to them.

For more practice with this topic, play ***Twenty Questions*** – download it from the website.

3 GRAMMAR FOCUS

Learning Objective: use the past continuous and the simple past to tell a story

[CD 2, Track 53]

- To explain the use of the past continuous, ask Ss to mime an action. Then suddenly turn off the light. Ask Ss: "What happened?" (Answer: You turned off the light.) Then ask Ss: "What were you doing when I turned off the light?" Help Ss to express their answers in the past continuous (e.g., *I was writing/typing/eating when you turned off the light.*).

TIP
To explain the use of a tense, use a simple memorable action or something visual like a time line (see below).

- Briefly explain the past continuous.

Past continuous vs. simple past

- Point out that the past continuous is often used with the simple past. Both actions happened at the same time, but one action (the past continuous) started earlier and was in progress when the other action (the simple past) happened.

Earlier action   Later action (interrupting the first)

8:00   8:15

I was eating when the phone rang.

- Point out that *when* and *while* are often interchangeable when referring to a point or a period in time – for example: *When/While* I *was waiting* in line, it started to rain. It started to rain *while/when* I *was waiting* in line.
- Refer Ss to the Perspectives section. Ask them to underline the simple past phrases (e.g., *I spilled a cup of coffee, I got a flat tire*).
- Ask Ss to look at the other half of each sentence (e.g., *I was having lunch, I was driving to the airport*). Elicit the form and explain that these are examples of the past continuous tense:

Subject +	*was/were +*	*verb + -ing*
I	*was*	*watching*

- Play the audio program to present the sentences in the box. Ss listen and repeat.

A

- Focus Ss' attention on the illustration and use the first item to model the task. Then have Ss work individually to complete the task. Go around the class and give help as needed.
- Ss compare answers in pairs. Then elicit answers from the class.

Answers

1. My sister **was texting** while she **was driving**, and she almost **crashed** her car.
2. While I **was cooking** dinner last night, a friend **called** and I **burned** the food.
3. My father **was skiing** when he **broke** his leg in several places.
4. We **had** our first child while we **were living** in a tiny apartment.
5. While I **was driving** in England a few years ago, I **realized** I was on the wrong side of the road!
6. Once I **was reading** a good book, but someone **told** me the ending.
7. My parents **met** each other while they **were working** at the same restaurant in Vancouver.

For more practice with the past continuous, play ***Mime*** – download it from the website. Write sentences on slips of paper and have Ss act them out for the rest of the class to guess.

B

- Point out that the past continuous is also used to say someone was in the middle of doing something at a certain time:

My family was living in Chile this time last year.
I was waiting for you at 8:00. Where were you?

- Explain the task and elicit sentences from the class. Write some of them on the board.
- Now Ss write sentences about themselves. Encourage them to include interesting information. Go around the class and check Ss' sentences before they begin part C.

C *Pair work*

- Explain the task and have two Ss model the example conversation. Then write these useful expressions on the board:

Oh, really? That's interesting.
Why were you/did you . . . ?
Wow! That's incredible./Oh, no! That's terrible.

- Ss take turns reading their sentences aloud in pairs. Remind them to respond and ask follow-up questions to get more information. Go around the class and write down any errors.
- Go over any errors you noticed with the whole class.

3 GRAMMAR FOCUS

Past continuous vs. simple past

Use the past continuous for an action in progress in the past.
Use the simple past for an action that interrupts it.

I **was having** lunch	when I **spilled** coffee on my clothes.
I **was driving** to the airport,	but I **got** a flat tire.
While I **was shopping** one day,	a celebrity **walked** into the store.

GRAMMAR PLUS *see page 143*

A Complete these sentences. Then compare with a partner.

1. My sister ______________ (text) while she ______________ (drive), and she almost ______________ (crash) her car.
2. While I ______________ (cook) dinner last night, a friend ______________ (call) and I ______________ (burn) the food.
3. My father ______________ (ski) when he ______________ (break) his leg in several places.
4. We ______________ (have) our first child while we ______________ (live) in a tiny apartment.
5. While I ______________ (drive) in England a few years ago, I ______________ (realize) I was on the wrong side of the road!
6. Once I ______________ (read) a good book, but someone ______________ (tell) me the ending.
7. My parents ______________ (meet) each other while they ______________ (work) at the same restaurant in Vancouver.

B Complete these statements with information about yourself. Use the simple past or the past continuous.

1. I was taking a selfie when . . .
2. While I was going home one day, . . .
3. I was . . .
4. While I was . . .
5. Last month, . . .
6. Some time ago, . . .

C **PAIR WORK** Take turns reading your sentences from part B. Then ask and answer follow-up questions.

A: I was taking a selfie when a man came and stole my phone.
B: Oh, no! What did you do?
A: I went to the police . . . and they told me to be more careful.

4 LISTENING How did it all begin?

A Listen to this story about a successful inventor. Put the sentences into the correct order from 1 to 8.

__1__ Mark Zuckerberg started writing computer programs.
____ His friends invested in Facebook.
____ He didn't accept Microsoft's offer.
____ He invented FaceMash.
____ Facebook became available to the public.
____ Zuckerberg wrote his very own messenger program.
____ He created a program that recommended music.
____ Three classmates asked for his help.

B Listen again. How did the invention change his life?

C **PAIR WORK** Think of other websites and apps that were successful inventions.

5 WORD POWER What happened?

A Some adverbs are often used in storytelling to emphasize that something interesting is about to happen. Which of these adverbs are positive (**P**)? Which are negative (**N**)? Which could be either (**E**)?

coincidentally	____	strangely	____
fortunately	____	suddenly	____
luckily	____	surprisingly	____
miraculously	____	unexpectedly	____
sadly	____	unfortunately	____

B **PAIR WORK** Complete these statements with adverbs from part A to make up creative sentences.

We were having a party when, . . .
I was walking down the street when, . . .
It started out as a normal day, but, . . .

A: We were having a party when, suddenly, the lights went out!
B: Once I was dancing at a party when, unfortunately, I fell down!

6 WRITING What's your story?

A Write a short story about something that happened to you recently. Try to include some of the adverbs from Exercise 5.

I was shopping at a big department store when, suddenly, I saw a little girl crying in a corner all by herself. The girl said she couldn't find her mother. I was taking her to the store manager when I saw an old school friend running towards me. Coincidentally, she was the girl's mother, and . . .

B **GROUP WORK** Take turns reading your stories. Answer any questions from the group.

4 LISTENING

Learning Objectives: listen for specific information; make inferences about stories

A *[CD 2, Track 54]*

- Explain the task and present the information in the chart. Ask Ss: "What do you know about Mark Zuckerberg?"
- Play the audio program. Ss listen and number the sentences. Then elicit Ss' answers.

Audio script

See page T-177.

Answers

1. Mark Zuckerberg started writing computer programs.
2. Zuckerberg wrote his very own messenger program.
3. He created a program that recommended music.
4. He didn't accept Microsoft's offer.
5. He invented FaceMash.
6. Three classmates asked for his help.
7. His friends invested in Facebook.
8. Facebook became available to the public.

B *[CD 2, Track 55]*

- Play the audio program again. Ss listen and answer the question. Then Ss compare their answers.

Answer

Mark Zuckerberg is now the chief executive of Facebook. Over 1 billion people use Facebook today, and Zuckerberg is worth over 24 billion dollars.

C *Pair work*

- Ss brainstorm in pairs and write down some inventions. Encourage them to ask each other additional questions like "Do you know who invented it?" or "Which ones do you use?"

5 WORD POWER

Learning Objective: use storytelling adverbs

A

- Read the instructions and model the task. Ask Ss to find a word that has a positive meaning and to write *P* next to it.
- Tell Ss to look for positive adverbs first and then negative words and words that could be either positive or negative, depending on context. Ss complete the chart individually. Go around the class and give help as needed. Then go over answers.

Answers

P: fortunately, luckily, miraculously
N: sadly, unfortunately
E: coincidentally, strangely, suddenly, surprisingly, unexpectedly

B *Pair work*

- Explain the task and model the example conversation with a S. Elicit other suggestions from the class.
- Ss form pairs and make up creative sentences. Then each pair joins another pair to share their ideas.

For more practice with adverbs, play the ***Chain Game*** – download it from the website. Have Ss add sentences to a story, rather than make one long sentence.

6 WRITING

Learning Objective: write a short story using adverbs and the simple past and past continuous

A

- Remind Ss that they have read and talked about coincidences and past events. Explain that now they are going to write a story about something that has happened to them.
- Ss read the example paragraph and write their own story. Remind Ss to use the past continuous and simple past, as well as the adverbs.

B *Group work*

- Ss exchange stories and read them aloud. Encourage them to ask follow-up questions and give additional information whenever possible.
- ***Option:*** Have Ss revise their stories and give them to you to check or grade.

End of Cycle 1

See the Supplementary Resources chart at the beginning of this unit for additional teaching materials and student activities related to this Cycle.

7 CONVERSATION

Learning Objective: use the present perfect continuous in a conversation between people catching up with each other

A *[CD 2, Track 56]*

- Focus Ss' attention on the picture. Ask: "Where are they? What do they look like? Do you think this is their first meeting?" Accept any reasonable answers.
- Books closed. Play the first few lines of the audio program. Ask: "Is this their first meeting? How do you know?" Then elicit answers. (Answers: No. They know each other, but haven't seen each other in ages.)
- Write these questions on the board:

  What are Steve and Luiza doing?
  How long have they been doing these things?
- Play the audio program. Have Ss listen and answer the questions. Then elicit answers. (Answers: Luiza: working two jobs and saving for a trip, for six months; Steve: spending money and acting, since he graduated)
- Books open. Play the audio program again. Focus Ss' attention on the pronunciation of been (= /bɪn/).
- Ask Ss to read the conversation and find examples of follow-up questions (e.g., *How long have you been trying?*), additional information (e.g., *Since I graduated. But I haven't had . . .*), and reactions (e.g., *Well, that's exciting.*).
- Ss practice the conversation in pairs.

B *[CD 2, Track 57]*

- Explain the task. Play the rest of the audio program. Ss listen and answer the question. Then elicit answers from the class.

Audio script

See page T-178.

Answers

The man has been looking for a house to buy and finally found one last month. The woman went to Italy last month. She's been taking some classes in Italian cooking.

8 GRAMMAR FOCUS

Learning Objective: use the present perfect continuous

[CD 2, Track 58]

- Refer Ss to the previous conversation. Ask them to find examples of statements with *have/haven't been.* Then write this chart on the board:

1	2	3	4	5
I	've	been	working	two jobs
I	haven't	been	doing	much

- Elicit how the present perfect continuous is formed by asking Ss what they see in each column:

  Subject + *have/has (not)* + *been* + verb + *-ing* + (rest)

  Briefly explain the use of the present perfect continuous and write the following on the board. Point out the use of time expressions (e.g., *for, since*):

  1. The present perfect continuous is used to describe an action that started in the past and continues into the present:
     I've been working two jobs for the last six months.
  2. The present perfect continuous can also be used without a time expression to describe an activity that started in the past but is still in progress:
     I've been trying to become an actor.
- Elicit additional sentences. Then play the audio program to present the examples in the box.

A

- Explain the task and model the first item. After Ss complete the task, elicit answers.

Answers

1. A: **Have** you **been learning** any new skills this year?
   B: Yes, I have. I'**ve been taking** some art courses.
2. A: What **have** you **been doing** lately?
   B: Well, I'**ve been looking for** a new job.
3. A: How **have** you **been feeling** recently?
   B: Great! I'**ve been running** three times a week. And I **haven't been drinking** as much coffee since I stopped working at the coffee shop.
4. A: **Have** you **been getting** enough exercise lately?
   B: No, I haven't. I'**ve been studying** a lot for a big exam.

B *Pair work*

- Ss work in pairs to practice the conversations in part A. They then ask the questions and respond with their own information.

7 CONVERSATION What have you been doing?

A Listen and practice.

Steve: Hey, Luiza! I haven't seen you in ages. What have you been doing lately?
Luiza: I haven't been going out much. I've been working two jobs for the last six months.
Steve: How come?
Luiza: I'm saving up money for a trip to Morocco.
Steve: Well, that's exciting!
Luiza: Yeah, it is. What about you?
Steve: Well, I've only been *spending* money. I've been trying to become an actor. I've been taking courses and going to a lot of auditions.
Luiza: Really? How long have you been trying?
Steve: Since I graduated. But I haven't had any luck yet. No one recognizes my talent.

B Listen to two other people at the party. What has happened since they last saw each other?

8 GRAMMAR FOCUS

Present perfect continuous

Use the present perfect continuous for actions that start in the past and continue into the present.

What **have** you **been doing** lately? — I**'ve been working** two jobs for the last six months.
How long **have** you **been trying**? — I**'ve been trying** since I graduated.
Have you **been saving** money? — No, I **haven't been saving** money. I**'ve been spending** it!

GRAMMAR PLUS *see page 143*

A Complete the conversations with the present perfect continuous.

1. **A:** ______________ you ______________ (learn) any new skills this year?
   B: Yes, I have. I ______________ (take) some art courses.
2. **A:** What ______________ you ______________ (do) lately?
   B: Well, I ______________ (look for) a new job.
3. **A:** How ______________ you ______________ (feel) recently?
   B: Great! I ______________ (run) three times a week. And I ______________ (not drink) as much coffee since I stopped working at the coffee shop.
4. **A:** ______________ you ______________ (get) enough exercise lately?
   B: No, I haven't. I ______________ (study) a lot for a big exam.

B **PAIR WORK** Read the conversations in part A together. Then read them again and answer the questions with your own information.

A: Have you been learning any new skills this year?
B: Yes, I've been taking guitar lessons.

9 PRONUNCIATION Contrastive stress in responses

A Listen and practice. Notice how the stress changes to emphasize a contrast.

A: Has your brother been studying German?
B: No, I've been studying German.

A: Have you been teaching French?
B: No, I've been studying French.

B Mark the stress changes in these conversations. Listen and check. Then practice the conversations.

A: Have you been studying for ten years?
B: No, I've been studying for two years.

A: Have you been studying at school?
B: No, I've been studying at home.

10 SPEAKING Tell me about it.

GROUP WORK Add three questions to this list. Then take turns asking and answering the questions. Remember to ask for further information.

Have you been . . . lately?

traveling
watching any good TV series
taking any lessons
working out
working long hours
going out a lot
staying up late
____
____
____

useful expressions

Really?
I didn't know that!
Oh, I see.
I had no idea.
Wow! Tell me more.

A: Have you been traveling lately?
B: Yes, I have. I've been going abroad about once a month.
C: Really? Lucky you!
B: Not exactly. I've been traveling for work, not on vacation.

11 INTERCHANGE 12 It's my life.

Play a board game. Go to Interchange 12 on page 126.

9 PRONUNCIATION

Learning Objectives: identify how stress is used in responses to emphasize contrast; sound more natural when giving responses that emphasize contrast

A *[CD 2, Track 59]*

- Explain that you can change the meaning of a sentence by stressing different words.
- Play the audio program. Point out the extra stress on the contrasting words in the example conversations.
- Remind Ss that stress is shown in English by making a word or syllable higher, longer, and louder.
- Play the audio program again, pausing after each line for Ss to repeat. Check individual Ss' pronunciation and proper use of contrastive stress.

TIP
During choral repetition, it is difficult to hear if Ss are using the correct pronunciation. It is important to interrupt the choral drill occasionally and ask individuals to try it.

B *[CD 2, Track 60]*

- Ss read the example conversations in pairs. Then they mark the words that need to be stressed to show contrast.
- Play the audio program and have Ss check their answers. Ask Ss to correct any errors they made.

Answers

A: Have you been studying for ten years?
B: No, I've been studying for **two** years.
A: Have you been studying at school?
B: No, I've been studying at **home**.

- Ss practice the conversations in pairs.

For more practice with contrastive stress, play ***True or False?*** – download it from the website. Ss look through the last two units and make sentences about the people and pictures. Partners use contrastive stress to correct the false statements.

10 SPEAKING

Learning Objective: discuss recent activities using the present perfect continuous

Group work

- Have Ss read the question prompts. Elicit suggestions for additional prompts. Ss choose three to add to the list.
- Elicit additional questions from Ss. Encourage them to use their imaginations. Write as many of the Ss' ideas as possible on the board (e.g., *Have you been cooking a lot/partying a lot/taking care of yourself?*).
- Point out the *useful expressions* box and ask Ss to add other expressions. Then write new expressions on the board for the class to use.
- Use the example conversation to model the task. Then ask Ss some of the questions in the list. Encourage Ss to ask follow-up questions and give additional information.
- Set a time limit of about ten minutes. Remind Ss to use contrastive stress when necessary.
- Ss form groups and take turns asking and answering questions. Go around the class and give help as needed.

TIP
To increase Ss' talking time, regroup them and have them share their ideas with other classmates. Possible ways to regroup Ss:
- have each group join another group
- have each group send one member to the next group
- assign a letter (a–e) to each S in a group and form new groups of all As, all Bs, etc.

- ***Option:*** For more practice, tell Ss to imagine they are going to a school reunion party. First, have Ss read the Conversation on page 81 again. Then have pairs role-play a similar conversation using their own words and information. Tell them to pretend that they haven't seen each other for several years.

! To make the role play more fun, try ***Musical Dialog*** – download it from the website.

11 INTERCHANGE 12

See page T-126 for teaching notes.

12 READING

Learning Objectives: skim an article about a unique musical group; read for specific information

A

- Books closed. Write the title on the board. Ask Ss to guess what the article might be about. Explain that *break down* means to put an end to something.
- Books open. Explain the task. Then give Ss one minute to answer the question. (Answers: All the musicians love music. They wanted to play music even though they were deaf. They show other deaf people that you can do whatever you want in life.)

! For another way to teach this reading, replace part A and part B with ***Reading Race*** – download it from the website. Books closed. Dictate the questions to Ss or write them on the board. Ss go around the class and answer them.

B

- Explain the task. Model the first word as an example. Ask Ss to read the first three sentences of the article. Then ask: "Did Beethoven stop composing after he went deaf?" (Answer: no, he continued) Then elicit the answer.
- Ss read the article and complete the task individually. Remind Ss to find the part of the article that refers to each sentence.
- Go over answers with the class and review any new vocabulary.
- ***Option:*** have Ss underline seven new words and look them up in their dictionaries. After that, have them write a sentence using each one.

Answers

1. continued
2. saw
3. understand
4. didn't want
5. before

Vocabulary

deaf: unable to hear
nightmare: a frightening dream
sign language: a system of communication using hand movements, used by people who are deaf (cannot hear)
hearing aid: a small piece of equipment worn inside or next to the ear by people who cannot hear well in order to help them to hear better

C

- Present the questions. Have Ss work individually to answer the questions and then discuss them in pairs. Go around the class and give help as needed.
- ***Option:*** Student A is a journalist. Student B is a member of the band Beethoven's Nightmare. Role-play an interview for a newspaper or TV program.

Answers

1. The Beatles
2. Headphones and powerful hearing aides
3. Knives and forks
4. At college, in Washington D.C
5. In 2001

D

- Have Ss discuss the question in small groups or in pairs. Give them five minutes to discuss and then have them present their ideas to the class.

End of Cycle 2

See the Supplementary Resources chart at the beginning of this unit for additional teaching materials and student activities related to this Cycle.

12 READING

A Skim the article. What is special about these musicians? How have they influenced other people?

BREAKING DOWN THE SOUND OF SILENCE

Ten years before he died, the composer Beethoven went deaf. He called this disability his "nightmare." Fortunately for thousands of classical music fans, he didn't stop writing brilliant music. One hundred and eighty years later, being deaf hasn't stopped three Americans – Steve Longo, Ed Chevy, and Bob Hiltermann – from playing music, either. In their case, the music is rock, and their band is called Beethoven's Nightmare.

The three boys grew up in different cities, but they all showed a surprising interest in music. Although they couldn't hear it, they were amazed by the energy of 1960s bands like the Beatles. They could see the effect the music had on the audiences – the happy faces of friends and family as they watched. Something exciting was obviously happening. "I'm going to do that, too," they all said. "Why? You can't hear," asked parents, teachers, and friends alike. Each boy used sign language to answer, "Because I can feel it."

Longo and Chevy started playing the guitar. They put on headphones and turned up the volume. With the help of powerful hearing aids, they could get some of the notes – the rest they felt through vibrations. Drummer Hiltermann came from a musical family. His parents thought that teaching their son to play an instrument was a waste of time. But they changed their minds after he nearly drove them crazy by using knives and forks to drum on the furniture of the house.

The three men first met in college in Washington, D.C. They started a band and played many concerts until they graduated in 1975. In 2001, Hiltermann had the idea to bring his old friends together again. They have been performing ever since. In 2013, a new member, Paul Raci, joined the band as a singer. At concerts, dancers put on a spectacular show and use sign language to explain the words of the songs to the audience. And, of course, the band plays very loudly!

The group has encouraged many deaf people, and people with other disabilities, to follow their dreams. Chevy says, "The only thing deaf people *can't* do is hear."

Dennis McCarthy, "Deaf band 'Beethoven's Nightmare' feels the music," *Los Angeles Daily News* (Oct. 31, 2013). Used with permission.

B Read the article. Choose the correct word(s) in the sentences below.

1. After going deaf, Beethoven **continued / refused** to compose music.
2. The boys knew music was powerful because of something they **read / saw.**
3. Many people didn't **understand / like** the boys' ambition to play music.
4. Hiltermann's parents **wanted / didn't want** him to learn to play at first.
5. The three young men started playing together **before / after** finishing college.

C Answer the questions.

1. Which band inspired the three boys to play music?
2. What did Longo and Chevy use to hear some parts of the music?
3. What did Hiltermann use to make noise in his house?
4. Where did the three men get to know each other?
5. When did Beethoven's Nightmare start playing?

D Do you think it's very difficult for people in your country to achieve their dreams? What new technology and facilities make it easier for them?

Units 11–12 Progress check

SELF-ASSESSMENT

How well can you do these things? Check (✓) the boxes.

I can . . .	Very well	OK	A little
Give information about books, movies, songs, etc. (Ex. 1)	☐	☐	☐
Understand information about countries (Ex. 2)	☐	☐	☐
Describe a situation (Ex. 3)	☐	☐	☐
Ask and answer questions about past events (Ex. 4, 5)	☐	☐	☐
Ask and answer questions about recent activities (Ex. 5)	☐	☐	☐

1 SPEAKING Trivia questions

A List six books, movies, songs, albums, or other popular works. Then write one *who* question for each of the six items.

Harry Potter books
Who wrote the *Harry Potter* books?

B **PAIR WORK** Take turns asking your questions. Use the passive with *by* to answer.

A: Who wrote the *Harry Potter* books?
B: I think they were written by J. K. Rowling.

2 LISTENING Did you know?

A Listen to a game show about Spain. Write the correct answers.

1. How many languages are officially recognized? ______________
2. What day is considered bad luck? ______________
3. What is the most valuable soccer team in the world? ______________
4. In how many countries is Spanish the official language? ______________
5. What fruit is thrown at the world's biggest food fight? ______________
6. What is Spain's famous dance called? ______________

B Listen again. Keep score. How much money does each contestant have?

Units 11–12 Progress check

SELF-ASSESSMENT

Learning Objectives: reflect on one's learning; identify areas that need improvement

- Ask: "What did you learn in Units 11 and 12?" Elicit Ss' answers.
- Ss complete the Self-assessment. Explain to Ss that this is not a test; it is a way for them to evaluate what they've learned and identify areas where they need additional practice. Encourage them to be honest, and point out they will not get a bad grade if they check (✓) "A little."
- Ss move on to the Progress check exercises. You can have Ss complete them in class or for homework using one of these techniques:
  1. Ask Ss to complete all the exercises.
  2. Ask Ss: "What do you need to practice?" Then assign exercises based on their answers.
  3. Ask Ss to choose and complete exercises based on their Self-assessment.

1 SPEAKING

Learning Objective: demonstrate one's ability to give information about popular entertainment

A

- Explain the task. Elicit some titles for the categories given and write them on the board. Then write a question using *who* (e.g., *Who played Edward in the* Twilight *movies? Who wrote . . . ? Who sang . . . ?*) next to each work listed on the board.
- Give Ss a few minutes to write six titles on a piece of paper. Then they should write one *who* question for each work. Remind Ss to underline titles of books, albums, and movies and to put titles of songs in quotation marks.

B *Pair work*

- Explain the task. Ask two Ss to read the example conversation. Point out that Ss must use the passive with *by* to answer the questions.
- Ss form pairs and take turns asking and answering their questions. Set a time limit of ten minutes. Go around the class and give help as needed.

2 LISTENING

Learning Objective: demonstrate one's ability to understand information about countries

A *[CD 3, Track 1]*

- In pairs, ask Ss to discuss what they know about Spain. Don't go over answers at this point.
- Explain the task. Ss listen to a game show and answer questions with information about Spain.
- Go over the questions. If Ss already know the information, tell them to write it on a separate piece of paper and check or correct it while they listen.
- Play the audio program. Ss complete the chart. After Ss compare notes in pairs, elicit answers from the class. Encourage Ss to use the passive to answer.

Audio script

See page T-178.

Answers

1. Four languages are officially recognized.
2. Tuesday the 13th is considered bad luck.
3. Real Madrid is the most valuable soccer team in the world.
4. Spanish is the official language in twenty-one countries.
5. Tomatoes are thrown at the world's biggest food fight.
6. Spain's famous dance is called *flamenco*.

B *[CD 3, Track 2]*

- Explain the task. Ss listen again to find out how much money each contestant has. Remind Ss to keep score on a piece of paper.
- Play the audio program again. Then go over answers with the class.

Answers

Contestant A: $100
Contestant B: $300
Contestant C: $200

- ***Option:*** Elicit other information about Spain.

3 GAME

Learning Objective: demonstrate one's ability to describe a situation

Group work

- Books closed. Model the task by demonstrating a sentence-making competition. Write this situation on the board:

  theft in a department store

- Elicit sentences from the class that explain what happened as a result of the situation. Ask a S to write them on the board (e.g., *some earrings were stolen, the police were called, a man was arrested*). If necessary, remind Ss that we use *steal* for objects and *rob* for places and people.
- Books open. Focus Ss' attention on the six situations and explain that Ss must use the passive without *by* to write as many sentences as possible for each situation.
- Ss work in small groups to write sentences for each situation. Set a time limit of ten minutes.
- Ask Ss to read the sentences they wrote for each situation. The group that wrote the most correct sentences wins.
- ***Option:*** Groups exchange papers and read each other's sentences to find out what they missed.

4 ROLE PLAY

Learning Objective: demonstrate one's ability to ask and answer questions about past events and recent activities

- Explain the task. Student A is a suspect, or a person the police believe has stolen the painting. Student B is a police detective.
- Have Ss form pairs. Tell Student As to make up an alibi, or a story to show they were in another place at the time of the crime. They should take notes to explain what they were doing when the painting disappeared.
- While Student As write notes, go over the questions.
- Ss work in pairs. If possible, have them stand on either side of a desk, which will represent the police station counter. Set a time limit of about ten minutes.
- During the role play, go around the class and listen. Take note of any common errors. When time is up, suggest ways the role plays could be improved. Give examples of good communication that you heard.
- Ss change roles and try the role play again.
- ***Option:*** Find out who had the most creative alibi.

5 DISCUSSION

Learning Objective: demonstrate one's ability to ask and answer questions about recent activities

A *Group work*

- Read the questions to model the correct pronunciation, intonation, and stress. Ss listen and repeat.
- Read the useful expressions in the box. Ask Ss to add other expressions.
- Model the activity by asking the class some of the questions in the list. Then ask follow-up questions and encourage Ss to give additional information.
- Ss form groups and take turns asking and answering questions. Set a time limit of about ten minutes.

B *Class activity*

- Ask Ss from each group to tell the class what they learned about their classmates.
- After each group presents their information, encourage the rest of the class to ask follow-up questions.

WHAT'S NEXT?

Learning Objective: become more involved in one's learning

- Focus Ss' attention on the Self-assessment again. Ask: "How well can you do these things now?"
- Ask Ss to underline one thing they need to review. Ask: "What did you underline? How can you review it?"
- If needed, plan additional instruction, activities, or reviews based on Ss' answers.

3 GAME What happened?

GROUP WORK Use the passive to write details about these situations. Then compare with the class. Which group wrote the most sentences?

The lights went out.	It snowed a lot yesterday.	Your roommate cleaned the apartment.
Our class was canceled.	Many roads were blocked.	The dishes were done.

4 ROLE PLAY Do you have an alibi?

A famous painting has been stolen from a local museum. It disappeared last Sunday afternoon between 12:00 P.M. and 4:00 P.M.

Student A: Student B suspects you stole the painting. Make up an alibi. Take notes on what you were doing that day. Then answer Student B's questions.

Student B: You are a police detective. You think Student A stole the painting. Add two questions to the notebook. Then ask Student A the questions.

Where were you last Sunday?
Where did you go for lunch?
Did anyone see you?
What were you wearing that day?
What were you doing between noon and 4:00 P.M.?
Was anyone with you?
____
____

Change roles and try the role play again.

5 DISCUSSION Is that so?

A GROUP WORK What interesting things can you find out about your classmates? Ask these questions and others of your own.

Have you been doing anything exciting recently?
Where do you live? How long have you been living there?
Have you met anyone interesting lately?
Who is your best friend? How did you meet? How long have you been friends?
Where were you living ten years ago? Did you like it there? What do you remember about it?

useful expressions

Really?
I didn't know that!
Oh, I see.
I had no idea.
Wow! Tell me more.

B CLASS ACTIVITY Tell the class the most interesting thing you learned.

WHAT'S NEXT?

Look at your Self-assessment again. Do you need to review anything?

Unit 13 Supplementary Resources Overview

	After the following SB exercises	You can use these materials in class	Your students can use these materials outside the classroom
CYCLE 1	**1 Snapshot**		
	2 Conversation		**SS** Unit 13 Speaking 1–2
	3 Grammar Focus		**SB** Unit 13 Grammar plus, Focus 1 **SS** Unit 13 Grammar 1 **GAME** Sentence Stacker (Participles as adjectives 1) **GAME** Speak or Swim (Participles as adjectives 2)
	4 Word Power	**TSS** Unit 13 Vocabulary Worksheet	**SS** Unit 13 Vocabulary 1–2
	5 Listening		
	6 Pronunciation		**GAME** Spell or Slime (Adjectives to describe movies)
	7 Discussion		**WB** Unit 13 exercises 1–4
CYCLE 2	**8 Perspectives**		
	9 Grammar Focus	**TSS** Unit 13 Grammar Worksheet	**SB** Unit 13 Grammar plus, Focus 2 **SS** Unit 13 Grammar 2 **GAME** Say the Word (Relative pronouns for people and things)
	10 Interchange 13		
	11 Speaking	**TSS** Unit 13 Extra Worksheet	
	12 Listening	**TSS** Unit 13 Listening Worksheet	
	13 Writing	**TSS** Unit 13 Writing Worksheet	
	14 Reading	**TSS** Unit 13 Project Worksheet **VID** Unit 13 **VRB** Unit 13	**SS** Unit 13 Reading 1–2 **SS** Unit 13 Listening 1–3 **SS** Unit 13 Video 1–3 **WB** Unit 13 exercises 5–10

Key **GAME:** Online Game **SB:** Student's Book **SS:** Online Self-study **TSS:** Teacher Support Site
VID: Video DVD **VRB:** Video Resource Book **WB:** Online Workbook/Workbook

My Plan for Unit 13

Use the space below to customize a plan that fits your needs.

With the following SB exercises	I am using these materials in class	My students are using these materials outside the classroom

With or instead of the following SB section	I am using these materials for assessment

13 That's entertainment!

- Discuss popular entertainment
- Discuss movies and famous Hollywood names

1 SNAPSHOT

MOVIE TRIVIA

Black Mass (2015)
Sienna Miller spent months rehearsing and filming, but in the end, the director decided to cut out all her scenes for "narrative reasons."

Django Unchained (2012)
In the movie, Leonardo DiCaprio was supposed to slam a table, but accidentally slammed a glass and cut his hand. The scene was so good that the director decided to incorporate it.

Furious 7 (2015)
Actor Paul Walker died while still shooting the movie. The director used computer technology and stunts to finish the remaining scenes.

Avatar (2009) The special effects were so expensive that director James Cameron had to wait 10 years to make the movie.

The Princess and the Frog (2009) After watching the movie, about fifty children got sick with salmonella from kissing frogs.

Paranormal Activity (2007)
This movie only cost $15,000 to make, but it made $9.1 million in its first week.

Which of the movie trivia do you find most interesting?
Do you know any other movie trivia?
Which of these movies have you seen? Did you enjoy it? Which would you like to watch?

2 CONVERSATION I think they're boring.

A Listen and practice.

Danny: It's so hot out. Do you want to stay in and watch a movie this afternoon?
Gina: Hmm. Maybe. What do you want to see?
Danny: How about an *X-Men* movie? I've heard that the early ones are really interesting.
Gina: For you, maybe. I'm not interested in action movies. Actually, I think they're boring.
Danny: What about that new movie based on one of Stephen King's novels?
Gina: I don't know. I'm always fascinated by his books, but I'm not in the mood for a horror movie.
Danny: Well, what do you want to see?
Gina: How about a *Game of Thrones* marathon? It's my favorite series ever.
Danny: OK, but only if you make us some popcorn.

B Listen to the rest of the conversation. What happens next? What do they decide to do?

13 That's entertainment!

Cycle 1, Exercises 1–7

In Unit 13, students discuss books, movies, and TV programs. By the end of Cycle 1, students will be able to discuss books, movies, and TV programs using participles as adjectives. By the end of Cycle 2, students will be able to discuss more about movies and famous Hollywood names using relative clauses.

1 SNAPSHOT

Learning Objective: discuss movies

- Focus Ss' attention on the pictures in the Snapshot. Ask them to identify the movies.
- Ss read the Snapshot. Ask Ss if anything surprises them about this information.
- Ss discuss the questions in small groups.
- Ss share any interesting trivia they learned in their groups.
- ***Option:*** Ask Ss to identify the genre of each movie in the Snapshot (drama, animation, western, fantasy/adventure, action, fantasy/action, horror). Some movies fall into more than one category. Ask for other genres and other examples of these genres (more on genres in Exercise 7).

! For another way to practice this vocabulary, try ***Vocabulary Steps*** – download it from the website. Ss rank the movie types in order from least favorite to favorite.

2 CONVERSATION

Learning Objective: use participles as adjectives in a conversation about entertainment

A *[CD 3, Track 3]*

- Books closed. Ask the class: "What movies are playing in theaters now? Which movies have you seen? Which are good? Bad?" If possible, bring or show movie listings to the class.

TIP
To help Ss see the value of what they are doing in class, link each exercise to the next (e.g., *You talked about movies in the Snapshot. Now you're going to hear two people talking about going to see a movie.*).

- Set the scene. Two people are trying to decide what movie to see tonight. Write these questions on the board: 1. Who is choosier? (more difficult to please) 2. What do they decide to see?
- Play the audio program. Then elicit Ss' answers to the questions on the board. (Answers: 1. the woman 2. a *Game of Thrones* marathon)
- ***Option:*** Ask Ss which of the three they would prefer to see.
- Play the audio program again. This time, ask Ss to listen and identify the adjectives Danny and Gina use for movies and TV shows. Then elicit answers from the class. (Answers: *Fast and Furious:* interesting, boring; *Game of Thrones:* favorite)
- Books open. Play the audio program again. Ss listen and read silently. Ask Ss to focus on how the two people reach an agreement.
- Ss practice the conversation in pairs.
- ***Option:*** Ss role-play a similar conversation. Student A makes suggestions. Student B is a bit choosy, but finally agrees. If possible, Ss talk about current movies.

B *[CD 3, Track 4]*

- Read the questions. Then play the rest of the audio program. Ss listen and take notes. After Ss compare their responses, elicit answers from the class.

Audio script

See page T-179.

Answers

The Internet is down so Gina and Danny decide to go to the movies and see a comedy.

3 GRAMMAR FOCUS

Learning Objective: use present participles and past participles as adjectives

[CD 3, Track 5]

Present and past participles as adjectives

- Draw a picture of a man on the board. Explain that the man is watching a boring movie on TV. Draw a TV next to the man and write *boring* inside the TV.
- Ask Ss how the man feels while watching TV. Elicit the word *bored* and write it inside the man's body.

- Draw a book on the other side of the man. Explain that now he is reading an interesting book. Write *interesting* on the book and elicit how the man feels. Write *interested* inside his body.
- Ask Ss to add five more examples of adjectives that end in *-ing* and *-ed* to the picture. In pairs, have Ss take turns making sentences.
- Refer Ss to the Grammar Focus box. Point out that the adjectives ending in *-ing* are called present participles. They are outside factors that cause a feeling. Past participles end in *-ed* and express the feeling or reaction.
- Play the audio program to present the sentences in the box. If necessary, play it again and have Ss listen for correct pronunciation and stress.

A

- Focus Ss' attention on the photo of Jennifer Lawrence and elicit adjectives about her. Then read the instructions and model the first item.
- Ss complete the task individually. After Ss compare their responses, elicit answers from the class.

Answers

1. John Cho is such an **amazing** actor. I'm always **amazed** by his incredible talent.
2. Most TV shows are really **boring**. I often get so **bored** watching them that I fall asleep.
3. I was **interested** in watching *The Martian* after I read the book. And I was surprised that the movie is really **interesting**.
4. I'm **excited** to watch *The Avengers*. Everybody has told me it's really **exciting**.
5. I find animated films very **amusing**. I've been **fascinated** by them since I was a little kid.
6. It's **surprising** that horror movies are so popular. I can't understand why people go to the movies to feel **terrified**.

B *Pair work*

- Explain the task. Then Ss work in pairs to complete the description. Give Ss a time limit before checking answers.

Answers

I had a terrible time at the movies last weekend. First, my ticket cost $25. I was really **shocked** by the price. By mistake, I gave the cashier two $5 bills instead of a twenty and a five. I was a little **embarrassed**. Then there was trash all over the theater. The mess was **disgusting**. The people behind me were talking during the movie, which was **annoying**. The story was hard to follow. I always find thrillers so **confusing**. I liked the special effects, though. They were **amazing**!

C *Pair work*

- Ss discuss the questions in pairs. Go around the class and help Ss when needed.

4 WORD POWER

Learning Objective: identify and classify synonyms for common adjectives

A *Pair work*

- Explain the task. Ss write similar adjectives, or synonyms, under the words in each heading.
- Ss complete the task individually, using a dictionary if necessary. Then elicit answers.

Answers

Awful	Wonderful	Stupid	Strange	Funny
disgusting	fantastic	dumb	bizarre	amusing
horrible	incredible	ridiculous	odd	hilarious
terrible	outstanding	silly	weird	hysterical

B *Group work*

- Explain the task. Refer Ss to Exercise 3. Then ask them to suggest similar sentences using the adjectives in the Word Power.
- Model a conversation with a S:

  T: Did you see the movie . . . ?
  S: Yes, I did.
  T: I didn't like it. I thought the special effects were horrible and the characters were bizarre. What did you think of it?
- Ss share opinions in groups.

3 GRAMMAR FOCUS

Participles as adjectives

Present participles	Past participles
That *X-Men* movie sounds **interesting**.	I'm not **interested** in action movies.
Stephen King's books are **fascinating**.	I'm **fascinated** by Stephen King's books.
I think action movies are **boring**.	I'm **bored** by action movies.

GRAMMAR PLUS *see page 144*

A Complete these sentences. Then compare with a partner.

John Cho

1. John Cho is such an ______________ actor. I'm always ______________ by his incredible talent. (amaze)
2. Most TV shows are really ______________. I often get so ______________ watching them that I fall asleep. (bore)
3. I was ______________ in watching *The Martian* after I read the book. And I was surprised that the movie is really ______________. (interest)
4. I'm ______________ to watch *The Avengers*. Everybody has told me it's really ______________. (excite)
5. I find animated films very ______________. I've been ______________ by them since I was a little kid. (amuse / fascinate)
6. It's ______________ that horror movies are so popular. I can't understand why people go to the movies to feel ______________. (surprise / terrify)

B **PAIR WORK** Complete the description below with the correct forms of the words.

amaze   annoy   confuse   disgust   embarrass   shock

I had a terrible time at the movies last weekend. First, my ticket cost $25. I was really ______________ by the price. By mistake, I gave the cashier two $5 bills instead of a twenty and a five. I was a little ______________. Then there was trash all over the theater. The mess was ______________. The people behind me were talking during the movie, which was ______________. The story was hard to follow. I always find thrillers so ______________. I liked the special effects, though. They were ______________!

4 WORD POWER How do you like it?

A **PAIR WORK** Complete the chart with synonyms from the list.

amusing	dumb	horrible	odd	silly
bizarre	fantastic	hysterical	outstanding	terrible
disgusting	hilarious	incredible	ridiculous	weird

Awful	Wonderful	Stupid	Strange	Funny

B **GROUP WORK** Share your opinions about a movie, an actor, an actress, a TV show, and a book. Use words from part A.

5 LISTENING What did you think?

A Listen to people talk about books, movies, and TV programs. Match each conversation to the statement that best describes the people's opinions.

1. ____ **a.** This special offers an amazing look into an exotic country.
2. ____ **b.** The new investigation into these creatures was a waste of time.
3. ____ **c.** The bad acting with this boring idea makes it terrible.
4. ____ **d.** She is excited to read more of this clever mystery series.

B Listen again. Write a reason each person gives to support his or her opinion.

1. ______________________ **3.** ______________________
2. ______________________ **4.** ______________________

6 PRONUNCIATION Emphatic stress

A Listen and practice. Notice how stress and a higher pitch are used to express strong opinions.

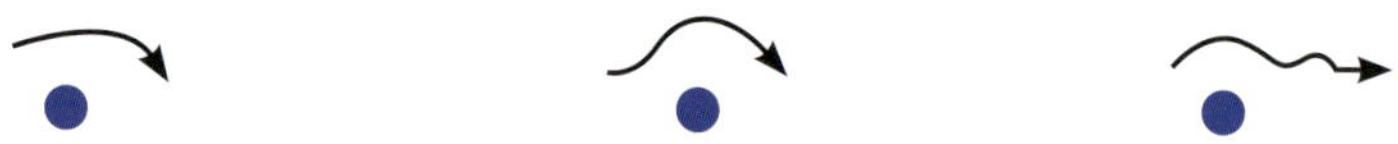

That was terrible!   He was amazing!   That's fascinating!

B **PAIR WORK** Write four statements using these words. Then take turns reading them. Pay attention to emphatic stress.

fantastic   horrible   ridiculous   weird

7 DISCUSSION I give it two thumbs up!

A **PAIR WORK** Take turns asking and answering these questions and others of your own.

What kinds of movies are you interested in? Why?
What kinds of movies do you find boring?
Who are your favorite actors and actresses? Why?
Are there actors or actresses you don't like?
What's the worst movie you've ever seen?
Are there any outstanding movies playing now?
Do you prefer to watch films dubbed or with subtitles? Why?

A: What kinds of movies are you interested in?
B: I like romantic comedies.
A: Really? Why is that?
B: They're entertaining! What about you?
A: I think romantic comedies are kind of dumb. I prefer . . .

B **GROUP WORK** Compare your information. Whose taste in movies is most like yours?

5 LISTENING

Learning Objective: make inferences about a conversation about popular entertainment

A *[CD 3, Track 6]*

- Explain the situation. Ss will hear people give opinions about books, movies, and TV programs. Then Ss will match the conversations to summary statements.
- Play the audio program. Ss listen and take notes. Then elicit answers from the class.

Audio script

See page T-179.

Answers

1. c 2. d 3. a 4. b

B *[CD 3, Track 7]*

- Explain the task. Ss listen to the audio program again and write down a reason for each person.
- Play the audio program again. Then elicit answers.

Possible answers

1. He walked out of the movie after half an hour. It was so boring he started falling asleep.
2. She stayed up until 4:00 in the morning to finish the first book. She's read all the books up to *K is for Killer* and says they're fantastic.
3. The photography was amazing. It showed many different kinds of animals.
4. It had the same silly stuff about visitors to Earth from other planets. It said nothing new.

6 PRONUNCIATION

Learning Objective: sound more natural when giving opinions by using emphatic stress

A *[CD 3, Track 8]*

- Remind Ss that in English words with more than one syllable, one syllable has the primary, or main, stress. Stress can be used to express strong opinions. Remind Ss that stress is shown by making the syllable higher, longer, and louder.
- Play the audio program. Ss listen and pay attention to the stress and pitch.
- Play the audio program again and have Ss repeat. Encourage them to exaggerate to show emotion.

B *Pair work*

- Explain the task. Ask Ss to write four sentences about movies. To show more emphatic stress, have Ss write two sentences about movies they hate and two about movies they love.
- Ss form pairs and take turns reading their sentences. Remind them to use stress and pitch to express their opinions.

TIP
To give Ss more practice with a pronunciation feature, ask them to practice or listen to other exercises (e.g., Conversation, Grammar Focus, Listening) again.

7 DISCUSSION

Learning Objective: discuss movies using participles as adjectives

A *Pair work*

- Books closed. Ask Ss to brainstorm questions about movies. Then write some of them on the board:

  What's your favorite . . . (musical/comedy/drama)?
  How many movies do you watch every month?
  Do you usually go to the theater, or do you usually watch movies on TV, on a computer, or on your phone?
- Books open. Ask Ss to read the list of questions and the example conversation. Encourage them to extend it as much as possible.
- Books closed. Ss form pairs and practice asking and answering their questions. Encourage them to ask follow-up questions and add emphatic stress. Set a time limit of about ten minutes. Go around the class and give help as needed.

! For more speaking practice, try the ***Onion Ring*** technique – download it from the website. Ss ask and answer questions about movies until you say, "Change!"

B *Group work*

- Each pair joins another pair. Ss compare their responses and decide who has similar taste in movies.

End of Cycle 1

See the Supplementary Resources chart at the beginning of this unit for additional teaching materials and student activities related to this Cycle.

8 PERSPECTIVES

Learning Objectives: listen for specific information in passages about entertainment; identify relative clauses in context

A *[CD 3, Track 9]*

- Books closed. Set the scene. Ss will hear four people talk about their favorite actress, actor, and movies.
- Play the audio program. Ss listen and guess what actress, actor, or movie each person is describing.

Answers

1. Ben Affleck
2. *Star Wars*
3. *Toy Story 3*
4. Meryl Streep

B

- Ask Ss if they are familiar with the movies and actors. What do they think of them?

Vocabulary

motion picture: a movie
blockbuster: a book, film, etc. that is very popular and successful

9 GRAMMAR FOCUS

Learning Objective: use relative clauses

[CD 3, Track 10]

Relative clauses

- Books closed. Read these sentences:

  She's an actress that is excellent in both dramas and comedies.
  He's a famous American actor who is also a successful director and producer.

- Point out that these sentences contain two clauses each: a main clause and a relative clause. Write this example on the board:

Main clause	Relative clause
It's a science fiction fantasy	that has become a blockbuster franchise.

- Ask Ss to identify the two clauses in the other sentences. Then elicit or explain that:
  1. A relative clause joins two sentences together.
  2. A relative clause gives information about something in the main clause.

***Relative pronouns:* who/which/that**

- Point out that the pronouns *who*, *which*, and *that* can be used to join two clauses together.
- Start with the relative pronoun *who*. Ask Ss to identify a sentence from the Perspectives section containing *who*.
- Ask Ss if the noun before *who* is a person or a thing. (Answer: a person)
- Repeat these steps for *which* and *that*.
- Write these rules on the board:
  1. Who is used to join clauses about people.
  2. Which is used to join clauses about things.
  3. That is used to join clauses about people or things.
- Play the audio program to present the sentences.

A

- Ask Ss to look over the sentences. Elicit or explain any new vocabulary (e.g., *adapted from* = based on). Ss complete the task. Then check answers.

Answers

1. Jennifer Hudson is a singer who/that has acted in several films.
2. *The Phantom of the Opera* is based on a French novel which/that was published in 1911.
3. *Spiderman* and *Transformers* are successful franchises which/that were adapted from comic books.
4. Michael Keaton is a famous Hollywood actor who/that began his career as a cameraman.
5. Dakota Fanning is an actress who/that made her first movie when she was only seven years old.
6. Wii Fit is a video game which/that helps people to get more exercise.
7. Stephenie Meyer is an American writer who/that wrote the *Twilight* series.
8. Many Hollywood stars live in Beverly Hills, which is a small city near Los Angeles, California.

- Ss compare their sentences with a partner.

B *Pair work*

- Explain the task. Use the first item to model a completed sentence. Ss complete the task in pairs and then share their sentences with the class.

10 INTERCHANGE 13

See page T-127 for teaching notes.

8 PERSPECTIVES And the Oscar goes to . . .

A Listen to people talk about some of their Hollywood favorites. Can you guess the actress, actor, or movie each person is describing?

1. He's a famous American actor who is also a successful director and producer. He won the Oscar for Best Motion Picture in 2013 with *Argo*, which he directed and co-produced.
2. The first movie in the series came out in 1977. It's a science fiction fantasy that has become a blockbuster franchise. The story takes place "a long time ago in a galaxy far, far away."
3. I really like animated movies, and the third one in this series is my favorite. It's about a boy's toys that have a secret life full of adventures when they are alone.
4. She's an actress that is excellent in both dramas and comedies. I loved her in *Mamma Mia!* and *The Devil Wears Prada*. In 2011, she won her third Oscar for her performance in *The Iron Lady*.

B Do you like the people and movies described in part A? What else do you know about them?

9 GRAMMAR FOCUS

Relative pronouns for people and things

Use *who* or *that* for people.	Use *which* or *that* for things.
He's an actor. He's also a director and producer.	It's a science fiction fantasy. It has become a blockbuster franchise.
He's an actor **who/that** is also a director and producer.	It's a science fiction fantasy **which/that** has become a blockbuster franchise.

GRAMMAR PLUS *see page 144*

Jennifer Hudson

A Combine the sentences using relative pronouns. Then compare with a partner.

1. Jennifer Hudson is a singer. She's acted in several films.
2. *The Phantom of the Opera* is based on a French novel. It was published in 1911.
3. *Spiderman* and *Transformers* are successful franchises. They were adapted from comic books.
4. Michael Keaton is a famous Hollywood actor. He began his career as a cameraman.
5. Dakota Fanning is an actress. She made her first movie when she was only seven years old.
6. Wii Fit is a video game. It helps people to get more exercise.
7. Stephenie Meyer is an American writer. She wrote the *Twilight* series.
8. Many Hollywood stars live in Beverly Hills. It's a small city near Los Angeles, California.

B **PAIR WORK** Complete these sentences. Then compare your information around the class.

1. Adele is a singer and songwriter . . .
2. *Fantastic Four* is a movie franchise . . .
3. *The Voice* is a reality show . . .
4. Scarlett Johansson is an actress . . .

10 INTERCHANGE 13 It was hilarious!

How do you like movies and TV shows? Go to Interchange 13 on page 127.

11 SPEAKING Pilot episode

A PAIR WORK A TV studio is looking for ideas for a new TV show. Brainstorm possible ideas and agree on an idea. Make brief notes.

What kind of TV show is it?
What's it about?
Who are the main characters?
Who is this show for?

B CLASS ACTIVITY Tell the class about your TV show.

"Our TV show is a comedy. It's about two very lazy friends who discover a time machine and travel to the time of the dinosaurs. Then . . ."

12 LISTENING At the movies

A Listen to two critics, Nicole and Anthony, talk about a new movie. Check (✓) the features of the movie that they discuss. (There are two extra features.)

	Nicole's opinion	Anthony's opinion
☐ acting		
☐ story		
☐ writing		
☐ music		
☐ love story		
☐ special effects		

B Listen again. Write Nicole and Anthony's opinions of each feature.

13 WRITING A movie review

A PAIR WORK Choose a movie you both have seen and discuss it. Then write a review of it.

What was the movie about?
What did you like about it?
What didn't you like about it?
How was the acting?
How would you rate it?

B CLASS ACTIVITY Read your review to the class. Who else has seen the movie?

Do they agree with your review?

MOVIE TALK LOGIN / REGISTER

We recently streamed *Birdman*, which won the Academy Award for Best Picture in 2015. It's about an actor who made successful movies in Hollywood in the past, and now tries to reinvent his career on Broadway.

It stars Michael Keaton and Emma Stone as a father and daughter. We liked the movie because it is both a drama and a comedy. I didn't like . . .

14 12

11 SPEAKING

Learning Objective: discuss ideas for a TV show using relative clauses

A *Pair work*

- Explain the task. Focus Ss' attention on the illustration and example in part B. Encourage Ss to be creative and use details to make their stories more exciting. Whenever possible, Ss should try to use relative clauses and adjectives.
- Read the questions that Ss should use during the activity. Elicit suggestions for other questions and write them on the board.

B *Class activity*

- Pairs take turns presenting their TV shows to the class. Encourage both Ss to add details. Other classmates ask follow-up questions.

TIP
To make their presentation smoother, ask each pair to assign information to one person or the other. For example, Student A describes the storyline of the show and the setting. Student B describes the main characters and their relationship to each other.

12 LISTENING

Learning Objective: listen for specific information and make inferences about a conversation about movies

A *[CD 3, Track 11]*

- As a class, brainstorm aspects of a movie that critics sometimes discuss (e.g., acting, story, costumes, music).
- Write this on the board and elicit meanings:

  1. *A standard story . . . nothing new.*
  2. *He was a totally believable character.*
  3. *The special effects were a weakness.*
  4. *It's just the same old stuff.*

- Ask Ss to decide if each expression means that the speaker liked the movie, didn't like it, or thought it was OK. (Answers: 1. OK 2. liked it 3. didn't like it 4. didn't like it)
- Explain the situation and the task. Make sure that Ss understand the rating system and words in the chart.
- Play the audio program. Ss listen and complete the chart. Ask Ss to compare answers in groups. If there are disagreements, go over those answers with the class.

Audio script

See page T-179.

Answers Parts A and B

acting: They both thought the new James Bond was great.
story: Nicole thought the story was very standard; nothing new. Anthony thought the story was unusually good and the surprise ending was great.
music: They both liked the music and thought it was interesting.
special effects: Nicole thought the special effects were the same old stuff. Anthony thought they were the best he's ever seen in a Bond film.

TIP
To avoid turning this into a "memory test," play the audio program a second time, segment by segment.

B *[CD 3, Track 12]*

- Explain the task. Play the audio program again and have Ss write the opinions. Elicit their answers.

13 WRITING

Learning Objective: write a movie review using relative clauses

A *Pair work*

- Explain the task and go over the questions. Try to pair up Ss who have recently seen the same movie.
- Ss use the questions to discuss the movie in detail.
- Ss form pairs and write the main points of their review.
- Ss read the example review and use their notes to write their own movie review. Remind Ss to practice the language they learned in this unit.

B *Class activity*

- Ss take turns reading their reviews to the class. Others who have seen the movie should say whether they agree.

14 READING

Learning Objectives: scan an article about special effects; identify sequence and text organization

A

- Books closed. Write *Acting* on the board and ask Ss to talk about what they think of the acting profession. Ask: "Do you think acting is an easy job or a difficult job? Can you think of a movie that was hard for the actor? Why?"
- Books open. Go over the questions with Ss. Then give them one minute to find the answers. Check the answers with the class. (Answer: The following films are mentioned: *The Machinist* (2005), *Batman Begins* (2005), *Saving Private Ryan* (1998), *Black Swan* (2010), and *The Dark Knight* (2008).)
- Ss read the article individually, underlining any words they don't understand. Tell them to choose three of these words to check in a dictionary. If they want to know any other words, they should wait until after they finish part A. This will help them focus on main ideas and general understanding, rather than on individual words.

B

- Explain the task. Elicit the location of the first sentence.
- Ss complete the task individually or in pairs. Then go over answers with the class.
- ***Option:*** Have Ss write an extra sentence for a paragraph, but without saying where it would go. Ss exchange sentences and try to guess where the extra sentence would go.

Answers

1. d
2. b
3. e
4. a
5. c

- Elicit or explain any new vocabulary.

Vocabulary

dress up: to wear special clothes in order to change your appearance
achieve: to succeed in doing something good, usually by working hard
unpleasant: not enjoyable or pleasant
part: a person in a film or play
boot camp: a military training camp for new recruits, with strict discipline

C

- Explain the task. The words could be anywhere in the article. Ss need to find them. Ss complete the task individually. Go around and give help as needed.
- Ss discuss their answers in pairs. Then go over answers with the class.

Answers

1. lines
2. producer
3. rib
4. critic

D

- Ss discuss the questions in pairs or small groups. Then ask them to share some of the ideas they discussed with the rest of the class.
- ***Option:*** Divide the class into two groups: interviewers and filmmakers. Interviewers write questions, and filmmakers answer based on information in the reading. Ss role-play in pairs. Tell filmmakers to make up answers they don't know.

End of Cycle 2

See the Supplementary Resources chart at the beginning of this unit for additional teaching materials and student activities related to this Cycle.

TIP

To raise Ss' awareness of their progress, occasionally discuss with the class how they feel they are progressing. Ask them what kinds of problems they face and how they learn best. Then suggest ideas or solutions. Encourage Ss to share their ideas.

14 READING

A Scan the article. Which movies are mentioned? When were they released?

THE REAL ART OF ACTING

Natalie Portman

1 Acting can bring fame, money, and success. But it's not always easy. Good acting is not only about learning lines and dressing up. It's also about convincing the audience that you really are somebody else. [a] To achieve this, good actors sometimes put themselves through unpleasant experiences.

2 Actors often have to lose or gain a lot of weight in order to play a part. In *The Machinist* (2005), Christian Bale plays an extremely thin factory worker who suffers from insomnia. [b] Four months before he began filming, Bale started a crazy diet.

Christian Bale

He only ate an apple and a can of tuna a day and lost 63 pounds. Although he wanted to lose another 20 pounds, the producers persuaded him to stop because they were worried about his health. When filming ended, he had just six months to gain the incredible 100 pounds he needed to play Bruce Wayne in *Batman Begins.* [c]

3 Physical training can also be a challenge. Steven Spielberg wanted to show the real horror of war in *Saving Private Ryan* (1998) and he wanted his actors to feel like real soldiers. So he sent a group of them, including Tom Hanks, to a 10-day military boot camp. [d] They ran miles every day, slept outside in the freezing cold, and were given little food. In the end, all of them were physically and mentally exhausted. Natalie Portman also had to make a great physical effort when she got the role of a ballerina in *Black Swan* (2010). Before filming, she spent a whole year training for eight hours a day, six days a week in order to learn to dance. Once filming began, things didn't get easier either. Portman dislocated a rib while dancing. Nevertheless, she bravely continued filming during the six weeks it took her to recover.

4 Sometimes "becoming" a character can mean saying goodbye to the real world and everybody in it completely. Actor Heath Ledger locked himself in a hotel room for six weeks when he was preparing to play the role of Joker in *The Dark Knight* (2008). He slept only two hours a day and he spent the rest of the time practicing how to walk, talk, and move like his character. [e] It seems he was successful in the end, as audiences and critics loved his work, and he won an Oscar for the part.

B Read the article. Where do these sentences belong? Write a–e.

1. The actors' lives became very hard. ____
2. Not sleeping is making him sick. ____
3. And he didn't speak to anybody at all. ____
4. The character has to be believable. ____
5. So he ate lots of pizza and ice cream. ____

C Find words in the text to match these definitions.

1. The words that actors say in a movie (paragraph 1) ______________
2. People who control how a movie is made (paragraph 2) ______________
3. A bone in a person's chest (paragraph 3) ______________
4. The people who write reviews of movies or books (paragraph 4) ______________

D Which of these unpleasant experiences is the worst? Do you think it's necessary for an actor to do this kind of thing for a part?

Unit 14 Supplementary Resources Overview

	After the following SB exercises	You can use these materials in class	Your students can use these materials outside the classroom
CYCLE 1	1 Snapshot		**SS** Unit 14 Vocabulary 1–2
	2 Word Power	**TSS** Unit 14 Vocabulary Worksheet	**SS** Unit 14 Speaking 1–2 **GAME** Spell or Slime (Vocabulary for body language)
	3 Conversation		
	4 Grammar Focus	**TSS** Unit 14 Listening Worksheet	**SB** Unit 14 Grammar Plus, Focus 1 **SS** Unit 14 Grammar 1 **GAME** Say the Word (Modals and adverbs)
	5 Pronunciation		
	6 Speaking		
	7 Interchange 14		**WB** Unit 14 exercises 1–5
CYCLE 2	8 Perspectives		
	9 Grammar Focus	**TSS** Unit 14 Grammar Worksheet **TSS** Unit 14 Extra Worksheet	**SB** Unit 14 Grammar Plus, Focus 2 **SS** Unit 14 Grammar 2 **GAME** Name the Picture (Permission, obligation, and prohibition 1) **GAME** Speak or Swim (Permission, obligation, and prohibition 2)
	10 Discussion		
	11 Listening		
	12 Writing	**TSS** Unit 14 Writing Worksheet	
	13 Reading	**TSS** Unit 14 Project Worksheet **VID** Unit 14 **VRB** Unit 14	**SS** Unit 14 Reading 1–2 **SS** Unit 14 Listening 1–3 **SS** Unit 14 Video 1–3 **WB** Unit 14 exercises 6–9

With or instead of the following SB section	You can also use these materials for assessment
Units 13–14 Progress Check	**ASSESSMENT PROGRAM** Units 13–14 Oral Quiz **ASSESSMENT PROGRAM** Units 13–14 Written Quiz

Key **GAME:** Online Game **SB:** Student's Book **SS:** Online Self-study **TSS:** Teacher Support Site
VID: Video DVD **VRB:** Video Resource Book **WB:** Online Workbook/Workbook

My Plan for Unit 14

Use the space below to customize a plan that fits your needs.

With the following SB exercises	I am using these materials in class	My students are using these materials outside the classroom

With or instead of the following SB section	I am using these materials for assessment

14 Now I get it!

- Discuss the meaning of gestures and body language
- Discuss rules and recognize common signs

1 SNAPSHOT

Do you use these emojis? In what situations do you use them?
What other expressions can you use emojis to convey?
What is the weirdest emoji you've ever seen? the funniest? the hardest to understand?

2 WORD POWER Body language

A What is this woman doing in each picture? Match each description with a picture. Then compare with a partner.

1. She's scratching her head. ______
2. She's biting her nails. ______
3. She's rolling her eyes. ______
4. She's tapping her foot. ______
5. She's pulling her hair out. ______
6. She's wrinkling her nose. ______

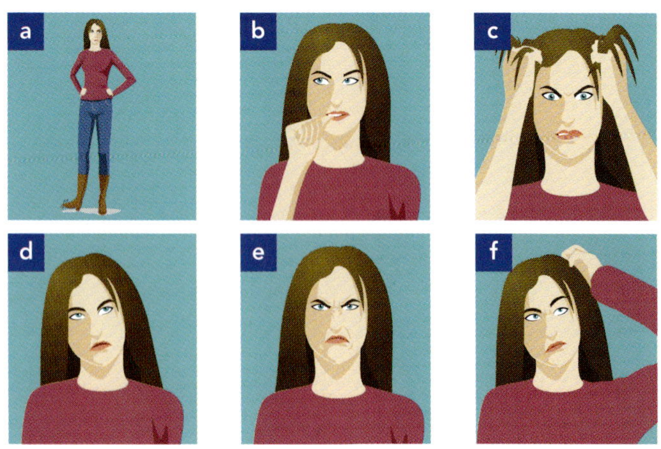

B GROUP WORK Use the pictures in part A and these adjectives to describe how the woman is feeling.

annoyed	confused	embarrassed	frustrated	irritated
bored	disgusted	exhausted	impatient	nervous

"In the first picture, she's tapping her foot. She looks impatient."

14 Now I get it!

Cycle 1, Exercises 1–7

In Unit 14, students discuss communication, including such topics as body language and gestures. They also discuss rules and recognize common signs. By the end of Cycle 1, students will be able to explain gestures using modals and adverbs. By the end of Cycle 2, students will be able to discuss signs using terms of permission, obligation, and prohibition.

1 SNAPSHOT

Learning Objective: discuss common symbols used in communication

- Books closed. Ask Ss if they know what emojis are and what they are used for. Ask if Ss know why they are called *emojis* and if they know any examples. (Answers: Emojis are picture symbols used in electronic messages and on Web pages. The word *emoji* comes from the Japanese words *e* ("picture") + *moji* ("character").
- Books open. Ss look at the emojis and read the definitions.
- Read the questions. Ss work in pairs or groups to discuss them. Go around the class and give help as needed. Then ask Ss to share their ideas.

2 WORD POWER

Learning Objective: describe feelings and the gestures used to express them

A

- Explain the task. Then model one example by asking Ss what the woman is doing in the first picture. (Answer: She's tapping her foot.) Tell Ss to write the letter *a* next to number *4*.
- Ss complete the task individually, without using their dictionaries. Remind them to look for clues (e.g., *hair, foot*) to help them find the answers. Go around the class and give help as needed. Then elicit Ss' answers.

Answers

1. f   2. b   3. d   4. a   5. c   6. e

- Model the pronunciation of each expression. Ss listen and repeat.
- ***Option:*** Ask Ss if they ever bite their nails, roll their eyes, pull their hair out, etc. Find out which are the most common gestures in the class.

For more practice with this vocabulary, play ***Mime*** – download it from the website.

B *Group work*

- Explain the task. Ss look at the pictures in part A and describe how the woman is feeling.
- Have Ss look at the adjectives and help with any new vocabulary. Model the pronunciation of each word.
- Point out that if the sound /t/ or /d/ appears before *-ed*, Ss should add an extra syllable (e.g., *disgusted* and *exhausted* have three syllables, while *annoyed* and *confused* have two syllables).

TIP
To show the number of syllables in a word, use your fingers (one for each syllable). If you hear a S make a mistake, like *em-bar-ras-sed,* indicate where the error lies by pointing to your fourth finger silently.

- To model the task, read the example sentence. Ask: "In the first picture, how do you think the woman feels?" Elicit suggestions (e.g., *frustrated, annoyed*).
- Ss discuss each picture in small groups. Tell Ss that there may be more than one answer. Go around the class and give help as needed. Then elicit Ss' answers.
- ***Option:*** Encourage Ss to explain to the class any gestures that represent different feelings in other cultures.

Possible answers

a. impatient, nervous, irritated
b. impatient, nervous
c. bored, frustrated, irritated, nervous
d. annoyed, frustrated, irritated
e. disgusted
f. bored, confused

For more practice with this vocabulary, play ***Bingo*** – download it from the website.

3 CONVERSATION

Learning Objective: use modals and adverbs in context in a conversation about body language

A *[CD 3, Track 13]*

- Focus Ss' attention on the illustration. Ask: "Where are they? What is the woman doing? How is the man reacting?" Elicit ideas.
- Books closed. Play the audio program and have Ss listen to check their answers. (Answers: They are in a restaurant. The Bulgarian woman is moving her head up and down and saying "no." The man is confused.)
- Write this on the board:

  Three people guess what Eva means. Which guess is correct?

  1. Maybe she wants to accept, but she thinks it's not polite.
  2. It might mean Eva is saying "no."
  3. It could mean she doesn't want anything but she thinks it's rude to say no.

- Play the audio program again. Ss listen to check their answer. Then ask Ss which guess is correct. (Answer: 2. It might mean Eva is saying NO.)
- Books open. Play the audio program again, pausing after each line so the class can repeat. Elicit or answer any questions about vocabulary.

Vocabulary

nod: move your head up and down as a way of agreeing or giving someone a sign
polite: behaving in a way that is not rude

- Ss practice the conversation in groups of three.
- ***Option:*** Challenge groups to substitute a different gesture and to use their own information when trying the conversation again.

B *[CD 3, Track 14]*

- Read the question aloud. Then play the second part of the audio program. Ss listen and take notes.

Audio script

See page T-180.

- Elicit answers from the class.

Answers

Elena finds the way people end a conversation unusual. For example, they'll say things like, "Hey, let's get together soon." She thought it was an invitation, but it's just a way of saying good-bye.

4 GRAMMAR FOCUS

Learning Objective: use modals and adverbs to discuss what gestures mean

[CD 3, Track 15]

Modals and adverbs

- Draw this on the board:

Slight Possibility

MODALS	↑	ADVERBS
It might/may mean		Maybe/Perhaps it means
It could mean		It probably means
It must mean	↓	It definitely means

Strong possibility

- Explain that when we are not sure about the meaning, we use modals of possibility (*might, may, could*) or adverbs (*maybe, perhaps, possibly, probably*). When we are sure about the meaning, we use the modal *must* or the adverb *definitely*.
- Ask: "Do modals use the base form of the verb or the infinitive?" Elicit the answer. (Answer: the base form)
- Explain that *maybe* and *perhaps* go at the beginning of the sentence. Elicit where *possibly*, *probably*, and *definitely* go in a sentence. (Answer: after the subject)
- Play the audio program to present the sentences in the box. Elicit additional examples from the class.

Pair work

- Explain the task. Ss look at the pictures and then match each gesture with a possible meaning in the box. Use the first gesture as a model.
- Ss work individually to write a sentence describing each gesture. Go around the class and give help as needed.
- When Ss finish, model the example conversation with a S. Then Ss work in pairs to compare their sentences.
- Find out which gestures Ss didn't agree on. Elicit other pairs' responses to check answers.

Answers

All answers include one of the modals or adverbs presented in the Grammar Focus.
1. I can't hear you.
2. I don't know.
3. Be quiet.
4. Come here.
5. Call me.
6. That sounds crazy!

3 CONVERSATION It's pretty confusing.

A Listen and practice.

Eva: How was dinner with the new Bulgarian student last night? What's her name – Elena?

Brian: Yeah, Elena. It was nice. We always have a good time, but I still don't understand her very well. You see, when we offer her something to eat or drink, she nods her head up and down. But, at the same time she says no.

Eva: It might mean she wants to accept it, but she thinks it's not polite. In some countries, you have to refuse any offer first. Then the host insists, and you accept it.

Brian: I don't know . . . It's pretty confusing.

Eva: It could mean she doesn't want anything, but she thinks it's rude to say no.

Jack: Actually, in some countries, when people move their heads up and down, it means "no."

Brian: Really? Now I get it!

B Now listen to Elena talk to her friend. What does she find unusual about the way people in North America communicate?

4 GRAMMAR FOCUS

Modals and adverbs

Modals	Adverbs
It **might/may** mean she wants to accept it.	**Maybe/Perhaps** it means she wants to accept it.
It **could** mean she doesn't want anything.	It **probably** means she doesn't want anything.
That **must** mean "no."	That **definitely** means "no."

GRAMMAR PLUS *see page 145*

PAIR WORK What do these gestures mean? Take turns making statements about each gesture. Use the meanings in the box or your own ideas.

possible meanings
I don't know.
Be quiet.
Call me.
That sounds crazy!
I can't hear you.
Come here.

A: What do you think the first gesture means?

B: It probably means . . . , OR It might mean . . .

5 PRONUNCIATION Pitch

A Listen and practice. Notice how pitch is used to express certainty or doubt.

	Certain	Uncertain
A: Do you think her gesture means "no"?	**B:** Definitely.	**B:** Probably.
A: Do you understand what her gesture means?	**B:** Absolutely.	**B:** Maybe.

B **PAIR WORK** Take turns asking yes/no questions. Respond by using *absolutely*, *definitely*, *maybe*, *probably*, and your own information. Pay attention to pitch.

6 SPEAKING What's the matter with me?

A **GROUP WORK** Imagine you have one of these problems. What could explain it?

A: I'm always exhausted at the end of the day.
B: It might mean you are not getting enough sleep.
C: It could mean you are working too hard.
D: That definitely means . . .

B **CLASS ACTIVITY** Who came up with the most interesting explanation in your group? the most unexpected?

7 INTERCHANGE 14 Casual observers

Interpret people's body language. Go to Interchange 14 on page 128.

5 PRONUNCIATION

Learning Objectives: identify the difference in pitch used to express certainty or doubt; sound more natural when expressing certainty or doubt

A *[CD 3, Track 16]*

Certain

- Point out that we can show certainty in three ways—by saying something higher, longer, or louder:
  1. We can raise our voice and say the main syllables at a higher pitch and end with a falling pitch.
  2. We can make the stressed syllable last longer.
  3. We can say the main syllables of each word more loudly.
- Have Ss practice saying *definitely* and *absolutely* using a high pitch. Listen carefully. Do the Ss sound certain when they say *definitely* and *absolutely*?

Uncertain

- Now explain that we express doubt or uncertainty in two ways:
  1. We do not release the start of the word quickly, i.e., lengthening the sound of the first syllable.
  2. We raise the pitch of the last syllable, as if asking a question.
- Have Ss practice saying *probably* and *maybe*.
- Play the audio program. Ss listen and practice.
- Play the audio program again. After they practice together, ask individual Ss to demonstrate for the class.

TIP
To make pronunciation practice more fun, involve Ss' senses. Have them exaggerate sounds (for word stress), stand up and sit down (for intonation), and blur syllables (for unreleased sounds). Above all, encourage Ss to have fun!

B *Pair work*

- Explain the task and elicit some examples of yes/no questions. Focus Ss' attention on illustrations in the unit and ask: "Is she angry? Do you think he's nervous?"
- Ss take turns asking and answering questions using the correct pitch and stress. Then ask a few Ss to demonstrate for the class.

6 SPEAKING

Learning Objective: discuss gestures using modals and adverbs

A *Group work*

- Explain the task. Use the first expression to model the task. Then ask a S to offer another explanation.
- Ss work in small groups to think of an explanation for each problem

B *Class activity*

- As the groups do part A, observe the Ss to see who offers the best explanations. Have them present their explanations to the class. Have Ss identify whose explanations are interesting or unexpected.

TIP
By closely observing Ss during the Speaking activity, you can decide if further grammar practice or clarification is needed.

7 INTERCHANGE 14

See page T-128 for teaching notes.

End of Cycle 1

See the Supplementary Resources chart at the beginning of this unit for additional teaching materials and student activities related to this Cycle.

Cycle 2, Exercises 8–13

8 PERSPECTIVES

Learning Objectives: discuss signs; identify terms of permission, obligation, and prohibition in context

A *[CD 3, Track 17]*

- Explain that Ss will talk about international signs. Draw a recognizable sign on the board and ask Ss what it means (e.g., a no parking sign). Elicit other common signs from Ss.
- Ask Ss to cover the sentences and look only at the pictures. In pairs, Ss guess what each sign means. During the task, help Ss with any new vocabulary.
- Explain the task. As you play the audio program, Ss listen and point to the appropriate sign. Play the first sentence to make sure Ss understand the instructions. Then play the rest of the audio program.
- Have Ss read descriptions a–h. Then play the audio program again. This time, Ss write the correct letter under the picture. Go over answers with the class.

Answers

1. d	2. a	3. g	4. e
5. h	6. c	7. b	8. f

B *Pair work*

- Explain the task and elicit suggestions for the first sign. Ss complete the task in pairs. Remind them to give two suggestions for each sign.

Possible answers

1. in a museum, in a Japanese restaurant
2. on a beach, at a public swimming pool
3. in a restaurant, food court
4. on the street, in a parking garage
5. on an airplane, in the movies
6. in a car, in a bus
7. in a mosque, in the movies
8. on the street, in a parking garage

9 GRAMMAR FOCUS

Learning Objective: use modals to express permission, obligation, and prohibition

[CD 3, Track 18]

***Prohibition:* can't, not be allowed to**

- Draw a man in jail on the board. Elicit ideas about things he can't or isn't allowed to do (e.g., *He can't visit his friends. He isn't allowed to go out.*). Then ask Ss what they can't or aren't allowed to do.

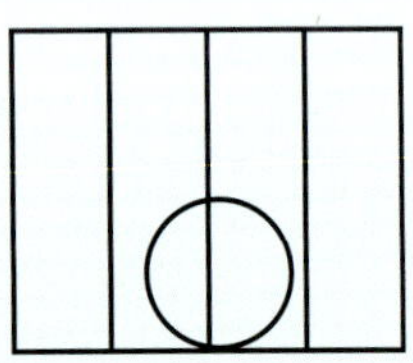

***Permission:* can, be allowed to**

- Elicit what he **can** or **is allowed to** do (e.g., *He's allowed to write letters. He can exercise every day.*). Then ask Ss what they can or are allowed to do.

***Obligation:* have to, have got to**

- Finally, ask what the prisoner **has (got) to** do, (e.g., *He has (got) to wear a prison uniform.*). Then elicit examples of obligations that Ss have.
- Play the audio program to present the sentences in the box. Refer Ss to the Perspectives section to find examples of the three functions.

A *Pair work*

- Ask Ss to look at the signs. Have Ss suggest what the first sign means.
- Explain any new vocabulary.
- Use the first school rule to explain and model the task. Then have Ss complete the task in pairs.
- Go over the answers with the class.

Answers

1. You **have to/You've got to** use the stairs in case of fire./You **can't** use the elevators.
2. You **can't/aren't allowed to** listen to music in class.
3. You **have to/You've got to** throw the trash in the garbage can.
4. You **have to/You've got to** put your cell phone on vibrate.
5. You **can't/aren't allowed to** eat or drink in this place.
6. You **can/are allowed to** park your bike here.
7. You **can't/aren't allowed to** record/tape the lessons.
8. You **have to/You've got to** show an ID with photo to enter.

B *Class activity*

- Explain the task and have two Ss read the example conversation. As a class, Ss discuss the rules found at the workplace or school. Remind them to use the language in the Grammar Focus box. Ask follow-up questions like "What rules do you think are good? Do you think there should be any other rules?"

8 PERSPECTIVES Rules and regulations

A What do you think these signs mean? Listen and match each sign with the correct meaning.

a. You can swim here.
b. You aren't allowed to take photos here.
c. You have to fasten your seat belts.
d. You've got to take off your shoes to enter.
e. You are allowed to park here.
f. You can't turn left.
g. Pets aren't allowed in this area.
h. You have to turn off electronic devices in this area.

B **PAIR WORK** Where might you see the signs in part A? Give two suggestions for each one.

"You might see this one by a lake . . ."

9 GRAMMAR FOCUS

Permission, obligation, and prohibition

Permission	Obligation	Prohibition
You **can** swim here.	You **have to** fasten your seat belt.	You **can't** turn left.
You**'re allowed to** park here.	You**'ve got to** take off your shoes.	Pets **aren't allowed** in this area.

GRAMMAR PLUS *see page 145*

A **PAIR WORK** Use the language in the grammar box to talk about these signs.

A: This first sign means you've got to use the stairs in case of a fire.
B: Yes, I think you're right. And the second one means you aren't allowed to . . .

B **CLASS ACTIVITY** What are some of the rules in your office or school?

A: In my office, we can't eat at our desks.
B: We can't either, but we're allowed to have water.
C: We're allowed to eat at our desks, but we have to clean up afterward.

10 DISCUSSION Play by the rules.

A **PAIR WORK** How many rules can you think of for each of these places?

at the gym	at a public swimming pool	on an airplane
in a museum	in a movie theater	at work

"At the gym, you have to wear sneakers or other athletic shoes. You're not allowed to wear regular shoes."

B **GROUP WORK** Share your ideas. Why do you think these rules exist? Have you ever broken any of them? What happened?

11 LISTENING Road signs

A Listen to four conversations about driving. Number the situations they are discussing in the correct order from 1 to 4.

____ Cars can't be in the bus and taxi lane.
____ Drivers must drive within the speed limit.
____ Drivers have to turn on car headlights on mountain roads.
____ Cars are allowed to park in this area after 6:00 P.M.

B Listen again. How did they find out about the traffic situation? Write what happened.

1. ______________________
2. ______________________
3. ______________________
4. ______________________

C **PAIR WORK** How do you move around your city? Give two examples of traffic laws you must obey.

12 WRITING Golden rules

A **GROUP WORK** Discuss the rules that currently exist at your school. How many can you think of? Are they all good rules?

B **GROUP WORK** Think of four new rules that you feel would be a good idea. Work together to write brief explanations of why each is necessary.

1. *You aren't allowed to use your first language. If you need to use it, you need to ask your teacher for permission.*
2. *You have to pay a small fine if you hand in your homework late.*
3. *You can be late, but you have to come in quietly so you don't disturb the lesson.*

C **CLASS ACTIVITY** Share your lists. Vote on the best new rules.

10 DISCUSSION

Learning Objective: discuss rules using terms of permission, obligation, and prohibition

A *Pair work*

- Explain the task. For each place, Ss think of as many rules as they can. Elicit ideas from Ss for the first place (e.g., *You can carry a towel with you. Children and pets are not allowed in.*).
- Ss work in pairs to think of rules for each place.
- Go over the answers with the class.

Possible answers

at a gym: You can carry a towel with you. Children and pets are not allowed in.
in a museum: You can't touch the exhibits. You're not allowed to take flash pictures.
at a public swimming pool: You are not allowed to dive. You can swim. You have to wear a swimsuit.
in a movie theater: You have to throw away your trash after the movie. You have to turn off or silence your cell phone. You can't talk loudly. You're allowed to sit anywhere you'd like.
on an airplane: You have to wear a seat belt. You can't bring sharp objects on board. You've got to turn off all electronic devices during takeoff and landing.
at work: You have to wear a uniform. You have to arrive on time. You aren't allowed to sleep. You can make personal calls sometimes.

B *Group work*

- Read the instructions and questions. Each pair joins another pair to discuss the questions.

For more speaking practice, play ***Vocabulary Tennis*** – download it from the website. Ss think of more places (e.g., at school, at home) and then brainstorm rules.

11 LISTENING

Learning Objective: listen for details and make inferences about some conversations about rules and laws

A *[CD 3, Track 19]*

- Set the scene. Ss will hear four conversations about driving. Ask the class: "Who knows how to drive?" Then brainstorm some rules of the road.
- Give Ss time to read the statements. Elicit or explain any new vocabulary.
- Play the audio program. Ss listen and complete the task. Then go over answers with the class.

Audio script

See page T-180.

Answers

2 Cars can't be in the bus and taxi lane.
4 Drivers must drive within the speed limit.
1 Drivers have to turn on car headlights on mountain roads.
3 Cars are allowed to park in this area after 6:00 P.M.

B *[CD 3, Track 20]*

- Explain the task. Play the audio program again. This time, Ss listen to find out what happened with each driver. Go over answers with the class.

Answers

1. She noticed that all the cars had their lights on. He saw a sign that says all cars need to have their headlights on for the next five miles.
2. The traffic officer was signaling her. There weren't any other cars in their lane.
3. He got a parking ticket. There was a sign that says you can't park there until after 6:00 P.M.
4. The other cars were flashing their lights. He saw a patrol car up ahead checking people's speed.

C *Pair work*

- Tell Ss to discuss in pairs how they get around in the city (e.g., by car, bus, train). Have Ss come up with two laws they obey and share them with the class.

12 WRITING

Learning Objective: write a list of rules using terms of permission, obligation, and prohibition

A *Group work*

- In groups, Ss discuss the rules that exist at their school and talk about whether the rules are good.
- Elicit any rules that Ss disagreed about in their groups and discuss them as a class.

B *Group work*

- Ss read the sample rules.
- In groups, Ss think of four new rules. Then they work together to write an explanation of each rule.

C *Class activity*

- Write Ss' new rules on the board. Then take a vote on which rules are best.

13 READING

Learning Objective: distinguish main ideas from supporting ideas in a reading about the meaning of some expressions

A

- ***Option:*** Books closed. Write an example of a common idiom on the board. Ask Ss: "What is this called?" Elicit the word *idiom* (a group of words used together with a meaning that you cannot guess from the meanings of the separate words).
- Books open. Read the title. Ask: "What do you think this article is about?" Elicit answers. (Possible answer: English idioms)
- Explain the task. Have students match each picture to the correct paragraph. Then go over answers with the class. (Answers: 1. B, 2. C, 3. A)

B

- Ss read the article. Tell them to circle or highlight words or expressions whose meanings they can't guess from context.
- When Ss finish, have them form small groups. Ask them to compare any words they couldn't guess and to help each other with definitions. Go around the class and give help as needed.

! For a new way to teach this Reading, try ***Vocabulary Mingle*** – download it from the website.

- Elicit any new words or expressions.

Vocabulary

reply: answer
sailor: someone who sails ships or boats as their job or as a sport
straw: the long, dried stems of plants such as wheat (a plant for grain), often given to animals for sleeping on and eating
take action: to do something
deal: cope with a situation

- Explain the task. Then model the first sentence as an example.
- Ss complete the exercise individually. Go over answers with Ss, asking them to justify their answers.
- Ask: "Does the article say it is important for language students to learn idioms?" (Answer: yes) "What can language learners do to help them remember idioms?" (Answer: know the idiom's origin). Explain that these are the article's main ideas.
- Ask: "What are the article's supporting ideas or examples?" (Answer: the origins of the three idioms included in the article)

Answers

1. You **can't** guess the meaning of an idiom if you understand each word.
2. In the past, people knew about important events when they heard **bells.**
3. A camel falls down if it has to carry too much **straw.**
4. Sailors used to feel **better** when they went to the bottom of the ship.

C

- Read the task. Read the sentences and explain any new vocabulary. Remind Ss that you may have to change the verbs to the correct form.
- Ss work individually to finish the task and check the answers in pairs.

Answers

1. Julie has a bad cold at the moment, and she's feeling under the weather.
2. I don't remember his face, but his name rings a bell.
3. When the neighbors' noisy kids broke my window with their ball, it was the last straw.

D

- Read the questions. If Ss are from different countries, have them explain an idiom to each other. If Ss are from the same country, ask them to tell you about some idioms and explain them in English.
- ***Option:*** Ask Ss to work in pairs to choose one idiom from the text and create a conversation using the idiom. For example:

  Son: Mom, can I stay home from school today?
  Mom: Why? Are you still feeling a little under the weather?
- Ask a few pairs to act out their conversation for the class.

End of Cycle 2

See the Supplementary Resources chart at the beginning of this unit for additional teaching materials and student exercises related to this Cycle.

A Skim the article. Match the pictures 1, 2, and 3 to the paragraphs.

UNDERSTANDING IDIOMS

Idioms can be a problem for language learners. They often seem to make absolutely no sense at all. For example, imagine your English friend Sam tells you his math exam was "a piece of cake." Do you imagine him at school, sitting in front of a sweet dessert with nothing but a pen to eat it with? In fact, he's saying that the exam was really easy. It's important to learn useful English idioms and knowing their origins helps us to remember them. Here are stories of three English idioms.

1

2

3

____ **A** If you ask a friend to hang out, you might hear, "Sorry, I can't tonight. I'm feeling a little under the weather." It may sound like rain is coming, but really, it means that your friend feels sick. This expression came from sailors, who often got seasick when bad weather tossed the ship from side to side. The sailors went down to the bottom part of the ship, away from the storm and where the ship's rocking was gentler.

____ **B** If you have a difficult roommate, you might say, "My roommate has loud parties every night, but last night was the last straw. They played music till 5 A.M.! I'm moving out." A "last straw" is a final problem that makes someone take action. This expression is a short form of the phrase "the straw that broke the camel's back." The idea is that even though a single piece of straw is very light, many pieces added together will be too heavy for the camel to carry.

____ **C** Have you ever asked someone if they know something, and they reply, "That rings a bell"? They're not hearing music! They mean that what you're saying sounds familiar, and they think they've heard it before. This idiom comes from the fact that bells are used to remind people of many things. Traditionally, bells would toll for an important event, like a wedding. School bells tell you that class is starting, and even the alarm chime on your phone reminds you that it's time to get up.

B Read the article and correct the false statements below.

1. You can guess the meaning of an idiom if you understand each word.
   ____
2. In the past, people knew about important events when they heard shouting.
   ____
3. A camel falls down if it has to carry too much water.
   ____
4. Sailors used to feel sicker when they went to the bottom of the ship.
   ____

C Complete the sentences with the correct form of one of the idioms.

1. Julie has a bad cold at the moment, and she's ______________________.
2. I don't remember his face, but his name ______________________.
3. When the neighbors' noisy kids broke my window with their ball, it ______________________.

D What idioms are commonly used in your country? Where do you think they come from?

Units 13–14 Progress check

SELF-ASSESSMENT

How well can you do these things? Check (✓) the boxes.

I can . . .	Very well	OK	A little
Ask about and express opinions and emotions (Ex. 1, 4, 5)	☐	☐	☐
Discuss movies (Ex. 2)	☐	☐	☐
Understand descriptions of rules and laws (Ex. 3)	☐	☐	☐
Speculate about things when I'm not sure and recognize emotions (Ex. 4)	☐	☐	☐
Describe rules and laws: permission, obligation, and prohibition (Ex. 5)	☐	☐	☐

1 SURVEY Personal preferences

A Complete the first column of the survey with your opinions.

	Me	My classmate
A fascinating book		
A confusing movie		
A boring TV show		
A shocking news story		
An interesting celebrity		
A singer you are amazed by		
A song you are annoyed by		

B **CLASS ACTIVITY** Go around the class and find someone who has the same opinions. Write a classmate's name only once.

"I thought *I am Malala* was a fascinating book. What about you?"

2 ROLE PLAY Movie night

Student A: Invite Student B to a movie. Suggest two movie options.
Then answer your partner's questions.
Start like this: *Do you want to see a movie?*

Student B: Student A invites you to a movie.
Find out more about the movie.
Then accept or refuse the invitation.

Change roles and try the role play again.

Units 13–14

Progress check

SELF-ASSESSMENT

Learning Objectives: reflect on one's learning; identify areas that need improvement

- Ask: "What did you learn in Units 13 and 14?" Elicit Ss' answers.
- Ss complete the Self-assessment. Explain to Ss that this is not a test; it is a way for them to evaluate what they've learned and identify areas where they need additional practice. Encourage them to be honest, and point out they will not get a bad grade if they check (✓) "A little."
- Ss move on to the Progress check exercises. You can have Ss complete them in class or for homework, using one of these techniques:
  1. Ask Ss to complete all the exercises.
  2. Ask Ss: "What do you need to practice?" Then assign exercises based on their answers.
  3. Ask Ss to choose and complete exercises based on their Self-assessment.

1 SURVEY

Learning Objective: demonstrate one's ability to ask about and express opinions and emotions

A

- Explain the task. Then go over the categories in the chart. Give Ss time to complete the column with their own opinions.

B *Class activity*

- Model the task by asking a S a question from the survey, like this:

T: What's the name of a book you think is fascinating?
S: Well, I thought the book *I am Malala* is fascinating.
T: (writes *I am Malala* in the My classmate column) Why is it fascinating?
S: Well, it tells a story about the Nobel Peace Prize winner and teenage activist from Pakistan.
T: Sounds interesting.

- Explain the rules before Ss begin. Ss should write the classmate's name and answer in the *My classmate* column. They can write each classmate's name only once. Ss should ask follow-up questions to try to find someone who has the same opinion.
- Ss stand up and move around the classroom, asking and answering questions about the categories in the chart. Go around the class and write down common errors.
- Elicit feedback from the class. Ask if anyone found another S with the same opinion. Go over any errors you noticed, and praise successful communication that you observed.

2 ROLE PLAY

Learning Objective: demonstrate one's ability to describe people and things

- Explain the task. Student A invites Student B to a movie. Student B finds out about two movie choices and then either accepts or refuses the invitation.
- Brainstorm the kinds of questions someone who is invited to a movie might ask. Write suggestions on the board (e.g., *What kind of movie is it? What's it about? Who's in it? What time is it playing? Where is it playing?*).
- Have Ss form pairs. Tell Student As to think of two movies they would like to see. Explain that they should be prepared to answer the questions on the board.
- While Student As prepare their answers, remind Student Bs how to politely accept or refuse an invitation.
- Ss work in pairs to complete the task. Set a time limit of about five minutes.
- During the role play, go around the class and listen. Take note of any common errors. When time is up, suggest ways the role plays could be improved. Give examples of good communication that you heard.
- Ss change roles and try the role play again.

3 LISTENING

Learning Objective: demonstrate one's ability to understand speculations and recognize emotions

A *[CD 3, Track 21]*

- Explain the task. Remind Ss that there are two extra topics.
- Play the audio program. Ss listen and complete the task. Then elicit answers.

Audio script

See page T-180.

Answers

1. Singapore: b. chewing gum
2. Kenya: f. carrying money
3. San Francisco: e. pigeons
4. Milan: a. smiling

B *[CD 3, Track 22]*

- Explain the task and give Ss time to read all the sentences.
- Play the audio program again, pausing after each person to give Ss time to write their answers.
- After Ss compare answers in pairs, go over answers.

Answers

1. In Singapore, you aren't allowed to chew gum on the metro.
2. In Kenya, you can't walk around without money.
3. In San Francisco, you aren't allowed to feed pigeons.
4. In Milan, you have to smile.

C *Pair work*

- Ss discuss the question in pairs.
- Ask Ss to share their opinions with the class.

4 GAME

Learning Objective: demonstrate one's ability to speculate about things when unsure

A

- Brainstorm some emotions and ideas that a person can communicate using only facial expressions and gestures. Write suggestions on the board (e.g., *I'm tired of waiting. I like that music a lot.*).
- Ss work individually to think of two emotions or ideas of their own. Tell them to write each one on a separate card or piece of paper.

B *Group work*

- Collect all the cards or pieces of paper. Then mix them up and place them face-down in one pile.
- Explain the rules. Ss take turns picking a card from the pile and acting out the meaning for the others in the group to guess. If Ss pick their own card, they should put it back and take another.
- Read the example conversation with Ss. Point out that Student B is the person acting out the meaning. He or she can speak only to say whether a guess is right, wrong, or close. Then ask a S to pick a card from the top of the pile to act out while the class guesses the meaning.
- Ss form small groups. Give each group some cards to place face-down in a pile. Remind Ss to use expressions with modals and adverbs (e.g., *could mean, might mean, may mean, probably means*).
- Ss take turns acting out meanings while the rest of the group guesses.

5 DISCUSSION

Learning Objective: demonstrate one's ability to describe rules and laws using terms of permission, obligation, and prohibition

Group work

- Explain the task. Give Ss time to read the laws silently. Answer any vocabulary questions.
- Explain the task. Give Ss time to read the laws silently. Answer any vocabulary questions.
- Ask three Ss to read the example conversation.
- Ss take turns discussing the other laws in small groups. Set a time limit of about ten minutes.

WHAT'S NEXT?

Learning Objective: become more involved in one's learning

- Focus Ss' attention on the Self-assessment again. Ask: "How well can you do these things now?"
- Ask Ss to underline one thing they need to review. Ask: "What did you underline? How can you review it?"
- If needed, plan additional instruction, activities, or reviews based on Ss' answers.

3 LISTENING Unusual laws around the world

A Listen to two people discuss an article about laws in different places. Match the topic to the place. (There are two extra topics.)

a. smiling	b. chewing gum	c. stealing
d. hospitals	e. pigeons	f. carrying money

1. Singapore ___ **2.** Kenya ___ **3.** San Francisco ___ **4.** Milan ___

B Listen again. Complete the sentences to describe each law.

1. In Singapore, you ______________________________.
2. In Kenya, you ______________________________.
3. In San Francisco, you ______________________________.
4. In Milan, you ______________________________.

C **PAIR WORK** Which law seems the strangest to you? the most logical? Why?

4 GAME Miming

A Think of two emotions or ideas you can communicate with gestures. Write them on separate cards.

B **GROUP WORK** Shuffle your cards together. Then take turns picking cards and acting out the meanings with gestures. The student who guesses correctly goes next.

A: That probably means you're disgusted.
B: No.
C: It could mean you're surprised.
B: You're getting closer . . .

I'm confused. I don't understand what you really want.

5 DISCUSSION What's the law?

GROUP WORK Read these laws from the United States. What do you think about them? Are they the same or different in your country?

- You aren't allowed to keep certain wild animals as pets.
- You're allowed to vote when you turn 18.
- In some states, you can get married when you're 16.
- You have to wear a seat belt in the back seat of a car in most states.
- Young men don't have to serve in the military.
- In some states, you can't drive faster than 65 miles per hour (about 100 kph).
- In most states, children have to attend school until they are 16 or 18.

A: In the U.S.A., you aren't allowed to keep certain wild animals as pets.
B: It's the same for us. You've got to have a special permit to keep a wild animal.
C: I've heard that in some countries, you can keep lions and tigers as pets.

WHAT'S NEXT?

Look at your Self-assessment again. Do you need to review anything?

Unit 15 Supplementary Resources Overview

	After the following SB exercises	You can use these materials in class	Your students can use these materials outside the classroom
CYCLE 1	**1 Snapshot**		
	2 Conversation		**SS** Unit 15 Speaking 1–2
	3 Grammar Focus		**SB** Unit 15 Grammar plus, Focus 1 **SS** Unit 15 Grammar 1 **GAME** Word Keys (Unreal conditional sentences with *if* clauses 1) **GAME** Sentence Runner (Unreal conditional sentences with *if* clauses 2)
	4 Listening	**TSS** Unit 15 Listening Worksheet	
	5 Interchange 15		**WB** Unit 15 exercises 1–4
CYCLE 2	**6 Word Power**	**TSS** Unit 15 Vocabulary Worksheet **TSS** Unit 15 Extra Worksheet	**SS** Unit 15 Vocabulary 1–2 **GAME** Sentence Stacker (Opposite Verbs)
	7 Perspectives		
	8 Grammar Focus		**SB** Unit 15 Grammar plus, Focus 2 **SS** Unit 15 Grammar 2 **GAME** Say the Word (Past modals)
	9 Pronunciation	**TSS** Unit 15 Grammar Worksheet	
	10 Listening		
	11 Speaking		
	12 Writing	**TSS** Unit 15 Writing Worksheet	
	13 Reading	**TSS** Unit 15 Project Worksheet **VID** Unit 15 **VRB** Unit 15	**SS** Unit 15 Reading 1–2 **SS** Unit 15 Listening 1–3 **SS** Unit 15 Video 1–3 **WB** Unit 15 exercises 5–9

Key **GAME:** Online Game **SB:** Student's Book **SS:** Online Self-study **TSS:** Teacher Support Site
VID: Video DVD **VRB:** Video Resource Book **WB:** Online Workbook/Workbook

My Plan for Unit 15

Use the space below to customize a plan that fits your needs.

With the following SB exercises	I am using these materials in class	My students are using these materials outside the classroom

With or instead of the following SB section	I am using these materials for assessment

15 I wouldn't have done that.

- Discuss imaginary situations
- Discuss difficult situations

1 SNAPSHOT

NEWS 4 YOU   NEW TODAY   MOST POPULAR   TRENDING   LOGIN | SIGN UP

FLORIDA MOM "CAUGHT" BEING HONEST

Nancy Bloom was caught on the security camera entering a convenience store while the owner was out to lunch. The door was unlocked, so Nancy walked in with her son, picked up some ice cream, and left the money on the counter.

MOST SHARED THIS WEEK

HONESTY IS ITS OWN REWARD

After driving for 20 miles to return a wallet lost in a park, Kate Moore gets only a half-hearted, "Oh. Thanks."

HOMELESS MAN FINDS $40,000 AND TURNS IT IN

When Tom Heart found a backpack full of cash, he didn't think twice. He took it straight to the police. After reading Tom's story, a stranger started a fundraising campaign for Tom that has already raised over $60,000.

Have you heard any stories like these recently?
Have you ever found anything valuable? What did you do?
Do you think that people who return lost things should get a reward?

2 CONVERSATION What would you do?

A Listen and practice.

Joon: Look at this. A homeless guy found a backpack with $40,000 inside!
Mia: And what did he do?
Joon: He took it to the police. He gave it all back, every single penny.
Mia: You're kidding! If I found $40,000, I wouldn't return it. I'd keep it.
Joon: Really? What would you do with it?
Mia: Well, I'd spend it. I could buy a new car or take a nice long vacation.
Joon: The real owner might find out about it, though, and then you could go to jail.
Mia: Hmm. You've got a point there.

B Listen to the rest of the conversation. What would Joon do if he found $40,000?

15 I wouldn't have done that.

Cycle 1, Exercises 1–5

In Unit 15, students discuss imaginary events and difficult situations. By the end of Cycle 1, students will be able to discuss imaginary situations using unreal conditional sentences with *if* clauses. By the end of Cycle 2, students will be able to discuss predicaments using the past modals *would have* and *should have*.

1 SNAPSHOT

Learning Objective: discuss examples of honesty

- Books closed. Ask the class: "Have you ever lost something valuable and had it returned? What happened?" Ss discuss in pairs. Encourage them to ask their partners follow-up questions.
- Books open. Ss read the information in the Snapshot. Ask them which story they find the most interesting. Why? Elicit or explain any new vocabulary.

Vocabulary

catch: discover someone doing something, usually something bad

fundraising: the activity of collecting money for a particular purpose

- Read the questions. Then have Ss discuss them in groups. After a few minutes, ask Ss to change groups and share their ideas again.
- ***Option:*** Follow up with a longer discussion. Ask the class: "Do you agree that honesty pays off? (It's best to be honest.) What should happen to people who cheat and then confess?"

2 CONVERSATION

Learning Objective: use unreal conditional sentences with *if* clauses in a conversation about a hypothetical situation

A *[CD 3, Track 23]*

- ***Option:*** Focus Ss' attention on the photo and and ask "Why do you think the mortarboard, the graduating cap, is made of dollars?" Elicit ideas. (e.g., You need a lot of money to go to college, you can make a lot of money after you go to college, etc).
- Books closed. Instead of Ss listening for specific information, tell Ss to simply listen carefully.
- Play the audio program. Then ask: "What kinds of things were the people talking about?" Have Ss write their answers on the board. (Answers: $40,000 returned; homeless guy took it to the police; she'd go back to college; she could go to jail)

TIP

To provide a break from sitting and involve Ss in their own learning, let Ss write their answers and brainstorm ideas on the board.

- Play the audio program again. Have Ss listen and take notes. Then have them work in pairs to compare their notes with those on the board.
- Books open. Have Ss check their own notes against the conversation. How many Ss feel that they got most of the main ideas? Some of the main ideas?
- Encourage Ss to check their dictionaries for the meanings of new words and expressions.
- Ss practice the conversation in pairs.

! For a new way to practice this Conversation, try ***Disappearing Dialog*** – download it from the website. Alternatively, use it with the Grammar Focus on page 101.

B *[CD 3, Track 24]*

- Read the question. Then play the rest of the audio program. Ss listen and write their answers.

Audio script

See page T-181.

- Elicit answers from the class.

Answer

Joon would take the money straight to the police.

- ***Option:*** Follow up with a discussion. Write these questions on the board:

  What can you buy with $40,000? With $10,000? What are the risks of keeping money that you find? How honest are you? Ss discuss in small groups or as a class.

3 GRAMMAR FOCUS

Learning Objective: use unreal conditional sentences with *if* clauses

[CD 3, Track 25]

Unreal sentences with if clauses

- Books closed. Write these sentences on the board:

  Mia: If I ______________ $40,000,
  I ______________ return it. I ______________ buy a new car.
  Joon: You ______________ go to jail.

- Have Ss fill in the blanks. To check answers, refer them to the previous conversation. (Answers: *found, wouldn't, could, could*)
- Ask Ss if Mia and Joon are talking about a real or an unreal situation. (Answer: unreal)
- Books open. Elicit or explain this rule for forming unreal conditional sentences:
  1. Two types of verb forms are used in the clauses:
     (1) the simple past form in the *if* clause (*found*),
     (2) a modal verb in the main clause (*would*).
     If I found $40,000, I wouldn't return the money so fast.
  2. The clauses can be used in either order. No comma is necessary when the *if* clause comes second.
     I wouldn't return the money so fast if I found $40,000.
  3. We can use various modals in the main clause. The most common is *would*, or its contraction, *'d*. We can also use *could* or *might*. *Might* expresses possibility, and *could* expresses ability:
     If I found $40,000, I might go to the police. (I'm not sure, but it's possible I would go to the police.)
     If I found $40,000, I could go back to college. (I would be able to go back to college.)

- Play the audio program to present the sentences in the box. Have Ss listen and repeat. Then elicit examples of sentences with *if* clauses and modals.

For more practice with unreal conditionals, play the ***Chain Game*** – download it from the website.

A

- Explain the task and model the first conversation with a S. Then Ss work individually to complete the task. Finally, elicit Ss' responses to check answers.

Answers

1. A: would . . . do
   B: 'd buy
2. A: had, would . . . go
   B: 'd fly
3. A: told, would . . . choose
   B: 'd go
4. A: Would . . . break, locked
   B: didn't have, 'd ask
5. A: wanted, would . . . say
   B: wouldn't say, 'd mind
6. A: would . . . do, saw
   B: wouldn't be, 'd ask

B *Pair work*

- Explain the task. Ss take turns asking the questions and giving their own answers.

4 LISTENING

Learning Objective: listen for the main idea and details in some conversations about difficult situations

A *[CD 3, Track 26]*

- Set the scene. Three friends are talking about predicaments, or unpleasant situations that are difficult to solve. Play the audio program. Have Ss listen and number the predicaments.

Audio script

See page T-181.

- Go over answers with the class.

Answers

1. Chris is addicted to the Internet.
2. Kari lost all her money in Europe.
3. Zoey saw her classmates cheating.

B *[CD 3, Track 27]*

- Explain the task. Ss listen and write the suggestions.
- Play the audio program again, pausing for Ss to take notes. Then discuss the best suggestions.

Answers

1. a. She wouldn't tell him he has a problem, and she would continue to suggest activities that don't involve the Internet.
   b. She would be honest and tell him what she thinks because it could affect his relationships with other people.
2. a. He'd call his parents and ask them to send money right away.
   b. She'd also call her parents, but would probably sell her watch or camera. She might get a job as a server until she made enough money to buy a plane ticket home.
3. a. She would talk to the teacher and ask him not to say that she told him.
   b. He wouldn't get involved. He'd pretend he didn't see anything.

C *Group work*

- Have Ss discuss the question in small groups. Then Ss share their answer with the class.

3 GRAMMAR FOCUS

Unreal conditional sentences with *if* clauses

Imaginary situation (simple past)	**Possible consequence (*would, could,* or *might* + verb)**
If I **found** $40,000,	**I would keep** it.
	I wouldn't return it.
	I could buy a new car.
	I might go to the police.
What **would** you **do if** you **found** $40,000?	

GRAMMAR PLUS see page 146

A Complete these conversations. Then compare with a partner.

1. **A:** What ____________ you ____________ (do) if you lost your sister's favorite sweater?
   B: Of course I ____________ (buy) her a new one.
2. **A:** If you ____________ (have) three months to travel, where ____________ you ____________ (go)?
   B: Oh, that's easy! I ____________ (fly) to Europe. I've always wanted to go there.
3. **A:** If your doctor ____________ (tell) you to get more exercise, which activity ____________ you ____________ (choose)?
   B: I'm not sure, but I think I ____________ (go) jogging two or three times a week.
4. **A:** ____________ you ____________ (break) into your house if you ____________ (lock) yourself out?
   B: No way! If I ____________ (not have) another key, I ____________ (ask) a neighbor for help.
5. **A:** If your friend ____________ (want) to marry someone you didn't like, ____________ you ____________ (say) something?
   B: No, I ____________ (not say) anything. I ____________ (mind) my own business.
6. **A:** What ____________ you ____________ (do) if you ____________ (see) your favorite movie star on the street?
   B: I ____________ (not be) shy! I ____________ (ask) to take a photo with them.

B **PAIR WORK** Take turns asking the questions in part A. Answer with your own information.

4 LISTENING Tough situations

A Listen to three people talk about predicaments. Check which predicament they are talking about.

1. ☐ Chris has relationship problems. ☐ Chris is addicted to the Internet.
2. ☐ Kari spent all her money in Europe. ☐ Kari lost all her money in Europe.
3. ☐ Zoey saw her classmates cheating. ☐ Zoey doesn't understand her math class.

B Listen again. Write the two suggestions given for each predicament.

1. a. ____________ b. ____________
2. a. ____________ b. ____________
3. a. ____________ b. ____________

C **GROUP WORK** Which suggestions do you agree with? Why?

5 INTERCHANGE 15 Tough choices

What would you do in some difficult situations? Go to Interchange 15 on page 130.

6 WORD POWER Opposites

A Find nine pairs of opposites in this list. Complete the chart. Then compare with a partner.

accept	borrow	dislike	find	lose	remember
admit	deny	divorce	forget	marry	save
agree	disagree	enjoy	lend	refuse	spend

accept	≠	*refuse*		≠			≠	
	≠			≠			≠	
	≠			≠			≠	

B **PAIR WORK** Choose four pairs of opposites. Write sentences using each pair.

I can't remember my dreams. As soon as I wake up, I forget them.

7 PERSPECTIVES That was a big mistake.

A Listen to people talk about recent predicaments. Then check (✓) the best suggestion for each one.

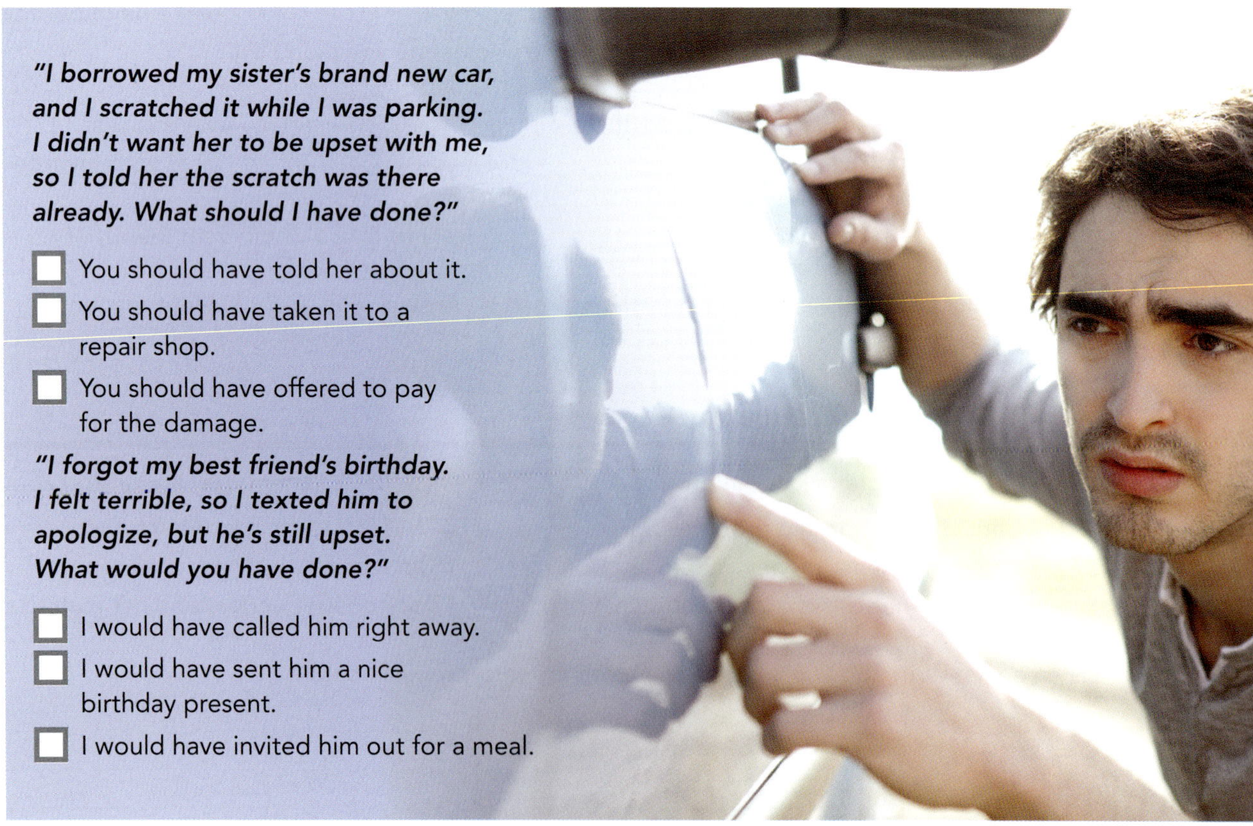

"I borrowed my sister's brand new car, and I scratched it while I was parking. I didn't want her to be upset with me, so I told her the scratch was there already. What should I have done?"

- ☐ You should have told her about it.
- ☐ You should have taken it to a repair shop.
- ☐ You should have offered to pay for the damage.

"I forgot my best friend's birthday. I felt terrible, so I texted him to apologize, but he's still upset. What would you have done?"

- ☐ I would have called him right away.
- ☐ I would have sent him a nice birthday present.
- ☐ I would have invited him out for a meal.

B **PAIR WORK** Compare with a partner. Do you agree with each other?

5 INTERCHANGE 15

See page T-129 for teaching notes.

End of Cycle 1

See the Supplementary Resources chart at the beginning of this unit for additional teaching materials and student activities related to this Cycle.

Cycle 2, Exercises 6–13

6 WORD POWER

Learning Objective: use verbs for describing events

A

- Explain the task and read the example answer in the chart. Ss complete the task individually and then compare answers in pairs. Go over answers with the class and help Ss with correct pronunciation and stress.

Answers

accept ≠ refuse
admit ≠ deny
agree ≠ disagree
borrow ≠ lend
dislike ≠ enjoy
divorce ≠ marry
find ≠ lose
forget ≠ remember
save ≠ spend

- ***Option:*** Ss work in pairs to brainstorm more verbs and their opposites (e.g., *come* and *go*, *give* and *take*).

TIP
Draw a line down one side of the board and use this as your "Vocabulary Column." Add new words to it throughout the lesson. Keep track of what you have taught your Ss by reviewing the list at the end of each class.

B *Pair work*

- Explain the task and read the example sentence. Point out that Ss can use a simple statement, a question, or an unreal conditional sentence with an *if* clause.
- Ss work in pairs to choose four sets of verbs from the chart in part A. Then they write sentences using each pair. Go around the class and check Ss' sentences for correct grammar.

7 PERSPECTIVES

Learning Objectives: discuss predicaments; identify past modals *would have* and *should have* in context

A *[CD 3, Track 28]*

- Focus Ss' attention on the picture and ask what happened. (Answer: He scratched his sister's car and is deciding what to do about it.) Explain that Ss will hear two predicaments that really happened, not imaginary situations.
- Draw this chart on the board and ask Ss to copy it:

Predicament	What went wrong?	What did he/she do about it?
#1		
#2		

- Books closed. Play the audio program. Have Ss listen and complete the chart. Then have Ss open their books, read the predicaments, and check their answers.
- Play the audio program again. Point out the reduction of *have*, which sounds like *of*.
- Ss check (✓) the best suggestion for each predicament.

B *Pair work*

- Ss work in pairs to compare answers. Encourage them to explain their answers. Then take a class vote to find out which suggestions were the most popular.
- ***Option:*** In pairs, Ss write new predicaments. Then each pair joins another pair, exchanges papers, and writes several suggestions for each predicament. The group then decides which suggestions are best.

8 GRAMMAR FOCUS

Learning Objective: use past modals to discuss actions in the past

[CD 3, Track 29]

- Refer Ss to the Perspectives section. Ask the class: "Did the man fix his sister's car? Did the man call his friend?" (Answer: no) Point out that the *would have* and *should have* actions were imaginary or hypothetical (they didn't really happen).
- Explain that we use *I would have* to give an opinion about an action in the past. We use *you should have* to make a suggestion about a past event. In both cases, our opinion or suggestion is too late.

Would have

- Ask Ss to find examples of *would have* from the Perspectives section. Ss write them on the board in columns, like this:

1	2	3	4	5
I	would	have	called	him…
I	would	have	sent	him…
I	would	have	invited	him…
What	would	you	have	done?

- Elicit the rules from Ss by asking what they can see in each column.

  Statement:
  Subject + *would have* + past participle + (rest)
  Question:
  Wh- + *would* + pronoun + *have* + past participle?
- Have Ss think of more examples of *would have* + past participle (e.g., *I would have told her "I'm sorry."*). Have Ss use the negative, too (e.g., *I wouldn't have called him.*).

Should have

- Repeat the above steps for *should have*.
- Play the audio program to present the sentences in the box. Ss listen and read silently.

A

- Explain the task and any new vocabulary (e.g., *cashier, trash, campsite*). You can copy and give the Ss the appendix on page T-151 so they can use more irregular past participles. Ss work individually to complete the sentences. Then go over answers with the class.

Answers

1. A: I was in a meeting at work when my girlfriend texted me saying she needed to see me right away. What should I have **done**?
   B: You should have **sent** her a message and **told** her you'd call back later.
2. A: The cashier gave me too much change. What should I have **done**?
   B: You should have **said** something. You shouldn't have **taken** the money.
3. A: I ignored an email from someone I don't like. What would you have **done**?
   B: I would have **replied** to the person. It just takes a minute!
4. A: We left all our trash at the campsite. What would you have **done**?
   B: I would have **taken** it with me and **thrown** it away later.

B

- Explain the task. Read the sentences in each column and explain any new vocabulary (e.g., *cheating, messy, comb, warn, leave a note, exchange*). Then Ss work individually to match the situations with the most appropriate suggestions. After Ss compare answers in pairs, go over answers with the class.

Answers

1. a, b, d　　2. b, d, e　　3. a
4. c, d, f　　5. d, g, h

C *Group work*

- Ss work in small groups to think of their own suggestions. Remind them to use past modals. Groups then choose their best suggestion for each situation.
- Ask groups to share their best ideas with the class.

9 PRONUNCIATION

Learning Objective: sound more natural when pronouncing the verb *have* in past modals

A *[CD 3, Track 30]*

- Play the audio program. Point out how the reduced form for *have* /əv/ sounds like *of*. Play the audio program again, pausing for the class to practice.

B *Pair work*

- In pairs, Ss practice the conversations in part A of Exercise 8 again. Go around the class and give help as needed. Then go over any errors you noticed.

TIP
To keep working on this feature, make it the "Sound of the Week" and focus on it for the next few classes.

8 GRAMMAR FOCUS

Past modals

Use *would have* or *should have* + past participle to give opinions or suggestions about actions in the past.

What **should** I **have done**?	You **should have told** her about it.
	You **shouldn't have lied** to your sister.
What **would** you **have done**?	I **would have called** him.
	I **wouldn't have texted** him.

GRAMMAR PLUS *see page 146*

A Complete these conversations. Then practice with a partner.

1. **A:** I was in a meeting at work when my girlfriend texted me saying she needed to see me right away. What should I have ______________ (do)?
   B: You should have ______________ (send) her a message and ______________ (tell) her you'd call back later.
2. **A:** The cashier gave me too much change. What should I have ______________ (do)?
   B: You should have ______________ (say) something. You shouldn't have ______________ (take) the money.
3. **A:** I ignored an email from someone I don't like. What would you have ______________ (do)?
   B: I would have ______________ (reply) to the person. It just takes a minute!
4. **A:** We left all our trash at the campsite. What would you have ______________ (do)?
   B: I would have ______________ (take) it with me and ______________ (throw) it away later.

B Read the situations below. What would have been the best thing to do? Choose suggestions. Then compare with a partner.

Situations

1. The teacher borrowed my favorite book and spilled coffee all over it. _____
2. I saw a classmate cheating on an exam, so I wrote her an email about it. _____
3. A friend of mine always has messy hair, so I gave him a comb for his birthday. _____
4. I hit someone's car when I was leaving a parking lot. Luckily, no one saw me. _____
5. My aunt gave me a wool sweater. I can't wear wool, so I gave it back. _____

Suggestions

a. You should have spoken to him about it.
b. I would have spoken to the teacher about it.
c. I would have waited for the owner to return.
d. I wouldn't have said anything.
e. You should have warned her not to do it again.
f. You should have left a note for the owner.
g. I would have told her that I prefer something else.
h. You should have exchanged it for something else.

C **GROUP WORK** Make another suggestion for each situation in part B.

9 PRONUNCIATION Reduction of *have*

A Listen and practice. Notice how ***have*** is reduced in these sentences.

What would you have (/əv/) done?   I would have (/əv/) told the truth.

B **PAIR WORK** Practice the conversations in Exercise 8, part A, again. Use the reduced form of ***have***.

10 LISTENING Problem solved!

A Listen to an advice podcast. Complete the chart.

	Problem	What the person did
Ronnie:		
Becca:		

B Listen again. According to Dr. Jones, what should each person have done?

Ronnie: ______________________

Becca: ______________________

C **PAIR WORK** What would you have done in each situation?

11 SPEAKING An awful trip

A **PAIR WORK** Imagine a friend has been on a really awful trip and everything went wrong. What should your friend have done? What shouldn't he or she have done?

Your friend spent hours in the sun and got a sunburn.
Your friend drank tap water and got sick.
Your friend stayed at a very bad hotel.
Your friend's wallet was stolen.
Your friend overslept and missed the flight back.

A: She shouldn't have spent so many hours in the sun.
B: She should have used sunscreen.

B **GROUP WORK** Have you ever had any bad experiences on a trip? What happened?

12 WRITING Advice needed

Write a post to a community blog about a real or imaginary problem. Put your drafts on the wall and choose one to write a reply to.

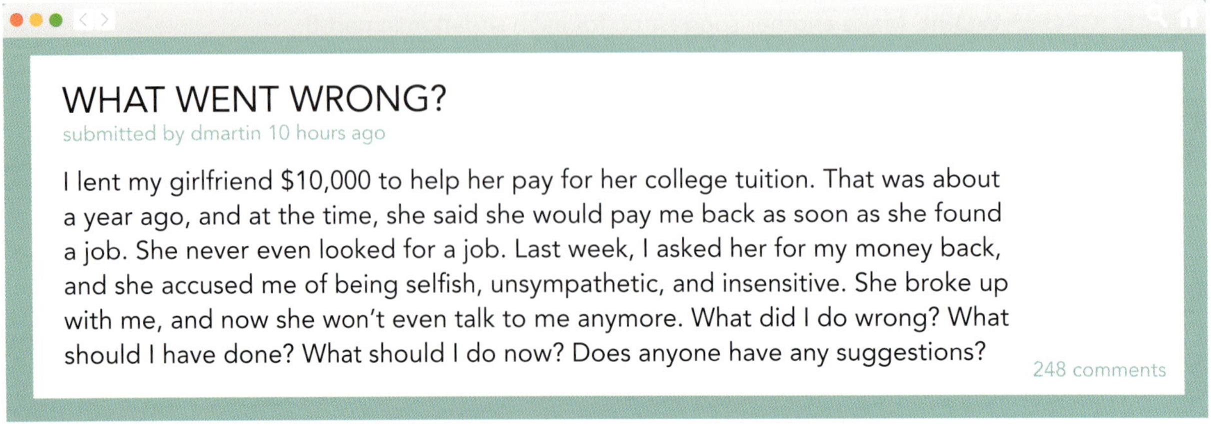

WHAT WENT WRONG?

submitted by dmartin 10 hours ago

I lent my girlfriend $10,000 to help her pay for her college tuition. That was about a year ago, and at the time, she said she would pay me back as soon as she found a job. She never even looked for a job. Last week, I asked her for my money back, and she accused me of being selfish, unsympathetic, and insensitive. She broke up with me, and now she won't even talk to me anymore. What did I do wrong? What should I have done? What should I do now? Does anyone have any suggestions?

248 comments

10 LISTENING

Learning Objective: listen for specific information in some conversations about difficult situations

- Set the scene. Explain that many people send messages to talk shows to ask for advice on personal problems. Ask Ss if they ever listen to such shows. If so, find out what kinds of problems people usually ask about.

A *[CD 3, Track 31]*

- Explain the task. Ss will hear two people's problems on a podcast. Ss take notes about each person's problem and complete the chart.
- Play the audio program, pausing after each email is read to give Ss time to take notes. Play the audio program again.

Audio script

See page T-181.

- Have Ss compare answers in pairs or groups. Then elicit responses from individual Ss.

TIP
To build Ss' confidence, have them compare answers before you ask them to speak in front of the whole class.

Answers

	Problem	What the person did
Ronnie	His dad wants him to study law, but he wants to study languages. They got in a fight.	He got really mad and told his dad he was selfish. Then he slammed the door.
Becca	Her boss welcomed a new employee for a new position, but she wanted a promotion or raise.	She never said anything to her boss about wanting a promotion or raise.

B *[CD 3, Track 32]*

- Play the audio program again. This time, tell Ss to listen for Dr. Jones's advice. Ask Ss to take notes.
- Go over answers with the class.

Answers

Ronnie: He shouldn't have told him he was selfish. He shouldn't have slammed the door.
Becca: She should have been more honest with her boss about wanting to grow in the company. She should have talked to him and expressed that a long time ago.

! For a new way to teach this Listening, try ***Stand Up, Sit Down*** – download it from the website.

C *Pair work*

- Ss discuss their opinions in pairs. Then ask Ss to share their ideas with the class.

11 SPEAKING

Learning Objective: discuss regrets using past modals

A *Pair work*

- Read the instructions and situations. Ss should think in pairs about what their friend should have done in each of the situations.
- Ss discuss what the friend should or shouldn't have done in the five situations. Go around the class and give help as needed.

B *Group work*

- Ss talk about their situations in small groups. Remind them to use the reduced form of *have* and to ask follow-up questions to get more details.

12 WRITING

Learning Objectives: write an email to an advice columnist; write a reply using past modals to give suggestions

- Write these questions on the board:
  Where were you? What happened?
  What was the problem? What did you do?
  How do you feel about the problem now?
- Explain the task. Ask a S to read the example post. Then tell Ss to think of a fun or interesting situation and make notes.
- Ss use their notes to write a short message to a community blog.
- Collect Ss' letters and give them to different Ss. Explain that Ss now play the role of the blogger and reply to someone else's message. When Ss finish, have them return the original message and their reply to the writer.

13 READING

Learning Objective: skim, scan, and identify meaning from context in online posts and comments

A

- Books closed. Explain that Ss are going to read posts on a message board. Some people are asking for advice about problems they are having, and others are giving it. Ask Ss to talk about what the kinds of problems people normally write about.
- Books open. Give Ss two minutes to skim the posts and determine what problem each person has. (Answers: Jack asks for advice about losing weight. Maya asks for advice about the best way to go sightseeing in Rio de Janeiro. Andrés asks for advice about whether to get a Master's or emigrate.)

B

- Explain the task. Ss match the names with the sentences.
- Check answers with the class.

TIP
To provide variety, have Ss check answers in groups of three. If their answers differ, find out why and give help as needed.

Answers

1. Andrés
2. Sarah
3. Marta
4. Jack
5. Dag
6. Maya

C

- Explain the task. Ss complete the task individually. Remind Ss to find the word in the article and to look at the context before guessing its meaning.
- Go over answers with the class.
- ***Option:*** For extra practice, ask Ss to write another sentence with these words or any other words they didn't know. Tell them to use their own information.

Answers

1. worth
2. fit in
3. be on the fence about

- Ask Ss if they have any questions about vocabulary. Encourage them to work together to explain any remaining words.

Vocabulary
overweight: too heavy or too fat
diet: a period when someone eats less food, or only particular types of food, because they want to become thinner
strict: must be followed or obeyed
give it a shot: try to do something, often for the first time
fit (something) in: find the time to see or do something
be on the fence: be unsure about what to do

! For another way to practice this vocabulary, try ***Vocabulary Mingle*** – download it from the website.

D

- Ss work in pairs or small groups to discuss the questions. After about five minutes, ask Ss to share their ideas with the class.
- ***Option:*** In pairs, Ss choose one of the posts. Then they role-play a conversation.

End of Cycle 2

See the Supplementary Resources chart at the beginning of this unit for additional teaching materials and student activities related to this Cycle.

13 READING

A Skim the three posts. What do Jack, Maya, and Andrés ask for advice about?

TOPTIPS.COM

HOME NEW ABOUT COMMUNITY SIGN IN

1 JACK – LONDON ♡ 12

I am overweight, and I'd really like to slim down. I've tried all kinds of diets, but none of them seem to work. And there's so much advice on the Internet – I don't know what to believe any more. What would you recommend?

I had the same problem until I tried a high protein/no carbohydrate diet. It was very strict – in the first couple of weeks you have to eat less than 40 grams of carbohydrates a day, so no bread, pasta, or potatoes! But I lost nine pounds in just 13 days, so for me it was worth it. I had a lot of meat and eggs and some butter, too, which was great! I'd give it a shot if I were you. (Sarah, Edinburgh)

2 MAYA – SAN FRANCISCO ♡ 22

I'm traveling to Rio de Janeiro next month, and I'd like to see as much of the city as possible. The problem is that I'm only going to be there for a couple of days, and I'm not sure how to fit everything in. Should I book an organized tour?

I was in Rio a couple of months ago. I travel a lot and like to be independent, so I chose to find my own way around the city. What a mistake! Rio's so big that I kept getting lost! And in the end, I didn't get to see the beach of Ipanema or the cathedral. It would have been nice to have somebody to talk to also. I really should have gone on a guided tour. (Dag, Oslo)

3 ANDRÉS – BOGOTÁ ♡ 11

I've just finished my degree, and I'm on the fence about what to do next. Here in Bogotá, there aren't many job possibilities right now. Should I go back to college to get a Master's? Or go stay with my cousin in New York and try to get a job there? (My English is not very good, by the way – a friend wrote this!)

Stay where you are! I moved to the United States from Poland and got a job as a server, but it's long hours and not much money. I haven't really made many friends, and I miss home. I should have stayed there and continued with my studies. (Marta, Krakow)

B Read the posts. Who would say these sentences? Write names from the posts.

1. Should I go abroad or stay where I am? ____________
2. It worked for me, so why don't you try it? ____________
3. I would have been happier if I hadn't moved. ____________
4. How can I choose the right eating plan? ____________
5. If I went there again, I'd definitely join a group. ____________
6. I don't have much time, so I need to be organized. ____________

C Find words or expressions in the posts to match these definitions.

1. Be an important or useful thing to do (post 1) ____________
2. Find enough time for something (post 2) ____________
3. To be unable to make a decision (post 3) ____________

D Do you agree with the advice given above? What advice would you give?

Unit 16 Supplementary Resources Overview

	After the following SB exercises	You can use these materials in class	Your students can use these materials outside the classroom
CYCLE 1	**1 Snapshot**	**TSS** Unit 16 Listening Worksheet	
	2 Perspectives		
	3 Grammar Focus		**SB** Unit 16 Grammar plus, Focus 1 **SS** Unit 16 Grammar 1 **GAME** Speak or Swim (Reported speech: requests)
	4 Speaking		
CYCLE 2	**5 Word Power**	**TSS** Unit 16 Vocabulary Worksheet	**SS** Unit 16 Vocabulary 1–2 **GAME** Say the Word (Verb-noun collocations)
	6 Conversation		**SS** Unit 16 Speaking 1
	7 Listening		
	8 Grammar Focus	**TSS** Unit 16 Grammar Worksheet	**SB** Unit 16 Grammar plus, Focus 2 **SS** Unit 16 Grammar 2–3 **GAME** Sentence Runner (Reported speech: statements)
	9 Pronunciation		**GAME** Sentence Stacker (*Had* and *would*)
	10 Writing	**TSS** Unit 16 Writing Worksheet	
	11 Speaking		
	12 Interchange 16		
	13 Reading	**TSS** Unit 16 Extra Worksheet **TSS** Unit 16 Project Worksheet **VID** Unit 16 **VRB** Unit 16	**SS** Unit 16 Reading 1–2 **SS** Unit 16 Listening 1–3 **SS** Unit 16 Video 1–3 **WB** Unit 16 exercises 1–8

With or instead of the following SB section	You can also use these materials for assessment
Units 15–16 Progress Check	**ASSESSMENT PROGRAM** Units 15–16 Oral Quiz **ASSESSMENT PROGRAM** Units 15–16 Written Quiz **ASSESSMENT PROGRAM** Units 9–16 Test

Key
GAME: Online Game
SB: Student's Book
SS: Online Self-study
TSS: Teacher Support Site
VID: Video DVD
VRB: Video Resource Book
WB: Online Workbook/Workbook

My Plan for Unit 16

Use the space below to customize a plan that fits your needs.

With the following SB exercises	I am using these materials in class	My students are using these materials outside the classroom

With or instead of the following SB section	I am using these materials for assessment

16 Making excuses

- Give reasons and explanations
- Discuss statements other people made

1 SNAPSHOT

Good Excuses, Poor Excuses

Not doing homework
- I was sure the assignment was due tomorrow.
- I emailed it to you, but it bounced back.

Arriving late to class
- My father didn't wake me up.
- My bike tire was flat because a dog bit it.

Missing work
- My cat was sick, and I had to take care of her.
- It was my birthday, and I always donate blood on that day.

Arriving late to work
- I worked on the new project until four in the morning, and then I overslept.
- My wife thinks it's funny to hide my car keys in the morning.

Arriving late for a date
- I was taking a telephone survey and lost track of the time.
- A horse running on the highway was holding up traffic.

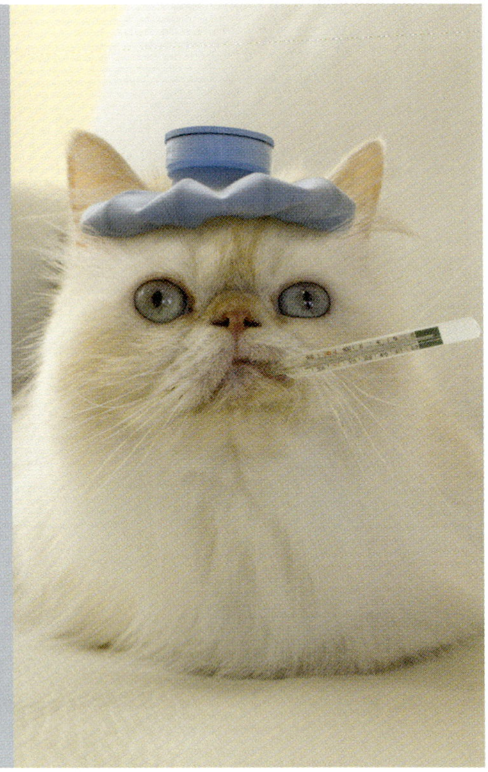

Which are good excuses? Which are poor ones?
What excuse do you usually use for these situations?
What excuses can you make for missing a date or party?

2 PERSPECTIVES At your request

A Who do you think made these requests? Listen and match.

1. She said to arrive on time for the meeting. ___
2. She asked me to pick up some food on the way home. ___
3. He said not to miss practice again. ___
4. She told me to hand in my homework before Friday. ___
5. She said to drink at least six glasses of water a day. ___
6. He asked me not to tell Mom about his new girlfriend. ___
7. He told me not to leave my bike in the apartment hallway. ___

a. my teacher
b. my boss
c. my brother
d. my doctor
e. my neighbor
f. my roommate
g. my coach

B PAIR WORK Can you think of another request each person might make?

A: Our teacher sometimes says, "Open your books."
B: A teacher could also say, "Repeat after me."

16 Making excuses

Cycle 1, Exercises 1–4

In Unit 16, students discuss statements other people made and practice giving reasons and explanations. By the end of Cycle 1, students will be able to discuss excuses and requests using reported speech. By the end of Cycle 2, students will be able to use reported speech to discuss statements that other people made.

1 SNAPSHOT

Learning Objective: discuss common excuses

- Books closed. Write these sentences on the board:

  I have to go. My battery is dying.
  I forgot to check my calendar. I'm sorry I'm late. I missed the bus.
  I can't go out with you. I have a boyfriend/girlfriend.

- Ask Ss what the sentences have in common. (Answer: They are all excuses.)
- Elicit some more excuses by giving situations (e.g., *being late for class, forgetting to do homework*).
- Books open. Focus Ss' attention on the cartoon. Ask: "What's happening? Why is she making an excuse? Do you think she's being honest?"
- Ss read the Snapshot silently. Answer any vocabulary questions (e.g., *assignment, due*) or elicit the meaning from other Ss.
- Give Ss a few minutes to look over the discussion questions and to think about their answers. Then Ss work in small groups to discuss them together. Go around the class and give help as needed.

2 PERSPECTIVES

Learning Objectives: discuss requests; identify reported speech for requests in context

A *[CD 3, Track 33]*

- Explain that Ss are going to hear some requests and decide who made each request.
- Play the first request in the audio program. Ask: "Who might make a request like this?" Elicit answers from the class.
- Play the audio program, pausing after each request to elicit ideas. Don't correct mistakes at this point.
- Ss read the sentences silently and match each request with a person.

TIP
Ask a S who finishes early to write the answers on the board.

Answers

1. b 2. f 3. g 4. a 5. d 6. c 7. e

- If necessary, explain or elicit the difference between the verbs *ask, tell,* and *say.*

  Ask leads to a question. Elicit the original questions from sentences 2 and 6, like this:

  She asked me, "Can you pick up some food on the way home?"
  He asked me, "Can you not tell Mom about my new girlfriend?"

  Point out that with *ask*, we have to say who we are asking (e.g., *she asked me/him/us*).

  Tell and *say* are very similar in meaning. The main difference is that *tell* is followed by a direct object, while *say* is not. For example:

  She told <u>me</u>, "Bring a dictionary tomorrow."
  She said, "Bring a dictionary tomorrow."

- Have Ss underline *asked me* and *told me* in the Perspectives section. Then play the audio program again. This time, focus Ss' attention on the use of *ask, tell,* and *say.*

B *Pair work*

- Explain the task. Ss look at the list of people. For each person, they think of another request they might make.
- Model the example conversation with a S and elicit more examples for a teacher. Remind Ss to use a direct object with *ask* and *tell.*
- Ss work in pairs to complete the task. Then each pair joins another pair to compare requests. Were there any similar requests? Which ones were different?
- Go around the class and write down any grammatical mistakes with *ask, say,* or *tell.* Then write the mistakes on the board and elicit corrections from the class.

3 GRAMMAR FOCUS

Learning Objective: use reported speech to make requests

[CD 3, Track 34]

TIP
To explain reported requests, it's helpful to draw pictures. If you have an artistic S, ask him or her to draw them for you.

- Draw a simple figure of a doctor on the board with a speech bubble coming from her mouth. In the bubble, write: "Drink six glasses of water a day."
- Then refer Ss to the Perspectives section. Ask: "What did the doctor say?" Write the reported request on the board:

  She said to drink six glasses of water a day.
- Explain that reported speech is used to talk about, or report, something that was asked or said in the past.
- Point out that the most common verbs for reporting requests are *ask*, *tell*, and *say*. They are used in the past tense to match the past action.
- Now draw another figure on the board with a speech bubble coming from his mouth. In the bubble, write: "Don't miss practice again." Elicit the reported request and write it on the board:

  He told me not to miss practice again.
- Make sure Ss understand how to form a reported request by explaining that:
  1. All three of these verbs are followed by an infinitive (e.g., *She asked me/told me/said to call her tonight.*).
  2. In a negative reported request, *not* is usually placed before the infinitive (e.g., *The coach asked/told me not to miss practice again.*).
- Play the audio program to present the sentences in the box. Ss listen and repeat.

A

- Ask Ss if they have ever thrown a surprise party. If so, have them say what happened. Encourage other Ss to ask follow-up questions for more information.
- Explain the situation. Then use the first request and example sentence to model the task.
- Ss work individually to write the reported requests before comparing answers with a partner. Elicit answers from the class.

Possible answers

2. He told them not to arrive late.
3. He asked them to bring some ice cream.
4. He asked them to help him make the sandwiches.
5. He asked them to bring a small gift for her.
6. He said not to spend more than $10 on the gift.
7. He told them to keep the party a secret.
8. He said not to say anything to the other teachers.

B *Group work*

- Tell Ss to imagine they are planning a party. Ss work individually to write four requests. Remind Ss to include requests with *Can you* and imperatives.
- Explain the task. Ss take turns reading their requests. Other Ss change the original requests into reported requests. Use the example conversation to model the task.
- Ss complete the task in small groups.

4 SPEAKING

Learning Objective: discuss recent requests using reported speech

A

- Explain the task. Ss think of two things they were asked to do and two things they were asked not to do.
- Ss work individually to complete the chart. Go around the class and give help as needed.

B *Group work*

- Go over the task. Ss use the information in the chart and reported speech to talk about recent requests. Others ask follow-up questions to get more information. Elicit useful expressions (e.g., *What request has someone made recently? Who made it? When? Why? Did you perform the request?*).
- Ss complete the activity in small groups.

End of Cycle 1

See the Supplementary Resources chart at the beginning of this unit for additional teaching materials and student activities related to this Cycle.

3 GRAMMAR FOCUS

Reported speech: requests

Original request	Reported request
Arrive on time for the meeting.	She **said to arrive** on time for the meeting. She **told me to arrive** on time for the meeting.
Don't leave your bike in the apartment hallway.	He **said not to leave** my bike in the hallway. He **told me not to leave** my bike in the hallway.
Can you pick up some food on the way home?	She **asked me to pick up** some food.

GRAMMAR PLUS *see page 147*

A Victor is organizing a surprise birthday party for his teacher. Look at what he told his classmates. Write each request using *say, tell,* or *ask*. Then compare with a partner.

1. Meet at my apartment at 7:30. *He told them to meet at his apartment at 7:30.*
2. Don't arrive late. ______
3. Can you bring some ice cream? ______
4. Can you help me make the sandwiches? ______
5. Can you bring a small gift for her? ______
6. Don't spend more than $10 on the gift. ______
7. Keep the party a secret. ______
8. Don't say anything to the other teachers. ______

B **GROUP WORK** Imagine you're planning a class party. Write four requests. Then take turns reading your requests and changing them into reported requests.

Edu: Bring something to eat to the party!
Eva: Edu told us to bring something to eat.

Aki: Can you help me clean up after the party?
Jim: Aki asked us to help her clean up.

4 SPEAKING That's asking too much!

A Think of requests that people have made recently. Write two things people asked you to do and two things people asked you *not* to do.

Person	Request
My boss	*shave off my beard*

B **GROUP WORK** Talk about the requests that each of you listed in part A. Did you do what people requested? Did you give an excuse? What was it?

5 WORD POWER Verb-noun collocations

A Find three more nouns that are usually paired with each verb. The same noun can be paired with more than one verb. Then compare with a partner.

an apology	an invitation	a request
a complaint	a joke	a solution
an excuse	a lie	a story
an explanation	an offer	a suggestion
an idea	a reason	the truth

make	*a request*			
give	*an excuse*			
tell	*a joke*			
accept	*an apology*			
refuse	*an invitation*			

B **PAIR WORK** How do you deal with the things in part A? Tell a partner.

A: What do you do when a close friend makes a difficult request?

B: I give a good explanation, and I offer to help in another way. What about you?

6 CONVERSATION Are you doing anything on Sunday?

A Listen and practice.

Gabriel Hi, Craig.

Craig Oh, hi, Gabriel. How are things?

Gabriel Just fine, thanks. Uh, are you doing anything on Sunday night?

Craig Hmm. Sunday night? Let me think. Oh, yes. My brother just called, and he told me he had tickets to the basketball finals. I said I would go with him.

Gabriel Oh, that's too bad! It's my birthday. I'm having dinner with Tina, and I thought I'd invite more people and make it a party.

Craig Oh, I'm really sorry, but I won't be able to make it.

Gabriel I'm sorry, too. But that's OK.

B **PAIR WORK** Act out the conversation in part A. Make up your own excuse for not accepting Gabriel's invitation.

5 WORD POWER

Learning Objective: discuss behaviors using *accept, give, make, offer, refuse,* and *tell*

A

- Explain the task. Elicit any new or unfamiliar vocabulary. If necessary, have Ss use their dictionaries.
- Help the class begin by asking about one or two of the verbs, like this:

  T: What word or phrase goes with the verb *make*?
  S: I think you can *make a complaint* in English.
  T: You're right. That's one. What's another?
- Ss complete the chart individually or in pairs.
- To check answers, write the verbs on the board and have Ss write their answers beside each verb.

Possible answers

make a complaint, an excuse, an invitation, a request, a suggestion
give an excuse, an explanation, a reason, a solution, a suggestion
tell the truth, a lie, a story, a joke
accept an invitation, an apology, an offer, an idea, a suggestion
refuse an invitation, an apology, an offer, an idea, a suggestion

B *Pair work*

- Go over the instructions. Ask Ss to write a sentence for each of the nouns in part A. Set a time limit. Then go around the class and give help as needed. To prepare for follow-up questions, tell Ss to include explanations in their sentences.
- Have two Ss read the example conversation to model the task. Remind Ss to ask follow-up questions. Elicit a few example questions and write them on the board:

  Do you normally make complaints? Where? Do you make written or verbal complaints?
  Do you like to tell jokes? Why don't you tell jokes more often?
  In what situation would you tell a lie?
- Ss take turns asking and answering their questions in pairs. After about five minutes, ask pairs to share some of their responses with the class.

For more practice with this vocabulary, play ***Tic-Tac-Toe*** – download it from the website.

6 CONVERSATION

Learning Objectives: practice a phone conversation between two friends; see examples of reported speech for statements in context

A *[CD 3, Track 35]*

- Books closed. Explain the situation. Gabriel is inviting Craig to his birthday party on Sunday, but Craig can't go because he has plans with his brother. Ask Ss what they would do if that happened to them. Would they cancel their plans or make another suggestion to celebrate the friend's birthday?
- Write these questions on the board:

  1. *Does Craig make an excuse? An apology?*
  2. *How does Gabriel respond? Does he express anger? Disappointment?*
- Play the audio program. Have Ss listen for the answers. (Answers: 1. He makes an excuse *and* an apology. 2. Gabriel expresses disappointment.)
- ***Option:*** Have a brief class discussion. Ask: "What would you have done if you were Craig?"
- Books open. Play the audio program again. Ss read silently as they listen. Ask Ss to listen for emotions expressed by the speakers (e.g., *That's too bad. Oh, I'm really sorry.*).
- Elicit or explain any new vocabulary.

Vocabulary
How are things?: How are you?
Oh, that's too bad!: I'm sorry to hear that something disappointing/bad has happened.
make it: go to an event

- Ss practice the conversation in pairs. To imitate the feeling of talking on the phone, have them sit back-to-back.

B *Pair work*

- Ss act out the conversation using their own words. Make sure the S playing Craig makes up a new excuse for not being able to make it to the party. Then have Ss change roles and repeat the task.

7 LISTENING

Learning Objective: listen for details in some conversations about a party

A *[CD 3, Track 36]*

- Focus Ss' attention on the picture of Gabriel on the phone. Set the scene. Ss will hear four phone conversations in which Gabriel's friends make excuses for not coming to his birthday party.
- Tell Ss to look at the four names and try to guess their excuses. Then play the audio program. Ss listen and complete the task.

Audio script

See page T-182.

- Elicit Ss' responses to check answers.

Answers

1. Grant: He said he was going with his parents to visit his aunt. She lives an hour outside the city.
2. Sayo: She said she was going to help her mom with the food and games for her little sister's birthday.
3. Diego: He said that he had to pick up his dad at the airport.
4. Carrie: She said that she was sick. She thought she had the flu.

B *[CD 3, Track 37]*

- Play the rest of the audio program. Ss listen and take notes.

Audio script

See page T-183.

- Elicit responses from the class. Play the audio program again if necessary.

Answer

Gabriel's friends surprise him and celebrate his birthday with him.

C *Pair work*

- Tell Ss to talk with their partners about the last party they went to.

8 GRAMMAR FOCUS

Learning Objective: use reported speech to make statements

[CD 3, Track 38]

- Write this excuse from Exercise 7 on the board:

Direct statement	Reported statement
"I'm going with my parents to visit my aunt."	He said he was going with his parents to visit his aunt.

- Ask Ss to look at the underlined verbs. Elicit what happens when we report a statement. (Answer: We don't use the same tense to report someone's original sentence. Here, the original sentences use the present tense and the reported statements use the past tense.)
- Have Ss look at the sentences in the Grammar Focus box. Go over the direct statements with present and past form verbs and modals to show how the verbs move back one tense in the reported statements.
- Write the following on the board:

Direct statement	Reported statement	
be →	was/were	present tense
have/go →	had/went	present tense
(made) →	had (made)	past tense
have (planned) →	had (planned)	present perfect
can	could	modal
will	would	modal
may	might	modal

- Play the audio program. Ss listen and repeat.

A

- Read the instructions and the first item, including the example answer. Ss work individually to write a reported statement for each excuse. Then Ss compare answers in pairs. Elicit Ss' responses.

Answers

1. Mason said/told her (that) he already had plans for Saturday.
2. Olivia said/told her (that) her in-laws were coming over for dinner that night.
3. Ben and Ava said/told her (that) they had been invited to a graduation party on Saturday.
4. Felipe said/told her (that) he had promised to help his sister with her homework.
5. Tae-yun said/told her (that) she couldn't come because she had broken her leg.
6. Osvaldo said/told her (that) he would be moving this weekend.
7. Lisa and Henry said/told her (that) they would have to pick someone up at the airport that evening.
8. Omar said/told her (that) he might have to work the night shift on Saturday.

B *Group work*

- Explain the task. Ss think of excuses to tell Isabella. In small groups, Ss take turns reading their excuses. Other Ss change the excuses into reported speech.

7 LISTENING Making excuses

A Listen to Gabriel invite his friends to his birthday party on Saturday. What excuses do they give for not going? Write them below.

1. Grant: ______________________
2. Sayo: ______________________
3. Diego: ______________________
4. Carrie: ______________________

B Listen. What happens on the night of Gabriel's birthday?

C **PAIR WORK** What was the last party you went to? Describe it to your partner.

8 GRAMMAR FOCUS

Reported speech: statements

Direct statements	Reported statements
I'm not feeling well.	She **said** (that) she **wasn't feeling** well.
I **have** houseguests for the weekend.	she **had** houseguests for the weekend.
I **made** a tennis date with Kim.	she **had made** a tennis date with Kim.
I **have planned** an exciting trip.	she **had planned** an exciting trip.
We **can't come** tomorrow.	They **told me** (that) they **couldn't come** tomorrow.
We **will be** out of town.	they **would be** out of town.
We **may go** out with friends.	they **might go** out with friends.

GRAMMAR PLUS see page 147

A Isabella is having a party at her house on Saturday. Look at these excuses. Change them into reported speech. Then compare with a partner.

1. Mason: "I already have plans for Saturday."
2. Olivia: "My in-laws are coming over for dinner that night."
3. Ben and Ava: "We've been invited to a graduation party on Saturday."
4. Felipe: "I promised to help my sister with her homework."
5. Tae-yun: "I can't come because I broke my leg."
6. Osvaldo: "I'll be moving this weekend."
7. Lisa and Henry: "We have to pick someone up at the airport that evening."
8. Omar: "I may have to work the night shift on Saturday."

Mason said he already had plans for Saturday. OR
Mason told her he already had plans for Saturday.

B **GROUP WORK** Imagine you don't want to go to Isabella's party. Take turns making excuses and changing them into reported speech.

A: I'm sorry, I can't go. I'm going camping this weekend.
B: Lucky guy! He said he was going camping this weekend.

9 PRONUNCIATION Reduction of *had* and *would*

A Listen and practice. Notice how *had* and *would* are reduced in the following sentences.

She said she**'d made** the bed. (She said she **had made** the bed.)
She said she**'d make** the bed. (She said she **would make** the bed.)

B Listen to four sentences. Check (✓) the reduced form that you hear.

1. ☐ had ☐ would **2.** ☐ had ☐ would **3.** ☐ had ☐ would **4.** ☐ had ☐ would

10 WRITING About my classmates

A Interview your classmates and take notes. Use your notes to write a report describing what people told you. Use reported speech.

	Name	Response
What did you do last night?		
What movie have you seen recently?		
Where are you going after class?		
What are your plans for the weekend?		
What will you do on your next birthday?		

B **GROUP WORK** Read your report, but don't give names. Others guess the person.

"Someone said that he'd go to Paris on his next vacation."

11 SPEAKING You can make it.

A **GROUP WORK** What are some things you would like to do in the future? Think of three intentions.

A: I'm going to take an English course abroad.
B: That sounds fun. Have you decided where?

B **CLASS ACTIVITY** Report the best intentions you heard. Then give suggestions.

B: Noriko said she was going to take an English course abroad, but she hadn't decided where.
C: She could go to Australia. My brother attended a very good school there. He told me he studied incredibly hard!

12 INTERCHANGE 16 Just a bunch of excuses

Make some plans. Student A, go to Interchange 16A on page 129; Student B, go to Interchange 16B on page 131.

9 PRONUNCIATION

Learning Objective: sound more natural by reducing *had* and *would* in reported speech statements

A *[CD 3, Track 39]*

- Write these contractions of *I had* and *I would* on the board:

  I had = I'd   I would = I'd
- Explain that these two are easily confused. Play the audio program. Have Ss listen to the pronunciation of the reduced forms of *had* and *would* in the sentences. Then play the audio program again, pausing after each sentence for Ss to practice.
- ***Option:*** Ss read reported speech sentences 3, 4, and 6 from Exercise 8A. Remind them to reduce *had* and *would*.

B *[CD 3, Track 40]*

- Explain the task. Ss listen to four sentences and check (✓) whether they hear a reduction of *had* or *would*. Point out that they can only decide this by paying attention to the verb that comes after the contraction.
- Play the audio program. Ss listen and check the boxes. Then elicit answers.

Audio script

See page T-183.

Answers

1. would 2. had 3. had 4. would

10 WRITING

Learning Objective: write a report with reported speech

A

- Explain the task. Ss walk around the room asking questions and completing the chart.
- Ss then write down the resulting responses in the form of reported statements.
- ***Option:*** Ss write their reports as homework.

B *Group work*

- Explain the task and read the example statement. In groups, Ss take turns reading their reports, one item at a time. They should not say the name of the person who responded. Group members guess who made each response. Walk around and help as needed.
- Ask Ss if any statements were very easy to guess.

11 SPEAKING

Learning Objectives: discuss future intentions; use reported speech

- Elicit or explain the meaning of the title *You can make it.* Then focus Ss' attention on the picture. Ask: "What do you think the man's intentions are?" Elicit answers from the class.

A *Group work*

- Explain the task. Ss think of three intentions. Then they discuss their intentions in small groups. Remind Ss to ask follow-up questions to get more information.
- ***Option:*** Award one point for every follow-up question a S asks. Ss keep track of their own scores.
- Go around the class and listen. Write down common errors. Then go over errors with the whole class.
- ***Option:*** Ss try the activity again in different groups.

TIP

To increase Ss' speaking time, have them complete a task a second time with a new challenge (e.g., focusing on pronunciation, grammar, fluency, or length of conversation).

! For another way to teach this Speaking exercise, try ***Moving Dialog*** – download it from the website. Ss begin like this:

S1: What would you like to do?
S2: I'm going to . . .

B *Class activity*

- Have Ss use reported speech to tell the class the best intentions they heard. Other Ss ask questions and make predictions about the intentions.

12 INTERCHANGE 16

See page T-130 for teaching notes.

13 READING

Learning Objective: summarize and make inferences in an article about communication

A

- Books closed. Ask Ss: "What are some good reasons for missing school or work?" Elicit answers from the class.
- ***Option:*** Books closed. Dictate the first paragraph to Ss. Read it twice at a normal speed. Ss take notes and then work in pairs to reconstruct the paragraph. When Ss finish, have them open their books to check their answers.
- Books open. Give Ss two minutes to skim the article and find three common reasons for missing work. (Answers: *health reasons, household accidents, transportation problems*)

B

- Ss read the article silently and then correct the summary. Tell them not to worry about new vocabulary. Go over answers with the class.

Answers

U.S. workers take just under a **week** in sick days a year. The **most** frequently used excuses are for health reasons. When employees take a sick day, it's important to explain the reason to their **employers**. It's OK to take a day off **only if there is actually something wrong with you**.

- Have Ss read the article again, underlining words or phrases they can't guess from context. When Ss finish, encourage them to check their dictionaries for the definitions.
- ***Option:*** Ss look up new words for homework.
- To make sure Ss understand important vocabulary, write the word or phrase on the board and tell the class to find it in the article. Have a S read the complete sentence in which it appears. Then ask Ss to give their own definition or an example for it.

Vocabulary

average: typical; normal
employee: someone who is paid to work for a person or company
fire: tell someone they must leave their job
stomachache: pain in your stomach
day off: a day when you do not work or go to school
household: connected with or belonging to a home
slip: to slide by accident and fall or almost fall

C

- Explain the task. Read the first sentence and point out the word in the text that matches the definition. Ask Ss to complete the task and compare their answers in pairs. Then go over answers with the class.

Answers

1. fired
2. excuse
3. privacy
4. sympathize
5. (advance) notice

D

- Ask each S to report a common excuse and a silly excuse they heard.

End of Cycle 2

See the Supplementary Resources chart at the beginning of this unit for additional teaching materials and student exercises related to this Cycle.

13 READING

A Scan the article. What are three common reasons for missing work?

A GOOD EXCUSE FOR A DAY OFF WORK

1 **On average, U.S. employees take 4.9 sick days per year. Usually this does not cause any particular problems. But when employees take sick leave without a good reason, it can quickly become an issue. In fact, in one survey, 18 percent of employers said that they had fired an employee for taking days off without a good reason. The key is to understand what reasons are acceptable and what reasons are not. Generally, most excuses for sick days fall into one of three categories.**

2 The most common reasons for not going to work are health-related. It would probably be OK to tell your boss that you ate something bad last night and that you have a stomachache. Of course you might not want to share the details of a health issue with your boss – after all, you do have the right to privacy. If you don't want to be too specific, you can just tell your boss that you have a small medical issue and need to take the day off.

3 Household accidents are the second category of reasons for not going in to work. You might call your boss to say you slipped in the shower and hurt your knee. This is a common accident and one that your boss will sympathize with. However, if you are going to be out of work for several days due to an injury, it's important to make arrangements with your employer. See if you can work from home, or at least make sure there is someone to cover your work.

4 The third type of sick day use isn't really about illness, but it's about something else you can't control: transportation problems. The car might not start, there may be a terrible traffic jam, or there could be delays on the subway. Some employers may be sympathetic to absences due to transportation problems, but others may not. It's important to know your boss and to understand whether he or she will accept an excuse like this.

5 Regardless of the reason for the sick day, there are a few things you can do to make missing work more acceptable to your employer. Try to keep sick days to a minimum. When you do need to take a sick day, give your employer as much advance notice as possible. Finally, never take a sick day if there isn't anything wrong with you – the only good excuses are the ones that are true.

B Read the article. Then correct four mistakes in the summary of the article.

U.S. workers take just under a month in sick days a year. The least frequently used excuses are for health reasons. When employees take a sick day, it's important to explain the reason to their colleagues. It's OK to take a sick day, even if you feel fine, as long as you give an excuse.

C Find words in the text to match these definitions.

1. told someone to leave his or her job (paragraph 1) ______
2. an explanation given for something (paragraph 1) ______
3. someone's right to keep information about his or her personal life secret (paragraph 2) ______
4. understand or care about someone's problems (paragraph 3) ______
5. a warning that something is about to happen (paragraph 5) ______

D What other excuses do people make for not going to work or class? What's the silliest excuse you have ever heard?

Units 15–16 Progress check

SELF-ASSESSMENT

How well can you do these things? Check (✓) the boxes.

I can . . .	Very well	OK	A little
Discuss imaginary events (Ex. 1)	☐	☐	☐
Ask for and give advice and suggestions about past events (Ex. 2)	☐	☐	☐
Understand and report requests (Ex. 3)	☐	☐	☐
Discuss statements other people made (Ex. 4)	☐	☐	☐

1 DISCUSSION Interesting situations

A What would you do in these situations? Complete the statements.

If I forgot to do my homework, ______________________________.
If I found a valuable piece of jewelry in the park, ______________________________.
If a friend gave me a present I didn't like, ______________________________.
If I wasn't invited to a party I wanted to attend, ______________________________.
If someone took my clothes while I was swimming, ______________________________.

B **GROUP WORK** Compare your responses. For each situation, choose one to tell the class.

A: What would you do if you forgot to do your homework?
B: I'd probably tell the teacher the truth. I'd ask her to let me hand it in next class.

2 SPEAKING Predicaments

A Make up two situations like the one below. Think about experiences you have had or heard about at work, home, or school.

"An old friend from high school visited me recently. We had a great time at first, but he became annoying. He made a big mess, and he left his things all over the place. After two weeks, I told him he had to leave because my sister was coming for the weekend."

B **PAIR WORK** Take turns sharing your situations. Ask for advice and suggestions.

A: What would you have done?
B: Well, I would have told him to pick up his clothes, and I would have asked him to clean up his mess.

Units 15–16

Progress check

SELF-ASSESSMENT

Learning Objectives: reflect on one's learning; identify areas that need improvement

- Ask: "What did you learn in Units 15 and 16?" Elicit Ss' answers.
- Ss complete the Self-assessment. Explain to Ss that this is not a test; it is a way for them to evaluate what they've learned and identify areas where they need additional practice. Encourage them to be honest, and point out they will not get a bad grade if they check (✓) "A little."
- Ss move on to the Progress check exercises. You can have Ss complete them in class or for homework, using one of these techniques:
  1. Ask Ss to complete all the exercises.
  2. Ask Ss: "What do you need to practice?" Then assign exercises based on their answers.
  3. Ask Ss to choose and complete exercises based on their Self-assessment.

1 DISCUSSION

Learning Objective: demonstrate one's ability to speculate about imaginary events

A

- Explain the task and answer any vocabulary questions.
- Tell Ss to think of interesting suggestions for the first situation (e.g., *I'd ask the teacher for an extension. I'd say my dog ate it.*).
- Ss work individually to write one suggestion for each situation. Set a time limit. Go around the class and give help as needed.

B *Group work*

- Explain the task. Ss work in groups to compare the statements they wrote in part A.
- Ask two Ss to read the example conversation. Encourage them to ask follow-up questions to continue the conversation.
- Explain that after discussing each situation, the group decides on the best suggestion. Then someone in the group writes it down.
- Ss form groups and choose a secretary. Set a time limit of about ten minutes for Ss to compare their suggestions and choose their favorites.
- Have groups read their best suggestions to the class. Encourage others to ask questions or to make comments.
- ***Option:*** Take a class vote on which suggestion they like most for each situation.

2 SPEAKING

Learning Objective: demonstrate one's ability to ask for and give opinions and suggestions about past events

A

- Present the situation in the example by focusing Ss' attention on the picture. Then tell Ss to think of two similar situations based on experiences they have had at work, home, or school.
- Ss work individually to write two situations. Go around the class and give help as needed.

B *Pair work*

- Ask two Ss to read the example conversation. Encourage Ss to ask follow-up questions. Remind them to use the reduced form of *have*.
- Ss work in pairs to take turns reading their situations and asking for advice and suggestions.
- Go around the class and write down any common errors, especially past modals. When time is up, write the errors on the board and have Ss correct them. Praise correct uses of past modals that you heard.

3 LISTENING

Learning Objective: demonstrate one's ability to understand and pass on requests

A *[CD 3, Track 41]*

- Explain the task. Ss listen to people making requests and match each request to the correct person.
- Play the audio program. Ss listen and complete the task. Then go over answers with the class.

Audio script

See page T-183.

Answers

1. parent	3. doctor	5. boss
2. neighbor	4. classmate	6. teacher

B *[CD 3, Track 42]*

- Explain the task. Ss write each request. Then play the audio program again, pausing after each conversation to give Ss time to write.
- Ss complete the task. Then go over answers with the class.

Answers

1. Please pick up your things.
2. Can you move your car?
3. Don't take more than three a day.
4. Can I borrow your notes?
5. Please come into my office.
6. Can we leave now?

C *Pair work*

- Explain the task. Then use the example to model the task for the class.
- Ss form pairs and take turns reporting the requests to each other. Go around the class and listen to make sure Ss are able to use reported requests.

4 GAME

Learning Objective: demonstrate one's ability to report what people say

A

- Explain the task and read the example. Give Ss time to think of and write three statements, one for each situation. Go around the class and give help as needed.

B *Class activity*

- Divide the class into groups of three. Tell each group to compare their statements and to choose one that they would like to talk about.
- ***Option:*** Ss continue to work in groups of three. The two Ss who did not experience the situation ask the third S detailed questions about it. They should find out as much as possible about the situation.
- Explain the task. In groups of three, Ss come to the front of the classroom and each read the same statement aloud. The rest of the class asks the three Ss questions. Make sure the class understands that only one of the Ss experienced the situation. The goal is to find out which of the three Ss really experienced the situation.
- Go over the three steps and the example questions with the class. Ask these questions to be sure that everyone in the class understands what to do: "How many contestants are telling the truth? How many are not? How can you find out who isn't telling the truth? What do you do when you discover someone isn't telling the truth?"
- Invite the first group to the front of the class to read their situation. Encourage the rest of the class to ask questions. Remind Ss to use reported speech when they discover who isn't telling the truth.

WHAT'S NEXT?

Learning Objective: become more involved in one's learning

- Focus Ss' attention on the Self-assessment again. Ask: "How well can you do these things now?"
- Ask Ss to underline one thing they need to review. Ask: "What did you underline? How can you review it?"
- If needed, plan additional instruction, activities, or reviews based on Ss' answers.

3 LISTENING A small request

A Listen to the conversations. Check (✓) the person who is making the request.

1. ☐ child ☐ parent **2.** ☐ neighbor ☐ teacher **3.** ☐ child ☐ doctor **4.** ☐ teacher ☐ classmate **5.** ☐ boss ☐ neighbor **6.** ☐ neighbor ☐ teacher

B Listen again. Complete the requests.

1. Please ______________________.
2. Can ______________________?
3. Don't ______________________.
4. Can ______________________?
5. Please ______________________.
6. Can ______________________?

C **PAIR WORK** Work with a partner. Imagine these requests were for you. Take turns reporting the requests to your partner.

"My dad told me to pick up my things."

4 GAME Who is lying?

A Think of situations when you expressed anger, gave an excuse, or made a complaint. Write a brief statement about each situation.

I once complained about the bathroom in a hotel.

B **CLASS ACTIVITY** Play a game. Choose three students to be contestants.

Step 1: The contestants compare their statements and choose one. This statement should be true about only one student. The other two students should pretend they had the experience.

Step 2: The contestants stand in front of the class. Each contestant reads the same statement. The rest of the class must ask questions to find out who isn't telling the truth.

Contestant A, what hotel were you in?

Contestant B, what was wrong with the bathroom?

Contestant C, what did the manager do?

Step 3: Who isn't telling the truth? What did he or she say to make you think that?
"I don't think Contestant B is telling the truth. He said the bathroom was too small!"

WHAT'S NEXT?

Look at your Self-assessment again. Do you need to review anything?

Interchange activities

INTERCHANGE 1

Learning Objectives: speak more fluently about the past using *used to*; ask follow-up questions with the past tense

A *Class activity*

- Focus Ss' attention on the title of this activity. Have Ss look at the information in the chart. Ask: "What do you think you have in common with your classmates?"
- Explain that the things Ss learn about one another in this activity will help them learn more about their classmates' personalities and past experiences.
- Read the instructions and go over the chart. Elicit questions 5–8.

Answers

5. Did you change schools when you were a child?
6. Did you use to argue with your brothers and sisters?
7. Did you get in trouble a lot as a child?
8. Did you use to have a favorite toy?

- Model the task with a S.

  T: Did you ever want to be a movie star?

  S: Yes. I used to want to be an actor.

  T: Did you use to act at school?

  S: No. But I wanted to.
- Write the S's name in the Name column and the information in the Notes column. Explain that if a classmate says "no," they should ask another S the same question.
- Check that the class understands the instructions by asking questions like these: "When someone says 'yes,' what do you do? Do you write the person's name or the word *yes* in the Name column?" (Answer: the person's name)

Interchange activities

INTERCHANGE 1 We have a lot in common.

A CLASS ACTIVITY Go around the class and find out the information below. Then ask follow-up questions and take notes. Write a classmate's name only once.

Find someone who . . .	Name	Notes
1. wanted to be a movie star **"Did you ever want to be a movie star?"**		
2. always listened to his or her teachers **"Did you always listen to your teachers?"**		
3. used to look very different **"Did you use to look very different?"**		
4. had a pet when he or she was little **"Did you have a pet when you were little?"**		
5. changed schools when he or she was a child "_______________?"		
6. used to argue with his or her brothers and sisters "_______________?"		
7. got in trouble a lot as a child "_______________?"		
8. used to have a favorite toy "_______________?"		

B GROUP WORK Tell the group the most interesting thing you learned about your classmates.

114 Interchange 1

- Set a time limit of about ten minutes. Remind Ss to ask follow-up questions to get more information.
- Encourage Ss to get up and move around the classroom. Go around the class and take note of any problems that Ss may be having. Go over any errors at the end of the activity.

B *Group work*

- In small groups, Ss take turns sharing the most interesting information they learned about their classmates.
- ***Option:*** If you have only one S, have the S ask you the questions about your life or you can think of a famous person and have your S ask questions to find out who it is.

INTERCHANGE 2 Top travel destinations

A **PAIR WORK** Look at the photos and slogans below. What do you think the theme of each tourism campaign is?

Possible themes

art	culture	entertainment
food	history	music
nature	shopping	sports

Cartagena
"The Colorful Caribbean"

New Orleans
"The Birthplace of Jazz"

Cairo
"The Earth's Mother"

Bangkok
"Thailand Old and New"

B **GROUP WORK** Imagine you are planning a campaign to attract more tourists to one of the cities above or to a city of your choice. Use the ideas below or your own ideas to discuss the campaign.

a good time to visit
famous historical attractions
special events or festivals
nice areas to stay
interesting places to see
memorable things to do

A: Do you know when a good time to visit Cartagena is?
B: I think between December and April is a good time because . . .

C **GROUP WORK** What will be the theme of your campaign? What slogan will you use?

Interchange 2 115

INTERCHANGE 2

Learning Objective: speak more fluently about tourism in one's town or city using indirect questions

- ***Option:*** Bring some English-language travel brochures to class. Have Ss discuss the ads in pairs or small groups. Then ask Ss to share the most interesting ads/brochures with the rest of the class.
- Books closed. Ask Ss if they know the slogan for their city or another city (e.g., *Quito, Ecuador, is called The City of Eternal Spring; New York City is called The Big Apple.*).
- Explain that to attract more tourists to a city, a tourism board uses a theme to build a campaign. This theme usually involves something special about the city. In this activity, Ss plan a campaign to attract tourists to a city.

A *Pair work*

- Books open. Present the slogans for each city listed and explain any new vocabulary. Be careful not to give away the theme of each campaign.

Vocabulary
colorful: having many different colors
birthplace: the place where a person or thing was born.

- Focus Ss' attention on the first photo and slogan. Ask: "What does this slogan mean? According to its slogan, what is special about Cartagena? Art? Culture? Food? Architecture?"
- Ss discuss each slogan and theme in pairs. Then have each pair join another pair to compare answers.

Answers

Cartagena – culture (history and architecture), nature, and entertainment
New Orleans – music, entertainment, culture (architecture and history)
Cairo – culture and history
Bangkok – culture (history and architecture)

B *Group work*

- Read the instructions, list of ideas, and example conversation. Explain the task. Ss work in groups to choose a city and discuss how it is special. Encourage Ss to be as creative as possible.
- Ss choose a city and discuss each idea on the list. Go around the class and give help as needed.

Tip
To make group work more effective, assign each student in the group a role (e.g., a note-taker, a language monitor, a leader, and a person who will report back to the class).

C *Group work*

- Explain the task. Ss work in the same groups from part B to discuss possible themes and slogans.
- Groups take turns sharing their ideas with the rest of the class.
- ***Option:*** To turn this activity into a project, have Ss research a city and prepare a poster with photos and maps or create a slide show with presentation software. Display Ss' work on a wall or bulletin board in the classroom or in a school magazine or website.

INTERCHANGE 3

Learning Objectives: speak more fluently about how people would like to change their lives using *wish*; ask follow-up questions

A

- Focus Ss' attention on the title of this activity. Explain that it refers to something you have wanted very much for a long time that has now happened. When people say "a dream come true," they mean that something finally becomes a reality.
- Explain the task and read the ten questions in the chart. Ss repeat for correct pronunciation, stress, and intonation. Tell Ss to write a complete sentence beginning with *I wish (that) I . . .* to answer each question. Go around the class and give help as needed. Tell Ss they can write either realistic or unrealistic wishes.
- ***Option:*** Ss can complete the chart in class or for homework.

B *Pair work*

- Explain the task and model the example conversation with Ss. Demonstrate how to keep the conversation going, like this:

  T: And how about you? What possession do you wish you had?

  S: Me? I really wish I had a small house far from the city.

  T: Really? Why?

  S: Well, I could go there on weekends, and I'd have time to relax and read a lot of books.
- Tell Ss to take notes while interviewing their partners to use later in part C.
- Ss form pairs and take turns asking and answering the questions in part A. Encourage Ss to extend their conversations by asking for additional information. Go around the class and give help as needed.

INTERCHANGE 3 **A dream come true**

A Complete this questionnaire with information about yourself.

My Wish List

1. What possession do you wish you had? I wish I had ________
2. What sport do you wish you could play? ________
3. Where do you wish you could live? ________
4. What skill do you wish you had? ________
5. What kind of home do you wish you could have? ________
6. What kind of vacation do you wish you could take? ________
7. What languages do you wish you could speak? ________
8. Which musical instruments do you wish you could play? ________
9. What famous person do you wish you could meet? ________
10. What kind of pet do you wish you could have? ________

B **PAIR WORK** Compare your questionnaires. Take turns asking and answering questions about your wishes.

A: What possession do you wish you had?
B: I wish I had a sailboat.
A: Really? Why?
B: Well, I could sail around the world!

C **CLASS ACTIVITY** Imagine you are at a class reunion. It is ten years since you completed the questionnaire in part A. Tell the class about some wishes that have come true for your partner.

"Victor is now a famous explorer and sailor. He has sailed across the Atlantic and to the South Pole. Right now, he's writing a book about his adventures on his boat."

116 Interchange 3

C *Class activity*

- Read the instructions and explain that a class reunion is a meeting of former classmates. Read the description of Victor, who is now a famous explorer and sailor.
- Model the activity by asking Ss about their partners. Write the information on the board and demonstrate how to use it to make an interesting description:

  Wish List - #3: Terry wishes he could live in the U.S. He wishes he could live near the beach so he could swim and windsurf every day.

  Ten-Year Reunion Statement: Terry moved to California five years ago. His dream has finally come true. He goes swimming and windsurfing every day!
- Give Ss a few minutes to go over their notes from part B. Then encourage them to make up one or two interesting or amusing sentences to describe their partner ten years from now. Go around the class and give help as needed.
- Ss take turns reading their descriptions to the class.

INTERCHANGE 4 Oh, really?

A How much do you really know about your classmates? Look at the survey and add two more situations to items 1 and 2.

	Name	Notes
1. Find someone who has . . . a. cooked for more than twenty people b. found something valuable c. lost his or her phone d. been on TV e. cried during a movie f. ____________ g. ____________		
2. Find someone who has never . . . a. been camping b. gone horseback riding c. fallen asleep at the movies d. played a video game e. baked cookies f. ____________ g. ____________		

B **CLASS ACTIVITY** Go around the class and ask the questions. Write the names of classmates who answer "yes" for item 1 and "no" for item 2. Then ask follow-up questions and take notes.

A: Have you ever cooked for more than 20 people?
B: Yes, I have. Last year I cooked for the whole family on Mother's Day.
A: How was it?
B: Well, my mother had to help me.

A: Have you ever been camping?
C: No, I haven't.
A: Why not?
C: Because I don't like mosquitoes.

C **GROUP WORK** Compare the information in your surveys.

Interchange 4 117

INTERCHANGE 4

Learning Objective: speak more fluently about past experiences

A

- Focus Ss' attention on the title. Explain that it is a phrase used to react to surprising information. In this activity, the phrase suggests that Ss might learn surprising things about their classmates.
- Read the question and instructions. Explain that a survey is a set of questions that you ask a large number of people to learn about their opinions or behavior. Ss will use this survey to discover what kinds of interesting experiences their classmates have had.
- Go over the situations listed in the chart. Elicit or explain any new vocabulary.
- Encourage Ss to be creative when they add two more situations to each item. Point out that this should be fun. The situations shouldn't embarrass or upset anyone.
- ***Option:*** Give some examples of things that people in the United States and Canada don't usually ask casual acquaintances about (e.g., *age, religion, politics, salary, cost of expensive or personal items*).
- Ss work individually to add four more situations. Go around the class and give help, especially on situations concerning cultural appropriateness.

B *Class activity*

- Explain the task and model the activity by reading the example conversations with Ss.
- Demonstrate when and how to write down classmates' names in the survey. If necessary, use the board to show how to take notes on additional information.
- ***Option:*** For lower-level classes, elicit the question for each item from the class.
- Set a time limit of about ten minutes. Ss stand up and move around the class to ask and answer each other's questions. Go around the class and give help as needed. Encourage Ss to change partners frequently.
- When time is up, see if Ss have filled in most of the chart. If not, give them a few more minutes to complete the task.

C *Group work*

- Ss compare their information in groups. Help them get started by writing these sentences on the board:

I found out that . . . (name) has . . .
Did you know that . . . (name) has never . . . ?
Did anyone find someone who has never . . . ?
When/Why/How did that happen?

INTERCHANGE 5A/B

Learning Objective: speak more fluently about vacation activities and plans using *be going to* and *will*

- Books closed. Ask: "Has anyone ever taken a hiking trip or a surfing trip?" If so, have the other Ss ask questions about the trip.
- Divide the class into pairs. Then assign each S an A or a B part.
- Books open. Tell Student As to look at Interchange 5A and Student Bs to look at Interchange 5B. Remind them not to look at each other's pages.
- Answer any questions about the instructions for the role play, the information in their brochures, or new vocabulary.

Vocabulary

Interchange 5A
beachfront: having a view of the sea
catamaran: boat with two side-by-side floating parts
hula: a traditional Hawai'ian dance
Interchange 5B
single room: a room for one person
double room: a room for two people
lodge: a small house in the country that is used especially by people on vacation
rafting: the sport or pastime of traveling down a river on a small boat
cruise: sailing from place to place on a ship
stargazing: looking at stars
sing-along: an informal occasion when people sing together in a group

- If necessary, separate the two groups. Go over Interchange 5A with Student As. When they understand what to do, they prepare their questions and roles. Then do the same with Student Bs and the information in Interchange 5B.

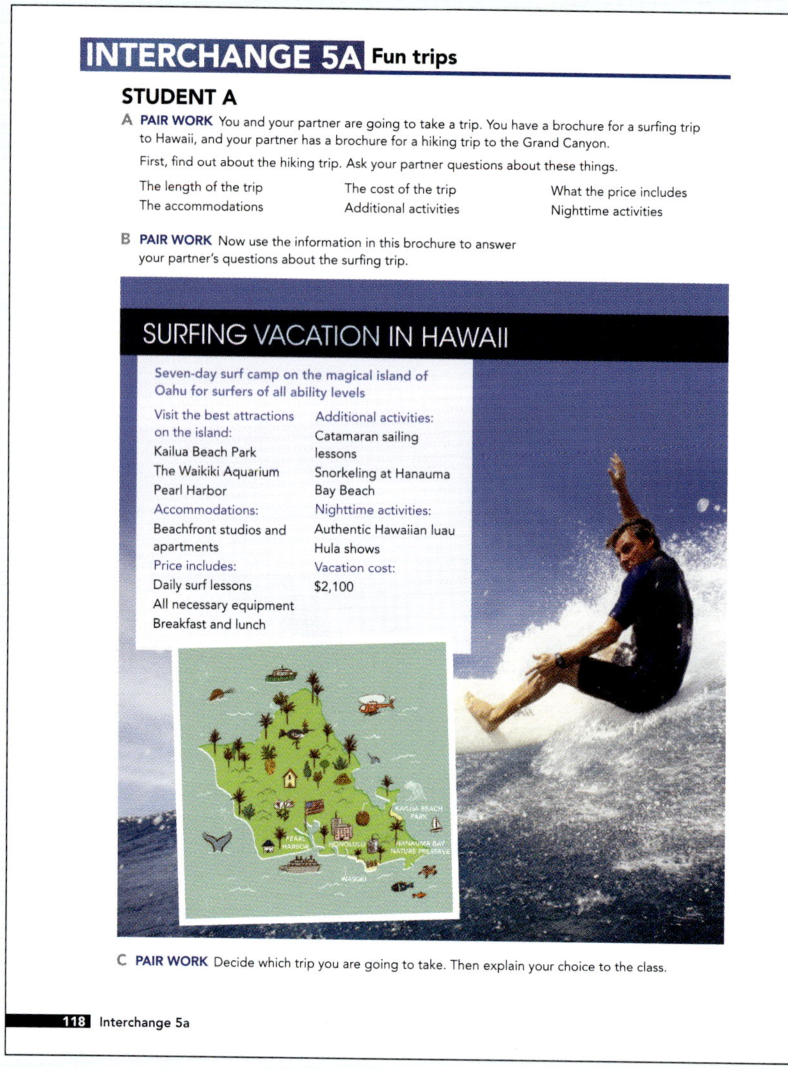

INTERCHANGE 5A Fun trips

STUDENT A

A **PAIR WORK** You and your partner are going to take a trip. You have a brochure for a surfing trip to Hawaii, and your partner has a brochure for a hiking trip to the Grand Canyon.

First, find out about the hiking trip. Ask your partner questions about these things.

The length of the trip	The cost of the trip	What the price includes
The accommodations	Additional activities	Nighttime activities

B **PAIR WORK** Now use the information in this brochure to answer your partner's questions about the surfing trip.

SURFING VACATION IN HAWAII

Seven-day surf camp on the magical island of Oahu for surfers of all ability levels

Visit the best attractions on the island:
Kailua Beach Park
The Waikiki Aquarium
Pearl Harbor

Accommodations:
Beachfront studios and apartments

Price includes:
Daily surf lessons
All necessary equipment
Breakfast and lunch

Additional activities:
Catamaran sailing lessons
Snorkeling at Hanauma Bay Beach

Nighttime activities:
Authentic Hawaiian luau
Hula shows

Vacation cost:
$2,100

C **PAIR WORK** Decide which trip you are going to take. Then explain your choice to the class.

118 Interchange 5a

A Pair work

- Model the role play with a Student B. Demonstrate how to start the activity by making up questions to ask about the hiking trip: "How much does the trip cost? What does the price include? What is the accommodation like? Are any additional activities available? Will there be any entertainment/ nightlife?"
- If Student B needs help answering the questions, elicit answers from other Student Bs.

INTERCHANGE 5B Fun trips

Student B

A **PAIR WORK** You and your partner are going to take a trip. You have a brochure for a hiking trip to the Grand Canyon, and your partner has a brochure for a surfing trip to Hawaii.

First, use the information in the brochure to answer your partner's questions about the hiking trip.

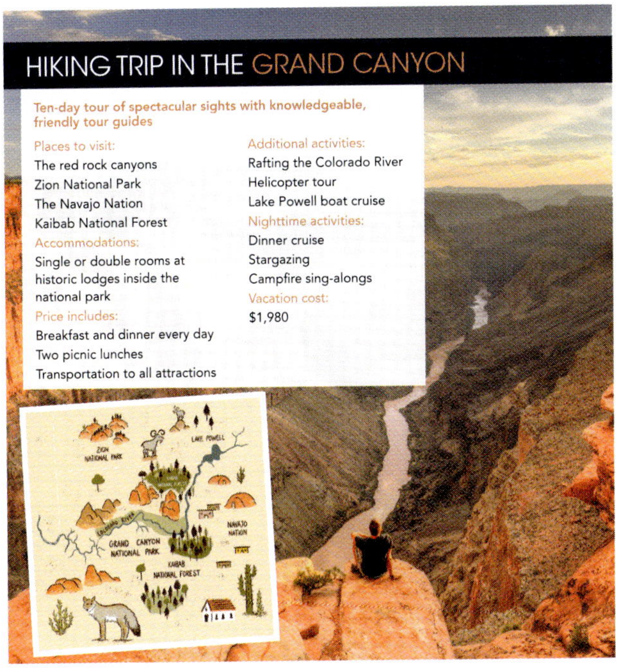

B **PAIR WORK** Now find out about the surfing trip. Ask your partner questions about these things.

The length of the trip	The cost of the trip	What the price includes
The accommodations	Additional activities	Nighttime activities

C **PAIR WORK** Decide which trip you are going to take. Then explain your choice to the class.

- Set a time limit of five minutes for part A of the role play. Student As start by asking questions about the hiking trip. Student Bs answer by using the information on their page and making up information. Go around the class and take note of any common errors.
- When time is up, go over any errors you observed with the class.

B *Pair work*

- Student Bs ask questions about the surfing trip. Set a time limit of five minutes. Go around the class and give help as needed. Remind Student As that they can make up additional information if they wish.

C *Pair work*

- Go over the instructions. Tell Ss to discuss what they would like to do and not do on their trips. Encourage Ss to ask follow-up questions and suggest additional information.
- Pairs take turns telling the class which trip they are going to take and why.

INTERCHANGE 6

Learning Objective: speak more fluently when apologizing and making requests

A *Pair work*

- Divide the class into pairs and assign each S an A or a B part.
- Explain the task. Point out that this activity is a series of four different role plays. Ss should use their own language, expressions, and vocabulary. Tell pairs to look at each picture while they perform that particular role play.
- Give the class a few minutes to look at the four situations and cues. Point out that Student A and Student B will each get two chances to make a complaint and two chances to apologize.
- Answer any questions that Ss may have about the situations or vocabulary they might want to use.
- ***Option:*** For each picture, brainstorm words and write Ss' suggestions on the board. If necessary, add some of these words to the board:

  Picture 1
  movie, phone, loud, pay attention, hear, reception

  Picture 2
  server, customer, problem, meal, order

  Picture 3
  meeting, late, presentation, car trouble, family problems, oversleep

  Picture 4
  host, vase, break, replace, pay, clumsy, embarrassed, upset

- Model the first example conversation with a S to show how Student A could begin and how Student B might reply. Try to keep the conversation going for at least a minute. Encourage Ss to have fun by using appropriate gestures and facial expressions.

INTERCHANGE 6 I'm terribly sorry.

A **PAIR WORK** Look at these situations. Act out conversations. Apologize and then give an excuse, admit a mistake, or make an offer or a promise.

useful expressions	
I'm sorry. / I didn't realize. / I forgot.	You're right. / I was wrong.
I'll . . . right away.	I'll make sure to . . . / I promise I'll . . .

1

Student A: You are trying to watch the movie.
Student B: You are talking on your phone.
A: Excuse me. I'm trying to watch the movie. Could you please turn off your phone?
B: I'm so sorry . . .

2

Student A: You are the server.
Student B: You are one of the customers.
A: Oh, I'm terribly sorry . . .
B: ______

3

Student A: You have just arrived for the meeting.
Student B: You are making a presentation.
A: I'm sorry I'm late . . .
B: ______

4

Student A: You are the host.
Student B: You broke the vase.
A: Oh, no! My vase.
B: ______

B **GROUP WORK** Have you ever experienced situations like these? What happened? What did you do? Share your stories.

Interchange 6 119

S: Excuse me. I'm trying to watch the movie. Could you please turn off your phone?
T: I'm so sorry, but I can't. It's my boss on the phone.
S: So can you go to the other room?
T: No, sorry, the reception is very bad there. I'm so sorry. I will be done in just five minutes, I promise.
S: Ok, I can wait, thank you.
T: Thank you. And I'm really sorry again.

- Have Ss practice each situation. Encourage Ss to stand up or move around.

B *Group work*

- Tell Ss to join another pair. Ss discuss experiences they have had that were similar to the situations in part A. Ss can also talk about other similar situations.
- ***Option:*** Call on one S from each group to share one of the stories from the group with the class. Ss can also write down their story for homework.

INTERCHANGE 7 Free advice

A **GROUP WORK** Look at the problems people have. What advice would you give each person? Discuss possible suggestions and then choose the best one.

1

"I'm moving to a new apartment with two roommates. How can I be sure we get along well and avoid problems?"

2

"A co-worker has asked to borrow my brand-new mountain bike for the weekend. I don't want to lend it. What can I say?"

3

"My family and I are going away on vacation for two weeks. How can we make sure our home is safe from burglars while we're gone?"

4

"I have an important job interview next week. How can I make sure to be successful and get the job?"

5

"I'm going to meet my future in-laws tomorrow for the first time. How can I make a good impression?"

6

"I'm really into social networking, but in the past week, five people I hardly know have asked to be my friends. What should I do?"

B **PAIR WORK** Choose one of the situations above. Ask your partner for advice. Then give him or her advice about his or her problem.

A: I'm moving to a new apartment with two roommates. How can I be sure we get along well?
B: Make sure you decide how you are going to split the household chores. And remember to . . .

Interchange 7 121

INTERCHANGE 7

Learning Objective: speak more fluently when giving advice using imperatives and infinitives

A *Group work*

- Books closed. To introduce the activity, ask Ss if they ever get advice from friends or family. Is the advice usually good?
- Books open. Focus Ss' attention on the pictures. Six people are talking about their problems. Have Ss look at the problems.
- Elicit or explain any new words and expressions (e.g., *roommates, get along, burglars, in-laws*) or have Ss check their dictionaries.
- Explain the task. Ss think of possible advice for each person. Elicit Ss' suggestions for the first person. Write some of their ideas on the board.

  - Make sure to be polite.
  - Don't forget to divide the household chores.
  - Talk about the house rules.
  - Respect their privacy.
  - Try to be friends.

- Ss form small groups and brainstorm advice for each person. Remind them that *advice* is a noncount noun. To make it plural, we say "pieces of advice." Then give Ss a time limit.

Tip
To keep Ss on task, remind them of the time throughout the activity (e.g., "You have two minutes left.").

- When time is up, have each group choose their best piece of advice for each situation.

B *Pair work*

- Explain that this activity gives each S a chance to ask for suggestions or give advice. Model the first person's problem with a S. Read the example conversation with the S. Then elicit additional suggestions.
- Divide the class into pairs and have them share their problems and advice. Set a time limit of five minutes. Remind the advice giver to give at least four suggestions for each situation. Encourage Ss to be creative, improvise, and have fun.
- In pairs, Ss take turns talking about their problems. The person with the problem starts first. Go around the class and listen. If Ss are having problems, stop the activity, go over the difficulties, and suggest solutions. If necessary, model a different situation.
- ***Option:*** Have Ss perform for the class.

INTERCHANGE 8

Learning Objectives: speak more fluently about holidays; ask follow-up questions and use common expressions to show interest

A *Class activity*

- Read the instructions. Then ask Ss to read the questions in the chart for unknown words. Explain any new vocabulary.

Vocabulary
traditional clothes: a costume or an outfit that is typical (or historical) in a particular country
get-together: a friendly, informal party

- Call on Ss to read the questions aloud, and check for correct pronunciation, stress, and rhythm. If necessary, model the correct pronunciation.
- Explain the task. Ss stand up and go around the room, asking classmates questions. If the classmate answers "yes," they write the classmate's name in the column and ask some follow-up questions. Then they write some notes before talking to another classmate. Remind them to talk to as many Ss as possible.
- Point out the need to ask follow-up questions and to give extra information when answering. Elicit some expressions to show interest (e.g., *That sounds like fun! That's interesting. Really? Tell me more! Wow!*).
- To practice asking follow-up questions, model the first two or three questions and elicit Ss' suggestions.
  1. Who was the party for? Did everyone arrive before the birthday boy/girl? Was the party a real surprise or did anyone tell?
  2. Who gave you the gift? Was it your birthday? Was it a gift you asked for?
  3. On what occasion? What do you wear? Does everybody wear the same thing?

INTERCHANGE 8 It's worth celebrating.

A CLASS ACTIVITY How do your classmates celebrate special occasions? Go around the class and ask the questions below. If someone answers "yes," write down his or her name. Ask for more information and take notes.

Question	Name	Notes
1. Have you ever given someone a surprise party?		
2. What's the best gift you have ever received?		
3. Do you ever wear traditional clothes?		
4. Have you bought flowers for someone special recently?		
5. Do you like to watch parades?		
6. Does your family have big get-togethers?		
7. Has someone given you money recently as a gift?		
8. Will you celebrate your next birthday with a party?		
9. Do you ever give friends birthday presents?		
10. What's your favorite time of the year?		
11. Do you ever celebrate a holiday with fireworks?		

A: Have you ever given someone a surprise party?
B: Yes. Once we gave my co-worker a surprise party on his birthday.
A: How was it?
B: It was great. He never suspected that we were planning it, so he was really surprised. And he was very happy that we got his favorite cake!

B PAIR WORK Compare your information with a partner.

122 Interchange 8

- Ss complete the activity. Set a time limit of about ten minutes. Go around the class and give help, particularly if there are communication problems.

B *Pair work*

- Ss form pairs and compare their information. With a S, model how they should begin their discussion.

T: Let's start with the first question. Have you ever given someone a surprise party?
S: Rodrigo's family loves to give surprise parties. Every birthday they call the whole family and try to surprise the birthday boy/girl with something special. He knows he is going to have a party every year, but he acts surprised anyway.

- ***Option:*** Ask pairs to tell the class some interesting things they learned about their classmates.

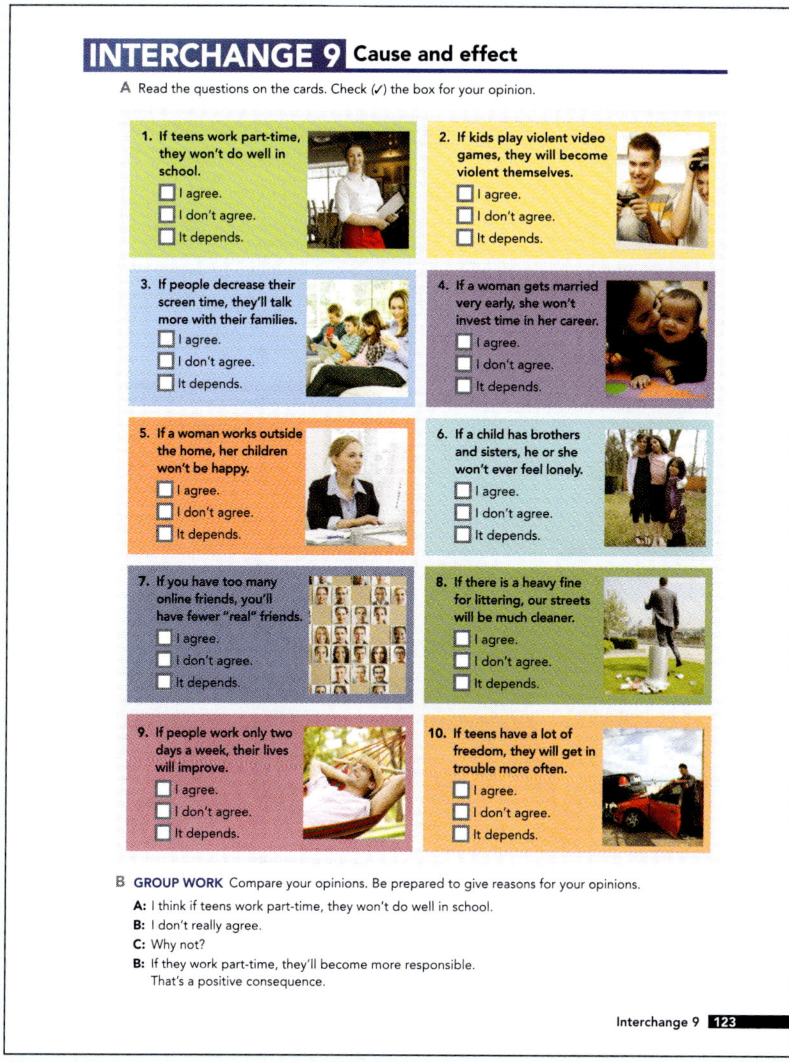

INTERCHANGE 9 Cause and effect

A Read the questions on the cards. Check (✓) the box for your opinion.

1. If teens work part-time, they won't do well in school.
   - ☐ I agree.
   - ☐ I don't agree.
   - ☐ It depends.
2. If kids play violent video games, they will become violent themselves.
   - ☐ I agree.
   - ☐ I don't agree.
   - ☐ It depends.
3. If people decrease their screen time, they'll talk more with their families.
   - ☐ I agree.
   - ☐ I don't agree.
   - ☐ It depends.
4. If a woman gets married very early, she won't invest time in her career.
   - ☐ I agree.
   - ☐ I don't agree.
   - ☐ It depends.
5. If a woman works outside the home, her children won't be happy.
   - ☐ I agree.
   - ☐ I don't agree.
   - ☐ It depends.
6. If a child has brothers and sisters, he or she won't ever feel lonely.
   - ☐ I agree.
   - ☐ I don't agree.
   - ☐ It depends.
7. If you have too many online friends, you'll have fewer "real" friends.
   - ☐ I agree.
   - ☐ I don't agree.
   - ☐ It depends.
8. If there is a heavy fine for littering, our streets will be much cleaner.
   - ☐ I agree.
   - ☐ I don't agree.
   - ☐ It depends.
9. If people work only two days a week, their lives will improve.
   - ☐ I agree.
   - ☐ I don't agree.
   - ☐ It depends.
10. If teens have a lot of freedom, they will get in trouble more often.
    - ☐ I agree.
    - ☐ I don't agree.
    - ☐ It depends.

B **GROUP WORK** Compare your opinions. Be prepared to give reasons for your opinions.

A: I think if teens work part-time, they won't do well in school.
B: I don't really agree.
C: Why not?
B: If they work part-time, they'll become more responsible. That's a positive consequence.

Interchange 9 123

INTERCHANGE 9

Learning Objective: speak more fluently about consequences in an informal debate

A

- Explain that Ss are going to have a chance to give their views on several different topics.
- Tell Ss to read the instructions and go over the ten statements in the questionnaire. If Ss have questions about any words or phrases in the questionnaire, tell them to check their dictionaries. If necessary, explain any new words or phrases.

Vocabulary

It depends: I would have different answers in different circumstances.
will become violent themselves: will be influenced by the violence they see and start doing things that hurt other people
heavy fine: a large amount of money that people must pay for doing something wrong
littering: throwing trash on the ground

- Model the task. Read the first statement and ask Ss to raise their hands if they agree. Then tell those Ss to check (✓) the first box. Ask the rest of the class: "How many of you don't agree? How many think it depends?"
- Ss work independently to complete the questionnaire. Go around the class and give help as needed.

B *Group work*

- Explain the task. Then model the example conversation with several Ss.
- Give Ss a few minutes to look back at the choices they made in part A. Tell Ss to make a few notes (e.g., examples, details, extra information) to explain the reasons for their opinions.
- Ss compare opinions in small groups. Go around the class and listen. Don't interrupt the discussions if Ss are communicating freely and easily with one another.

INTERCHANGE 10

Learning Objective: speak more fluently about job skills in an interview

A *Pair work*

- Explain the activity. Ss read the example job description *Activities Director*. Focus Ss' attention on the categories *Requirements* and *Responsibilities*. Tell pairs to think about some jobs and choose one.
- ***Option:*** Before Ss start the activity, brainstorm some job names and write them on the board. Ss choose one of them to do the exercise.

Vocabulary

activities director: an employee on a cruise ship that is in charge of all onboard entertainment
experience: knowledge or skill that you gain from doing a job or an activity
people person: a person who enjoys or is particularly good at interacting with others
outgoing: friendly, sociable; enjoys meeting people
responsibility: a task you must do
ship: a large luxury boat that people ride for travel and entertainment
onboard: available or situated on a ship, aircraft, or other vehicle
entertainment: shows, films, television, or other performances or activities that entertain people

- Tell Ss to think about what experience applicants need and what the job responsibilities are.

B *Pair work*

- Present the useful questions box. Then model how to start the role play with a S.

T: Well, let's start with work experience. What kind of degree do you have?
S: Uh, I have a bachelor's degree in business.
T: Oh? That sounds good. Where did you go to school?
S: At the University of Miami.
T: That's a good school. Do you have any work experience?
S: Actually, I don't have any, but I learn fast . . .

INTERCHANGE 10 **You're hired.**

A **PAIR WORK** Look at the following job description. Write an ad for your ideal job.

JOB FINDER | About | Careers | Education | Job search

Activities Director

Requirements:	*Responsibilities:*
Experience working with tourists A "people person" Outgoing and creative personality	Organize all leisure activities on a popular cruise ship, including planning daily tours, special onboard activities, and nightly entertainment

B **PAIR WORK** Take turns interviewing your classmates for the job you have created. Get as much information as you can to find the right person for the job.

useful questions
What kind of degree do you have?
What work experience do you have?
What hours can you work?
Do you mind . . . ?
Are you interested in . . . ?
Why should I hire you for the job?

C **GROUP WORK** Who would you hire for the job you posted? Why?

D **CLASS ACTIVITY** Compare the ideal jobs you created in part A. How are they similar? How are they different?

124 Interchange 10

- Ss form pairs and decide who will interview first and for which job. Set a time limit of about five minutes. Encourage Ss to have fun and to be creative during their discussion. Go around the class and take note of things that pairs are doing well or that could be improved.
- When time is up, go over your observations with the class.
- Ss exchange roles and try the interview again. Go around the class and give help as needed.

C *Group work*

- Tell Ss that their next task is to discuss their interview notes and decide who to hire for each job. Remind them to explain their reasons.
- ***Option:*** You may want to share some cultural information about hiring practices in North America. For example, by law, an employer is not allowed to discriminate against a person because of race, religion, age, gender, or marital status. To avoid this, employers cannot ask personal questions.

D *Class activity*

- Ask Ss what jobs they chose to write about and write job titles on the board. Ask Ss to describe how the listed jobs are similar and different.
- ***Option:*** As homework, ask Ss to research their job further. Where can they work? What kind of extra courses should they take? Ss bring answers to class and share what they learned.

INTERCHANGE 11 True or false?

A List one movie, one TV show, one song, and one book.

B **GROUP WORK** Take turns making statements about each item. Does everyone agree with each statement?

A: *Titanic* was filmed on a small lake in Mexico.
B: Are you sure? Wasn't it filmed on the ocean?
C: I'm pretty sure it was filmed in a plastic pool. I read it on the Internet.

C Now think of other famous creations and creators. Complete the chart. Make some of the items true and some false.

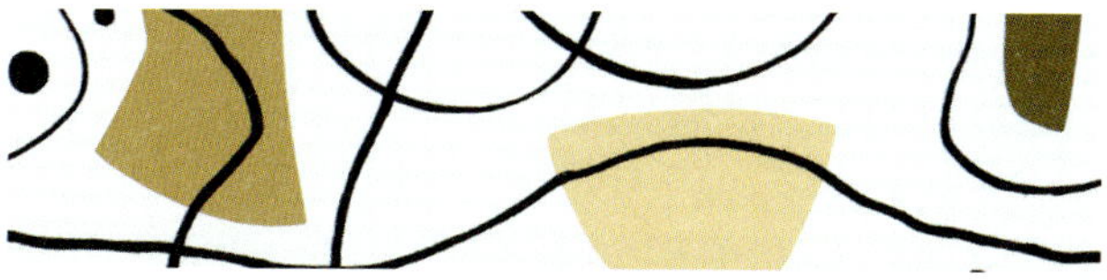

1.	The Martian movie	direct	director
2.	painting	was painted by paint	painter
3.	play	write	William Shakespeare playwright
4.	song	record	singer
5.	book	write	writer
6.	invention	invent	inventor

D **GROUP WORK** Make a statement about each item to your group members. Ask them to decide which statements are true and which are false.

A: The movie *The Martian* was directed by Steven Spielberg.
B: I think that's true.
C: No, that's false. It was directed by Ridley Scott. I'm sure of it.

Interchange 11 125

INTERCHANGE 11

Learning Objective: speak more fluently about works of art using the passive with and without *by*

A

- Explain that Ss are going to make up statements about movies, books, songs, inventions, and works of art. First, Ss write down the name of a movie, a TV show, a song, and a book. Set a time limit.

B *Group work*

- Explain that Ss have to make one statement about each item they listed. Point out the first line of the example conversation ("*Titanic* was filmed in a small lake in Mexico") as an example.
- To help Ss, draw the following chart on the board:

The movie The song The book	was	written directed produced sung filmed recorded	in by	(date) (name)
(name)	won	an Oscar a Grammy an award	in for	(movie) (song)
(name)	played	the role of the guitar/ drums	(name) in on	(movie) (song)

- When Ss have written one sentence about each item, explain the task. In groups, Ss take turns making their statements. The others in the group listen and agree or disagree.
- Model the example conversation with Ss. Point out some ways to disagree politely with someone (e.g., *Are you sure?/I'm not sure. I think . . ./Wasn't it . . . ?/I don't agree.*). Then Ss begin the discussion.
- ***Option:*** If a group disagrees about a statement but doesn't know the answer, tell them to check the answer before the next class.
- ***Option:*** Have Ss share some new and interesting facts they learned with the class.

C

- Ask Ss to read the instructions silently and to look at the chart. Elicit or explain any new vocabulary.
- Point out the first example (The Martian *was directed by . . .*). Elicit films and directors from the class. Then give Ss time to complete the statements. Remind them to include some false statements.
- ***Option:*** Ss may do this part for homework.

D *Group work*

- Explain the task. Ask three Ss to read the example conversation.
- Ss form groups. Tell them to take turns reading the statements aloud and deciding which are true. If a statement is false or if Ss don't agree, they should discuss. Set a time limit of about five minutes. Go around the class and give help as needed.
- When time is up, Ss share their statements with the class.
- ***Option:*** Groups can compete against each other by reading their statements aloud. Other groups say which are true and get one point for each correct answer. After all groups have read their statements, total the points. The group with the most points wins.

INTERCHANGE 12

Learning Objective: speak more fluently about one's life experiences

A *Group work*

- Divide the class into groups of four or five Ss each. Then go over the instructions to make sure the class understands how to play.
- Give Ss a few minutes to make small markers with their own initials on them. Tell Ss that the markers must be small enough to fit on the squares of the board game. Then make sure that each group has a coin to toss. Go around the class and help the Ss decide which side of the coin is "heads" (face up) and which side is "tails" (face down).
- Model the example conversation with Ss. Then start again with a new sentence (e.g., *During middle school, I played the clarinet.*) and have Ss ask you follow-up questions.
- Set a time limit of about 20 minutes for the game. Ss take turns tossing the coins and moving their markers forward around the board. Go around the class and give help as needed. Remind groups to ask at least two follow-up questions after each S makes a statement.
- If more than one group finishes early, have them change players to form new groups and play again giving different answers.
- ***Option:*** Ss earn one point for each follow-up question they ask. Ss keep track of their own score.
- Stop the activity when time is up or, if the Ss are enjoying the game, let them continue playing until one S in each group finishes.

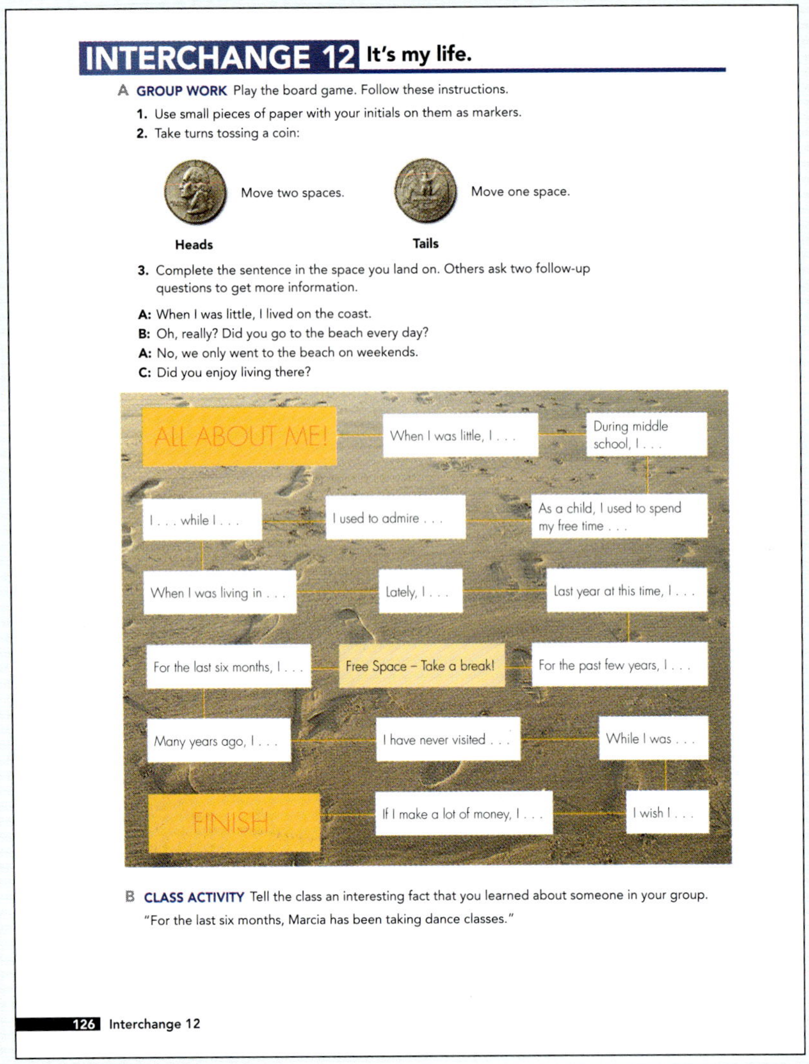
INTERCHANGE 12 It's my life.

A GROUP WORK Play the board game. Follow these instructions.

1. Use small pieces of paper with your initials on them as markers.
2. Take turns tossing a coin:

Heads — Move two spaces.
Tails — Move one space.

3. Complete the sentence in the space you land on. Others ask two follow-up questions to get more information.

A: When I was little, I lived on the coast.
B: Oh, really? Did you go to the beach every day?
A: No, we only went to the beach on weekends.
C: Did you enjoy living there?

B CLASS ACTIVITY Tell the class an interesting fact that you learned about someone in your group.
"For the last six months, Marcia has been taking dance classes."

126 Interchange 12

B *Class activity*

- Read the example sentence to model the activity. Then ask groups or individual Ss to share something interesting they learned about their classmates.

INTERCHANGE 13 It was hilarious!

A Complete the questionnaire.

What is the name of a TV show or movie . . . ?

1. that made you laugh a lot
2. that made you feel sad
3. that you have seen more than once
4. which had great music
5. that was about a silly story

What is the name of a TV or movie star . . . ?

6. who is very talented
7. who is famous but not very talented
8. who does things to help society
9. who is an excellent comedian
10. that reminds you of someone you know

B **PAIR WORK** Compare your questionnaires. Ask follow-up questions of your own.

A: What's the name of a TV show or movie that made you laugh a lot?
B: *Grown Ups 2.*
A: Really? Why?
B: I thought the movie was hilarious.
A: Who was in it?
B: Adam Sandler. I always enjoy his movies.
A: Well, I liked his earlier movies better.

INTERCHANGE 13

Learning Objective: speak more fluently about popular entertainment

A

- Write these topics on the board:

  TV stars *movie stars*
  TV shows *movies*

- Ss form pairs and brainstorm names associated with one of the topics. Give Ss a time limit of one or two minutes.
- Read the question and phrases in the questionnaire aloud. Explain any new vocabulary or have Ss check their dictionaries.
- ***Option:*** Model each of the ten questions in the chart (e.g., *What is the name of a TV show or movie that made you laugh a lot?*). Have Ss repeat to practice good pronunciation, intonation, and word stress. Ss complete the task individually. Go around the class and give help as needed.
- Ss complete the questionnaire individually. Give Ss a time limit of one or two minutes.

B *Pair work*

- Explain the task. Have two Ss read the example conversation. Elicit more follow-up questions and write the suggestions on the board.
- Ss compare the information in their questionnaires in pairs. Encourage them to ask follow-up questions to get more details and information from their partners. Go around the class and take note of problems and successes.
- Share your observations and possible solutions with the class. Be sure to praise examples of good communication and fluent speech.

INTERCHANGE 14

Learning Objective: speak more fluently about gestures using modals and adverbs

A *Pair work*

- Pre-teach some useful language by writing these phrases on the board:

  It might/may mean . . .
  It could mean . . .
  Maybe/Perhaps it means . . .
  It possibly means . . .

- Explain the task and give Ss a few minutes to look at the situations again.
- Model the example conversation with a S.
- Ss discuss the situations in pairs. Go around the class and give help as needed.

B *Group work*

- Each pair joins another pair to compare their ideas about what is happening in each situation. Explain that they should give reasons why they agree or disagree with one another.
- Set a time limit of about five minutes for groups to compare opinions. Go around the class and take note of how Ss are doing. If Ss have problems expressing their ideas, let them check their dictionaries.
- When time is up, elicit Ss' interpretations for each situation. Remind them that there are no right or wrong answers.

INTERCHANGE 14 Casual observers

A PAIR WORK Look at this scene of an airport. What do you think is happening in each of the situations? Look at people's body language for clues.

A: Why do you think the couple in situation 1 looks upset?
B: Well, they might be having a fight. They look . . .
A: Who do you think the woman in situation 6 is?
B: She must be famous. She might . . .

B GROUP WORK Compare your interpretations. Do you agree or disagree?

128 Interchange 14

Possible answers

1. The couple is arguing and they look upset. Maybe the man is angry with the woman for bringing so much luggage.
2. A man looks extremely satisfied. A woman is looking at the guy with an amazed look. She may think he is eating too much.
3. The young couple looks very happy and excited. Perhaps they are on their honeymoon.
4. A woman is pulling her hair out and looks very nervous. She could have a lot of work to do or she may be late for a meeting.
5. The little girl is sitting in a corner and crying. She looks desperate. Perhaps she is lost and can't find her parents.
6. The woman looks vain and proud. Maybe she is famous.
7. The two friends look very tired. They may have been backpacking for a long time.

INTERCHANGE 15 Tough choices

A What would you do in each of these situations? Circle **a**, **b**, or **c**.
If you think you would do something else, write your suggestion next to **d**.

1 If I saw someone shoplifting in a store, I would . . .
a. pretend I didn't notice.
b. talk to the store manager.
c. talk to the shoplifter.
d. ______________________.

2 If I saw an elderly woman trying to cross a street, I would . . .
a. keep walking.
b. offer to help.
c. try to stop traffic for her.
d. ______________________.

3 If I saw someone standing on a highway next to a car with smoke coming from the engine, I would . . .
a. continue driving.
b. stop and help.
c. use my cell phone to call the police.
d. ______________________.

4 If I saw my friend's boyfriend or girlfriend with someone other than my friend, I would . . .
a. say nothing.
b. talk to my friend.
c. talk to my friend's boyfriend or girlfriend.
d. ______________________.

5 If I were eating dinner in a restaurant and I found a hair in my food, I would . . .
a. remove it and continue eating.
b. mention it to the server.
c. demand to speak to the manager.
d. ______________________.

B **GROUP WORK** Compare your choices for each situation in part A.
A: What would you do if you saw someone shoplifting in a store?
B: I'm not sure. Maybe I would pretend I didn't notice.
C: Really? I wouldn't. I would . . .

C **CLASS ACTIVITY** Take a class survey. Find out which choice was most popular for each situation. Talk about any other suggestions people added for **d**.

INTERCHANGE 15

Learning Objective: speak more fluently about difficult situations

A

- Explain the task. Briefly go over the five situations and the choices to make sure that Ss understand any new words or phrases.

Vocabulary
shoplift: the crime of stealing things from a store

- Give Ss a few minutes to complete the task individually. Remind them to write their own idea next to *d* if they don't choose *a*, *b*, or *c*. Go around the class and give help as needed, particularly with the Ss' own suggestions for *d*.

B *Group work*

- Divide the class into groups. Use the example conversation to model how Ss should compare choices and extend the discussion.
- Set a time limit of about ten minutes. Encourage groups to ask one another follow-up questions during their discussions. Go around the class and give help as needed.

C *Class activity*

- Read the first situation and choices. Ask Ss to raise their hands to show which answer they chose. Continue with the other situations, writing the numbers on the board to keep track of the Ss' choices. Are Ss surprised at the choices that were most popular? If so, ask some follow-up questions to discover why.
- For each situation, elicit suggestions for *d*. Encourage the rest of the class to give their comments and opinions.

INTERCHANGE 16A/B

Learning Objective: speak more fluently about schedules and free time

- To introduce the topic of giving excuses, have Ss look at the reading on page 111. Ask: "What are some good excuses for missing work or school?"
- Divide the class into pairs. Then assign each S an A or a B part. Tell Student As to look at page 129 and Student Bs to look at page 131.

A *Pair work*

- Read the situation to the class. Then give pairs a few minutes to look over their calendars and to think of interesting excuses for the days they don't want to meet. Remind Ss not to look at their partner's page. Answer any questions about the instructions or the information in the calendars.
- Model the example conversation with a S to demonstrate how to ask questions and make excuses.
- Tell Ss to write the excuses that their partners give on their calendars. Ss will need these notes for the pair work in part B.
- Encourage Ss to have fun and not to give up until they agree on a date. Go around the class and give help as needed.
- Stop the activity when time is up or when all the pairs have agreed on a date.

B *Pair work*

- Divide the class into new pairs. Ask Student As to work together and Student Bs to work together.
- Explain the task. Ss use reported speech to tell their new partner about what their partner from part A said.

INTERCHANGE 16A Just a bunch of excuses

Student A

A PAIR WORK You and your partner want to get together. Ask and answer questions to find a day when you are both free. You also want to keep time open for other friends, so give excuses for those days. Write your partner's excuses on the calendar.

A: Do you want to meet on the 2nd?
B: I'm sorry. I'm going to an engagement party. Are you free on the 1st?
A: Well, I . . .

Calendar

Day Week Month Year

September

Today

Sunday	Monday	Tuesday	Wednesday	Thursday	Friday	Saturday
					1 dinner with Pat	2
3	4 class	5	6	7 You want to keep this date free. Make an excuse.	8 party at Sam's	9
10	11 You want to keep this date free. Make an excuse.	12 bowling with Chris	13	14 movie with Haru	15	16
17 dinner with office friends	18 class	19	20	21 study for tomorrow's exam	22 You want to keep this date free. Make an excuse.	23
24	25	26 You want to keep these dates free. Make excuses.	27	28 dinner for Dad's birthday	29 go dancing with Jess & Bo	30 You might have a date. Give an excuse.

B PAIR WORK Now work with another student. Discuss the excuses your partner gave you in Part A. Decide which excuses were probably true and which ones were probably not true.

A: Pablo said that on the 7th he had to take care of his neighbors' cats. That was probably not true.
B: I agree. I think . . .

- Tell Ss to look at the excuses they wrote on their calendars in part A. Explain that they should use these notes to make statements with reported speech. Model the example conversation with a S. Then elicit a few additional examples from Ss and write them on the board.
- Pairs report the excuses they heard in part A and discuss whether the excuses were real or not. Go around the class and give help as needed.

INTERCHANGE 16B Just a bunch of excuses

Student B

A **PAIR WORK** You and your partner want to get together. Ask and answer questions to find a day when you are both free. You also want to keep time open for other friends, so give excuses for those days. Write your partner's excuses on the calendar.

A: Do you want to meet on the 2nd?
B: I'm sorry. I'm going to an engagement party. Are you free on the 1st?
A: Well, I . . .

Calendar

September

Sunday	Monday	Tuesday	Wednesday	Thursday	Friday	Saturday
					1	2 Kelly's engagement party
3 You want to keep this date free. Make an excuse.	4 movie with Alex	5	6 You want to keep these dates free. Make excuses.	7	8	9
10 visit Mom and Dad	11 office party	12	13 photography workshop at school	14	15 You want to keep these dates free. Make excuses.	16
17 visit Grandma	18	19 jogging with Andie	20	21	22 party at Cameron's	23 dinner with Farah
24 family get-together	25 You need a break. Make an excuse.	26 study group meeting	27	28 work late: big report due Friday	29	30

B **PAIR WORK** Now work with another student. Discuss the excuses your partner gave you in Part A. Decide which excuses were probably true and which ones were probably not true.

A: Maria said that on the 9th she had to help her brother paint his kitchen. That might be true.
B: I agree. I think . . .

Grammar plus

UNIT 1

1 Past tense page 3

■ Use a form of *be* with *born*: I **was born** here. (NOT: I ~~born~~ here.) Don't use a form of *be* with the verb *die*: He **died** last year. (NOT: He ~~was died~~ last year.)

Complete the conversation.

1. **A:** Do you live around here?
   B: No, I don't. I'm from Costa Rica.
   A: Really? *Were you born* ______ in Costa Rica?
   B: No. Actually, I was born in San Miguelito, Panama.
2. **A:** That's interesting. So where ____________?
   B: I grew up in Costa Rica. My family moved there when I was little.
3. **A:** ____________ in the capital?
   B: No, my family didn't live in a city. We lived in a small town called Puerto Viejo.
4. **A:** ____________ away from Puerto Viejo?
   B: Oh, about eight years ago. I left Puerto Viejo to go to college.
5. **A:** Where ____________ to college?
   B: I went to college in San Jose, and I live there now.
6. **A:** And ____________ to Miami?
   B: I got here a few days ago. I'm visiting my cousin.

2 *Used to* page 5

■ Use the base form of *used to* in questions and negative statements: Did you **use to** play sports? (NOT: Did you ~~used to~~ play sports?) I didn't **use to** like bananas. (NOT: I didn't ~~used to~~ like bananas.)

■ Don't use *never* in negative statements: I **never used to** wear sunglasses. (NOT: I never ~~didn't use to~~ wear sunglasses.)

Complete the conversations with the correct form of *used to*.

1. **A:** Hey, Dad. What kinds of clothes *did you use to* ______ wear – you know, when you were a kid?
   B: Oh, we ____________ wear jeans and T-shirts – like you kids do now.
   A: Really? ____________ Mom ____________ dress like that, too?
   B: No, not really. She never ____________ like wearing pants. She always ____________ wear skirts and dresses.
2. **A:** ____________ you ____________ play a sport when you were a kid?
   B: Well, I ____________ be a swimmer. My sister and I ____________ swim on a team.
   A: Wow, that's cool! Were you good?
   B: Yeah. I ____________ win gold medals all the time. And my sister ____________ be the fastest swimmer on the team.

UNIT 2

1 Expressions of quantity page 9

■ Count nouns have a plural form that usually ends in -*s*. Noncount nouns don't have a plural form because you can't separate and count them: Are there any **parking garages** around here? BUT Is there any **parking** around here? (NOT: Are there any ~~parkings~~ around here?)

Complete the conversations with the correct words in parentheses.

1. **A:** There's ______________ (too many / too much) traffic in this city. There should be ______________ (fewer / less) cars downtown.
   B: The problem is there ______________ (aren't / isn't) enough public transportation.
   A: You're right. We should have more ______________ (bus / buses). There ______________ (aren't / isn't) enough of them during rush hour.
2. **A:** How do you like your new neighborhood?
   B: It's terrible, actually. There's ______________(too many / too much) noise and ______________ (too few / too little) parking.
   A: That's too bad. There ______________ (aren't / isn't) enough parking spaces in my neighborhood either.
3. **A:** Did you hear about the changes to the city center? Starting next month, there will be more bicycle ______________ (lane / lanes) and ______________ (fewer / less) street parking.
   B: That's good. There ______________ (are too many / is too much) pollution downtown. I'm sure there will be ______________ (fewer / less) accidents, too.
   A: That's true.

2 Indirect questions from Wh-questions page 11

■ Indirect questions are often polite requests for information. *Can you tell me how much this magazine costs?* sounds more polite than *How much does this magazine cost?*

Complete the conversation with indirect questions.

1. **A:** Excuse me. Can you *tell me where the post office is* ______________?
   B: Yes, of course. The post office is on the next corner.
2. **A:** And could you ______________?
   B: You can find a really good restaurant on Central Avenue.
3. **A:** OK. Do you ______________?
   B: Yes. The restaurant is called Giorgio's.
4. **A:** Thanks. Can you ______________?
   B: Yes. They serve Italian food.
5. **A:** Oh, good! Do you ______________?
   B: It opens at 5:00. Tell them Joe sent you!
   A: OK, Joe. Thanks for everything! Bye now.

UNIT 3

1 Evaluations and comparisons page 17

- In evaluations, *enough* goes after adjectives and before nouns.
- adjective + *enough*: This house isn't **bright enough**. (NOT: This house isn't ~~enough bright~~.)
- noun + *enough*: This house doesn't have **enough light**. (NOT: This house doesn't have ~~light enough~~.)

A Read each situation. Then write two sentences describing the problem, one sentence with *not . . . enough* and one with *too*.

1. Our family needs a big house. This house is very small.
  a. This house isn't big enough for us.
  b. This house is too small for us.

2. We want to live on a quiet street. This street is very noisy.
  a. ______
  b. ______

3. We need three bedrooms. This house has only two.
  a. ______
  b. ______

4. We want a spacious living room. This one is cramped.
  a. ______
  b. ______

B Rewrite the comparisons using *as . . . as*. Use *just* when possible.

1. My new apartment is smaller than my old one.
My new apartment isn't as large as my old one.

2. This neighborhood is safer than my old one.
______

3. This apartment has a lot of privacy. My old one did, too.
______

4. My rent is reasonable now. It was very high before.
______

2 *Wish* page 20

- Use *could* (the past of *can*) and *would* (the past of *will*) with *wish*: I **can't** move right now, but I wish I **could**. My landlord **won't** paint my apartment, but I wish he **would**.

Match the problems with the wishes.

1. My house isn't very nice. c
2. It costs a lot to live here. ____
3. My landlord won't call me back. ____
4. I have noisy neighbors. ____
5. I don't like living alone. ____
6. The buses don't run very often. ____

a. I wish I could find a good roommate.
b. I wish he'd return my calls.
c. I wish it were more attractive.
d. I wish I could afford a car.
e. I wish their music weren't so loud.
f. I wish it weren't so expensive.

UNIT 4

1 Simple past vs. present perfect page 23

■ Use the simple past – not the present perfect – when you say when an event ended: I had sushi last night. (NOT: I~~'ve had~~ sushi last night.)

Complete the conversations. Choose the best forms.

1. **A:** What ________________ (did you have / have you had) for dinner last night?
   B: I ________________ (tried / have tried) Indian food for the first time. ________________ (Did you ever have / Have you ever had) it?
   A: A friend and I ________________ (ate / have eaten) at an Indian restaurant just last week. It ________________ (was / has been) delicious!
2. **A:** ________________ (Did you ever take / Have you ever taken) a cooking class?
   B: No, I ________________ (didn't / haven't). How about you?
   A: I ________________ (took / have taken) a few classes. My last class ________________ (was / has been) in December. We ________________ (learned / have learned) how to make some wonderful Spanish dishes.
3. **A:** I ________________ (watched / have watched) a great cooking show on TV yesterday.
   B: Really? I ________________ (never saw / have never seen) a cooking show. ________________ (Was it / Has it been) boring?
   A: No, it ________________ (wasn't / hasn't). It ________________ (was / has been) very interesting!

2 Sequence adverbs page 25

■ *Then*, *next*, and *after that* mean the same. *First* comes first, and *finally* comes last; you can use the other adverbs in any order: **First,** put some water in a pan. **Then/Next/After that,** put the eggs in the water. **Finally,** boil the eggs for 7 minutes.

Unscramble the steps in this recipe for hamburgers. Then write the steps in order.

salt and pepper add in the bowl to the meat then

________ : ________________________________

2 pounds of chopped beef put in a bowl first,

Step 1 : First, put 2 pounds of chopped beef in a bowl.

put the burgers in a pan finally, and cook for 10 minutes

________ : ________________________________

next, the meat and the salt and pepper mix together

________ : ________________________________

into four burgers after that, with your hands form the meat

________ : ________________________________

UNIT 5

1 Future with *be going to* and *will* page 31

- Use the base form of the verb – not the infinitive (*to* + base form) – with *will*:
  I think I**'ll go** to Hawaii next winter. (NOT: I think I'll ~~to~~ go to Hawaii next winter.)
- Use *be going to* – not *will* – when you know something is going to happen:
  Look at those black clouds. It**'s going to** rain. (NOT: It ~~will~~ rain.)

Complete the conversation with the correct form of *be going to* or *will* and the verbs in parentheses.

A: It's Friday – at last! What *are you going to do* (do) this weekend?
B: I'm not sure. I'm really tired, so I probably ______________ (not do) anything exciting. Maybe I ______________ (see) a movie on Saturday. How about you? How ______________ (spend) your weekend?
A: My wife and I ______________ (do) some work on our house. We ______________ (paint) the living room on Saturday. On Sunday, we ______________ (clean) all the rugs.
B: ______________ (do) anything fun?
A: Oh, I think we ______________ (have) a lot of fun. We like working around the house. And Sunday's my birthday, so we ______________ (have) dinner at my favorite Italian restaurant.
B: Now that sounds like fun!

2 Modals for necessity and suggestion page 33

- Some modals for necessity and suggestion are stronger than others.
  Weak (for advice or an opinion): *should, ought to*
  Stronger (for a warning): *had better*
  Strongest (for an obligation): *must, need to, have to*

Choose the correct word or words to complete the advice to travelers.

1. You ______________ (must / should) show identification at the airport. They won't allow you on a plane without an official ID.
2. Your ID ______________ (needs to / ought to) have a picture of you on it. It's required.
3. The picture of you ______________ (has to / ought to) be recent. They won't accept an old photo.
4. Travelers ______________ (must / should) get to the airport at least two hours before their flight. It's not a good idea to get there later than that.
5. All travelers ______________ (have to / had better) go through airport security. It's necessary for passenger safety.
6. Many airlines don't serve food, so passengers on long flights probably ______________ (must / ought to) buy something to eat at the airport.

UNIT 6

1 Two-part verbs; *will* for responding to requests page 37

- Two-part verbs are verb + particle.
- If the object of a two-part verb is a noun, the noun can come before or after the particle: **Take out** the trash./**Take** the trash **out**.
- If the object is a pronoun, the pronoun must come before the particle: **Take** it **out**. (NOT: Take ~~out it~~.)

Write conversations. First, rewrite the request given by changing the position of the particle. Then write a response to the request using *it* or *them*.

1. Put away your clothes, please.
   A: Put your clothes away, please.
   B: OK. I'll put them away.
2. Turn the lights on, please.
   A: ______
   B: ______
3. Please turn your music down.
   A: ______
   B: ______
4. Clean up the kitchen, please.
   A: ______
   B: ______
5. Turn off your phone, please.
   A: ______
   B: ______

2 Requests with modals and *Would you mind . . . ?* page 39

- Use the base form of the verb – not the infinitive (*to* + base form) – with the modals *can*, *could*, and *would*: **Could** you **get** me a sandwich? (NOT: Could you ~~to~~ get me a sandwich?)
- Requests with modals and *Would you mind . . . ?* are polite – even without *please*. *Can you get me a sandwich?* sounds much more polite than *Get me a sandwich.*

Change these sentences to polite requests. Use the words in parentheses.

1. Bring in the mail. (could)
   Could you bring in the mail?
2. Put your shoes by the door. (would you mind)
   ______
3. Don't leave dishes in the sink. (would you mind)
   ______
4. Change the TV channel. (can)
   ______
5. Don't play ball inside. (would you mind)
   ______
6. Clean up your mess. (would you mind)
   ______
7. Put away the clean towels. (can)
   ______
8. Pick up your things. (could)
   ______

UNIT 7

1 Infinitives and gerunds for uses and purposes page 45

- Sentences with infinitives and gerunds mean the same: *I use my cell phone to send text messages* means the same as *I use my cell phone for sending text messages.*
- Use a gerund – not an infinitive – after *for*: Satellites are used **for studying** weather. (NOT: Satellites are used for ~~to study~~ weather.)

Read each sentence about a technology item. Write two sentences about the item's use and purpose. Use the information in parentheses.

1. My sister's car has a built-in GPS system. (She use / get directions)
   - a. She uses the GPS system to get directions.
   - b. She uses the GPS system for getting directions.
2. I love my new smartphone. (I use / take pictures)
   - a. ______
   - b. ______
3. That's a flash drive. (You use / back up files)
   - a. ______
   - b. ______
4. My little brother wants his own laptop. (He would only use / watch movies and play games)
   - a. ______
   - b. ______
5. I'm often on my computer all day long. (I use / shop online and do research)
   - a. ______
   - b. ______

2 Imperatives and infinitives for giving suggestions page 47

- With imperatives and infinitives, *not* goes before – not after – *to*: Try **not to** talk too long. (NOT: Try ~~to not~~ talk too long.)

Rewrite the sentences as suggestions. Use the words in parentheses.

1. When you go to the movies, turn off your phone. (don't forget)
   When you go to the movies, don't forget to turn off your phone.
2. Don't talk on the phone when you're in an elevator. (try)
   ______
3. Don't eat or drink anything when you're at the computer. (be sure)
   ______
4. Clean your computer screen and keyboard once a week. (remember)
   ______
5. Don't use your tablet outside when it's raining. (make sure)
   ______
6. When the bell rings to start class, put your music player away! (be sure)
   ______

UNIT 8

1 Relative clauses of time page 51

- Relative clauses with *when* describe the word *time* or a noun that refers to a period of time, such as *day, night, month,* and *year.*

Combine the two sentences using *when.*

1. Thanksgiving is a holiday. Entire families get together.
   Thanksgiving is a holiday when entire families get together.
2. It's a wonderful time. People give thanks for the good things in their lives.
   ______
3. It's a day. Everyone eats much more than usual.
   ______
4. I remember one particular year. The whole family came to our house.
   ______
5. That year was very cold. It snowed all Thanksgiving day.
   ______
6. I remember another thing about that Thanksgiving. My brother and I baked eight pies.
   ______

2 Adverbial clauses of time page 54

- An adverbial clause of time can come before or after the main clause. When it comes before the main clause, use a comma. When it comes after the main clause, don't use a comma: When Ginny and Tom met, they both lived in San Juan. BUT: Ginny and Tom met when they both lived in San Juan.
- The words *couple* and *family* are collective nouns. They are usually used with singular verbs: When a couple **gets** married, they often receive gifts. (NOT: When a couple ~~get~~ married, they often receive gifts.)

Combine the two sentences using the adverb in parentheses. Write one sentence with the adverbial clause before the main clause and another with the adverbial clause after the main clause.

1. Students complete their courses. A school holds a graduation ceremony. (after)
   a. After students complete their courses, a school holds a graduation ceremony.
   b. A school holds a graduation ceremony after students complete their courses.
2. Students gather to put on robes and special hats. The ceremony starts. (before)
   a. ______
   b. ______
3. Music plays. The students walk in a line to their seats. (when)
   a. ______
   b. ______
4. School officials and teachers make speeches. Students get their diplomas. (after)
   a. ______
   b. ______
5. The ceremony is finished. Students throw their hats into the air and cheer. (when)
   a. ______
   b. ______

UNIT 9

1 Time contrasts page 59

■ Use the modal *might* to say something is possible in the present or future: In a few years, movie theaters **might** not exist. = In a few years, maybe movie theaters won't exist.

Complete the conversation with the correct form of the verbs in parentheses. Use the past, present, or future tense.

A: I saw a fascinating program last night. It talked about the past, the present, and the future.

B: What kinds of things did it describe?

A: Well, for example, the normal work week in the 19th century ____________ (be) over 60 hours. Nowadays, many people ____________ (work) around 40 hours a week.

B: Well, that sounds like progress.

A: You're right. But on the show, they said that most people ____________ (work) fewer hours in the future. They also talked about the way we shop. These days, many of us ____________ (shop) online. In the old days, there ____________ (be) no supermarkets, so people ____________ (have to) go to a lot of different stores. In the future, people ____________ (do) all their shopping from their phones.

B: I don't believe that.

A: Me neither. What about cars? Do you think people ____________ (still drive) cars a hundred years from now?

B: What did they say on the show?

A: They said that before the car, people ____________ (walk) everywhere. Nowadays, we ____________ (drive) everywhere. And that ____________ (not change).

2 Conditional sentences with *if* clauses page 61

■ The *if* clause can come before or after the main clause: **If** I change my eating habits, I'll feel healthier./I'll feel healthier **if** I change my eating habits. Always use a comma when the *if* clause comes before the main clause.

■ For the future of *can*, use *will be able to*: If you save some money, you**'ll be able to buy** a car. (NOT: . . . you~~'ll can buy~~ a car.)

■ For the future of *must*, use *will have to*: If you get a dog, you**'ll have to take care** of it. (NOT: . . . you~~'ll must take~~ care of it.)

Complete the sentences with the correct form of the verbs in parentheses.

1. If you *exercise* (exercise) more often, you'*ll feel* ____________ (feel) more energetic.
2. If you ____________ (join) a gym, exercise ____________ (become) part of your routine.
3. You ____________ (not have to) worry about staying in shape if you ____________ (work out) three or four times a week.
4. If you ____________ (ride) a bike or ____________ (run) a few times a week, you ____________ (lose) weight and ____________ (gain) muscle.
5. You ____________ (sleep) better at night if you ____________ (exercise) regularly.
6. If you ____________ (start) exercising, you ____________ (might/not have) as many colds and other health problems.

UNIT 10

1 Gerunds; short responses page 65

■ Short responses with *so* and *neither* are ways of agreeing. The subject (noun or pronoun) comes after the verb: I love traveling. So **do I**. (NOT: So ~~I do~~.) I can't stand talking on the phone. Neither **can I**. (NOT: Neither ~~I can~~.)

Rewrite A's line using the words given. Then write an agreement for B.

1. I hate working alone. (can't stand)
   A: I can't stand working alone.
   B: Neither can I.
2. I don't like reading about politics or politicians. (interested in)
   A: ______
   B: ______
3. I can solve problems. (good at)
   A: ______
   B: ______
4. I have no problem with working on weekends. (don't mind)
   A: ______
   B: ______
5. I love learning new things. (enjoy)
   A: ______
   B: ______
6. I can't develop new ideas. (not good at)
   A: ______
   B: ______

2 Clauses with *because* page 68

■ Clauses with *because* answer the question "Why?" or "Why not?": Why would you make a good flight attendant? I'd make a good flight attendant **because** I love traveling, and I'm good with people.

Complete the sentences with *because* and the phrases in the box.

I don't write very well
I love arguing with people
I'm afraid of flying
✓ **I'm much too short**
I'm not patient enough to work with kids
I'm really bad with numbers

1. I could never be a fashion model because I'm much too short.
2. I wouldn't make a good high school teacher ______.
3. I wouldn't want to be a flight attendant ______.
4. I could never be an accountant ______.
5. I would make a bad journalist ______.
6. I'd be an excellent lawyer ______.

UNIT 11

1 Passive with *by* (simple past) page 73

- The past participle of regular verbs is the same form as the simple past: Leonardo da Vinci **painted** *Mona Lisa* in 1503. *Mona Lisa* was **painted** by Leonardo da Vinci in 1503.
- The past participle of some – but not all – irregular verbs is the same form as the simple past: The Egyptians **built** the Pyramids. The Pyramids were **built** by the Egyptians. BUT Jane Austen **wrote** *Pride and Prejudice*. *Pride and Prejudice* was **written** by Jane Austen.

Change the sentences from active to passive with *by*.

1. The Chinese invented paper around 100 C.E.
   Paper was invented by the Chinese around 100 C.E.
2. Marie Curie discovered radium in 1898.
   ______
3. Dr. Felix Hoffmann made the first aspirin in 1899.
   ______
4. Tim Berners-Lee developed the World Wide Web in 1989.
   ______
5. William Herschel identified the planet Uranus in 1781.
   ______
6. Georges Bizet wrote the opera *Carmen* in the 1870s.
   ______

2 Passive without *by* (simple present) page 75

- When it is obvious or not important who is doing the action, don't use a *by* phrase: Both the Olympics and the World Cup are held every four years. (NOT: . . . are held ~~by people~~ . . .)

Complete the information with *is* or *are* and the past participle of the verbs in the box.

base	know
export	✓ speak
import	use

1. Portuguese – not Spanish – is spoken ______ in Brazil.
2. Diamonds and gold from South Africa ______ by countries all over the world.
3. The U.S. dollar ______ in Puerto Rico.
4. Colombia ______ for its delicious coffee.
5. Many electronic products ______ by Japan and South Korea. It's an important industry for these two countries.
6. The economy in many island countries, such as Jamaica, ______ on tourism.

UNIT 12

1 Past continuous vs. simple past page 79

■ When the past continuous is used with the simple past, both actions happened at the same time, but the past continuous action started earlier. The simple past action interrupted the past continuous action.

Earlier action — 6:00 — *I was watching TV*

Later action — 6:20 — *when the phone rang.*

Complete the conversations with the correct form of the verbs in parentheses. Use the past continuous or the simple past.

1. **A:** What happened to you?
   B: I ___*fell*___ (fall) while I ___*was jogging*___ (jog) in the park.
2. **A:** ________ you ________ (see) the storm yesterday?
   B: Yes! It ________ (start) while I ________ (drive) to work.
3. **A:** We finally ________ (move) to a larger apartment.
   B: That's good. I know you ________ (live) in a tiny place when your daughter ________ (be) born.
4. **A:** My sister ________ (have) a bad accident. She ________ (hurt) her back when she ________ (lift) weights at the gym.
   B: That ________ (happen) to me last year, but I ________ (not lift) weights. I ________ (take) a boxing class, and I ________ (trip).

2 Present perfect continuous page 81

■ The same time expressions used with the present perfect can also be used with the present perfect continuous. Don't confuse *for* and *since*: I've been working here **for** 5 years./I've been working here **since** 2010.

Complete the sentences with the present perfect continuous form of the verbs in parentheses.

1. **A:** What ___*have*___ you ___*been doing*___ all day?
   B: I ________ (clean) the house, and Peter ________ (watch) TV. He ________ (not feel) very well lately.
   A: How ________ you ________ (feel) these days?
   B: I ________ (feel) great. I ________ (not eat) any junk food, and I ________ (exercise) a lot. I ________ (take) really good care of myself.
2. **A:** How long ________ you and Joe ________ (date)?
   B: We ________ (go out) together for almost a year. Can you believe it?
   A: Maya and I ________ (date) for even longer. I think it's time to get married. We ________ (talk) about it a lot lately.
   B: Joe and I ________ (not talk) about marriage, but I ________ (think) about it.

UNIT 13

1 Participles as adjectives page 87

■ Adjectives ending in *–ing* are present participles. They are things that *cause* a feeling. Adjectives ending in *–ed* are past participles. They *express* the feeling.

Complete the sentences with the correct participle.

1. Why are we watching this ____boring____ movie? Aren't you ____bored____ with it? (boring / bored)
2. Kristen Stewart is an ____________ actress. I'm ____________ by her talent. (amazing / amazed)
3. Are you ____________ in computer-generated special effects? The latest 3-D movies are very ____________. (interesting / interested)
4. I had an ____________ experience the last time I went to the movies. I started to cough, and I couldn't stop. I was really ____________. (embarrassing / embarrassed)
5. Julie and I saw an Italian comedy yesterday. I found it ____________, but Julie didn't seem very ____________ by it. (amusing / amused)
6. Oh, I'm really ____________ with Jeremy right now. He took me to the most ____________ movie last night. I wanted to walk out after half an hour, but he wouldn't leave! (disgusting / disgusted)
7. Do you think sci-fi movie directors make their films ____________ intentionally? I get so ____________ by the complicated storylines and weird characters. (confusing / confused)
8. I think that great books make great movies. If I find a book ____________, I'm usually ____________ by the movie, too. (fascinating / fascinated)

2 Relative pronouns for people and things page 89

■ Relative clauses give information about nouns. Don't use a personal pronoun in a relative clause: He's an actor **that** won two Oscars. (NOT: He's an actor that ~~he~~ won two Oscars.)

Complete the conversations. Use *that* for things and *who* for people.

A: How did you like the movie last night? Was it any good?

B: It wasn't bad, but it's not the kind of movie ____that____ makes you think. I like films ____________ have a strong message and interesting storylines.

A: How about the acting? Did you like the actors ____________ star in it?

B: Jessica Biel is pretty good, actually.

A: Oh, she's that beautiful actress ____________ is married to Justin Timberlake.

B: Justin who? Who's that?

A: Oh, you know him. He's the one ____________ was in the band 'NSync years ago. It was a "boy band" ____________ was popular in the 1990s.

B: I remember 'NSync, but I don't remember the names of the guys ____________ were in the band.

A: Well, I loved Justin Timberlake when I was a kid. And he's not a bad actor. Did you see the movie *The Social Network*?

B: I did see that. It's about the guys ____________ started Facebook, right? I didn't realize Justin Timberlake was in it. Now I'll have to see it again!

UNIT 14

1 Modals and adverbs page 93

- Use the modals *might/may, could,* and *must* and the adverbs *maybe/perhaps, probably,* and *definitely* when you aren't sure about what you're saying:
  Slight possibility: *might, may, maybe, perhaps*
  Possibility: *could, probably*
  Strong possibility: *must, definitely*

Rewrite each sentence in different ways, using the words in parentheses.

1. Perhaps it means she doesn't agree with you.
   a. (maybe) Maybe it means she doesn't agree with you.
   b. (might) ______________________
   c. (may) ______________________
2. That gesture could mean, "Come here."
   a. (probably) ______________________
3. That almost definitely means he doesn't understand you.
   a. (must) ______________________

2 Permission, obligation, and prohibition page 95

- Use *have/has* with *got to*: You**'ve got to** keep the door closed. (NOT: You ~~got to~~ keep the door closed.)

Complete the conversations with the words and phrases in the box.
Use each word or phrase only once.

are allowed to	**✓ can't**
aren't allowed to	**have to**
can	**have got to**

1. **A:** Oh, no! That sign says, "No fishing." That means we ____can't____ fish here.
   B: You're right. We ______________ go somewhere else to fish. I think you ______________ fish in the pond on Cedar Road. Let's go there.
2. **A:** What does that sign mean?
   B: It means bad news for us. It means you ______________ bring dogs to the beach. We'd better take Buddy home.
3. **A:** Please don't leave your garbage here. You ______________ put it in the trash room down the hall. That's one of the building's rules.
   B: I'm really sorry.
4. **A:** You ______________ put your bike in the bike room downstairs, if you want. It's much safer than locking it up outside.
   B: Oh, that's great! I'll do that. I didn't know about the bike room.

UNIT 15

1 Unreal conditional sentences with *if* clauses page 101

- The clauses in unreal conditional sentences can come in either order. Don't use a comma when the *if* clause comes second: **If** I won the lottery, I'd share the money with my family./I'd share the money with my family **if** I won the lottery.

Complete the conversation with the correct form of the verbs in parentheses.

1. **A:** If a friend ________________ (ask) to borrow some money, what ________________ you ________________ (say)?
   B: Well, if I ________________ (have) any extra money that month, I ________________ probably ________________ (give) it to her.
2. **A:** What ________________ you ________________ (do) if someone ________________ (give) you a million dollars?
   B: Hmm, I'm not sure. I ________________ (buy) a lot of nice clothes and jewelry, or I ________________ (spend) some and ________________ (give) some away, or I ________________ (put) it all in the bank.
3. **A:** If you ________________ (think) a friend was doing something dangerous, ________________ you ________________ (say) something to him, or ________________ you ________________ (keep) quiet?
   B: I ________________ definitely ________________ (talk) to my friend about it.
4. **A:** What ________________ you ________________ (do) if you ________________ (have) a problem with your boss?
   B: That's a hard one. If that ________________ (happen), I ________________ (talk) to the human resources department about it, or I ________________ just ________________ (sit down) with my boss and ________________ (talk) about the situation.

2 Past modals page 103

- Use *should have* and *would have* for all subjects. They don't change form: He **should have called** sooner. (NOT: He should ~~has~~ called sooner.)

Read the situations. Use the words in parentheses to write opinions and suggestions.

1. My neighbor had a party last night. It was very loud, so I called the police.
   (you / speak / to your neighbor first)
   You should have spoken to your neighbor first.
2. The mail carrier put someone else's mail in my box. I threw it away.
   (you / write / a note and leave / the mail in your box)
   ____
3. My sister asked if I liked her new dress. It didn't look good on her, but I said it did.
   (I / tell her the truth)
   ____
4. A salesperson called me last night. I didn't want to buy anything, but I let her talk to me for almost half an hour.
   (I / tell her I'm not interested / hang up)
   ____

UNIT 16

1 Reported speech: requests page 107

- When a reported request is negative, *not* comes before *to*: Don't leave your wet towel on the floor. She told me **not to leave** my wet towel on the floor. (NOT: She told me ~~to not~~ leave my wet towel on the floor.)

Harry's roommate, Tyler, is making some requests. Read what Tyler said to Harry. Write the requests with the verbs in parentheses and reported speech.

1. "Can you put away your clean clothes?" (ask)
   Tyler asked Harry to put away his clean clothes.
2. "Meet me in the cafeteria at school at noon." (say)
   ______
3. "Don't leave your shoes in the living room." (tell)
   ______
4. "Hang up your wet towels." (say)
   ______
5. "Could you stop using my phone?" (ask)
   ______
6. "Make your bed on weekdays." (tell)
   ______
7. "Don't eat my food." (say)
   ______
8. "Be a better roommate!" (tell)
   ______

2 Reported speech: statements page 109

- The tense of the introducing verb (*ask, say, tell*) changes when the sentence is reported: simple present → simple past; present continuous → past continuous; present perfect → past perfect. Modals change, too: *can* → *could*; *will* → *would*; *may* → *might*.

Bill and Kathy are having a barbecue on Sunday. They're upset because a lot of their friends can't come. Read what their friends said. Change the excuses into reported speech.

1. Lori: "I have to visit my grandparents that day."
   Lori said that she had to visit her grandparents that day.
2. Mario: "I'm going to a play on Sunday."
   ______
3. Julia: "I've promised to take my brother to the movies that day."
   ______
4. Daniel: "I can't come. I have to study for a huge exam on Monday."
   ______
5. The neighbors: "We'll be out of town all weekend."
   ______
6. Alice: "I may have to babysit my nephew."
   ______

Grammar plus answer key

Unit 1

1 Past tense

2. did you grow up/are you from
3. Did you live
4. When did you move
5. did you go
6. when did you come/get

2 Used to

1. A: Hey, Dad. What kinds of clothes **did you use to** wear – you know, when you were a kid?
   B: Oh, we **used to** wear jeans and T-shirts – like you kids do now.
   A: Really? **Did** Mom **use to** dress like that, too?
   B: No, not really. She never **used to** like wearing pants. She always **used to** wear skirts and dresses.
2. A: **Did** you **use to** play a sport when you were a kid?
   B: Well, I **used to** be a swimmer. My sister and I **used to** swim on a team.
   A: Wow, that's cool! Were you good?
   B: Yeah. I **used to** win gold medals all the time. And my sister **used to** be the fastest swimmer on the team.

Unit 2

1 Expressions of quantity

1. A: There's **too much** traffic in this city. There should be **fewer** cars downtown.
   B: The problem is there **isn't** enough public transportation.
   A: You're right. We should have more **buses**. There **aren't** enough of them during rush hour.
2. A: How do you like your new neighborhood?
   B: It's terrible, actually. There's **too much** noise and **too little** parking.
   A: That's too bad. There **aren't** enough parking spaces in my neighborhood either.
3. A: Did you hear about the changes to the city center? Starting next month, there will be more bicycle **lanes** and **less** street parking.
   B: That's good. There **is too much** pollution downtown. I'm sure there will be **fewer** accidents, too.
   A: That's true.

2 Indirect questions from *Wh*-questions

Answers may vary. Some possible answers:

2. And could you **tell me where I can find a good restaurant**?
3. Do you **know what the name of the restaurant is**?
4. Can you **tell me what type of food they serve**?
5. Do you **know what time the restaurant opens**?

Unit 3

1 Evaluations and comparisons

A

Answers may vary. Some possible answers:

2. This street isn't quiet enough./This street is too noisy.
3. This house doesn't have enough bedrooms./This house is too small for us./This house has too few bedrooms for us.
4. This living room isn't spacious enough./This living room doesn't have enough space./This living room is too cramped/small.

B

Answers may vary. Some possible answers:

2. My old neighborhood isn't as safe as this one.
3. This apartment has (just) as much privacy as my old one.
4. My rent isn't as high as it used to be.

2 Wish

2. f 3. b 4. e 5. a 6. d

Unit 4

1 Simple past vs. present perfect

1. A: What **did you have** for dinner last night?
   B: I **tried** Indian food for the first time. **Have you ever had** it?
   A: A friend and I **ate** at an Indian restaurant just last week. It **was** delicious!
2. A: **Have you ever taken** a cooking class?
   B: No, **I haven't**. How about you?
   A: I **have taken** a few classes. My last class **was** in December. We **learned** how to make some wonderful Spanish dishes.
3. A: I **watched** a great cooking show on TV yesterday.
   B: Really? I **have never seen** a cooking show. **Was it** boring?
   A: No, it **wasn't**. It **was** very interesting!

2 Sequence adverbs

Step 1: First, put 2 pounds of chopped beef in a bowl.
Step 2: Then add salt and pepper to the meat in the bowl.
Step 3: Next, mix the meat and the salt and pepper together.
Step 4: After that, form the meat into four burgers with your hands.
Step 5: Finally, put the burgers in a pan and cook for 10 minutes.

Unit 5

1 Future with *be going to* and *will*

B: I'm not sure. I'm really tired, so I probably **won't do** anything exciting. Maybe I**'ll see** a movie on Saturday. How about you? How **are you going to spend** your weekend?
A: My wife and I **are going to do** some work on our house. We**'re going to paint** the living room on Saturday. On Sunday, we**'re going to clean** all the rugs.
B: **Are(n't) you going to do** anything fun?
A: Oh, I think we**'ll have/'re going to have** a lot of fun. We like working around the house. And Sunday's my birthday, so we**'re going to have** dinner at my favorite Italian restaurant.
B: Now that sounds like fun!

2 Modals for necessity and suggestions

1. You **must** show identification at the airport. They won't allow you on a plane without an official ID.
2. Your ID **needs to** have a picture of you on it. It's required.
3. The picture of you **has to** be recent. They won't accept an old photo.
4. Travelers **should** get to the airport at least two hours before their flight. It's not a good idea to get there later than that.
5. All travelers **have to** go through airport security. It's necessary for passenger safety.
6. Many airlines don't serve food, so passengers on long flights probably **ought to** buy something to eat at the airport.

Unit 6

1 Two-part verbs; *will* for responding to requests

2. A: Turn on the lights, please.
   B: OK. I'll turn them on.
3. A: Please turn down your music.
   B: OK. I'll turn it down.
4. A: Clean the kitchen up, please.
   B: OK. I'll clean it up.
5. A: Turn your phone off, please.
   B: OK. I'll turn it off.

2 Requests with modals and *Would you mind . . . ?*

2. Would you mind putting your shoes by the door?
3. Would you mind not leaving dishes in the sink?
4. Can you change the TV channel?
5. Would you mind not playing ball inside?
6. Would you mind cleaning up your mess?
7. Can you put away the clean towels?
8. Could you pick up your things?

Unit 7

1 **Infinitives and gerunds for uses and purposes**

2. a. I use my smartphone/it to take pictures.
   b. I use my smartphone/it for taking pictures.
3. a. You use a flash drive/it to back up files.
   b. You use a flash drive/it for backing up files.
4. a. He would only use a laptop/it to watch movies and play games.
   b. He would only use a laptop/it for watching movies and playing games.
5. a. I use my computer/it to shop online and do research.
   b. I use my computer/it for shopping online and doing research.

2 **Imperatives and infinitives for giving suggestions**

2. Try not to talk on the phone when you're in an elevator.
3. Be sure not to eat or drink anything when you're at the computer.
4. Remember to clean your computer screen and keyboard once a week.
5. Make sure not to use your tablet outside when it's raining.
6. When the bell rings to start class, be sure to put your music player away!

Unit 8

1 **Relative clauses of time**

2. It's a wonderful time when people give thanks for the good things in their lives.
3. It's a day when everyone eats much more than usual.
4. I remember one particular year when the whole family came to our house.
5. That year was very cold when it snowed all Thanksgiving day.
6. I remember another thing about that Thanksgiving when my brother and I baked eight pies.

2 **Adverbial clauses of time**

2. a. Before the ceremony starts, students gather to put on robes and special hats.
   b. Students gather to put on robes and special hats before the ceremony starts.
3. a. When music plays, the students walk in a line to their seats.
   b. The students walk in a line to their seats when music plays.
4. a. After school officials and teachers make speeches, students get their diplomas.
   b. Students get their diplomas after school officials and teachers make speeches.
5. a. When the ceremony is finished, students throw their hats into the air and cheer.
   b. Students throw their hats into the air and cheer when the ceremony is finished.

Unit 9

1 **Time contrasts**

A: I saw a fascinating program last night. It talked about the past, the present, and the future.
B: What kinds of things did it describe?
A: Well, for example, the normal work week in the 19th century **was/used to be** over 60 hours. Nowadays, many people **work/are working** around 40 hours a week.
B: Well, that sounds like progress.
A: You're right. But on the show, they said that most people **will work/might work** fewer hours in the future. They also talked about the way we shop. These days, many of us **shop** online. In the old days, there **were** no supermarkets, so people **had to go/used to have to go** to a lot of different stores. In the future, people **will do/might do/are going to do** all their shopping from their phones.
B: I don't believe that.
A: Me neither. What about cars? Do you think people **will still drive/are still going to drive** cars a hundred years from now?
B: What did they say on the show?
A: They said that before the car, people **walked/used to walk** everywhere. Nowadays, we **drive** everywhere. And that **won't change/isn't going to change/'s not going to change**.

2 **Conditional sentences with *if* clauses**

2. If you **join** a gym, exercise **will become** part of your routine.
3. You **won't have to** worry about staying in shape if you **work out** three or four times a week.
4. If you **ride** a bike or **run** a few times a week, you**'ll lose** weight and **gain** muscle.
5. You**'ll sleep** better at night if you **exercise** regularly.
6. If you **start** exercising, you **might not have** as many colds and other health problems.

Unit 10

1 **Gerunds; short responses**

2. A: I'm not interested in reading about politics or politicians.
   B: Neither am I.
3. A: I'm good at solving problems.
   B: So am I.
4. A: I don't mind working on weekends.
   B: Neither do I.
5. A: I enjoy learning new things.
   B: So do I.
6. A: I'm not good at developing new ideas.
   B: Neither am I.

2 **Clauses with *because***

2. I wouldn't make a good high school teacher **because I'm not patient enough to work with kids**.
3. I wouldn't want to be a flight attendant **because I'm afraid of flying**.
4. I could never be an accountant **because I'm really bad with numbers**.
5. I would make a bad journalist **because I don't write very well**.
6. I'd be an excellent lawyer **because I love arguing with people**.

Unit 11

1 **Passive with *by* (simple past)**

2. Radium was discovered by Marie Curie in 1898.
3. The first aspirin was made by Dr. Felix Hoffmann in 1899.
4. The World Wide Web was developed by Tim Berners-Lee in 1989.
5. The planet Uranus was identified in 1781 by William Herschel.
6. The opera *Carmen* was written by Georges Bizet in the 1870s.

2 **Passive without *by* (simple present)**

2. Diamonds and gold from South Africa **are imported** by countries all over the world.
3. The U.S. dollar **is used** in Puerto Rico.
4. Colombia **is known** for its delicious coffee.
5. Many electronic products **are exported** by Japan and Korea. It's an important industry for these two countries.
6. The economy in many island countries, such as Jamaica, **is based** on tourism.

Unit 12

1 **Past continuous vs. simple past**

2. A: **Did** you **see** the storm yesterday?
   B: Yes! It **started** while I **was driving** to work.
3. A: We finally **moved** to a larger apartment.
   B: That's good. I know you **were living** in a tiny place when your daughter **was** born.
4. A: My sister **had** a bad accident. She **hurt** her back when she **was lifting** weights at the gym.
   B: That **happened** to me last year, but I **wasn't lifting** weights. I **was taking** a boxing class, and I **tripped**.

2 **Present perfect continuous**

1. A: What **have** you **been doing** all day?
   B: **I've been cleaning** the house, and Peter **has been watching** TV. He **hasn't been feeling** very well lately.
   A: How **have** you **been feeling** these days?
   B: **I've been feeling** great. I **haven't been eating** any junk food, and I**'ve been exercising** a lot. I**'ve been taking** really good care of myself.

2. A: How long **have** you and Joe **been dating**?
   B: We**'ve been going out** together for almost a year. Can you believe it?
   A: Maya and I **have been dating** for even longer. I think it's time to get married. We**'ve been talking** about it a lot lately.
   B: Joe and I **haven't been talking** about marriage, but I**'ve been thinking** about it.

Unit 13

1 Participles as adjectives

2. Kristen Stewart is an **amazing** actress. I'm **amazed** by her talent.
3. Are you **interested** in computer-generated special effects? The latest 3-D movies are very **interesting**.
4. I had an **embarrassing** experience the last time I went to the movies. I started to cough, and I couldn't stop. I was really **embarrassed**.
5. Julie and I saw an Italian comedy yesterday. I found it **amusing**, but Julie didn't seem very **amused** by it.
6. Oh, I'm really **disgusted** with Jeremy right now. He took me to the most **disgusting** movie last night. I wanted to walk out after half an hour, but he wouldn't leave!
7. Do you think sci-fi movie directors make their films **confusing** intentionally? I get so **confused** by the complicated storylines and weird characters.
8. I think that great books make great movies. If I find a book **fascinating**, I'm usually **fascinated** by the movie, too.

2 Relative pronouns for people and things

A: How did you like the movie last night? Was it any good?
B: It wasn't bad, but it's not the kind of movie **that** makes you think. I like films **that** have a strong message and interesting storylines.
A: How about the acting? Did you like the actors **who** star in it?
B: Jessica Biel is pretty good, actually.
A: Oh, she's that beautiful actress **who** is married to Justin Timberlake.
B: Justin who? Who's that?
A: Oh, you know him. He's the one **who** was in the band 'NSync years ago. It was a "boy band" **that** was popular in the 1990s.
B: I remember 'NSync, but I don't remember the names of the guys **who** were in the band.
A: Well, I loved Justin Timberlake when I was a kid. And he's not a bad actor. Did you see the movie *The Social Network*?
B: I did see that. It's about the guys **who** started Facebook, right? I didn't realize Justin Timberlake was in it. Now I'll have to see it again!

Unit 14

1 Modals and adverbs

1. a. Maybe it means she doesn't agree with you.
   b. It might mean she doesn't agree with you.
   c. It may mean she doesn't agree with you.
2. a. That gesture probably means, "Come here."
3. a. That must mean he doesn't understand you.

2 Permission, obligation, and prohibition

1. A: Oh, no! That sign says, "No fishing." That means we **can't** fish here.
   B: You're right. We**'ve got to/have to** go somewhere else to fish. I think you**'re allowed to/can** fish in the pond on Cedar Road. Let's go there.
2. A: What does that sign mean?
   B: It means bad news for us. It means you **aren't allowed to** bring dogs to the beach. We'd better take Buddy home.
3. A: Please don't leave your garbage here. You**'ve got to/ have to** put it in the trash room down the hall. That's one of the building's rules.
   B: I'm really sorry.
4. A: You **can** put your bike in the bike room downstairs, if you want. It's much safer than locking it up outside.
   B: Oh, that's great! I'll do that. I didn't know about the bike room.

Unit 15

1 Unreal conditional sentences with *if* clauses

1. A: If a friend **asked** to borrow some money, what **would** you **say**?
   B: Well, if I **had** any extra money that month, I **would** probably **give** it to her.
2. A: What **would/could** you **do** if someone **gave** you a million dollars?
   B: Hmm, I'm not sure. I **could/might buy** a lot of nice clothes and jewelry, or I **could/might spend** some and **give** some away, or I **could/might put** it all in the bank.
3. A: If you **thought** a friend was doing something dangerous, **would** you **say** something to him, or **would** you **keep** quiet?
   B: I **would** definitely **talk** to my friend about it.
4. A: What **would** you **do** if you **had** a problem with your boss?
   B: That's a hard one. If that **happened**, I **might/could talk** to the human resources department about it, or I **might/ could** just **sit down** with my boss and **talk** about the situation.

2 Past modals

2. You should have written a note and left the mail in your box.
3. I would have told her the truth.
4. I would have told her I wasn't interested and hung up (the phone).

Unit 16

1 Reported speech: requests

2. Tyler said to meet him in the cafeteria at school at noon.
3. Tyler told him/Harry not to leave his shoes in the living room.
4. Tyler said to hang up his wet towels.
5. Tyler asked him/Harry to stop using his/Tyler's phone.
6. Tyler told him/Harry to make his bed on weekdays.
7. Tyler said not to eat his/Tyler's food.
8. Tyler told him/Harry to be a better roommate.

2 Reported speech: statements

1. Lori said (that) she had to visit her grandparents that day. Lori told them (that) she had to visit her grandparents that day.
2. Mario said/told them (that) he was going to a play on Sunday.
3. Julia said/told them (that) she had promised to take her brother to the movies that day.
4. Daniel said/told them (that) he couldn't come because he had to study for a huge exam on Monday.
5. The neighbors said/told them (that) they would be out of town all weekend.
6. Alice said/told them (that) she might have to babysit her nephew.

Appendix

Countries and nationalities

This is a partial list of countries, many of which are presented in this book.

Argentina	Argentine
Australia	Australian
Austria	Austrian
Bolivia	Bolivian
Brazil	Brazilian
Canada	Canadian
Chile	Chilean
China	Chinese
Colombia	Colombian
Costa Rica	Costa Rican
Czech Republic	Czech
Ecuador	Ecuadorian
Egypt	Egyptian
England	English
France	French
Germany	German
Greece	Greek
Hungary	Hungarian
India	Indian
Indonesia	Indonesian
Ireland	Irish
Italy	Italian
Japan	Japanese
Malaysia	Malaysian
Mexico	Mexican
Morocco	Moroccan
New Zealand	New Zealander
Paraguay	Paraguayan
Peru	Peruvian
the Philippines	Filipino
Portugal	Portuguese
Russia	Russian
Singapore	Singaporean
South Korea	South Korean
Spain	Spanish
Switzerland	Swiss
Thailand	Thai
Turkey	Turkish
the United Kingdom	British
the United States	American
Uruguay	Uruguayan
Vietnam	Vietnamese

Irregular verbs

Present	Past	Participle
(be) am / is, are	was, were	been
break	broke	broken
bring	brought	brought
build	built	built
buy	bought	bought
come	came	come
do	did	done
drink	drank	drunk
drive	drove	driven
eat	ate	eaten
fall	fell	fallen
feel	felt	felt
find	found	found
fly	flew	flown
forget	forgot	forgotten
give	gave	given
go	went	gone
grow	grew	grown
have	had	had
hear	heard	heard
keep	kept	kept
lose	lost	lost
meet	met	met
put	put	put
ride	rode	ridden
ring	rang	rung
run	ran	run
see	saw	seen
send	sent	sent
set	set	set
speak	spoke	spoken
stand	stood	stood
steal	stole	stolen
swim	swam	swum
take	took	taken
teach	taught	taught
tell	told	told
think	thought	thought
wear	wore	worn
write	wrote	written

Comparative and superlative adjectives

Adjectives with *-er* and *-est*

big, bright, busy, cheap, clean, dark, dingy, dirty, far, fast, heavy, hot, huge, large, long, loud, messy, near, neat, new, nice, noisy, old, quiet, safe, short, slow, small, tall, young

Adjectives with *more* and *most*

attractive, beautiful, boring, comfortable, convenient, cramped, crowded, dangerous, delicious, difficult, exciting, expensive, famous, important, inconvenient, interesting, modern, patient, popular, private, run-down, serious, spacious, special, terrible, unusual

Irregular adjectives

good → better → best

bad → worse → the worst

1 Language summary

VOCABULARY

Nouns
achievement
award
(summer) camp
(body) cast
chess
childhood
comic book
contact information
courage
headline
hide-and-seek
hobby
hometown
illness
immigrant
interest
memory
outdoors
pet
playground
politics
possession
profile
recreation
relatives
role
scary movies
self-portrait
social networking
specialist
stickers
superhero
taste
teddy bear
thriller
toy car
video game

Adjectives
basic
current
far
fit
good (at)
messy
neat
online
outdoor

Verbs
argue
collect
direct (a movie)
donate
follow
get (in trouble)
keep fit
produce (a movie)
refer
remember
skate
take up
notice
urge
worry (about something)

Adverbs
afterwards
regularly

EXPRESSIONS

Introducing yourself
My name is . . . ./I'm . . . .
Nice to meet you.

Exchanging personal information
Could you tell me (a little) about yourself?
Are you from . . . ?
  Yes, I am./No, I'm not.
Where were you born?
  I was born in . . . .
Did you grow up there?
  Yes, I did./No, I didn't.

Talking about past activities
Where did you learn to . . . ?
What/Where did you use to . . . ?
  When I was a kid, I used to . . . .
Did you use to . . . ?
  Yes, I did./Yes, I used to . . . .
  No, I didn't./No, I didn't use to . . . , but now . . . .

Apologizing
I'm (really) sorry.

Asking for and agreeing to a favor
Can you . . . ?
  Sure.
  It's a deal!

2 Language summary

VOCABULARY

Nouns
ATM
bicyclist
birthplace
block
campaign
capacity
certificate
CO_2 (= carbon dioxide)
commute
crowd
daycare
downtown
facilities
fare
government
healthcare
issue
marvel
message
board
nature
paradise
passenger
pedestrian
pollution
post
restroom
resident
rush
service
shopping mall
sign
slogan
speed
tip
theme
tourism
traffic

Compound nouns
bicycle lane
bicycle stand
bus lane
bus station
bus stop
bus system
green space
parking garage
parking space
police officer
public transportation
recycling center
recycling system
rush hour
streetlight
subway line
subway station
subway stop
subway system
taxi lane
taxi service
taxi stand
traffic jam
train station
train stop
train system
Wi-Fi hotspots

Adjectives
affordable
colorful
cheerful
duty-free
eco-friendly
family-friendly
healthy
inexpensive
live
memorable
pre-paid (phone)
silly

Verbs
apply (for something)
appreciate
attract
catch (a bus)
cause
earn
improve
lend
provide
run (= operate)
stay (open)
take (forever)

Adverbs of quantity
fewer
less
more
not enough
too many
too much

EXPRESSIONS

Expressing concern
There are too many . . . /There is too much . . .
There should be fewer . . . /There should be less. . .
We need more . . .
There aren't enough . . . /There isn't enough . . . .

Getting someone's attention
Excuse me.

Asking for information
Could you tell me where . . . ?
Can you tell me how often . . . ?
Do you know what time/when . . . ?
Just one more thing.
What time does . . . ?

Thanking someone
Thanks (a lot).

3 Language summary

VOCABULARY

Nouns
(room and) board
contact lenses
damage
evaluation
expense
housework
(musical) instrument
mobile home
personality
PIN
privacy
progress
questionnaire
reminder
rent
reunion
safari
seaweed
seeds
(closet) space
suburb
vegetable
wish
wish list
wishful thinking

Adjectives
afraid
average
bright
comfortable
common
convenient
cramped
dingy
huge
inconvenient
modern
private
run-down
separate
spacious
two-car/2-car (garage)
wild

Verbs
achieve
add
expect
grow (one's own)
make (changes)
move (out/away)
park (a car)
rent
waste

Adverb
abroad

Preposition
per

EXPRESSIONS

Giving an opinion
The . . . isn't . . . enough.
The . . . is too . . . .
There aren't enough . . . ./There isn't enough . . . .
It's not as . . . as . . . .
It doesn't have as many . . . as . . . ./It has just as many . . . as . . . .
There is too much . . .

Expressing regret about a present situation
I'm afraid so.
I wish (that) I could . . . .
I wish I didn't . . . .
I wish life were easier.

Agreeing
Me, too.

4 Language summary

VOCABULARY

Nouns

Food and beverages

check
cilantro
coconut
comfort foods
curry
eggplant
fish
garlic
knowledge
lamb
lime
lobster
meat
oil
onion
(an) order
(chili) pepper
popcorn
pork
ramen
salt
sauce
shellfish
snail
soda
soy sauce
spice
squid
takeout
tuna
topping

Other

appetizer
(the) blues
bowl
brain
bunch
competition
cookbook
diet
dish
dough
driver's license
free time
grill
mixture
model (= example)
order
pan
password
plate
recipe
server
side
slice
stew
survey
tablespoon

Adjectives

For food and beverages

delicious
ethnic
juicy
lean
marinated
melted
rich
soothing
strange
tempting
tough

Other

anxious
clay
depressed
irritable
low (= unhappy)
secure
stressed

Verbs

Cooking methods

bake
boil
fry
grill
roast
steam
toast

Other

calm down
cheer up
chop
close
contain
cool
cover
cry
cut up
fit
heat
influence
marinate
mash
mix
not care for (= not like)
order
outsmart
pop
pour
refrigerate
relieve (stress)
roll out
shake
spread
squeeze
stand up
stir
turn over

Adverbs

from time to time
lightly
powerfully

Conjunction

as well as

EXPRESSIONS

Talking about food and beverages

Have you ever eaten . . . ?
  Yes, I have./No, I haven't.
It was/They were . . . !
This/It sounds . . . ./
They sound . . . .

Ordering in a restaurant

Have you decided yet?
  Yes. I'll have . . . .
And you?
  I think I'll have . . .

Making and declining an offer

Why don't you try some?
  No, thanks./No, I don't think so.

Describing a procedure

First, . . .
Then . . .
Next, . . .
After that, . . .
Finally, . . .

5 Language summary

VOCABULARY

Nouns

Activities

bike tour
camping
cruise
eat at stalls (on the street)
hang out
hula
rafting
sightseeing
sing-along
stargazing
surfing
take the train

Other

accommodations
ATM card
brochure
camper
carry-on bag
catamaran
condition
copy
credit card
cruise
danger
document
double room
first-aid kit
health
identification
lodge
luggage
medication
money belt
opportunity
plane ticket
reindeer
rental
safety
sandals
single room
specialty
stall
sub-zero
suitcase
surfboard
swimsuit
tap
tour
vaccination
visa
wildlife

Adjectives

beachfront
checked
excited
foreign
necessary
pleasant
round-trip
whole

Verbs

Modals

had better
must
ought to
should

Other

avoid
bring back
carry
check out
discover
hang out
pick (someone) up
rent
sunbathe

Adverbs

by myself
fairly
in advance
right away

EXPRESSIONS

Talking about definite plans

Have you made any plans?
 I'm going to . . . .
How are you going to spend . . . ?

Talking about possible plans

I guess I'll . . . .
Maybe I'll . . . .
I think I'll . . . .
I probably won't . . . .

Asking about length of time

For how long?
How long are you going to . . . ?

Describing necessity

You must/You need to/You (don't) have to . . . .

Giving suggestions

You'd better/You ought to/You should/You shouldn't . . . .

Making and accepting an offer

Why don't you . . . ?
Do you mean it? I'd love to!
The more the merrier!
That sounds like fun.

6 Language summary

VOCABULARY

Nouns
chore
expense
groceries
guest
laptop
magazine
mess
noise
parking space
staff
stranger
survey
trash

Adjectives
clumsy
embarrassed
loud
(un)reasonable
sure
tasty

Verbs
Two-part verbs
clean up
drive (someone) crazy
go through
hang up
keep (something) clean
let (something or someone) out
look after
make sure
pick up (after yourself)
put away
take off
take out
throw out
turn down
turn off
turn on

Other
admit
apologize
bother
criticize
gain (weight)
lend
lock
make
mind
promise
realize
refuse
respect
text

Adverbs
almost
as soon as
quietly
sincerely

EXPRESSIONS

Making and agreeing/objecting to a request
Please . . ./. . . , please.
In a minute.
OK. No problem!
Oh, but . . . .
All right. I'll . . . .
Can/Could you . . . ?
  Sure, no problem. I'd be glad to.
Would you please . . . ?
  OK. I'll . . . .
Would you mind . . . ?
  Sorry. I'll . . . right away.

Giving an excuse
I'm sorry. I didn't realize . . . .

Admitting a mistake
I'm sorry. I forgot.
You're right./I was wrong.

Making an offer
I'll . . . right away.
Feel free to . . .

Making a promise
I promise I'll . . . ./
I'll make sure to . . . .

7 Language summary

VOCABULARY

Nouns

Machines/Appliances/ Technology

app
computer crash
drone
flash drive
gadget
GPS system
identity theft
passcode
robot
smartphone
smart device
tablet
touchscreen
video call

Other

assignment
burglar
computer whiz
digital native
directions
doubt
employee
early adopter
fee
hacker
invention
task
technology

Adjectives

frozen
strict
worth

Verbs

back up
create
entertain
freeze
influence
lend
perform
post
protect
recharge
rent
(get a) ride
set
understand

EXPRESSIONS

Describing a use or purpose

How do you use . . .?
 I use it for . . . .

Giving advice

Be sure (not) to . . . .
Don't forget to . . . .
Make sure (not) to . . . .
Remember to . . . .
Try (not) to . . . .

8 Language summary

VOCABULARY

Nouns

Holidays, festivals, and celebrations

April Fool's Day
Carnival
Children's Day
Chinese New Year
Day of the Dead
Labor Day
Mother's Day
New Year's Eve
Saint Patrick's Day
Thanksgiving
Valentine's Day
wedding anniversary

Other

ancestor
barbecue
boyfriend
bride
candles
ceremony
costumes
custom
doll
fall
fireworks
get-together
groom
honeymoon
loaf of bread
(good/bad) luck
marriage
mask
parade
picnic
reception
relatives
(engagement) ring
samba
sari
sculpture
skeleton
spring
summer
tradition
trick
winter

Adjectives

lunar
messy
national
romantic
surprise
traditional

Verbs

(be) like
book
date
destroy
dress
dress up
explode
fill
get engaged/married
get lost
get together
look forward to
occur
put on
strike

EXPRESSIONS

Describing holidays, festivals, and celebrations

. . . is a day/a night when . . . .
. . . is the day when . . . .
. . . is the month when . . . .
. . . is the season when . . . .
A/An . . . is a time when . . . .
After . . . , ...
Before . . . , ...
When . . . , ...

Asking about customs

How long does it last?
Is/Are there . . . ?
What do people wear?
What happens?
What happens during the . . . ?
What kind of food is served?
When is it?
Why do they do that?

9 Language summary

VOCABULARY

Nouns
advantage
advertisement
assembly line
builder
bunch
(common) cold
communication
consequence
cure
degree
disadvantage
entertainment
environment
fashion
grocery store
gym
healthcare
housing
loan
meal
national team
neighborhood
ocean liner
office tower
pupil
shame
situation
steam train
takeout
tax
teleportation

Adjectives
attracted to
bright
brilliant
dark
driverless
embarrassed
empty
falling down
high-paying
in shape
intelligent
jealous
multiple
non-polluting
popular
serious
shy
two-hour
virtual

Verbs
Modals
can
may
might
would

Other
admit
be able
become
begin
consider
die
earn
exist
fall in love
feel
fight
fly
get
hang out
improve
join
look after
meet
miss
move
offer
order
receive
shout
spend
tear down
travel

Adverbs
anymore
anywhere
nowadays
sadly
soon
still

Conjunction
so

EXPRESSIONS

Talking about the past
In the past, ...
People used to . . . .
. . . years ago, ...

Talking about the present
These days, ...
Today, people . . . .
Nowadays, people . . . .

Talking about the future
Soon, there will be . . . .
In . . . years, people might/may . . . .
In the future, people are going to . . . .

Describing situations and possible consequences
If I . . . , I won't be able to . . . .
If you don't . . . , you'll have to . . . .
If they . . . , they might . . . .
If you . . . , you may have to . . . .

10 Language summary

VOCABULARY

Nouns

Jobs/Occupations
accountant
activities director
agent
architect
artist
flight attendant
journalist
marine biologist
reporter
stockbroker
teacher
video game tester

Other
agreement
applicant
article
bug
career
co-worker
deadline
(business) deal
decision
device
employee
experience
honesty
overseas
overtime
personality trait
pressure
public speaking
relationship
résumé
(special) skills
stock market
straight talk
timetable

Adjectives

attentive
broke
creative
critical
cross-cultural
developing (country)
disorganized
efficient
forgetful
generous
hardworking
impatient
lazy
level-headed
moody
nine-to-five
organized
patient
punctual
reliable
rude
serious
short-tempered
strict
unfriendly

Verbs

agree
analyze
apply
be fed up (with something/someone)
chat
check (something) out
design
develop
do for a living
draw
enjoy
evaluate
go over
hire
interview
laugh
lighten up
make a decision
make up (your mind)
manage
place (one's trust in)
realize
release
sell
sign

Preposition

besides

EXPRESSIONS

Talking about possible occupations
I'd make a good/bad . . . because . . . .
I wouldn't want to be a/an . . . because . . . .
I could (never) be a/an . . . because . . . .
I wouldn't mind working as a/an . . . because . . . .
The best job for me is . . . because . . . .

Expressing feelings and opinions
I like/hate/enjoy . . . .
I'm (not) interested in . . . .
I'm (not) good at . . . .
I don't mind . . . .
I can't stand . . . .

Agreeing with feelings and opinions
So do I.
So am I.
Neither am I.
Neither do I.
Neither can I.

Disagreeing with feelings and opinions
I don't.
Really? I . . . .
Oh, I'm not.
I am!
Well, I am.
Oh, I don't mind.

11 Language summary

VOCABULARY

Nouns
B.C.E. (Before the Common Era)
canal
cattle
chess set
clue
construction
crop
currency
dialects
drawing
euro
exhibit
feta cheese
Flemish
handicraft
lobster
microscope
needle
northwest
novel
pin
revolution
rice
seabed
sheep
souvenir
soybeans
textiles
variety
wheat
World Heritage City
wonder

Adjectives
agricultural
amazing
corrupt
digital
food-processing
life-size
manual (typewriter)
medieval
official
tiny
traditional
unique
warm
wide

Verbs
catch
consume
cultivate
direct
employ
export
feature
film
manufacture
preserve
produce
raise
record
wonder

Adverb
officially

EXPRESSIONS

Describing works of art, inventions, and discoveries
. . . was/were built/composed/created/designed/directed/painted/recorded/written by . . . .
. . . was/were developed/discovered/invented/produced by . . . .

Asking about a country
Where is it located?
What languages are spoken?
What currency is used?
What famous tourist attraction is found there?
What products are exported?
What cities are found there?
Is English spoken (much) there?
Are credit cards accepted (everywhere)?

12 Language summary

VOCABULARY

Nouns
audience
audition
bunch
celebrity
childhood
classical music
deaf
disability
effect
ending
flat tire
fork
headphones
hearing aid
influence
knife
luck
nightmare
selfie
sign language
vibration
wallet

Adjectives
accidental
amazed
brilliant
calm
normal
powerful
quiet
spectacular
surprising
tiny
worth

Verbs
achieve
act
break
burn
compare
crash
drive (someone) crazy
drum
hear
pick up
realize
recognize
reply
save (money)
ski
slip
spend (money)
spill

Adverbs
accidentally
coincidentally
fortunately
immediately
luckily
miraculously
obviously
sadly
strangely
suddenly
surprisingly
unexpectedly
unfortunately

EXPRESSIONS

Talking about past events
I was . . . , but I . . . .
I was . . . when I . . . .
While I was . . . , ...

Exchanging personal information
What have you been doing lately? I've been . . . .
How long have you been doing that?
For . . . .
Since I graduated.

Greeting someone after a long time
I haven't seen you in ages. What have you been up to?

Expressing interest and surprise
Wow! Tell me more.
Oh, really?
Really? I didn't know that!
Oh, I see.
I had no idea.
Well, that's exciting.

Asking for a reason
How come?

13 Language summary

VOCABULARY

Nouns

Movie types

action
adventure
animated
(romantic) comedy
documentary
drama
horror
musical
science fiction
thriller

Other

acting
audience
bill
boot camp
character
critic
director
lines
motion picture
producer
rib
special effects
story
studio
thumb
trivia

Adjectives

amazing
amusing
awful
bizarre
blockbuster
choosy
disgusting
dumb
excellent
fascinating
horrible
main
odd
outstanding
ridiculous
silly
stupid
talented
terrible
terrifying
unpleasant
weird
wonderful

Verbs

amaze
amuse
annoy
be based (on)
bore
confuse
disgust
dress up
embarrass
excite
fascinate
interest
laugh
put through
rate
shock
surprise
terrify

Adverbs

by mistake
mentally
physically

EXPRESSIONS

Giving opinions about movies, books, and people

I'm (not) interested in . . . .
I thought . . . .
I'm fascinated by . . . .
I (don't) think . . . .
I (don't) find . . . .
I was bored by . . . .

Describing movies, books, and people

It's the movie which/ that . . . .
It was a great book which/that . . . .
It's about a man/woman who/that . . . .
He's/She's . . . who/that . . . .

14 Language summary

VOCABULARY

Nouns
body language
garbage can
gesture
lane
nail
obligation
permission
prohibition
regulation
rule
sailor
seat belt
speed limit
stairs
trash
thumbs up

Adjectives
annoyed
bored
broke
confused
disgusted
embarrassed
exhausted
flushed
frustrated
heart-shaped
irritated
late
nervous
polite
reserved
rude

Verbs
argue
bite
break
clap
exist
fasten
nod
park
pull out
raise
roll
scratch
scream
tap
turn off
wink

Adverbs
absolutely
definitely
maybe
perhaps
possibly
quickly

Preposition
side to side

EXPRESSIONS

Hypothesizing
It might/may mean . . . .
It could mean . . . .
Maybe/Perhaps it means . . . .
It possibly means . . . .

Making a logical assumption
That must mean . . . .
That probably means. . . .
That definitely means. . . .

Disagreeing
I don't think so.

Expressing permission
You can . . . .
You're allowed to . . . .

Expressing prohibition
You can't. . . .
You aren't allowed to. . . .

Expressing obligation
You have to . . . .
You've got to . . . .

15 Language summary

VOCABULARY

Nouns
campsite
cashier
comb
diet
fundraising
honesty
jail
owner
predicament
problem
repair shop
reward
trash
truth

Adjectives
honest
overweight
selfish
strict
valuable

Verbs
accept
admit
agree
borrow
catch
cheat
complain
confess
demand
deny
dislike
disqualify
divorce
enjoy
exchange
find
fit (something) in
forget
ignore
lend
lose
marry
oversleep
pay off
refuse
reply
save
spend
spill
text
trust
warn

Adverbs
meanwhile
straight

EXPRESSIONS

Describing imaginary situations and consequences in the present
What would you do if . . . ?
　If I . . . , I'd/I could/I might/I wouldn't . . . .

Saying someone is right
Hmm. You've got a point there.

Expressing disbelief
You're kidding!

Giving opinions or suggestions about actions in the past
What should I have done?
　You should have . . . . /You shouldn't have . . . .
What would you have done?
　I would have . . . . /I wouldn't have . . . .

16 Language summary

VOCABULARY

Nouns
apology
assignment
coach
complaint
day off
employee
excuse
guy
hallway
highway
houseguest
(good/bad) intentions
invitation
joke
lie
request
stomachache
suggestion
sympathy
truth

Adjectives
average
due
flat (tire)
funny
household

Verbs
bounce
donate
fire
hide
lose track
make up
pick up
slip
sympathize
take care

Adverbs
quickly
out of town
past (= later than)

EXPRESSIONS

Reporting requests
. . . asked/told me to . . . .
. . . said to . . . .
. . . asked/told me not to . . . .
. . . said not to . . . .

Reporting statements
. . . said (that) . . . .
. . . told me (that) . . . .

Exchanging personal information
How are things?
Just fine, thanks.

Talking on the phone
Hi, ... This is . . . .
Oh, hi.

Expressing regret
That's too bad.
I'm really sorry.
I'm sorry, too.

Audio scripts

1 Good memories

2 Conversation (p. 2)

B Listen to the rest of the conversation. What are two more things you learn about Isabel?

Isabel: Hey, that was fun. Thanks for the lesson!
Nico: No problem. So, tell me a little about yourself. What do you do?
Isabel: I work in a hospital.
Nico: Really! What do you do there?
Isabel: I'm in charge of their computers.
Nico: Oh, so you're a computer specialist.
Isabel: Well, sort of. Yeah, I guess so.
Nico: That's great. Then maybe you can give me some help with a computer course I'm taking.
Isabel: Oh, sure . . . but only if you promise to give me some more skateboarding lessons.
Nico: It's a deal!

4 Listening (p. 3)

A Listen to interviews with two immigrants to the United States. Why did they move to the U.S.A.?

1. Enrique

Interviewer: So where are you from originally, Enrique?
Enrique: I'm from Mexico . . . near Chiapas.
Interviewer: And when did you move here to New York?
Enrique: When I was 18 years old. I came here to study.
Interviewer: What did you study?
Enrique: I studied business. I wanted to return to Mexico afterwards, but I found a great job here in New York.
Interviewer: I see. So you're an immigrant to the United States.
Enrique: That's right.
Interviewer: What was the most difficult thing about moving to the U.S.?
Enrique: Well, I don't have any relatives here and in the beginning, it was hard. You see, in Mexico, we spend a lot of time with family. But now I have a lot of friends here and it's easier.
Interviewer: So what things do you miss the most from home?
Enrique: Oh, that's easy—the food! There are some great Mexican restaurants here, but it's not the same as my mother's cooking.

2. Jessica

Interviewer: Hi, Jessica. Where are you from?
Jessica: Hi! I'm from South Korea, but I've lived here in the U.S. since I was a teenager.
Interviewer: And why did you move to the U.S.?
Jessica: I came here to go to high school and improve my English.
Interviewer: And are you studying now?
Jessica: No, I finished college last year and now I'm working as an engineer in New York.
Interviewer: That's great! And what was it like when you first came here? Was it difficult?
Jessica: Yeah, it was at times. The biggest change was the school system. They organize classes differently here. I think students have more free time here than in South Korea, but I like it!
Interviewer: And what do you miss the most from South Korea?
Jessica: My family. I try to go home often, but it's expensive and far. I miss the music too, but fortunately I can listen to a lot of it online.

B Listen again and complete the chart.

2 Life in the city

4 Listening (p. 9)

A Listen to a city resident talk to her new neighbor about the city. Check (✓) True or False for each statement.

Sophia: Hi, there. I'm Sophia. You must be my new neighbor!
Jacob: Yes, hi! My name's Jacob.
Sophia: Welcome to the building! Are you all moved in?
Jacob: I am! Tomorrow I start my new job downtown.
Sophia: That's great. So you have a car?
Jacob: No, I don't. I was planning to take the bus there.
Sophia: Oh, you don't want to do that. It'll take forever. There aren't enough buses in this city. We really need more public transportation.
Jacob: Really?
Sophia: Yeah, everyone has a car. And in summer there are way too many tourists, so there are even more cars than usual right now. And don't even ask about parking!
Jacob: Well, I really don't want to buy a car. Is it safe to ride a bike?
Sophia: Yeah, people ride their bikes a lot, actually. Do you have one?
Jacob: No, I don't, but I guess I'll buy one.
Sophia: If you want, you can borrow my bike tomorrow. And I know a great bike shop I can recommend.
Jacob: Wow, thanks, Sophia! I appreciate it.

B Listen again. For the false statements, write the correct information.

8 Conversation (p. 11)

B Listen to the rest of the conversation. Check the information that Rachel asks for.

Rachel: Excuse me. It's me again. I'm sorry. I need some more information – if you don't mind. Do you know how much the bus costs?
Clerk: It's $10. You can buy a ticket on the bus.
Rachel: $10? Wow.
Clerk: Well, a taxi costs about $25.
Rachel: Hmm, OK. And do you know where a bookstore is? I'd like to get a city guide.
Clerk: Go two blocks down and turn right. You'll see one on your left.
Rachel: Thanks very much. Have a nice day.
Clerk: You, too.

Units 1–2 Progress check

1 Listening (p. 14)

A Listen to an interview with Charlotte, a fashion designer. Answer the questions in complete sentences.

Interviewer: Thanks for taking the time to speak with me, Charlotte.
Charlotte: Oh, it's my pleasure.
Interviewer: So you're not from New York. Where did you grow up?
Charlotte: I grew up in Australia, in a city called Melbourne.
Interviewer: How do you spell that?
Charlotte: M-E-L-B-O-U-R-N-E.
Interviewer: What was that like?
Charlotte: Fantastic. It's a really fun city, right on the ocean. My family still lives there. My father owns a restaurant, and my mother teaches.
Interviewer: What did you want to be when you grew up?
Charlotte: Well, I never thought I'd be a fashion designer! I wanted to be a teacher or maybe a writer.
Interviewer: Why not a fashion designer?
Charlotte: Well, I never thought people would like my ideas.
Interviewer: I can't imagine it. Were you popular when you were growing up?
Charlotte: Not really. I wasn't unpopular, but I wasn't in the popular crowd at school. I had a nice group of friends, though.
Interviewer: How did you like school?
Charlotte: Oh, I loved school. I was a great student. My mother actually taught at my primary school. I always thought that was fun.
Interviewer: What about your free time as a child? Did you have a hobby?
Charlotte: I used to love to draw. Later I learned to paint, and I still do that. Actually, I have some paintings in a gallery right now.
Interviewer: That's impressive.
Charlotte: Well, it's a very small exhibit. But it's something I really enjoy when I'm not designing clothes.
Interviewer: Did you have a favorite sport when you were growing up?
Charlotte: I used to play basketball a lot as a kid. My friends and I used to watch our favorite teams play and then play our own games, too. I really liked basketball.
Interviewer: What about a favorite place?
Charlotte: Hmm. My favorite place? I used to go to a summer camp on a lake. I loved that. I got to go horseback riding almost every day.
Interviewer: Do you still ride horses?
Charlotte: No. Not very often.

3 Making changes

5 Listening (p. 18)

A Listen to Josh describe a "capsule hotel." Check True or False for each statement.

Host: Welcome to the program "A Home Away from Home." Our guest tonight is Josh Philips from Tennessee. Josh, tell us a little bit about yourself. What do you do?
Josh: Well, at the moment, I'm working as an English teacher in Tokyo, Japan. Tokyo is an exciting city, but sometimes it feels too big. It can take hours to go from one part of the city to another. When I don't feel like going all the way home, I sometimes stay in a capsule hotel.
Host: A capsule hotel? Can you explain what that is?
Josh: Yeah. It's a hotel with lots of small rooms. Actually, they're not really rooms. They're spaces that are two meters by one meter, and only a meter high, so they're very cramped! But the hotel is just as convenient as a regular hotel, and not as expensive.
Host: And what's inside each little room, or should I say, each space?
Josh: Well, inside every capsule there's a bed, a TV . . .
Host: A TV? Really?
Josh: Yeah, and a reading light, a radio, and an alarm clock. The hotel also has lockers for your personal belongings.
Host: Interesting. So what kind of people stay in a capsule hotel?
Josh: Well, probably people like me. People who miss the last train home or don't want to go all the way home. Sometimes you're just too busy and tired, especially if you have to work early the next morning.
Host: Interesting. So, would you recommend a capsule hotel to other people?
Josh: Sure! The rooms are small, but you get used to it. But I wouldn't recommend a capsule hotel to people who can't relax in small, cramped spaces. There just isn't enough space.

B Listen again. For the false statements, write the correct information.

8 Conversation (p. 19)

B Listen to the rest of the conversation. What changes would Harry like to make in his life?

Harry: Yeah! It's sometimes pretty hard to pay the rent. I'm thinking of finding a new job.
Dylan: Really? What kind of job would you like?
Harry: I'm not sure, but I wish I worked somewhere else. I'm tired of this place. I need to live somewhere more exciting.
Dylan: I know what you mean. Hey, maybe we could move to a different city. We could even be roommates!
Harry: Yeah. Uhh. Maybe . . .

4 Have you ever tried it?

2 Conversation (p. 22)

B Listen to the rest of the conversation. How did Aiden like the snails? What else did he order?

Claire: Oh, good! Here comes our server now!
Server: Here are your frog legs. And for you, sir . . . the snails.
Aiden: Thank you.
Claire: Mmm, these frog legs are delicious! How are the snails?
Aiden: Well, I think they're . . . yuck! Oh, sorry, I guess snails are too strange for me. Um, I think I'm going to order something else, if you don't mind.
Claire: Oh, sure. Go ahead.
Aiden: Excuse me!
Server: Yes?
Aiden: Um, I really don't care for this appetizer. Could you bring me something else?
Server: Yes, of course. What would you like instead?
Claire: Try the frog legs.
Aiden: No, I don't think so. I'll tell you what. Just forget an appetizer for me, and bring me a nice, juicy steak . . . with French fries and a large soda.

5 Listening (p. 23)

A Listen to six people ask questions in a restaurant. Are they talking about these items? Write Y (yes) or N (no).

1.

Woman: Have you finished with this?
Man: No, I'm still drinking it. Thanks.

2.

Man: Have you tried this before?
Woman: Yes, I have. Mm, and it's just as delicious as it smells!

3.

Man: Did you taste it?
Woman: No, not yet. I'm waiting for the waitress to bring me a fork.

4.

Man: Have you ever eaten this here?
Woman: I ate it once, but I didn't like it. I think it was cooked for too long.

5.

Woman: How is it?
Man: Great. Just the way I like it: black and strong.

6.

Man 1: Did you ask the waiter for it?

Man 2: Yes, and it's my treat this time. You paid last time.

B Listen again. For the *no* items, write what they might be talking about.

11 Listening (p. 26)

A Listen to people explain how to make these snacks. Which snack are they talking about? Number the photos from 1 to 4. (There is one extra photo.)

1.

Man: This snack is one of my favorites. First, take a couple tomatoes and chop them. Next, chop half an onion and a little cilantro and put them in with the tomato. After that, you chop a small jalapeño pepper and add that in. Then, put in some lemon or lime juice. Finally, add a little salt and pepper. Mm, it's healthy and great with chips!

2.

Woman: This is really easy. First, you put a little oil in a pan. Then heat the oil. Next, put in the kernels and cover the pan. When the kernels start to pop, shake the pan gently every few seconds. In about a minute, the popping will slowly stop. After that, turn off the heat, and pour it into a bowl. Finally, put a little salt on it and enjoy!

3.

Man: My grandpa taught me how to make this easy breakfast. First, put egg, vanilla, and cinnamon in a bowl and mix them together. Stir in the milk. Then dip slices of bread in the mixture so both sides of the bread are wet. Cook the bread in a pan on medium heat until both sides are golden. It's delicious with maple syrup!

4.

Woman: My mom and I always used to make these. You need butter, sugar, egg, flour, and salt. Oh, and chocolate, of course! First, mix the butter, sugar, and egg together. Then add the flour and salt. Next, add the chocolate and mix it all together. Finally, make balls with the mixture and put them on a tray. Bake in the oven for eight minutes. I love to eat them with a glass of milk!

B Listen again. Check the steps you hear for each recipe.

Units 3–4 Progress check

2 Listening (p. 28)

A Listen to three people talk about things they wish they could change. Check the topic each person is talking about.

1.

Woman: I don't like where I'm living. I need a change. I wish I could move to a big city. There are lots of things to do and see. I would love being in a new place.

2.

Man: I wish I spoke Spanish. I really need it if I want to travel to Central America. And I know that if I speak another language, I can get a better job, too.

3.

Woman: I've been really worried about money. I wish I could find a better job. I could save a little money every month. I could even buy a few things that I need, too.

B Listen again. Write one change each person would like to make.

5 Hit the road!

2 Conversation (p. 30)

B Listen to the rest of the conversation. Where are they going to stay? How will they get there?

Lily: By the way, where are we going to stay?
Nora: Oh. There's a small hotel near the beach where we can stay. I stayed there last year and it's very nice, clean, and not too expensive.
Lily: Do you think they still have vacancies?
Nora: They probably have at least one room available. We can share a room and save some money.
Lily: Sounds good. And when are we going to go?
Nora: There is a bus that leaves at 6:00 in the morning. Is that too early for you?
Lily: That's fine with me. I think I'll be too excited to sleep!

9 Listening (p. 34)

A Listen to an interview with a spokeswoman from the London Visitor Center. Number the topics she discusses in the correct order from 1 to 4.

Interviewer: What should people do to make their trip to London pleasant?
Spokeswoman: Well, don't try to do too much in a short time. That's very important. You should start planning before you get here. You ought to decide in advance which sights you most want to see.
Interviewer: Is it easy to get around on public transportation?
Spokeswoman: Oh, yes, there are buses, trains, the metro, taxis. There are plenty of options. But you ought to go online and investigate. There are websites that will show you the best route to get where you want to go. Oh! And don't be afraid to ask questions. Even British visitors have to ask for help when they come here. You'll find that people from London are happy to help. They like welcoming visitors to their city and are willing to give directions.
Interviewer: I see. And is London a safe city for tourists?
Spokeswoman: It's safer than many cities in the world. But just like in any big city, you should still be careful. For example, don't go off on your own, especially at night. And never carry much cash on you.
Interviewer: One last thing – is it an expensive city to visit?
Spokeswoman: Yes, it can be, but there are a lot of places in the city where you don't have to spend a lot of money. If you're a student, you should bring your student ID card with you. That way, you can get a discount at museums and galleries.
Interviewer: Is there anything else you'd like to add?
Spokeswoman: Yeah, just that most people have a great time when they come to London. And I'm sure you will, too!

B Listen again. Write one piece of advice that she gives for each topic.

6 Sure! I'll do it.

2 Conversation (p. 36)

B Listen to the rest of the conversation. What complaints do Nolan and Rodrigo have about Ken?

Nolan: Whose clothes are these, anyway?
Rodrigo: They must be Ken's. He never puts his clothes away.
Nolan: He never puts *anything* away, you mean. He's so messy. There was a pile of dirty dishes in the sink this morning. He just leaves them there. He never washes his dishes.
Rodrigo: We have to sit down and find a way to divide the work around here. We are all messy *and* lazy, actually.
Nolan: You know what? I'm beginning to miss home.

6 Listening (p. 38)

A Listen to the results of a survey about family life. Check the answer to each question. Sometimes more than one answer is possible.

Natalie: Welcome to this week's program, "Who Has It Harder?", where we'll take a look at the roles and responsibilities of men, women, boys, and girls in families. First, thanks to everyone who responded to our survey. Rob?

Rob: Thanks, Natalie. Later on in the program, we'll be taking your phone calls and talking to Dr. Harris, a family psychologist, who will answer your questions. And now for the results of the survey. Natalie?
Natalie: Well, in response to the first question – "Who is the messiest in the house?" – the answer was boys! Eighty-five percent of you said that your sons or brothers don't help much around the house. They don't pick up their things, don't hang up their clothes, and leave their clothes lying around.
Rob: Interesting. And what about the second question, Natalie? "Who does most of the work in the kitchen?"
Natalie: Well, 84 percent of you answered "women." Many of you also explained that the boys and men usually take out the garbage. The girls and women tend to cook, do the dishes, and clean up. Both boys and girls put the groceries away.
Rob: And what about general chores inside and outside the house, Natalie?
Natalie: Well, according to our results, women usually clean up inside the house, while men usually clean up the yard. Both men and women contribute here, it seems.
Rob: That's good that everyone helps out. So what else do the men do?
Natalie: Ah, well, that's our next question, "Who worries most about expenses?" Our survey results indicate that men worry most about household expenses. One young man wrote to us saying, "My dad always tells my sister and me to turn off the lights if we're not in a room, not to spend so much time on the computer, to turn off the TV, well, everything really. I guess he's really worried about money." So, Rob, it appears dads worry the most about money.
Rob: Yes, very interesting. Well, now I'd like to introduce Dr. Harris . . .

B Listen again. According to the survey, what specific chores do men, women, boys, and girls usually do? Take notes.

Units 5–6 Progress check

1 Listening (p. 42)

A Listen to Lily, Tyler, and Abby describe their summer plans. What is each person going to do?

1. Lily

Man: So, what are you planning to do on your vacation, Lily?
Lily: Oh, I'm going to do something relaxing this year. Last year I went white-water rafting and mountain climbing.
Man: Wow, that sounds exciting.
Lily: Yeah, it was fun, but I was exhausted at the end. I think this year I'll just go to the beach and maybe go snorkeling.
Man: You should go to Holbox Island in Mexico! I hear the water is amazing.

2. Tyler

Woman: What are your plans for the summer, Tyler?
Tyler: Oh, I'd love to go lie on a beach somewhere, but I need to save some money for school. I think I'll stay home and get a job.
Woman: That doesn't sound like much fun.
Tyler: Oh, it won't be so bad. Some of my friends are going to work this summer, too, so we'll have a good time on the weekends.

3. Abby

Man: Have you planned anything for the summer, Abby?
Abby: Yeah. I'm going to work the first month and save some money. Then I'm going to Thailand to visit my sister. She's working in Bangkok. She says it's really interesting there, so I want to see what it's like. I'm really looking forward to it!

B Listen again. What is the reason for each person's choice?

7 What do you use this for?

6 Listening (p. 46)

A Listen to two people talk about the best apps for travel. Check the four app categories. (There are two extra categories.)

Jamie: Hey, Alan, I know you love your phone, but can you play with it later? We have to talk about our trip to Indonesia!
Alan: Sorry, Jamie. I love this new app I found. It's perfect for planning our trip.
Jamie: I found an app too! This one helps me pack for the trip. It looks at the weather and area you're going to visit and recommends items you need.
Alan: An app for packing? Wow, they have thought of everything. Well, you can use this app to choose specific attractions in cities. The pictures are amazing.
Jamie: I would love to see more pictures.
Alan: I know! So other people use this app to save pictures they've taken on trips or just pictures they like. Then they share the pictures and you can search them to get ideas. And the best part is you don't even need to know the people. If they make the pictures public, you just search by the country, city, or attraction. So I've looked at other people's pictures and saved them.
Jamie: So what have you found? Show me!
Alan: Look at these waterfalls! They're only one hour outside the city.
Jamie: They look beautiful! I didn't see those waterfalls in the guide book.

Alan: I know, this app is better than any guide book. But I wish it recommended more hotels.
Jamie: Oh, they have a lot of apps for finding good hotels! My sister uses one for finding inexpensive rooms when she's traveling for work. You put how much money you want to spend and it gives you available options in the area. Sometimes it gives you a discount, too.
Alan: That's great!
Jamie: Now we just need to plan our music.
Alan: I know the perfect app! If we like new songs on the radio, we can use an app to save them and add them to a list. And we don't even need to know who sings it! The app tells us.
Jamie: Perfect! They really have thought of everything!

B Listen again. What can you use the apps for? Write the uses next to the categories you checked above.

7 Conversation (p. 47)

B Listen to the rest of the conversation. What else does Justin want help with? What does Allie suggest?

Justin: You know so much about technology. Can you help me with something else?
Allie: Sure. What do you need?
Justin: I'm thinking about getting a new tablet computer. Which do you think I should get?
Allie: I don't know. That depends on what you want it for.
Justin: I need it for work. You know, emails, video calls with clients . . . And I also want to use it to read e-books when I travel.
Allie: Hey, why don't we go to a store on Saturday and we can compare a few different options.
Justin: Yeah! Thanks! I'll buy you lunch afterwards.
Allie: It's a deal.

9 Listening (p. 48)

A Listen to people give suggestions for using three of these things. Number them 1, 2, and 3. (There are two extra things.)

1.

Man: Be sure to back up your photos at least once a month. You're going to take lots, and it's important to have them in another place in case you lose it. And remember to put your favorite apps on the home screen. That will save you a lot of time.

2.

Woman: Type in where you are now. Then type in where you want to go. Make sure to get the exact address. Then just listen to the directions. Be sure to watch the road. You don't want to have an accident!

3.

Man: Be sure to put it in correctly. Then punch in your secret code. Remember to press "Enter." And don't forget to count your money before you walk away from the machine.

B Listen again. Write two suggestions you hear for each thing. Then compare with a partner.

8 Time to celebrate!

5 Listening (p. 52)

A Listen to Vanessa talk about her trip to Carnival in Brazil. Write three facts about Carnival that she mentions.

Vanessa: Isn't this music great? It's from a samba CD that I got when I was in Brazil for Carnival last year. Carnival is a big party or celebration in late February or early March. It lasts for four days. People celebrate Carnival all over Brazil, but the most famous party is in Rio de Janeiro. That's where I went. I had to book my hotel six months early because hotels fill up really quickly. But it was amazing! There were colorful decorations all over the city. And everyone was very friendly. I got lost and didn't even have to ask for directions. People came up to me and offered to help! My favorite part was the big parade. The costumes and the dancing were amazing. People work on the costumes and practice the samba dances for months as part of a competition. There were people dancing everywhere. I'd really recommend you try to go to Rio for Carnival. I can't wait to go back!

B Listen again and answer these questions about Vanessa's experience.

8 Conversation (p. 53)

B Listen to the rest of the conversation. What does Anusha say about her wedding reception?

Julia: And was this picture from your wedding reception?
Anusha: Yes, sort of. This is actually from the *second* reception. After the wedding ceremony, my parents had a small celebration for family and close friends. Then, the next day, my husband's family hosted this huge party for all our friends and relatives.
Julia: Another party, the day after the wedding?
Anusha: Yes, it's an Indian tradition.
Julia: And what was it like?
Anusha: It was fantastic. They hired a band and some dance performers. And there was lots of excellent food. We had a great time.
Julia: It sounds like your wedding was a lot of fun.
Anusha: It really was!

Units 7–8 Progress check

4 Listening (p. 57)

A Listen to two people discuss a book about marriage customs. Match each country to the title that describes its marriage custom.

1.

Man: You know, this book about marriage customs is really interesting.
Woman: Oh yeah?
Man: Listen to this. In Sweden, at a wedding reception, when the groom leaves the table, all the male wedding guests take turns kissing the bride at her table.
Woman: So if you and I are getting married and you go to the bathroom, all the men at the wedding will come kiss me?
Man: Yeah, that's right. And if you leave the room, all the women will kiss me.
Woman: How funny! I would love to see that!

2.

Woman: Hmm. What about China?
Man: Uh, I haven't read anything about China.
Woman: Well, I have heard that in one region, before the wedding, the bride starts crying every day for one month.
Man: Crying? I thought weddings were a good thing.
Woman: They say they are tears of happiness. Then the mother joins in and the grandmother, too. At the end of the month, every woman in the family is crying with the bride. They say all the crying together sounds like a song.
Man: Hmm. That's different.

3.

Man: Oh, here's another one. This one is really interesting.
Woman: Oh, yeah?
Man: Yeah. Listen to this. It talks about this native tribe in Paraguay.
Woman: Uh-huh.
Man: When two women in the tribe want to marry the same man, guess what they do.
Woman: I have no idea. What?
Man: They have a boxing match and fight until one of them wins.
Woman: And the prize is the husband?
Man: Of course!

4.

Man: And here's an interesting custom from Germany.
Woman: Let's hear it.
Man: The wedding guests bring dishes to the wedding as gifts for the couple.
Woman: That doesn't sound that different.
Man: Well, then the same guests that brought the dishes break all of them.
Woman: Why do they do that?
Man: They say that the loud noise from the dishes breaking scares away evil spirits. So the wedding guests are helping protect the couple and wishing them good luck.
Woman: Interesting.

B Listen again. Complete the sentences to describe the custom.

9 Only time will tell.

2 Conversation (p. 58)

B Listen to the rest of the conversation. What else has changed in their neighborhood?

Tom: Well, what about that old bookstore? Do you know if it's still there?
Mia: No, it's not. Now it's a cell phone repair store.
Tom: Really? What about the Thai restaurant next to it? I loved that place.
Mia: Oh, that's still there.
Tom: Let's go there this weekend. I'll drive. I can pick you up.
Mia: Great!

5 Listening (p. 60)

A Listen to Katie talk to her grandfather about an upcoming trip. Check the three concerns her grandfather has about the trip.

Grandpa: Katie, I can't believe you're leaving for Japan next week! You're going so far away.
Katie: Oh, Grandpa, you don't need to worry! I'll be fine.
Grandpa: Well, you're a young girl going by yourself to the other side of the world. When I was your age, we used to take the train to another city or state, but that was it. Not a lot of people flew internationally.
Katie: Yeah, but flying to other countries is really common now, Grandpa. And these days lots of people work and live overseas.
Grandpa: Yes, but you don't know anyone. When I moved to Chicago at your age, it took me months to make friends.
Katie: Well, big international cities like Tokyo have people from all over the world. I've already gone online and found two groups of people from the U.S. who meet up at different places in the city. It will be easy for me to make friends.
Grandpa: Okay, but promise me that we'll talk often! We'll want to know how you are. Your grandma and I can coordinate times that work for you.
Katie: I promise.
Grandpa: I love that we can see you with video calls, and that they're free! I remember even calling someone in another part of the country used to be expensive. Now we can talk to you and see your face on the other side of the world for nothing.

Katie: I know, it's great! [*pause*] You know, Grandpa, flying isn't as expensive either nowadays. You and Grandma could come visit me in Tokyo. I'm going to be there for six months.
Grandpa: Your grandma does love Japanese food. And I would love for you to be our tour guide! Hmm. I'll look at tickets.
Katie: Great idea! We could plan everything over our video calls! It would be great to see you on the other side of the world.

B Listen again. Write what Katie says in response to these concerns.

10 I like working with people.

2 Conversation (p. 64)

B Listen to the rest of the conversation. What is one problem with the job? What does Jeff decide to do?

Jeff: What do they say about the job?
Mai: Let's see. You must have experience using different devices and platforms, because you have to test the games to see if there are any bugs . . . and you need to be able to work well with a team.
Jeff: That's no problem.
Mai: Look. It says that sometimes you may need to work overtime and on weekends.
Jeff: Well, that *is* a problem.
Mai: But the pay is really good. And I think you'd enjoy it.
Jeff: You've got a point. I guess it *is* an interesting opportunity. Yeah, I'll apply for it.

6 Listening (p. 66)

A Listen to people talk about the kind of work they are looking for. Then check each person's ideal job.

1. Alex

Alex: What kind of job do I have in mind? Well, I don't want a regular nine-to-five job and eventually, I'd like to work for myself. I'm good at drawing, and I think it would be fun to design people's homes and businesses. I've actually been reading blogs about designing and am looking into programs at universities.
Woman: That sounds great. Have you tried designing anything?
Alex: Well, yes, I've actually done some drawings recently of my dream house. Would you like to see them?
Woman: Definitely.

2. Evelyn

Woman: What kind of career are you planning for yourself?
Evelyn: I don't know. I think I'd like to have a job where I can help people. Everybody else in my family is in business, and I'm not good at selling or negotiating. It's just not for me. I know I'd love working overseas, though. Maybe in a children's hospital in a developing country. But that's a long way away. I have to get into medical school first, and that's not going to be easy!

3. Edward

Woman: So what kind of job are you looking for?
Edward: Well, I haven't made up my mind. I enjoy working with people, and I love traveling. I don't want a job where I'm stuck in an office all day.
Woman: Are you interested in working in business? That's where you can sometimes make good money.
Edward: I'm not really interested in making a lot of money at this point in my life. I just want to get out and see the world. I'll worry about money later.

B Listen again. Write two reasons each person gives for his or her ideal job.

8 Word Power (p. 67)

C Listen to four conversations. Then check the adjective that best describes each person.

1. A boss

Woman: How do you like your new boss?
Man: She's OK. I just wish she'd learn to lighten up a little.
Woman: What do you mean?
Man: Oh, she never enjoys a joke. She never laughs. It's hard to even get a smile out of her.

2. A co-worker

Man: Look what Mary gave me! Isn't this a great book?
Woman: Yeah, it is! Mary's so sweet – she's always giving her friends and co-workers presents. And she's so helpful with her time.

3. A teacher

Woman: What do you think of the new French teacher?
Man: Well, she's kind of strange. She's happy one minute, and the next minute she's not.

4. A relative

Man: Hey, what's wrong?
Woman: I'm fed up with my brother! It seems like he's always angry at me about something.
Man: Really?
Woman: Yeah. He gets upset so easily. I don't know what's the matter with him.

Units 9–10 Progress check

3 Listening (p. 71)

A Listen to Michelle and Robbie discuss four jobs. Write down the jobs and check if they would be good or bad at them.

1. Michelle

Robbie: I don't know what classes to take this semester. I can't decide what I want to do with my life. Have you thought about it, Michelle?
Michelle: A little bit. My history professor says I should think about a career in politics. But I don't think I'd make a good politician.
Robbie: Why not?
Michelle: Oh, you know me. I'm not good at working with other people. I'm too moody. And politicians have to work with people all the time.
Robbie: That's true. So what do you think you want to do?
Michelle: Well, honestly. I think I'd make a good computer engineer.
Robbie: Oh, you would! You've always helped me with my computer problems.
Michelle: I love solving problems and making new things. Plus, then I'd get to work alone a lot.

2. Robbie

Robbie: That reminds me of a problem I'm having.
Michelle: What is it?
Robbie: You know my parents have a restaurant, right? Well, my father wants me to be the manager.
Michelle: And you don't want to?
Robbie: No way! Restaurant managers have to manage other people. I'd be terrible. I'm too disorganized.
Michelle: So, what do *you* want to do?
Robbie: Well, I think I could be a good teacher. I like working with kids, and I'm pretty patient.
Michelle: That's true. And you're very hardworking.

B Listen again. Write down the reasons they give.

11 It's really worth seeing!

2 Perspectives (p. 72)

A How much do you know about the Walt Disney Company and theme parks? Find three mistakes in the statements below. Then listen and check your answers.

1. The Walt Disney Company was founded in 1923 in California by Walt Disney and his brother Roy.
2. Their most famous character, Mickey Mouse, first appeared in a movie in 1928.
3. The first Disney theme park, Disneyland, was opened in 1955 in California and soon became an international attraction.
4. The official opening was broadcast live by the ABC television network.
5. In 1971, the company opened their second park, Disney World.
6. Some of their most popular parks in Florida include Magic Kingdom, Animal Kingdom, and Epcot Center.
7. In 1983, the company opened their first foreign park, Tokyo Disneyland.
   Later, theme parks were opened in Paris, Hong Kong, and Shanghai.

6 Listening (p. 74)

A Listen to three tour guides describe some famous monuments. Take notes to answer the questions below. Then compare with a partner.

1. The Taj Mahal. Why was it built? What do the changing colors of the building represent?

Woman: What would you do for love? Would you take 17 years to build a place to remember someone? That's what Emperor Shah Jahan did when he built the Taj Mahal. This incredible building was designed for his wife when she died. She was his third wife, but also his favorite. The colors of the building change with the time of day, and they say that the different colors represent the different moods of women. So, ladies, you can change your mood three times a day and it's accepted! Now, this was built almost 400 years ago, before modern construction equipment, so think about all the work that went into building this. More than 1,000 elephants were used to transport materials and around 20,000 people were hired to build the Taj Mahal. Now, if we walk closer, you'll see . . .

2. Palace of Versailles. What did King Louis XIV want the Hall of Mirrors to show? What problem did the candles cause? How did the mirrors help?

Man: Now we come to the Hall of Mirrors, one of the most famous rooms in the Palace of Versailles. King Louis XIV wanted this room to show all the riches and power of France: the paintings on the wall, the beautiful detail of the room, the gardens outside. They were all made more visible with the mirrors. But electricity didn't exist in those days, so candles were used. Any idea what problems the candles caused? Anyone?
Tourist: Candles make smoke?
Man: That's right! Candles make smoke, and smoke can damage paintings. The mirrors reflected the light of the candles, so they didn't have to use as many. Fewer candles meant less smoke and less smoke damage to the room. Pretty smart, right? Now let's go see some of the 350 rooms and apartments for visitors . . .

3. La Sagrada Familia. What did the architect think about man-made structures versus nature? Why are no straight lines used?

Woman: Folks, I am so excited today to show you La Sagrada Familia! Construction on this church started in 1882, and over 130 years later, it's still not finished! The architect, Antoni Gaudí, felt very strongly that architecture should reflect nature, and you can see this in his buildings. For example, you may notice that hill over there. La Sagrada Familia is exactly one meter shorter because Gaudí believed that no man-made structure should be taller than its natural surroundings. And notice the curves of the church. This is another example of how Gaudí copied nature. He said if straight lines don't exist in nature, they shouldn't exist in architecture, either.

8 Conversation (p. 75)

B Listen to the rest of the conversation. What other suggestion does Erik give Lisa?

Erik: So, when is your conference in Amsterdam?
Lisa: In April.
Erik: Great. You'll be there for the Tulip Festival. I think it's the most beautiful spring garden in the world.
Lisa: Yeah, I've heard about it. It's in the city, right?
Erik: No, actually, it's located in Lisse, about an hour south of Amsterdam.
Lisa: How do I get there?
Erik: You can take a bus or you go on a day tour. The tulips are gorgeous. They're really worth seeing.
Lisa: I'm sure they are. Thanks for the tips.

10 Listening (p. 76)

A Listen to a news report about tourism in Costa Rica. Select the six effects of mass tourism that are mentioned. (There are two extra effects.) Indicate if they are positive or negative.

Reporter: We're coming to you live from the ecotourism conference in San José, Costa Rica. Ecotourism is a form of responsible tourism that aims to raise awareness of and protect the local environment and culture. Alberto Rodriguez, an environmental studies professor from the local university, is here with us to explain. Good morning, Mr. Rodriguez. Can you tell us how tourism has changed Costa Rica over the last ten years?

Mr. Rodriguez: Good morning, Emily. Well, tourism has been good for the country in many ways. English is now spoken more than ever, and many Costa Ricans are bilingual. Tourism jobs are available all over the country, and more foreigners are investing here, so it's been good for our economy. But there have been costs to the country, too. With mass tourism, acres of jungle are cut down so high-rise hotels can be built. Fish and lobster are hunted in our waters to feed to tourists. Twenty-five percent of Costa Rican land is protected, but what about the other seventy-five percent? Ecotourism has become the answer to that question. The government reviews businesses and decides if they qualify in the ecotourism category. Then they put them on a list so travelers can choose them when they visit our beautiful country.

Reporter: What makes a business an "ecotourism" business? What are the criteria?

Mr. Rodriguez: Well, let's look at this hotel where we're having the conference. It fulfills some of the most common criteria to be a certified ecotourism business here. Local Costa Ricans are employed, waste is recycled, energy-saving devices are used, and visitors are educated about our culture and environment.

Reporter: Fantastic. Before we go, Mr. Rodriguez, is there anything you'd like to say to all the travelers listening to you right now?

Mr. Rodriguez: I would encourage all travelers to visit ecotourism businesses when traveling. They can learn about nature without disturbing it. Together we can make a difference!

Reporter: Thank you, Mr. Rodriguez. Live from San José, Costa Rica, Emily Jameson reporting.

B Listen again. Write down three criteria the hotel fulfills in order to be an ecotourism business in Costa Rica.

12 It's a long story.

4 Listening (p. 80)

A Listen to this story about a successful inventor. Put the sentences into the correct order from 1 to 8.

Woman: Around fifteen years ago, Mark Zuckerberg was a normal high school student. He was living in a quiet town in New York. Today, he is the founder and CEO of Facebook, the world's most popular social networking site. So how did it all begin?

When Zuckerberg was only ten years old, he was already writing computer programs. His father taught him how to program computers, and he loved it! A couple of years later, he wrote his very own messenger program. His program "Zucknet" connected the computers in his home to the computers in his father's office.

While he was studying in high school, he developed a computer program that looked at people's favorite music and recommended new music. Microsoft wanted to buy the program, but Zuckerberg did not accept the offer.

In 2002, he entered Harvard University. One night while he was playing on his computer, he invented a program called FaceMash. FaceMash compared pictures of Harvard students. The program was a success, but the university suddenly shut down the site a couple of days later.

Many people at Harvard now knew who Zuckerberg was. Three classmates asked for his help to develop a social networking site for Harvard students. While he was working on that site, he got the idea for Facebook.

At first, Facebook started was only for Harvard students, but soon people from other universities were using it. Zuckerberg wanted more people to use Facebook, but he needed more money. His friends were also interested in Facebook. Coincidentally, they had the money he needed to create the site! They invested in the site, and Facebook expanded so that anyone who was 13 or older could use it.

Today, Mark Zuckerberg lives in California, where he is the chief executive of Facebook. Over 1 billion people use Facebook today, and Zuckerberg is worth over 24 billion dollars!

B Listen again. How did the invention change his life?

7 Conversation (p. 81)

B Listen to two other people at the party. What has happened since they last saw each other?

Maggie: Hey, Bob, how's it going?
Bob: Pretty good, thanks.
Maggie: I haven't seen you for a while. What have you been up to?
Bob: Well, I've been looking for a house to buy. I finally found one last month.
Maggie: That's terrific!
Bob: Yeah. I'm really tired of renting. So what have you been doing lately?
Maggie: Well, I went to Italy last month.
Bob: Really? What were you doing there?
Maggie: I was taking a short Italian course. But guess what! I fell in love.
Bob: You did? Who's the lucky guy?
Maggie: Actually I fell in love with the food there. So I've been taking some classes in Italian cooking. That pizza you're eating – I made it!

Units 11–12 Progress check

2 Listening (p. 84)

A Listen to a game show about Spain. Write the correct answers.

Host: Welcome to today's show! The rules of the game are simple: I will ask a question, and the first contestant to hit the buzzer gets to answer that question. Each correct answer is worth $100. Today's topic is "Spain." Are you ready, contestants? Now, we all know that Spanish is spoken in Spain, but is that it? The first question, for $100, is: How many languages are officially recognized in Spain? Contestant A!
Woman 1: Two? Castilian Spanish and Catalan?
Host: Sorry, Contestant A, that is not entirely correct. Anyone else want to try? Contestant B?
Man: I think it's four. Castilian Spanish, Catalan, Galician, and Basque?
Host: Excellent! Castilian Spanish is spoken everywhere, but depending on the region, three other languages are also recognized by the government. And Basque is one of the oldest living languages in the world! How about that? Anyway, contestant B is first on the board with $100. And now for the next question: What day is considered bad luck in Spain? Contestant A!
Woman 1: Tuesday the 13th?
Host: Correct! While most Western countries think Friday the 13th is bad luck, in Spain it's a Tuesday! And I'd agree that Tuesdays are usually worse than Fridays, right? Next question: What is the most valuable soccer team in the world? Contestant B!
Man: Barcelona!
Host: Nice try, Contestant B, but Barcelona is the second most valuable soccer team in the world. Other contestants? Contestant C?
Woman 2: Real Madrid?
Host: Correct! OK, we're all tied up at $100. Let's see how you do with our next question: Let's remember that Spain used to be very powerful. In how many countries is Spanish spoken as the official language? Yes, Contestant C!
Woman 2: 21?
Host: Yes, that's right! If we include Puerto Rico where Spanish is official with English, there are 21 countries with Spanish as the official language. Quite a lot, right? OK. There are only two questions left. Let's go, players! Next question: Spain is an agricultural country, but in one village, people have a festival where they throw a lot of this fruit at each other all day. What fruit is it? Contestant C!
Woman 2: Olives?
Host: Oooh, no, although they love their olives. Contestant B?
Man: Tomatoes!
Host: Good for you! Yes, at La Tomatina festival near Valencia, tomatoes are thrown in one of the world's largest food fights. We only have one more question left, contestants. And remember, the winner of this round will be back here tomorrow for the championship playoff! And now for our last question: What is the name of Spain's most famous dance? Contestant B!
Man: I think it's flamenco.
Host: Yes! That's correct. The flamenco dance comes from Spain, but it is now practiced and taught all over the world. So, contestants, let's look at your scores. Contestant A, you answered . . .

B Listen again. Keep score. How much money does each contestant have?

13 That's entertainment!

2 Conversation (p. 86)

B Listen to the rest of the conversation. What happens next? What do they decide to do?

Gina: OK. I'll go make the popcorn. You get the show set up.
Danny: Sure. . . . Ugh. Hey, Gina?
Gina: Yeah? What happened?
Danny: The Internet is down.
Gina: I can't believe it. It's the second time this month.
Danny: I guess we are going to have to go out.
Gina: All right. But if we go out in this heat, I think I want to see something light and fun.
Danny: How about a comedy, then?
Gina: Sounds good. Should we check what's in the theaters?
Danny: No, let's just go! Whatever you like best is fine . . . but I'm in charge of snacks!

5 Listening (p. 88)

A Listen to people talk about books, movies, and TV programs. Match each conversation to the statement that best describes the people's opinions.

1.

Woman: What did you think of the movie?
Man: Pretty terrible. I walked out after half an hour.
Woman: You did?
Man: Yeah, it was so boring that I started falling asleep! And I've never seen such bad acting! I think I'm going to start reading movie reviews online so I don't waste my money.

2.

Man: What do you think of Sue Grafton's books?
Woman: I love those mysteries! When I started to read *A Is for Alibi*, I couldn't put it down. I stayed up till 4:00 in the morning to finish it!
Man: Wow! Have you read any of the other books in the series?
Woman: Oh, yeah. They're fantastic. *B Is for Burglar, C Is for Corpse*, . . . I'm already up to *K Is for Killer*. Using the alphabet to build a mystery series is such a clever idea. I can't wait to read all 26 books! I wonder what *Z* will be!

3.

Man 1: Did you see that documentary on TV last night, the one about Australia?

Man 2: I did. It was fascinating! I didn't know they had so many different kinds of animals there. And the photography!

Man 1: Yeah, it was pretty amazing, wasn't it?

Man 2: Yeah, it was. It made me really want to go there and see it for myself.

4.

Woman 1: Are you reading that book, too? It seems everyone's reading it now. When did UFOs become so popular anyway?

Woman 2: Actually, I just finished it. What a waste of time! Just the same silly stuff about visitors to Earth from other planets.

Woman 1: I know. It said absolutely nothing new.

Woman 2: You know, I'm tired of hearing stories about little green creatures. If they're real, how come no one can ever take a picture of them?

B: Listen again. Write a reason each person gives to support his or her opinion.

12 Listening (p. 90)

A Listen to two critics, Nicole and Anthony, talk about a new movie. Check the features of the movie that they discuss. There are two extra features.

Nicole: Welcome to *At the Movies*! I'm Nicole Reeves . . .
Anthony: And I'm Anthony Hale. Good evening!
Nicole: Tonight we're going to review the new James Bond film. Well, I really liked this new James Bond actor very, very much!
Anthony: Mm-hmm.
Nicole: He's the best actor that's ever had the role – warm, human, even funny. A totally believable character.
Anthony: I have to agree, a perfect 007 type. Nicole, what did you think of the story?
Nicole: It was the standard Bond movie that has the usual beautiful women, the usual evil villain – nothing new.
Anthony: Well, I'm surprised. I have to say that I thought the story was unusually good. The race car scenes were exciting, and the surprise ending was great.
Nicole: Well, I can't agree with you there.
Anthony: Really? What did you think about the music?
Nicole: I was impressed by the music. It was the classic James Bond theme with a modern twist.
Anthony: I couldn't agree more! I haven't heard such interesting music in a movie in a long time. It really added to the action scenes.
Nicole: Yes, but unfortunately that brings up a weakness in the film for me: the special effects. Again, it's just the same old stuff . . . the car that flies, the pen that's really a gun. You get tired of that kind of thing.
Anthony: Nicole, I have to disagree with you there. I have to say that the special effects were the best that I've ever seen in a Bond film.
Nicole: So, Anthony, overall how do you rate this new James Bond movie?

Anthony: Well, Nicole, I'd have to say that I'm proud to give this movie my highest rating . . . four stars . . . and I would like to encourage everyone to go and see it! How about you, Nicole? You did like the new actor who plays James Bond.
Nicole: That part's true, Anthony; however, I have to give the movie only two stars . . . a rating of "fair."
Anthony: Hmm. Well, that's all from us tonight. See you next week.

B Listen again. Write Nicole and Anthony's opinions of each feature.

14 Now I get it!

3 Conversation (p. 93)

B Now listen to Elena talk to her friend. What does she find unusual about the way people in North America communicate?

Freddy: So how are things at school, Elena?
Elena: Oh, pretty good, actually.
Freddy: Do you find it easy to communicate with people?
Elena: Most of the time, yes, although there are some things that seem strange to me. For instance, sometimes when a conversation is ending, people say, "Hey, let's get together soon." I used to say, "OK! When?", and it always surprised people. Eventually, I realized "Let's get together soon" is just a way of saying good-bye.
Freddy: Right! It's not really an invitation at all. It's more like, a way to say that you want to stay in touch.
Elena: Yeah. I know that now!

11 Listening (p. 96)

A Listen to four conversations about driving. Number the situations they are discussing in the correct order from 1 to 4.

1.

Woman: Huh, that seems strange.
Man: What is it?
Woman: All these cars have their lights on. It's the middle of the day and the sun is shining!
Man: Well, we are driving in the mountains and these roads are pretty narrow. Oh, and look at that sign! It says all cars need to have their headlights on for the next five miles.
Woman: Oh, you're right. I guess lights can only help us in these conditions.

2.

Woman: I wonder why that traffic officer is signaling me?
Man: Perhaps he means you're driving too fast.
Woman: No, I don't think so. The speed limit is 60, and I'm only going 55.
Man: Hmm. I wonder why there are no other cars in this lane.
Woman: What do you mean?
Man: Well, you see how all the other cars are in the lane next to us.
Woman: You're right. I think this one is just for buses and taxis. They really should put up better signs around here.

3.

Man: Oh, no. Not another parking ticket. That's the second one this week. Why did I get a ticket for parking here? I thought this was a free parking zone.
Woman: Maybe you can only park here after working hours. Is there a sign around anywhere?
Man: Oh, you're right. There's one over there. I didn't even notice it. Looks like you can't park here till after 6:00 P.M.
Woman: How much is the fine?
Man: Sixty dollars! Can you believe that?

4.

Man: That's weird. The last few cars driving toward us were flashing their lights.
Woman: I see what you mean. There's another one.
Man: Maybe my lights are on or something. Let me check. No, they're off.
Woman: Do you think there's an accident up ahead? Maybe you'd better slow down.
Man: Oh, now I see what's happening. There's a patrol car up ahead checking people's speed. How nice of those other drivers to let me know! Well, I'm within the speed limit!

B Listen again. How did they find out about the traffic situation? Write what happened.

Units 13–14 Progress check

3 Listening (p. 99)

A Listen to two people discuss an article about laws in different places. Match the topic to the place. (There are two extra topics.)

1.

Woman: You know, this article about strange international laws is fascinating.
Man: Oh yeah? Let's hear some.
Woman: For example, take Singapore. You aren't allowed to chew gum on the metro there. And chewing gum in general is hard to find in Singapore.
Man: I think I like that. It's so annoying when you step on old chewing gum. I bet the city is a lot cleaner!

2.

Woman: Oh, here's another one. In Kenya, you can't walk around without money.
Man: Hm, so you always have to carry some cash?
Woman: Yes, according to this, the logic is that if you don't have money, then you want to steal.
Man: Interesting. I wonder if an ATM card is accepted.
Woman: Good question!

3.

Man: Anything about the U.S.?
Woman: I haven't found anything yet, but I'm sure there are lots of odd laws.
Man: I know in San Francisco, California, you aren't allowed to feed pigeons.
Woman: You can't feed those birds? They're everywhere there!
Man: I think that's the problem. The government says pigeons are birds that damage property and have diseases.

4.

Woman: And here's a strange one from Italy.
Man: Oh yeah?
Woman: In the city of Milan, you have to smile.
Man: Are you serious? That's a law?
Woman: They say you can only look sad at a funeral or a hospital.
Man: How bizarre!

B Listen again. Complete the sentences to describe each law.

15 I wouldn't have done that.

2 Conversation (p. 100)

B Listen to the rest of the conversation. What would Joon do if he found $40,000?

Mia: So, what would you do if you found $40,000?
Joon: Oh, you know me. I hate breaking rules, and I'd feel nervous keeping the money. So I'd take the money straight to the police.
Mia: I guess that wouldn't be such a bad idea. Maybe you'd be lucky, and the owner of the money would give you a big reward.
Joon: Well, they say honesty is its own reward. But I could use a new bike!

4 Listening (p. 101)

A Listen to three people talk about predicaments. Check which predicament they are talking about.

1.

Blake: You know, I'm really worried about Chris.
Zoey: Why?
Blake: Well, this may sound silly, but he spends too much time on the Internet. I think he might be addicted to it.
Jane: Really? Why do you think so?
Blake: We went to the movies yesterday and during the whole movie he was on his phone. He couldn't even take a two-hour break to watch this movie he's wanted to see! Then I suggested we go to the mountains this weekend for a hike, and he said no. He said if he didn't have WiFi service in the mountains, he wouldn't go.
Jane: Wow, that is pretty bad. We all need time away from technology.
Blake: So what would you do if you were in my position? Would you say something to him?
Jane: I wouldn't tell him he has a problem. He wouldn't like that. I would continue to suggest activities that don't involve the Internet. He can't say no forever.
Zoey: Oh, I would be honest and tell him what I think. He will make excuses until you're direct with him. It's a problem that could affect his relationships with other people and he needs to know that.

2.

Jane: I just got an email from my friend Kari. She lost all her money on vacation in Europe. Isn't that horrible?
Zoey: Yeah, that's terrible.
Jane: Blake, what would you do if you were on vacation overseas and you lost all your money and credit cards?
Blake: I guess I'd call my parents and ask them to send me some money right away. What about you, Zoey?
Zoey: Yeah, I'd probably do the same thing . . . though I guess I'd probably sell my watch and camera . . . or I might get a job as a server somewhere till I made enough money to buy a plane ticket home.

3.

Zoey: You know, something happened to me this morning and I don't know what I should do.
Jane: What happened?
Zoey: Well, I was taking a test in math and I saw two classmates cheating in front of me.
Jane: How were they cheating?
Zoey: Well, I heard some noise, so I looked over there, and they both were looking at their arms. Their arms had writing all over them.
Blake: Oh, so they wrote the answers on their arms?
Zoey: Yeah, and then after class they were laughing and talking all about it. What would you do if you saw two people cheating on a test?
Jane: If I were in your position, I would talk to the teacher. I would tell him what you saw and ask him not to say that you told him. It's not fair if they get a good grade and they didn't spend any time studying like you did.
Blake: I wouldn't get involved. I would pretend I didn't see anything. It's not your business and sooner or later they'll get caught.

B Listen again. Write the two suggestions given for each predicament.

10 Listening (p. 104)

A Listen to an advice podcast. Complete the chart.

Cole: Good morning and welcome to *Problem Solved*, a podcast where we find great solutions to your problems. Life is full of predicaments, but there's always a solution! I'm Cole Williams and today we have Dr. Jones with us. Thanks for being here, Dr. Jones.
Dr. Jones: Hello, everyone. Thanks for having me.

Cole: Now let's get started with our first problem, from a listener named Ronnie. In his email, he says, "Dear *Problem Solved*, I'm a senior in high school and am starting to apply to college. My dad really wants me to study law. He's a lawyer and loves it. But I love languages and want to be a language teacher. We got in a huge fight about it. I got really mad and told him he was selfish. Then I slammed the door. Now we're not talking. What should I do? Thanks, Ronnie." Dr. Jones, what advice would you give to Ronnie?

Dr. Jones: Well, Ronnie, I understand your frustration. You know what you want to do and you feel you don't have your father's support. But you shouldn't have told him he was selfish, and you definitely shouldn't have slammed the door. He's thinking about your future and wants what's best for you. You need to apologize and tell him that you appreciate his opinion, but that studying languages is your passion. If I were you, I would've said that from the start. But don't worry, your dad will understand and eventually let you decide your career. Be patient with him.

Cole: Patience is always excellent advice. Let's go to the next problem, from Becca, a listener in New York. In her email, she says, "Dear *Problem Solved*, I have a problem at work. I've been at my company for five years and have always arrived on time and even worked overtime to get the job done right. My boss often congratulates me on my work and I was sure I would get a promotion or raise soon. But I never said anything to him about wanting those things. Then last week, my boss welcomed a new employee. The company created a new position and this new guy is taking it! They gave him his own office and I know he's making more money. Why didn't they ask me? Now I feel unmotivated and unhappy at work. What should I do? Becca."

Dr. Jones: Becca, thanks for writing in. While there are plenty of things you should do now, let's first look at what you should have done before this new employee arrived. You said your boss always appreciated your work, but maybe you should have been more honest with him about wanting to grow in the company. I would have talked to him and expressed that a long time ago. It's possible he thought that you weren't interested. But don't worry, there are plenty of things you can do now. Why don't you talk to your new co-worker? Find out about his education and work history. Look at him as a colleague and someone you can learn from, not as competition. He might suggest a course you could take or have some good advice. And then, talk to your boss, but be positive. Let him know how much you like working there and how much you'd like to grow more in the company. He might have some good advice too and in the end, he will appreciate your honesty and ambition.

Cole: I think honesty and patience are two good lessons we can learn from today's podcast. That's all the time we have for today. Thank you, Dr. Jones, for being here with us. And listeners, remember, life is full of predicaments, but there's always a solution. I'm Cole Williams and thank you for joining us today. Don't miss the next episode of our podcast, *Problem Solved*, next week!

B Listen again. According to Dr. Jones, what should each person have done?

16 Making excuses

7 Listening (p. 109)

A Listen to Gabriel invite his friends to his birthday party on Saturday. What excuses do they give for not going? Write them below.

1. Grant

Grant: Hello?
Gabriel: Hi, Grant! This is Gabriel. How's it going?
Grant: Oh, hi, Gabriel. Not too bad.
Gabriel: Um, you know, it's my birthday on Saturday, and I thought maybe you'd like to come to my party.
Grant: Oh, this Saturday? I really wish I could, but I won't be around this weekend. I'm going with my parents to visit my aunt. She lives about an hour outside the city.
Gabriel: Oh.
Grant: I'm sorry, Gabriel. Have a great party, though, and happy birthday.
Gabriel: Oh, thanks. And you have a great weekend with your family, Grant.
Grant: Thanks. See you next week.
Gabriel: OK.
Grant: Bye.

2. Sayo

Sayo: Hello?
Gabriel: Sayo? Hi, it's Gabriel. How are you?
Sayo: Hey, I'm doing okay. How are you?
Gabriel: Oh, I'm good. So, Saturday is my birthday, and I was wondering if you'd like to come to my party.
Sayo: Oh. What time?
Gabriel: Say around 7:30?
Sayo: Oh, I'm sorry. Um, Saturday is my little sister's birthday too, and she's having a party. My mom asked me to help her with the food and games.
Gabriel: Oh, OK, Sayo. Well, I hope you have a good time. Tell your sister happy birthday for me.
Sayo: Thank you. And happy birthday to you! I hope your party's fun.
Gabriel: Yeah, well, I hope so, too. Uh, see you in class on Monday?
Sayo: Sure! Bye-bye!
Gabriel: Bye.

3. Diego

Diego: Hello?
Gabriel: Hello, Diego?
Diego: Hi, Gabriel. How's it going?
Gabriel: It's going pretty well. How about you?
Diego: Not too bad. What's up?
Gabriel: Well, my birthday is Saturday and I'm having a little party with some friends, and I thought maybe you'd like to come.
Diego: Saturday?
Gabriel: Yeah. Around 7:30.
Diego: Oh, you know, my dad told me to pick him up at the airport at 8:30.
Gabriel: Oh, I didn't know your dad was out of town.
Diego: Yeah, he travels a lot for work. And it's really expensive for him to take a taxi home.
Gabriel: Yeah, of course. I understand. Don't worry about it.
Diego: I'm really sorry. OK, well –
Gabriel: See you soon.
Diego: Take care, Gabriel. And happy birthday.
Gabriel: Thanks Diego. Talk to you soon.
Diego: Bye.

4. Carrie

Carrie: Hello?
Gabriel: Hello? Carrie? This is Gabriel.
Carrie: Oh, hi, Gabriel [*coughs*].
Gabriel: What's wrong?
Carrie: I . . . I think I've got the flu.
Gabriel: Oh, I'm sorry to hear that. I guess you won't be coming to my party on Saturday, huh?
Carrie: No, I guess not. I'm feeling pretty run-down.
Gabriel: Oh, I'm sorry. Well, hey, take care of yourself, Carrie. I hope to see you next week.
Carrie: Yeah, me, too [*coughs*]. Bye.

B Listen. What happens on the night of Gabriel's birthday?

Gabriel: Well I guess I'll have some cake. Happy birthday to me, happy birthday to me –
Grant: Surprise!
Sayo: Happy birthday!
Diego: Surprise, Gabriel!
Carrie: Happy birthday, Gabriel!
Gabriel: Oh, wow! Oh my gosh! Grant, Sayo . . . Wow, what a surprise! Diego, Carrie! Man, you really fooled me! I had no idea! Carrie, did you set this up? Wow, you're the best. I can't believe it.

9 Pronunciation (p. 110)

B Listen to four sentences. Check the reduced form that you hear.

1.

Man: She told me that she'd bring some drinks.

2.

Woman: He said that he'd taken a taxi.

3.

Man: She said that she'd bought a gift.

4.

Woman: He told me that he'd tell all of his friends.

Units 15–16 Progress check

3 Listening (p. 113)

A Listen to the conversations. Check the person who is making the request.

1.

Woman: Please pick up your things.
Girl: In a minute. I'm on the phone.

2.

Man: Excuse me. Can you move your car? You're blocking my driveway.
Woman: Oh, sure. I'm sorry, I didn't realize.

3.

Woman: How many of these should I take?
Man: Don't take more than three a day.

4.

Teenager 1: I missed English yesterday. Can I borrow your notes?
Teenager 2: No problem. They're right here in my bag.

5.

Man 1: Jake, please come into my office.
Man 2: Yes, sir. I'll be right in.

6.

Girl: Can we leave now?
Man: Please don't go until the bell rings.

B Listen again. Complete the requests.

Workbook answer key

1 Good memories

Exercise 1

A

Verb	**Past tense**	**Verb**	**Past tense**
be	was/were	hide	hid
become	became	laugh	laughed
do	did	lose	lost
email	emailed	move	moved
get	got	open	opened
have	had	scream	screamed

B

My best friend in school was Michael. He and I were in Mrs. Gilbert's third-grade class, and we were friends. We often did crazy things in class, but I don't think Mrs. Gilbert ever really got mad at us. For example, Michael had a pet lizard named Peanut. Sometimes he hid it in Mrs. Gilbert's desk drawer. Later, when she opened the drawer, she always screamed loudly, and the class laughed. After two years, Michael's family moved to another town. We emailed each other for a few years, but then we lost contact. I often wonder what he's doing now.

Exercise 2

Sarah: Welcome to the building. My name's Sarah Walker.
Benedito: Hello. I'm Benedito Peres. It's nice to meet you.
Sarah: Nice to meet you, too. Are you from around here?
Benedito: No, I'm from Brazil.
Sarah: Oh, really? *Were you born* in Brazil?
Benedito: No, I wasn't born there, actually. I'm originally from Portugal.
Sarah: That's interesting. So, when did you move to Brazil?
Benedito: I moved to Brazil when I was in elementary school.
Sarah: Where did you live?
Benedito: We lived in Recife. It's a beautiful city in northeast Brazil. Then I went to college.
Sarah: Did you go to school in Recife?
Benedito: No, I went to school in São Paulo.
Sarah: And what did you study?
Benedito: Oh, I studied engineering. But I'm here to go to graduate school.
Sarah: Great! When did you arrive?
Benedito: I arrived last week. I start school in three days.
Sarah: Well, good luck. And sorry for all the questions!

Exercise 3

Answers will vary. Examples:

1. I was born in Seoul, Korea.
2. No, we didn't move.
3. Yes, my favorite teacher was Miss Kim.
4. I played tennis when I was a kid.
5. I began to study English when I was six years old.

Exercise 4

A

He is from Guadalajara, Mexico. He is an actor.

B

1. True
2. False. The director was Mexican.
3. True
4. False. He directed a movie called *Déficit*.
5. False. He plays a conductor.
6. False. He works in films in many different languages.

Exercise 5

2. My favorite pet was a cat called Felix.
3. We used to go to summer camp for two weeks during our summer vacations. It was really fun.
4. There was a great playground on my street. We used to go there every afternoon to play.

Exercise 6

2. They also used to ride bikes. Their dog Bruno always used to follow them.
3. Allie used to go to the beach every weekend during summer vacation. She hardly ever goes now.
4. Robert used to collect comic books. Now they're worth a lot of money.
5. They used to have a rabbit. They don't have any pets now.

Exercise 7

2. A: Did you collect shells?
   B: No, we didn't collect shells. We used to build sand castles.
3. A: Did you use to swim?
   B: Yes, we did. We used to swim for hours. Then we played all kinds of sports.
4. A: Really? What did you use to play?
   B: Well, we used to play beach volleyball with some other kids.
5. A: Did you use to lose?
   B: No, we didn't. We used to win!

Exercise 8

Answers will vary. Examples:

1. I used to ride my bike.
   Now I swim.
2. I used to like pop music.
   Now I like rock music.
3. I used to wear casual clothes.
   Now I wear work clothes.

Exercise 9

Paola: I'm an immigrant here. I was born in Chile and grew up there. I came here in 2011. I wasn't very happy at first. Things were difficult for me. I didn't speak English, so I went to a community college and studied English there. My English got better, and I found this job. What about you?

Exercise 10

1. A: Are you from Toronto:
   B: No, I'm originally from Morocco.
2. A: Tell me a little about yourself.
   B: What do you want to know?
3. A: How old were you when you moved here?
   B: About 16.
4. A: Did you learn English here?
   B: No, I studied it in Morocco.
5. A: By the way, I'm Lucy.
   B: Glad to meet you.

2 Life in the city

Exercise 1

2. bus stop
3. bicycle lane
4. traffic jam
5. subway station
6. taxi stand

Exercise 2

A

2. dark streets: install modern streetlights
3. no places to take children: build more parks
4. crime: hire more police officers
5. car accidents: install more traffic lights
6. traffic jams: build a subway system

B

Answers may vary. Examples:

2. There are too many traffic jams.
3. There isn't enough public transportation.
4. There is too much crime.
5. There aren't enough places to take children.
6. There isn't enough light.

C

Answers may vary. Examples:

2. There should be fewer traffic jams.
3. There should be more public transportation.
4. There should be less crime.
5. There should be more places to take children.
6. There should be more light.

Exercise 3

A

2. business district
3. green spaces
4. parking garages
5. bicycle lanes
6. public transportation
7. rush hour

B

Life in this city needs to be improved. For one thing, there are too many cars, and there is too much bad air, especially during *rush hour*. The air pollution is terrible. This problem is particularly bad downtown in the business district. Too many people drive their cars to work. Also, the city doesn't spend enough money on public transportation. There should be more buses and subway trains so people don't have to drive.

We also need fewer parking garages downtown. It's so easy to park that too many people drive to work. Instead, the city should create more parks and green space so people can relax and get some fresh air when they're downtown. There should also be more bicycle lanes so people can ride to work and get some exercise.

C

Answers will vary.

Exercise 4

A

1. tram
2. ferry
3. subway
4. cable railway

B

	cable railway	*ferry*	*subway*	*tram*
1. How old is it?	nearly 130 years old	NG	NG	over 115 years old
2. How many people use it?	NG	NG	4 million a day	180,000 a day
3. How safe is it?	very	very	NG	NG
4. Where can you go?	Victoria Peak	Kowloon, other islands, Macau, Guangdong	airport, major centers	NG

Exercise 5

1. A: Could you tell me where I can buy some perfume?
   B: You should try *the duty-free shop*.
2. A: Can you tell me where I can find a good place to stay?
   B: Yeah, there is a nice hotel on the next street.
3. A: Do you know where I can change money?
   B: There's a money exchange on the second floor. There's also an ATM over there.
4. A: Do you know what time the last train leaves for the city?
   B: No, but I can check the schedule.
5. A: Could you tell me where the taxi stand is?
   B: Sure. Just follow that sign.

Exercise 6

Guest: Could you *tell me where the gym is*?
Clerk: Sure, the gym is on the nineteenth floor.
Guest: OK. And can you tell me where the coffee shop is?
Clerk: Yes, the coffee shop is next to the gift shop.
Guest: The gift shop? Hmm. I need to buy something for my wife. Do you know what time it closes?
Clerk: It closes at 6:00 P.M. I'm sorry, but you'll have to wait until tomorrow. It's already 6:15.
Guest: OK. Oh, I'm expecting a package. Could you call me when it arrives?
Clerk: Don't worry. I'll call you when it arrives.
Guest: Thanks. Just one more thing. Do you know how often the airport bus leaves?
Clerk: The airport bus leaves every half hour. Anything else?
Guest: No, I don't think so. Thanks.

Exercise 7

2. There should be less traffic downtown.
3. Could you tell me where the subway station is?
4. There should be more parking garages.
5. Do you know how often the bus comes?
6. Can you tell me what time the last train leaves?

Exercise 8

Answers will vary. Examples:

1. Yes, there is a traffic-free zone downtown.
2. Most people drive to and from work.
3. Rush hour is very busy and there is a lot of traffic.
4. The biggest problem is traffic.
5. The city has improved the subways.
6. The city could provide more buses and subway lines.

3 Making changes

Exercise 1

A

1. convenient / *inconvenient*
2. cramped / spacious
3. dangerous / safe
4. big / small
5. bright / dark
6. modern / old
7. quiet / noisy
8. cheap / expensive

B

2. The rooms are too dark.
3. The living room is too cramped for the family.
4. The bathroom isn't modern enough.
5. The yard is too small for our pets.
6. The street isn't quiet enough for us.
7. The neighborhood isn't safe enough.
8. The location is too inconvenient.

Exercise 2

2. There aren't enough bedrooms.
3. It's not modern enough.
4. There aren't enough parking spaces.
5. The neighborhood doesn't have enough streetlights.
6. There aren't enough closets.
7. It's not private enough.
8. The living room isn't spacious enough.

Exercise 3

Client: Well, it's *not as convenient as* the apartment on Main Street.
Realtor: That's true, the house is less convenient.
Client: But the apartment doesn't have as many rooms as the house.
Realtor: Yes, the house is more spacious.
Client: But I think there are just as many closets as in the apartment.
Realtor: You're right. The closet space is the same.
Client: The wallpaper in the apartment is not as dingy as the wallpaper in the house.
Realtor: I know, but you could change the wallpaper in the house.
Client: Hmm, the rent on the apartment is almost as expensive as the rent on the house, but the house is much bigger. Oh, I can't decide. Can you show me something else?

Exercise 4

A

Answers will vary.

B

Answers will vary.

Exercise 5

A

be	***play***	***have***	***move***
healthy	guitar	my own room	somewhere else
happier	soccer	more free time	to a new place

B

2. I wish I had my own room.
3. I wish I played soccer.
4. I wish I had more free time.
5. I wish were happier.
6. I wish I played guitar.

Exercise 6

2. A: I wish I could retire.
B: I know what you mean.
3. A: Where do you want to move?
B: Somewhere else.
4. A: I wish I could find a bigger house.
B: It's very nice, though.

Exercise 7

2. This neighborhood is too dangerous.
3. My apartment should be more private.
4. Our house has just as many bedrooms as yours.
5. I wish I had more closet space.
6. We wish we could move somewhere else.
7. That apartment isn't big enough.
8. I wish housework weren't difficult.

Exercise 8

A

Italy, China, Turkey

B

	Rome	***Huangshan***	***Turkey***
1. People make wishes only once a year.			✓
2. You need a lock and key.		✓	
3. You put your wish on a tree.			✓
4. You need a coin to make your wish.	✓		
5. Wish-making is only for couples.		✓	
6. The money from the wishes goes to poor people.	✓		
7. Some people make their wishes on the Internet.			✓

4 Have you ever tried it?

Exercise 1

Margo: I went to Sunrise Beach last week. <u>*Have you ever been*</u> to Sunrise Beach, Chris?
Chris: Yes, <u>I have</u>. It's beautiful. <u>Did you go</u> to the restaurant on the beach?
Margo: Yeah, <u>I did</u>. I <u>went</u> on Saturday. <u>I had</u> the sea snails.
Chris: Wow! <u>I've never eaten</u> sea snails!
Margo: Oh, they were delicious. On Sunday I <u>got</u> to the beach early to see the sun come up. <u>Have you ever seen</u> a sunrise on a beach, Chris?
Chris: No, <u>I haven't</u>.
Margo: Then I <u>went</u> swimming around 6:00, but there were some strange dark shadows in the water. <u>Have you ever heard</u> of sharks at Sunrise Beach?
Chris: Yes, <u>I have</u>. I <u>heard</u> a news report about sharks last summer.
Margo: Wow! Maybe I <u>had</u> a lucky escape on Sunday morning! Why don't you come with me next time?
Chris: Are you kidding?

Exercise 2

A
Answers will vary.

B
Answers will vary. Possible answers:
2. Have you ever gone horseback riding?
3. Have you ever traveled abroad?
4. Have you ever read a novel in English?
5. Have you ever taken a cruise?

C
Answers will vary. Possible answers:
2. Yes, I have. I rode a horse on the beach last summer.
3. Yes, I have. I went to Mexico last year, and I went to Germany five years ago.
4. Yes, I have. I read *To Kill a Mockingbird* when I was a teenager.
5. Yes, I have. I took a cruise to Hawaii two years ago.

Exercise 3

A
pollen, cats, foods

B and C

	Problem	*What didn't work*	*What worked*
Andrew:	sneezing all the time	aspirin	anti-allergy medicine, air filter
Mariana:	red and irritated eyes	petting cat less	changing where cat could go
Eric:	red skin with a painful itch	eating less peanut butter	eating other foods

Exercise 4

A
<u>4</u> After that, pour the eggs into a frying pan. Add the mushrooms and cook.
<u>2</u> Then beat the eggs in a bowl.
<u>1</u> First, slice the mushrooms.
<u>3</u> Next, add salt and pepper to the egg mixture.
<u>5</u> Finally, fold the omelet in half. Your omelet is ready. Enjoy!

B
Answers will vary.

Exercise 5

Alexa: I <u>went</u> to a Thai restaurant last night.
Pedro: Really? I <u>have/'ve never eaten</u> Thai food.
Alexa: Oh, you should try it. It's delicious!
Pedro: What <u>did</u> you <u>order</u>?
Alexa: First, I <u>had</u> soup with green curry and rice. Then I <u>tried</u> pad thai. It's noodles, shrimp, and vegetables in a spicy sauce.
Pedro: I <u>have not/haven't</u> tasted pad thai before. <u>Was</u> it very hot?
Alexa: No. It <u>was</u> just spicy enough. And after that, I <u>ate</u> bananas in coconut milk for dessert.
Pedro: Mmm! That sounds good.
Alexa: It was.

Exercise 6

2. I had a huge lunch, so I <u>skipped</u> dinner.
3. What <u>ingredients</u> do you need to cook crispy fried noodles?
4. First, fry the beef in oil and curry powder, and then <u>pour</u> the coconut milk over the beef.
5. We need to leave the restaurant now. Could we have the <u>check</u>, please?

Exercise 7

1. A: Have you ever tried barbecued chicken? You marinate the meat in barbecue sauce for about an hour and then cook it on the grill.
B: <u>Mmm! That sounds good!</u>
2. A: Here's a recipe called Baked Eggplant Delight. I usually bake eggplant for an hour, but this says you bake it for only five minutes!
B: <u>That sounds wrong.</u>
3. A: Look at this dish – frogs' legs with bananas! I've never seen that before.
B: <u>Yuck! That sounds awful.</u>

Exercise 8

2. I <u>brought</u> all the ingredients with me.
3. <u>Did</u> you eat a huge dinner last night?
4. We <u>took</u> my mother to the new Chilean restaurant.
5. I haven't <u>given</u> a birthday gift to my father yet.
6. We have never <u>been</u> to a Chinese restaurant.
7. I have never <u>eaten</u> snails. What are they like?
8. Have you <u>decided</u> what kind of pizza you would like?
9. I <u>bought</u> this chicken sandwich for $5.
10. Oh, I'm sorry. I just <u>broke</u> a glass. What a mess!
11. Victor <u>made</u> gogi gui for dinner.
12. I wasn't hungry this morning, so I <u>skipped</u> breakfast.
13. Oh, no! I <u>forgot</u> to buy rice.
14. Have you ever <u>driven</u> a sports car?
15. I <u>tried</u> Greek food for the first time last night.
16. Have you ever <u>fallen</u> asleep at the movies? It's really embarrassing.

5 Hit the road!

Exercise 1

A

take	*do*	*go*	*rent*
long walks	a lot of hiking	camping	a camper
sailing lessons	some fishing	on vacation	a car
a vacation	something exciting	swimming	a condominium

B

Answers will vary.

C

Answers will vary.

Exercise 2

Scott: So, Elena, do you have any vacation plans?
Elena: Well, *I'm going to paint my apartment* because the walls are a really ugly color. What about you?
Scott: I'm going to rent a car and take a long drive.
Elena: Where are you going to go?
Scott: I'm not sure. I'll probably visit my sister Jeanne. I haven't seen her in a long time.
Elena: That sounds nice. I like to visit my family, too.
Scott: Yes, and maybe I'll go to the mountains for a few days. I haven't been hiking in months. How about you? Are you going to do anything else on your vacation?
Elena: I'll probably catch up on my studying. I have a lot of work to do before school starts.
Scott: That doesn't sound like much fun.
Elena: Oh, I am planning to have some fun, too. I'm going to relax on the beach. I love to go surfing!

Exercise 3

A

2. A: How are you going to get there?
B: I'm going to drive.
3. A: Where are you going to stay?
B: I'm going to stay in a condominium. My friend has one near the beach.
4. A: Is anyone going to travel with you?/Are you going to travel with anyone?
B: No, I'm going to travel by myself.

B

2. Maybe I'll take the train.
3. I won't stay at a hotel.
4. I think I'll ask a friend.

Exercise 4

A

Rio de Janeiro and Iguaçu Falls

B

1. True
2. False. Buenos Aires has the widest avenue in the world.
3. False. Iguaçu Falls is bigger than Niagara Falls.
4. True
5. False. Rio de Janeiro has great beaches.

Exercise 5

2. You should never leave cash in your hotel room.
3. You need to take your credit card with you.
4. You have to pay an airport tax.
5. You should let your family know where they can contact you.
6. You'd better not go out alone late at night.
7. You must get a vaccination if you go to some countries.

Exercise 6

A

2. hiking boots
3. a first-aid kit
4. a swimsuit

B

Answers will vary. Possible answers:
2. They need to take hiking boots.
3. They ought to take a first-aid kit.
4. He should take a swimsuit.

Exercise 7

Answers will vary. Possible answers:
2. You need to buy good quality camping equipment.
3. You ought to buy maps and travel guides.
4. You shouldn't forget a first-aid kit.
5. You don't have to take a lot of cash.
6. You should get a GPS system for your car.
7. You'd better remember to bring insect spray.
8. You must take your driver's license.
9. You should remember to bring a jacket.
10. You don't have to pack a lot of luggage.

Exercise 8

1. I'm not going to go on vacation alone.
2. I want to travel by myself.
3. You should travel with a friend.
4. You must get a vaccination.

Exercise 9

A

Answers will vary. Possible answer:

I'm going to arrive in Lisbon, Portugal, on July 6 and check in at the Tivoli Hotel. Then maybe I'll go shopping. I'm going to spend three days in Lisbon sightseeing. Then I'm going to take a tour bus across the border to Seville in Spain. I'll probably visit the cathedral. I'm going to see some flamenco dancing in the evening. Then I'm going to rent a car and drive to Málaga on the Costa del Sol. I guess I'll visit the old city center. Maybe I'll spend time on the beach. Then I'm going to fly to Madrid on July 19. I'll probably visit some museums there. I'm going to take a tour of the city and see the sights. I'm going to go home on July 22.

B

Answers will vary.

6 Sure! I'll do it.

Exercise 1

2. OK, I'll put them away.
3. OK, I'll hang them up.
4. OK, I'll turn them off.
5. OK, I'll turn it on.

Exercise 2

A

Answers will vary. Possible answers:

2. hang up
3. let down
4. pick up
5. put away
6. take out
7. take off
8. throw away
9. turn off
10. turn up

B

Answers will vary. Possible answers:

2. Please hang up your jacket. The floor is dirty.
3. Please take out the trash. It smells bad.
4. Please pick up the phone. It's ringing.
5. Please turn off the TV. No one is watching it.
6. Please throw away the chair. It's broken.

Exercise 3

2. Take out the trash.
3. Turn down the TV.
4. Pick up your things.
5. Put away your clothes.
6. Turn on the radio.

Exercise 4

A

2. The milk is getting warm.
3. The bag is almost full.
4. It's a mess.
5. It's too loud.

B

Answers will vary. Possible answers:

2. Sorry, I had to answer the phone.
3. Sorry, I didn't know the garbage bag was full.
4. Sorry, I made a cake today.
5. Sorry, I didn't realize it was so loud.

Exercise 5

A

One is for young children, and the other is for teenagers; one is a reward system, the other is a system for frustrating computer users.

B

Answers will vary.

Exercise 6

2. Would you mind taking this form to the office?
3. Could you turn the TV down?
4. Would you mind not leaving wet towels on the floor?
5. Would you text me today's homework assignment?
6. Can you pass me that book, please?

Exercise 7

2. A: Would you mind helping me?
B: Sorry, I can't right now.
3. A: Excuse me, but you're sitting in my seat.
B: Oh, I'm sorry. I didn't realize that.
4. A: Would you like to come in?
B: All right. Thanks.
5. A: Would you mind not leaving your clothes on the floor?
B: Oh, all right. I'll put them away.
6. A: Can you hand me the remote control?
B: No problem.

Exercise 8

Answers will vary. Possible answers:

2. *Benjamin:* You're late! I've been here for half an hour!
Jen: I'm really sorry. My car broke down.
3. *Customer:* I brought this laptop in last week, but it's still not working right.
Salesperson: Oh, I'm sorry. I'll fix it for you.
4. *Father:* You didn't take out the garbage this morning.
Son: I'm sorry. I didn't want to be late for the school bus.
5. *Customer:* This steak is very tough. I can't eat it.
Waiter: I'm really sorry. I'll bring you another one.
6. *Neighbor 1:* Could you do something about your dog? It barks all night and it keeps me awake.
Neighbor 2: I'm sorry. I won't leave him outside at night anymore.
7. *Resident:* Would you mind moving your car? You're parked in my parking space.
Visitor: Sorry. I won't do it again.
8. *Teacher:* Please put away your papers. You left them on your desk yesterday.
Student: I'm sorry. I forgot I put them there.

Exercise 9

1. Throw that old food away. Put it in the trash can.
2. Would you mind picking up some groceries? We need coffee, milk, and rice.
3. Turn the lights off. Electricity costs money!
4. My neighbor made a promise. He said, "I'll be sure to stop my dog from barking."

Exercise 10

A

2. don't criticize my friends
3. mail these bills
4. don't talk so loudly
5. put away the groceries
6. take off your sunglasses
7. turn down the TV
8. clean up your bedroom

B

Answers will vary. Possible answers:

2. Could you not criticize my friends?
3. Would you mail these bills?
4. Would you mind not talking so loudly?
5. Can you put away the groceries?
6. Could you take off your sunglasses?
7. Would you turn down the TV?
8. Can you clean up your bedroom?

Exercise 11

Answers will vary.

7 What do you use this for?

Exercise 1

2. A robot is used for doing boring jobs.
3. A digital camera is used for taking and deleting photos easily.
4. A flash drive is used for storing and sending data.
5. A GPS system is used for determining your exact location.

Exercise 2

Answers will vary. Possible answers:
2. flash drive, back up files
A flash drive is used to back up files.
3. GPS system, places
GPS systems are used to find places.
4. videos, video camera
A video camera is used to take videos.
5. the Internet, information
The Internet is used to find information.

Exercise 3

2. download
3. watching
4. pay
5. backing up
6. find

Exercise 4

2. People used to write letters, but now they usually send emails instead.
3. A cell phone is used to make calls and send texts.
4. I used to have a desktop computer, but now I just use a laptop.
5. We download all of our movies. We used to buy DVDs, but we don't buy them anymore.
6. Wi-Fi networks are used to access the Internet wirelessly.

Exercise 5

A

Answers will vary. Possible answers:
prices, size, what the item does

B

Answers will vary.

Exercise 6

A

_d_ question and answer sites
_g_ blogs
_f_ gaming sites
_h_ media sharing sites
_a_ news sites
_e_ search engines
_b_ social media sites
_c_ shopping sites

B

Answers will vary.

Exercise 7

_3_ Next, check what the site has to offer you. Don't worry if you can't understand all its functions.
_1_ First of all, join a social networking site. Choose a site where you already know people.
_4_ After that, use the site's search features to find friends. Be sure to browse through groups who share your interests.
_5_ Finally, invite people to be your friend. Try not to be shy! A lot of people may be waiting to hear from you.
_2_ Then customize your profile page. For example, play with the colors to make the page reflect your personality. Now you're ready to start exploring!

Exercise 8

Answers may vary. Possible answers:
2. Be sure to charge your cell phone/smartphone.
3. Remember to turn off the light.
4. Try not to eat when you're at the computer.
5. Try to check the weather before your trip.
6. Make sure to get gas.

Exercise 9

My brother just bought a smartphone. It's really great. It has a lot of high-tech features. In fact, it's an amazing handheld computer, not just a cell phone. For example, it has Wi-Fi connectivity, so my brother can connect to the Internet in most places. He can send a message to a friend by email or through a social networking site. He can also find out where he is because it has a GPS app. That's perfect for my brother because he likes mountain climbing. He'll never get lost again! His smartphone also has an excellent camera, so he can take photos of his climbing trips. And, of course, it's a phone. So he can talk to his girlfriend anytime he wants!

Exercise 10

Answers may vary. Possible answers:
2. It's fragile.
3. Unplug it.
4. Don't spill anything on it.
5. Recharge the battery.

Exercise 11

A: What a day! First, my microwave didn't work.
B: What happened?
A: *It burned my lunch.* Then I tried to use my computer, but that didn't work either.
B: Why not?
A: I couldn't get a Wi-Fi signal. After that, I tried to use the vacuum cleaner.
B: Let me guess. It didn't pick up the dirt.
A: Worse! It spread dirt around the room.
B: Did you take the vacuum cleaner to get it fixed?
A: Well, I tried, but my car wouldn't start.
B: Oh, no! Do you need a ride to work tomorrow?

8 Time to celebrate!

Exercise 1

One of the most important national holidays in the United States is Independence Day. This is the day when Americans celebrate winning their independence from Britain almost 250 years ago. There are many customs for Independence Day. Most towns, big and small, mark this holiday with parades and fireworks. They put up a lot of decorations usually in red, white, and blue, the colors of the U.S. flag. Bands play patriotic music. It's also a day when many Americans get together with family and friends to celebrate with a barbecue or a picnic.

Exercise 2

1. I hate April 15! In the United States, it's the day when people have to pay their taxes. I always owe the government money.
2. June is my favorite month. It's the month when summer vacation begins. I always go straight to the beach.
3. September is my least favorite month. It's the month when school starts. Good-bye, summer!
4. I've never liked winter. It's a season when I feel sad and depressed. The cold weather always affects my mood negatively.

Exercise 3

A

2. We always have a party at our house on New Year's Eve.
3. Janice and Nick are getting married soon. They plan to have a small wedding with just a few family members.
4. Valentine's Day is on February 14th every year.
5. My friends and family gave me some very nice presents on my birthday.
6. People like to play tricks on each other on April Fools' Day.
7. On the Fourth of July, many people shoot fireworks into the sky at night.
8. Tomorrow is my parents' 25th wedding anniversary.

B

2. Spring is the season when the flowers start to bloom.
3. New Year's Eve is a night when people celebrate new beginnings.
4. The weekend is a time when people relax.
5. Father's Day is a day when children spend time with their fathers.
6. Winter is the season when we go skiing.

Exercise 4

A

Answers will vary.

B

	Americans give gifts on:	*Americans don't give gifts on:*
Martin Luther King Jr. Day		✓
Valentine's Day	✓	
April Fools' Day		✓
Mother's Day	✓	
Father's Day	✓	
Independence Day		✓
Labor Day		✓
Thanksgiving		✓

Exercise 5

Answers will vary. Possible answers:

2. When someone has a birthday, friends and family go out to dinner.
3. After a couple moves into a new home, they have a housewarming party.
4. After a student graduates, he/she starts looking for a job.
5. When a woman gets engaged, she usually receives an engagement ring.
6. When a couple has their first child, their friends and family cook for them for the first few months.

Exercise 6

Newly married couples often leave on their honeymoon before the wedding reception ends. When they go on their honeymoon, most couples like to be alone. After they come back from their honeymoon, many newlyweds have to live with relatives. They can only live in their own place when they have enough money to pay for it.

Exercise 7

Answers will vary.

Exercise 8

1. Wedding celebrations are often held in a restaurant or hotel.
2. Children's Day is a day when people in many countries honor their children.
3. Fall is the season when people in the U.S. celebrate Thanksgiving.
4. In Indonesia, on Nyepi Day, Balinese people observe a day of silence to begin the new year.

Exercise 9

2. New Year's Eve is a night when many people have parties.
3. At the end of the year, Japanese people exchange *oseibo* presents to show their appreciation for the people in their lives.
4. Many Brazilians celebrate the Festa Junina in June.
5. In Sweden, Midsummer's Day occurs around June 21.

Exercise 10

Answers will vary. Possible answers:

2. What is going to happen at midnight?
3. Will there be fireworks?
4. Are people going to sing and dance?
5. What kind of clothes should I wear?
6. Are you going to make special food?

9 Only time will tell.

Exercise 1

Answers will vary. Possible answers:

In many countries nowadays, food shopping takes very little time. In the past, people *used to go* to a different shop for each type of item. For example, you bought meat at a butcher's shop and fish at a fish market. A fruit market sold fruits and vegetables. For dry goods, like rice or beans, you had to go to grocery stores. Today, the supermarket or superstore sells all these things. Once every week or two, people drive in their cars to these huge stores to buy everything – not only food, but also clothes, electronic goods, furniture, and medicine. But in the future, the way we shop is going to change again. Nowadays, people do a lot of their shopping online. Soon, maybe, no one will leave home to go shopping. People will use their computers to order everything online.

Exercise 2

1. A: When did people travel by horse and carriage?
   B: About 100 years ago.
2. A: When might doctors find a cure for the fl u?
   B: In the next 50 years.
3. A: When did the first man go to the moon?
   B: About 50 years ago.
4. A: When is everyone going to buy everything online?
   B: Soon.

Exercise 3

2. In the past, people used to collect CDs. Nowadays, they listen to music online.
3. A few years ago, people used to use desktop computers. Today, they use tablets.
4. Fifty years ago, people used to wear business suits to work. These days, they wear casual clothes.
5. Nowadays, people drive their own cars. Sometime in the future, they will ride in cars that drive themselves.

Exercise 4

A

Answers will vary. Possible answer:

It changed from jazz to swing to rock 'n' roll. Rock 'n' roll changed into disco, punk, and hip-hop.

B

Answers will vary.

Exercise 5

1. A: What if I get in shape this summer?
   B: You might be able to come rock climbing with me.
2. A: What will happen if I stop exercising?
   B: Well, you might gain weight.
3. A: What if I get a better job?
   B: You'll be able to buy some new clothes.
4. A: What will happen if I don't get a summer job?
   B: You probably won't have enough money for your school expenses.

Exercise 6

A

feel	***get***	***join***	***spend***
energetic	a cold	a group	money
relaxed	married	a gym	time

B

Answers will vary.

Exercise 7

Answers will vary. Possible answers:

2. if I eat more fruits and vegetables.
3. I'll be in better shape.
4. I won't get into a good college.
5. if I drink less coffee.
6. if I get a good job.

Exercise 8

A

Noun	***Adjective***	***Noun***	***Adjective***
energy	energetic	medicine	medical
environment	environmental	success	successful
health	healthy		

B

2. There are a lot of environmental problems in my country. There's too much air pollution, and the rivers are dirty.
3. My health is not as good as it used to be. So, I've decided to eat better food and go swimming every day.
4. My party was a great success. I think I might have another one soon!
5. If I start exercising more often, I might have more energy.

Exercise 9

Answers will vary. Possible answers:

2. If I go on a diet, I may be able to lose weight.
3. In the future, few people will use cash to buy things.
4. If I get a better job, I'll be able to buy an apartment.
5. I'll arrive at noon.

Exercise 10

Answers will vary.

10 I like working with people.

Exercise 1

1. A: I enjoy working in sales.
   B: <u>So do I.</u>
2. A: I like working the night shift.
   B: <u>Well, I don't.</u>
3. A: I can't stand getting to work late.
   B: <u>Neither can I.</u>
4. A: I'm interested in using my language skills.
   B: <u>So am I.</u>

Exercise 2

2. Takiko is a novelist. He writes all his books by hand because he hates <u>using a laptop</u>.
3. Sarah usually works alone all day, but she enjoys <u>working with a team</u>, too.
4. Jennifer works for a large company, but she's interested in <u>starting her own business</u>.
5. Pablo has to use Portuguese and Japanese at work, but he's not very good at <u>learning languages</u>.
6. Annie has to drive to work every day, but she doesn't like <u>commuting</u>.

Exercise 3

Answers will vary. Possible answers:

2. I'm not good at making decisions quickly.
3. I can't stand making mistakes.
4. I enjoy working with a team.

Exercise 4

Answers will vary. Possible answers:

2. I can't stand <u>commuting on the bus.</u>
3. I don't mind <u>taking the train.</u>
4. I'm interested in <u>learning to paint.</u>
5. I'm not interested in <u>joining a gym.</u>
6. I'm good at <u>making small talk.</u>
7. I'm not very good <u>at speaking to large groups of people.</u>

Exercise 5

1. Eric hates waiting in line. He's a very <u>impatient</u> person.
2. You can trust Marta. If she says she's going to do something, she'll do it. She's very <u>reliable</u>.
3. Kevin isn't good at remembering things. Last week, he missed another important business meeting. He's so <u>forgetful</u>.

Exercise 6

A

1. journalist
2. stockbroker
3. flight attendant
4. language teacher

B

Answers will vary. Possible answers:

1. computers, world news, under pressure
2. make decisions quickly, good with numbers, level-headed, money
3. long hours, punctual, reliable, traveling
4. foreign language, speaking, communicate well

C

Answers will vary.

Exercise 7

Answers will vary. Possible answers:

2. Olivia could be a carpenter because she enjoys doing things with her hands. She couldn't be a factory worker because she doesn't enjoy working in the same place every day.
3. Margo would make a good model because she enjoys wearing different clothes every day. She would make a bad lawyer because she's not good at organizing her time.
4. Ha-joon could be a salesperson because he loves helping people. He wouldn't make a good detective because he's not good at solving problems.
5. Eddie would make a good nurse because he's good at taking care of people. He wouldn't want to be an accountant because he's not good with numbers.

Exercise 8

1. Mike could never be <u>a</u> nurse or <u>a</u> teacher because he is very short-tempered and impatient with people. On the other hand, he's <u>an</u> efficient and reliable person. So he would make <u>a</u> good bookkeeper or accountant.
2. Scott would make <u>a</u> terrible lawyer or executive. He isn't good at making decisions. On the other hand, he'd make <u>an</u> excellent actor or artist because he's very creative and funny.

Exercise 9

A

1. efficient / <u>*disorganized*</u>
2. friendly / <u>unfriendly</u>
3. punctual / <u>late</u>
4. interesting / <u>boring</u>
5. level-headed / <u>moody</u>
6. patient / <u>impatient</u>
7. quiet / <u>outgoing</u>
8. reliable / <u>forgetful</u>

B

1. Mingyu is an <u>outgoing</u> person. She really enjoys meeting new people.
2. Hannah is very <u>moody</u>. One day she's happy, and the next day she's sad.
3. I can't stand working with <u>forgetful</u> people. I like having reliable co-workers.
4. Charles is an <u>interesting</u> person. I'm never bored when I talk to him.

Exercise 10

A

2. Ed would make a great nurse because he's so <u>level-headed</u>. He never gets anxious or upset when things go wrong.
3. A good lawyer has to remember facts. Nathan is a terrible lawyer because he's very <u>forgetful</u>.
4. My favorite teacher at school was Mrs. Wilson. She was pretty <u>strict</u>, so no one misbehaved in her class.
5. My boss is very <u>generous</u>. She gave me a big holiday bonus.
6. June's assistant is very <u>efficient</u>. She works fast and never wastes time.
7. My boss complains about everything I do. He's so <u>critical</u>.
8. Julie is so <u>impatient</u>. She can't stand waiting for anything.

B

1. A: I'm not very good at video games. How about you?
   B: Oh, <u>I am</u>. I play video games every weekend.
2. A: Jake is not punctual.
   B: <u>Neither is</u> Karen. She's always late.
3. A: I'm so disorganized!
   B: <u>So am</u> I. My desk is a mess. I can never fi nd anything.
4. A: I don't mind traveling for work.
   B: <u>Neither do</u> I. I think it's kind of fun.
5. A: I can't stand working in the evening.
   B: <u>Neither can</u> I. I prefer to work during the day.
6. A: I'm not very outgoing at parties.
   B: <u>Neither am</u> I. I'm usually pretty quiet at social events.
7. A: I hate taking the train to work.
   B: <u>I don't mind</u>. I usually read or listen to music when I'm on the train.
8. A: Stella is really creative.
   B: <u>So is</u> Robert. He always has great ideas

11 It's really worth seeing!

Exercise 1

2. The play *Romeo and Juliet* was written by William Shakespeare in the 1590s.
3. The microwave oven was invented by Percy Spencer in 1947.
4. The picture *Sunflowers* was painted by Vincent van Gogh in 1888.
5. In 1960, a 1,000-year-old Viking settlement in eastern Canada was discovered by Norwegian explorer Helge Ingstad.
6. The song "Let It Go" from the movie *Frozen* was composed by a married couple, Robert Lopez and Kristen Anderson-Lopez.

Exercise 2

2. The box-office hit *Star Wars: The Force Awakens* was directed by J.J. Abrams.
3. The first satellite was launched into space by the Soviet Union in 1957.
4. The children's novel *Charlotte's Web* was written by E.B. White.
5. The Guggenheim Museum in New York City was designed by Frank Lloyd Wright.

Exercise 3

2. The Blue Mosque was designed by Mehmet Aga in 1616.
3. Buckingham Palace was built by the Duke of Buckingham in 1705.
4. Canberra, Australia was planned by Walter Burley Griffin in 1913.
5. The Vasco da Gama Bridge was designed by Armando Rito in 1998.
6. The Burj Khalifa was built by 12,000 workers in 2010.

Exercise 4

A

Ottawa, Canada This capital city's name . . .
Valparaiso, Chile The Spanish explorer . . .
Rio de Janeiro, Brazil The name of this city, . . .
Cusco, Peru The name of this city . . .
Montevideo, Uruguay The most popular belief . . .
Bogota, Columbia The name of this city . . .

B

1. False. Neither city was named after a person.
2. True
3. False. It was named after a hero in a myth who grew wings and became a rock.
4. True

Exercise 5

Ecuador *is* situated on the equator in the northwest of South America. It is made up of a coastal plain in the west and a tropical rain forest in the east. These two areas are separated by the Andes mountains in the center of the country.

The economy is based on oil and agricultural products. More oil is produced in Ecuador than any other South American country except Venezuela. Bananas, coffee, and cocoa are grown there. Many of these products are exported. Hardwood is also produced and exported.

Many people in Ecuador are of Incan origin. Several native languages are spoken there, such as Quechua. Spanish is spoken in Ecuador, too.

Exercise 6

2. The peso is the currency that is used in Chile.
3. Millions of people visit Italy every year. Tourism is a very important industry there.
4. A lot of meat, especially beef, is exported by Argentina.
5. Gold mining is an important industry in South Africa.
6. Much of the world's wheat is grown in the Canadian prairies. It's used to make foods like bread and pasta.
7. A lot of computers are exported by Taiwan. In fact, the electronics industry is an important part of many East Asian economies.

Exercise 7

Answers will vary. Possible answers:

Every year, millions of tourists visit California. California is known for its beautiful scenery, warm climate, and excellent food. There are many national parks in California. They are visited by over 30 million people every year. Many world-famous museums are located there, including the Getty Center in Los Angeles and the San Francisco Museum of Modern Art.

The state is divided into two parts, called Northern California and Southern California. San Francisco and Yosemite National Park are found in Northern California.

San Francisco is bordered by water on three sides. It is a city with a beautiful bay and two famous bridges. San Francisco's streets are always filled with tourists. On the north end of the bay is the world-famous Napa Valley. South of San Francisco, there is an area that is famous for its computer industries; it is called Silicon Valley. Many computer industries are located there. Los Angeles, Hollywood, and Disneyland are located in Southern California. Southern California is known for its desert areas, which are sometimes next to snowcapped mountains.

Exercise 8

1. The Montjuic Tower in Barcelona was designed by Santiago Calatrava.
2. Four official languages are spoken in Switzerland.
3. In South Korea, a lot of people are employed in the automobile industry.
4. Malaysia is governed by a prime minister.

Exercise 9

A

1. What was invented by Alexander Graham Bell?
2. Where is Acapulco located?
3. When was Santiago, Chile founded?
4. What is grown in Thailand?

B

1. Do you know where the Golden Gate Bridge is located?
2. Can you tell me who *Don Quixote* was written by?
3. Do you know when antibiotics were first used?
4. Could you tell me who the tea bag was invented by?

Exercise 10

1829 was established
1863 was opened
1964 was introduced
1990 was reached
1995 were tested
2006 was finished
2011 was reduced

12 It's a long story.

Exercise 1

2. Peter was studying/was reading when the fire alarm went off.
3. The Mitchells were watching television/a movie when the fire alarm went off.
4. Isabella and Carlos were playing chess/a game when the fire alarm went off.
5. Mr. Yang was cooking when the fire alarm went off.
6. Paula was talking on the phone when the fire alarm went off.

Exercise 2

Answers will vary.

Exercise 3

Matt: How did you get your first job, Sonia?
Sonia: Well, I got a summer job in a department store while I was studying at the university.
Matt: No, I mean your first full-time job.
Sonia: But that is how I got my first full-time job. I was working during summer when the manager offered me a job after graduation.
Matt: Wow! That was lucky. Did you like the job?
Sonia: Well, I did at first, but then things changed. I was doing the same thing every day, and they weren't giving me any new responsibilities. I was getting really bored when another company asked me to work for them.

Exercise 4

Answers will vary. Possible answers:

2. I saw an old friend last week while I was running.
3. My car was giving me a lot of trouble, so I took it to a mechanic.
4. Coffee arrived while I was talking on the phone.

Exercise 5

A

Answers will vary. Possible answers:
She sings in many languages. / She sings very well. / She sang in the film *Frida*.

B

1. False. Lila's father was a professor of art and film.
2. True
3. False. She wrote a musical based on the book.
4. False. She learned to sing from listening to her mother.
5. True

Exercise 6

A

2. Carrie and Alex have been going to graduate school since August.
3. Tom has been studying Chinese for a year.
4. Linda has not been teaching since she had a baby.
5. Lori has not been living in Los Angeles for very long.
6. Luis and Silvina have been traveling in South America for six weeks.

B

Answers will vary.

Exercise 7

Mark: What have you been doing lately?
Andrew: I've been working a lot and trying to stay in shape.
Mark: Have you been jogging?
Andrew: No, I haven't been jogging. I've been playing tennis in the evenings with friends.
Mark: Really? Have you been winning?
Andrew: No, I've been losing most of the games. But it's fun. How about you? Have you been exercising?
Mark: No, I haven't been getting any exercise. I've been working long hours every day.
Andrew: Have you been working on weekends?
Mark: Yes, I've even been working on weekends. I've been working Saturday mornings.
Andrew: Well, why don't we play a game of tennis on Saturday afternoon? It's great exercise!

Exercise 8

1. A: When I was a kid, I lived on a farm.
   B: Really? Tell me more.
2. A: I haven't been ice-skating in ages.
   B: Neither have I.
3. A: I was a teenager when I got my first job.
   B: Really? That's interesting.
4. A: I haven't seen you for a long time.
   B: Not since we graduated.

Exercise 9

2. A: Were you living in Europe before you moved here?
   B: No, I was living in South Korea.
3. A: How long have you been studying English?
   B: I have been studying it for about a year.
4. A: What were you doing before you went back to school?
   B: I was selling real estate.
5. A: What have you been doing since I last saw you?
   B: I have been traveling around the country.

Exercise 10

Answers will vary. Possible answers:

2. While I was getting dressed, my friend arrived.
3. I've been a fan of that TV show for a long time.
4. I've had a part-time job since last year.
5. I haven't been saving enough money lately.
6. I haven't seen you in ages.

13 That's entertainment!

Exercise 1

This action movie is dumb. It has amazing action scenes, but the story is really boring. I think the other Indian Jones movies were exciting, but I think this one is ridiculous.

This drama is based on a fascinating true story. It's about Brian Piccolo, a football player who develops a terrible disease, and his friend Gayle Sayers. Maybe it doesn't sound interesting, but it's a must-see. The film has great acting and a wonderful script. I was very moved by the story of the friendship between Piccolo and Sayers.

Exercise 2

2. I really enjoyed all of the Hunger Games movies. In fact, I think they're wonderful.
3. The special effects were great in that sci-fi movie we saw last week. They can do such incredible things with 3-D technology these days.
4. The latest Star Wars movie was fantastic, and I'd love to see it again.

Exercise 3

2. A: His new movie is the dumbest movie I've ever seen.
   B: I didn't like it either.
3. A: It's weird that they don't show more classic movies on TV. I really like them.
   B: I know. It's strange.
4. A: I think Tina Fey is hilarious.
   B: Yeah, she's excellent.
5. A: The movie we saw last night was ridiculous.
   B: Well, I thought it was pretty good.

Exercise 4

Answers will vary.

Exercise 5

A

2. *Pan's Labyrinth* fantasy
4. *The Bridge on the River Kwai* war movie
1. *Casablanca* romantic drama
3. *2001: A Space Odyssey* science fiction

B

1. a movie with an unusual "star": *2001: A Space Odyssey*
2. two lovers in a difficult situation: *Casablanca*
3. where dreams and reality meet: *Pan's Labyrinth*
4. its music is unforgettable: *The Bridge on the River Kwai*

C

1. you won't be disappointed c. you're going to like it
2. out of this world d. outstanding
3. it's a must a. you need to see it
4. steals the show b. becomes the center of attention

Exercise 6

A

2. *The Theory of Everything* is a movie which is based on a true story about Stephen Hawking.
3. Elizabeth Taylor was an actress who won two Academy Awards.
4. Akira Kurosawa was a director who was one of the most influential filmmakers in history.
5. *The Miracle Worker* is a great movie which won a lot of awards.
6. Jennifer Lopez is an actress, a dancer, and a singer who also appears on TV.

B

Answers will vary.

Exercise 7

Karen: Who is Mark Twain?
Carlos: Oh, you know him. He's an author who wrote a lot of novels about life in America in the 1800s.
Heather: Oh, I remember. He wrote several stories that people have to read in literature classes, right?
Carlos: Yes, but people love reading them for pleasure, too.
Heather: What's his most popular book?
Carlos: I guess *Adventures of Huckleberry Finn* is the one that is most famous. It's a work that has been very popular since it was published in 1885.
Heather: Ah, yes, I think I've heard of it. What's it about?
Carlos: It's about a boy who has a lot of adventures with his friend Tom Sawyer. It was one of the first American novels that was written in the first person. It's Huck Finn himself who tells the story.
Heather: Now, that's a story that I'd like to read.

Exercise 8

A

2. A romance is a movie that has a love story.
3. A comedy is a movie that makes you laugh.
4. An action film is a movie has a lot of excitement.
5. A horror film is a movie that is scary.
6. A biography is a movie that is about a real person.
7. A documentary is a movie that shows real events.

B

Answers will vary.

Exercise 9

1. I thought the special effects in the *Jurassic Park* movies were cool. It's incredible what they can do with computers.
2. Have you ever seen the 1965 film *Doctor Zhivago*? The cinematography is beautiful, especially the lighting.
3. Hermione Granger is my favorite character in the *Harry Potter* books.
4. I've forgotten the name of the composer who wrote *Rhapsody in Blue*. Was it George Gershwin?

Exercise 10

The Hunger Games is a series of science fiction films that started to come out in 2012. The first one was directed by Gary Ross who also wrote the screenplay. The films include Jennifer Lawrence and Woody Harrelson who are famous actors. The films are about a young girl who is called Katniss. She joins a contest to save her community in the near future which is very dark and dangerous. Will she save her community?

14 Now I get it!

Exercise 1

A

1. e. **2.** d **3.** a **4.** c **5.** b

B

Answers will vary. Possible answers:

2. Maybe it means they need help.
3. It probably means he wants everyone to stop.
4. Perhaps it means they need a taxi.
5. It could mean she wants to turn.

Exercise 2

2. That sign is really confusing. What does it mean? It's not clear at all.
3. I got stuck behind a really slow bus on a narrow mountain road. I felt frustrated because I couldn't pass it.
4. I drove for eight hours on a straight, flat road where the scenery never changed. I've never been so bored!
5. I couldn't get into the parking space, and everyone was looking at me. It was pretty embarrassing.
6. I went bicycling all day. Now I'm so exhausted that I'm going to sleep for 12 hours!
7. I asked the taxi driver to turn off his radio because the loud music was very annoying.

Exercise 3

1. That sounds crazy!
2. Shh. Be quiet!
3. Come here.
4. Where's the restroom?

Exercise 4

A

_3_ If you eat the right food you will be healthy.
_6_ People with the same interests become friends.
_1_ We may think we will be happier in a different situation, but it is not necessarily true.
_4_ Don't worry if you love someone who doesn't return your love. You can always find someone else.
_2_ It is easier to fix something before there is a problem than after the problem has occurred.
_5_ It is preferable to do something with some delay than to never do it at all.

B

1. A: I really don't understand what Miriam sees in Bill.
B: Oh, I do. They both love movies from other countries and they like learning languages.
A: Ah, I see! Birds of a feather flock together.

2. A: It's 10 o'clock already! Do you think I can get to the party on time?
B: That depends on whether you can catch the bus.
A: But what if I don't?
B: Well, getting there is the important thing. Better late than never.

3. A: A penny for your thoughts.
B: I was just thinking about what it's like to be a movie star.
A: Do you think they're any happier than you are?
B: They must be, don't you think?
A: Oh, I don't know. The grass is always greener on the other side of the fence.

4. A: It's cold outside. Why don't you put on your new coat?
B: Do you think I need to, dear?
A: Well, you don't want to catch a cold like the one you had last month, do you?
B: OK, you're right. Like they say, an ounce of prevention is worth a pound of cure.

Exercise 5

Answers will vary. Possible answers:

1. It could mean you shouldn't get upset over small problems.
2. Maybe it means you shouldn't judge a person before you know them better.
3. It might mean that you always have to pay people back in some way when they do something for you.
4. It probably means that people like to gossip about negative things.

Exercise 6

Teacher: OK, class. This afternoon, we're going to take the school bus to the science museum.
Student 1: Great! I'm going to take some photos.
Teacher: I'm afraid *you're not allowed to* take photos.
Student 1: But how can they stop me? I'll use my cell phone, not a camera.
Teacher: You have to check all your things with security.
Student 2: Can I take my jacket into the museum?
Teacher: I'm not sure. It might be best to leave it on the bus.
Student 2: But what about my wallet? It might not be safe on the bus.
Teacher: Oh, it's definitely a good idea to keep your money with you. Keep it in your pocket.
Student 3: And what about touching things in the museum?
Teacher: There are "Don't touch!" signs next to some of the things. But you can touch things if there is no sign.

Exercise 7

1. *Student:* This is great!
Instructor: Hey, slow down! You *aren't allowed to* go above the speed limit.
2. *Student:* Uh, what does that sign mean?
Instructor: It means you can't turn left.
3. *Instructor:* You look confused.
Student: What . . . what does that sign mean?
Instructor: It means you are allowed to do two things. You can turn right or go straight.
4. *Instructor:* Why are you stopping?
Student: The sign says to stop.
Instructor: Actually, you don't have to stop. Just be prepared to, if necessary.
5. *Instructor:* Hey, stop! Didn't you see that sign? It means you have to come to a complete stop.
Student: What sign? I didn't see any sign.

Exercise 8

2. It must mean you're not allowed to light a fire here.
3. That sign might mean you're not allowed to swim here.
4. That sign probably means you can get food here.
5. It could mean you have got to be quiet after 10:00 P.M.

Exercise 9

1. A: I went to the movies last night. A couple who sat behind me talked during the entire movie.
B: That's irritating!
2. A: I fell asleep during class this afternoon. The teacher had to wake me up.
B: Oh, that's embarrassing!
3. A: I drove all night to get there on time.
B: Oh, that's exhausting! How can you keep your eyes open?
4. A: Did Sara give you directions to the party?
B: She did, but they're really confusing. Hey, can I get a ride with you?
5. A: This movie is taking forever to download. Why does it have to take so long?
B: You are so impatient! There, look. It's done!

15 I wouldn't have done that.

Exercise 1

A

Answers will vary.

B

Answers will vary. Possible answers:

2. If someone climbed through my neighbor's window, I'd probably call the police.
3. If my boss made things difficult for me at work, I guess I'd talk to my boss.
4. If a friend sounded unhappy on the phone, I'd ask my friend if he or she had a problem.

Exercise 2

Answers will vary. Possible answers:

1. If a relative asked to borrow some money, I'd probably lend them some.
2. If I had three wishes, I would wish for a new car, a million dollars, and good health.
3. If I could have any job I wanted, I would be a singer.
4. If I had a year of vacation time, I would travel around the world.
5. If I could change one thing about myself, I would be taller.

Exercise 3

2. My friend confessed to cheating on the biology exam, but his teacher still failed him.
3. I'm in a difficult predicament at work. I don't know whether to talk to my boss about it or just quit.
4. If I saw someone shoplifting in a store, I'd tell the store manager immediately.
5. My uncle died and left me $20,000. I'm going to invest most of it.
6. When I went back to the parking lot, I tried to get into someone else's car by mistake.
7. There is so much great music to download from the Internet. I don't know what to choose.
8. My aunt won't let me use her car because she thinks I'm a terrible driver. She has a point. I had two accidents last year!

Exercise 4

A

6 I guess I'd take it back to the store and exchange it for something else.
1 I guess I'd write a letter of complaint to the manufacturer.
5 Maybe I'd ask them to repair it.
4 I think I'd make an appointment to see the instructor to talk about it.
2 I'd probably wait until the next month to see if the mistake is corrected.
3 I'd write a letter to the city council and ask them to pay for the damage.

B

Answers will vary.

Exercise 5

Answers will vary. Possible answers:

2. I wouldn't have asked her to speak more quietly. I would have moved to a different seat.
3. I wouldn't have asked them to come back the next day. I would have asked them to stay and ordered food from a restaurant.
4. I wouldn't have called the police. I would have asked them to turn the TV down.
5. I wouldn't have given her a bill. I would have asked her to leave.
6. I wouldn't have stayed quiet about it. I would have apologized.

Exercise 6

Answers will vary.

Exercise 7

A

Dear Harriet,

I've never written to an advice columnist before, but I have a big problem. I'm going out with this really nice guy. He's very sweet to me, and I really want to *marry* him. In fact, we plan to have our wedding next summer. But he has a problem with money. He spends money like crazy! Sometimes he borrows money from me, but he never pays it back. I want to save money because I want us to buy an apartment when we get married. However, if I tell him he has a problem with money, he denies it. He says, "I disagree with you. You never want to go out and enjoy yourself." I don't want to lose him, but what can I do? – J.M., Seattle

Dear J.M.,

You and your boyfriend must *agree* on how you spend your money *before* you get married. If you both admit that there is a problem, you could probably find an answer. He should accept your idea of saving some money. And you shouldn't always refuse to go out and have fun. Don't forget that talking can really help. Good luck! – Harriet

B

Answers will vary.

Exercise 8

A

Carly: Guess what, Kristin! A university in New Zealand has offered me a scholarship.
Kristin: Great! When are you going?
Carly: That's just it. I may not go. What *would* you *do* if your boyfriend asked you not to go?
Kristin: Well, I would try to convince him that it's a good opportunity for me.
Carly: I've tried that. He said I could study the same thing here.
Kristin: If I were you, I would talk to him again. You know, I once missed a big opportunity.
Carly: Oh? What happened?
Kristin: I was offered a job in Los Angeles, but my husband disliked the idea of moving, so we didn't go. I should have taken the job. I've always regretted my decision. In my situation, what would you have done?
Carly: Oh, I would have accepted the offer.
Kristin: Well, there's the answer to your predicament. Accept the scholarship!

B

Answers will vary.

Exercise 9

Answers will vary. Possible answers:

2. I wouldn't put it on my finger.
3. I could take it to a jewelry store to see if it is valuable.
4. I might bring it to the police.
5. I might not pick it up.

16 Making excuses

Exercise 1

2. Julie asked Eric to do an Internet search for her.
3. Andrew asked Eric to check a flash drive for viruses.
4. Tanya told Eric to put some information on a spreadsheet.
5. Carla said not to forget to add paper to the copier.
6. Alan told Eric to reformat a text file as a PDF file.
7. Bruce told Eric to get him some coffee.
8. Cindy told Eric to make five copies of the agenda before the meeting.
9. Jack asked Eric to give him a ride home.
10. Robin said not to be late to work again.

Exercise 2

A

Noun	*Verb*	*Noun*	*Verb*
acceptance	accept	explanation	explain
apology	apologize	invitation	invite
complaint	complain	offer	offer
excuse	excuse	suggestion	suggest

B

2. I accepted an invitation to Billy and Kate's house for dinner.
3. I didn't want to go to Jenny's party, so I made up an excuse.
4. I was rude to my teacher. I must apologize to him.
5. Can you explain the end of the movie? I didn't understand it.
6. Steve said he'd take me to the airport. It was really nice of him to offer.
7. Thank you for your helpful suggestion on how to fix my essay. The teacher really liked it!
8. I received an invitation to Mindy's party. I can't wait to go.

Exercise 3

2. I made a complaint to the police because our neighbors' party was too noisy.
3. I couldn't go to the meeting, so I expressed my concerns in an email.
4. Jake gave an excuse for being late for work. He said there had been a traffic jam on the highway.
5. Lori was very funny at the class party. As usual, she told a lot of jokes.

Exercise 4

A

Hi, William. It would be wonderful if you could come to our party next Friday! It's Mick's birthday and I really think that he would appreciate it if you could be there. All of his friends will be there. The best part is that Mick doesn't know everyone is going to be there. It's a surprise birthday party! So please come and be part of the surprise.

Hi, Eileen. Thank you for the invitation. You know I would love to come if I could, but unfortunately I am working late on Friday. I have to study for my examination next week. So, have a great time without me, and of course I will send a present to Mick.

Oh, William, come on! Please come. The best present you can give to Mick is being with him on his birthday. I know everyone would really enjoy seeing you, too.

Eileen, I really should study for the test. I know I will probably regret not going, but I think I should stick to my plan.

William, you are so right when you say you will regret it if you don't come to Mick's birthday party. All of your friends will be there. As a matter of fact, I mentioned you to Penelope and she said she is looking forward to talking to you at the party. We will all be disappointed if you don't come. Especially Penelope!

Eileen, I've given it some thought and you are right! I should go to Mick's party. In fact, wild horses couldn't stop me. See you on Friday!

B

Answers will vary. Possible answers:

1. She called him to invite him to Mick's birthday party.
2. He has to study for a test.
3. He wants to talk to Penelope at the party.

Exercise 5

A

2. Teresa said her sister was having a baby shower.
3. Bill said he might have some houseguests on Saturday.
4. Miyako and Yoshiko said they were going camping this weekend.
5. Marco said he was sorry, but he would be busy on Saturday afternoon.

B

2. Paul and James told her they would be moving into their new apartment that day.
3. Luis told her he watches the football game on TV every Saturday.
4. Sandra told her she had already made plans to do something else.

C

Answers will vary.

Exercise 6

A

2. a **3.** d **4.** e **5.** b

B

2. Brian: "The game was canceled because of bad weather."
3. Nina: "I'll be studying on Saturday night."
4. Carl: "I can't come for dinner on Friday. I have to work late."
5. Max: "I don't want to go to the party because Kayla will be there."

Exercise 7

1. A: We're going to go hiking. Do you want to join us?
   B: Sorry, I won't be able to.
2. A: I'm really sorry. We'll be out of town this weekend.
   B: No problem.
3. A: Meet us at 7:00. OK?
   B: OK, sounds like fun.
4. A: I'm sorry. I won't be able to make it.
   B: Well, never mind.

Exercise 8

A

	Accept	*Refuse*
1. I'm really sorry.		✓
2. Great.	✓	
3. Sounds like fun.	✓	
4. I've made other plans.		✓
5. I won't be able to make it.		✓
6. I'm busy.		✓
7. Thanks a lot.	✓	
8. I'd love to.	✓	

B

Answers will vary.

CREDITS

The authors and publishers acknowledge the following sources of copyright material and are grateful for the permissions granted. While every effort has been made, it has not always been possible to identify the sources of all the material used, or to trace all copyright holders. If any omissions are brought to our notice, we will be happy to include the appropriate acknowledgements on reprinting and in the next update to the digital edition, as applicable.

Texts

Text on p. 13 adapted from 'The 4 Happiest Cities on Earth' by Ford Cochran. Copyright © National Geographic Creative. Reproduced with permission; Mark Boyle for the text on p. 21 adapted from 'Living without money changed my way of being'. Reproduced with kind permission of Mark Boyle; Text on p. 41 adapted from 'World's weirdest hotel requests and complaints' by James Teideman. Copyright © www.skyscanner.net. Reproduced with the kind permission; Text on p. 83 adapted from 'Deaf band 'Beethoven's Nightmare' feels the music' by Dennis McCarthy. Copyright © Los Angles Daily News. Reproduced with permission.

Key: B = Below, BC = Below Centre, BL = Below Left, BR = Below Right, B/G = Background, C = Centre, CL = Centre Left, CR = Centre Right, L = Left, R = Right, T = Top, TC = Top Centre, TL = Top Left, TR = Top Right.

Illustrations

337 Jon (KJA Artists): 39, 92(B), 97; **Mark Duffin:** 18, 25(C), 37, 43(T); **Pablo Gallego** (Beehive Illustration): 43(B); **Thomas Girard** (Good Illustration): 2, 22, 41, 93; **John Goodwin** (Eye Candy Illustration): 40; **Daniel Gray**: 75, 118, 120; **Quino Marin** (The Organisation): 36, 80, 128; **Gavin Reece** (New Division): 58, 81, 119; **Paul Williams** (Sylvie Poggio Artists): 16, 114.

Photos

Back cover (woman with whiteboard): Jenny Acheson/Stockbyte/GettyImages; Back cover (whiteboard): Nemida/GettyImages; Back cover (man using phone): Betsie Van Der Meer/Taxi/GettyImages; Back cover (woman smiling): PeopleImages.com/DigitalVision/GettyImages; Back cover (name tag): Tetra Images/GettyImages; Back cover (handshake): David Lees/Taxi/GettyImages; p. x: PeopleImages.com/DigitalVision/GettyImages; p. x: Betsie Van Der Meer/Taxi/GettyImages; screenshots on p. xi, xii, xiii, xiv, xix from Interchange 5e Student's Book 2, Jack C. Richards, Jonathan Hull and Susan Proctor; p. xv: Betsie Van Der Meer/Taxi/GettyImages; p. xvi: PeopleImages.com/DigitalVision/GettyImages; screenshot on p. xvi (B) from Interchange 5e Games, Jack C. Richards, Jonathan Hull and Susan Proctor; screenshots on p. xvii Interchange 5e Workbook 2, Jack C. Richards, Jonathan Hull and Susan Proctor; screenshots on p. xviii from Interchange 5e Teacher's Edition 2 and Complete Assessment Program, Jack C. Richards, Jonathan Hull and Susan Proctor; p. xix (woman): Jenny Acheson/Stockbyte/GettyImages; p. xix (whiteboard): Nemida/GettyImages; screenshots on p. xx from Interchange 5e Intro Teacher's Resource Worksheets & Supplementary Resources Overview; p. xxiii (TL): Hero Images/Getty Images; p. xxiii (TR): Cultura RM Exclusive/dotdotred/Getty Images; p. xxiii (CL): vitchanan/iStock/Getty Images Plus/Getty Images; p. xxiii (CR): Svetlana Braun/iStock/Getty Images Plus/Getty Images; p. xxiii (BL): Hero Images/Getty Images; p. xxiii (BR): Cultura RM Exclusive/dotdotred/Getty Images; p. iv (Unit 1), p. 2 (header): Ekaterina Borner/Moment Open/Getty Images; p. 2 (TL): Juanmonino/E+/Getty Images; p. 2 (TR): Purestock/Getty Images; p. 6 (TR): GlobalStock/E+/Getty Images; p. 6 (CL): Alistair Berg/DigitalVision/Getty Images; p. 7 (TL): Bettmann/Getty Images; p. 7 (BR): Alberto Pizzoli/AFP/Getty Images; p. iv (Unit 2), p. 8 (header): Martin Polsson/Maskot/Getty Images; p. 8 (traffic jam): Roevin/Moment/Getty Images; p. 8 (green space): Yutthana Jantong/EyeEm/Getty Images; p. 8 (Ex 2a.a): Sergiy Serdyuk/Hemera/Getty Images Plus/Getty Images; p. 8 (Ex 2a.b): AvalancheZ/iStock/Getty Images Plus/Getty Images; p. 8 (Ex 2a.c): Peeterv/iStock/Getty Images Plus/Getty Images; p. 8 (microphone): Darryn van der Walt/Moment/Getty Images; p. 9: Kentaroo Tryman/Maskot/Getty Images; p. 10: arnaudbertrande/RooM/Getty Images; p. 11: Tim Bieber/Photodisc/Getty Images; p. 13 (photo 1): peder77/iStock/Getty Images Plus/Getty Images; p. 13 (photo 2): Sollina Images/The Image Bank/Getty Images; p. 13 (photo 3): Panoramic Images/Getty Images; p. 13 (photo 4): Jonathan Drake/Bloomberg/Getty Images; p. 14: Three Lions/Stringer/Getty Images; p. 15: Mark Edward Atkinson/Blend Images/Getty Images; p. iv (Unit 3), p. 16 (header): Hill Street Studios/Blend Images/Getty Images; p. 16 (BR): Lihee Avidan/Photonica World/Getty Images; p. 17 (L): Leren Lu/Taxi Japan/Getty Images; p. 17 (R): Aliyev Alexei Sergeevich/Blend Images/Getty Images; p. 18: Coneyl Jay/Stockbyte/Getty Images; p. 19 (T): laflor/iStock/Getty Images Plus/Getty Images; p. 19 (B): XiXinXing//iStock/Getty Images Plus/Getty Images; p. 20: Jose Luis Pelaez Inc/Blend Images/Getty Images; p. 21: © Mark Boyle; p. iv (Unit 4), p. 22 (header): Yuri_Arcurs/DigitalVision/Getty Images; p. 22 (L): Anna Pustynnikova/iStock/Getty Images Plus/Getty Images; p. 22 (CL): John Ibarra Photography/Moment/Getty Images; p. 22 (CR): PuspaSwara/iStock/Getty Images Plus/Getty Images; p. 22 (R): trindade51/iStock/Getty Images Plus/Getty Images; p. 23: Dan Dalton/DigitalVision/Getty Images; p. 24 (TR): bdspn/iStock/Getty Images Plus/Getty Images; p. 24 (bake): Mark_KA/iStock/Getty Images Plus/Getty Images; p. 24 (boil): Dorling Kindersley/Getty Images; p. 24 (fry): Chris Everard/The Image Bank/Getty Images; p. 24 (grill): Dave Bradley Photography/The Image Bank/Getty Images; p. 24 (roast): Lew Robertson/Photographer's Choice/Getty Images; p. 24 (steam): Aberration Films Ltd/Science Photo Library/Getty Images; p. 25 (TR): Lauri Patterson/E+/Getty Images; p. 25 (photo 1): Simon Wheeler Ltd/Photolibrary/Getty Images; p. 25 (photo 2): jacktherabbit/iStock/Getty Images Plus/Getty Images; p. 25 (photo 3): Dave King/Dorling Kindersley/Getty Images; p. 25 (photo 4): Bruce James/StockFood Creative/Getty Images; p. 25 (photo 5): robdoss/iStock/Getty Images Plus/Getty Images; p. 26 (spaghetti): Lauri Patterson/E+/Getty Images; p. 26 (cookies): 4kodiak/E+/Getty Images; p. 26 (salsa): Douglas Johns/StockFood Creative/Getty Images; p. 26 (toast): DebbiSmirnoff/iStock/Getty Images Plus/Getty Images; p. 26 (popcorn): Michael Deuson/Photolibrary/Getty Images; p. 26 (CR): Plattform/Getty Images; p. 26 (BL): AD077/iStock/Getty Images Plus/Getty Images; p. 27 (TR): stevecoleimages/E+/Getty Images; p. 27 (BL): Lombardis Pizza of New York City; p. 29 (CR): Lauri Patterson/E+/Getty Images; p. 29 (BR): Echo/Cultura/Getty Images; p. iv (Unit 5), p. 30 (header): Hero Images/Getty Images; p. 30 (Ex 1: photo 1): Gary John Norman/Cultura Exclusive/Getty Images; p. 30 (Ex 1: photo 2): Yuri_Arcurs/DigitalVision/Getty Images; p. 30 (Ex 1: photo 3): LuckyBusiness/iStock/Getty Images Plus/Getty Images; p. 30 (Ex 1: photo 4): Yellow Dog Productions/The Image Bank/Getty Images; p. 30 (BR): AID/a.collectionRF/Getty Images; p. 31: Ed Freeman/The Image Bank/Getty Images; p. 33: AngiePhotos/E+/Getty Images; p. 34 (CR): John W Banagan/Photographer's Choice/Getty Images; p. 34 (BR): annebaek/iStock/Getty Images Plus/Getty Images; p. 35 (photo 1): Brian Bailey/The Image Bank/Getty Images; p. 35 (photo 2): Matteo Colombo/Moment/Getty Images; p. 35 (photo 3): Adam Woolfitt/robertharding/Getty Images; p. iv (Unit 6), p. 36 (header): B and G Images/Photographer's Choice/Getty Images; p. 36 (TL): Westend61/Getty Images; p. 38 (CR): Stockbyte/Getty Images; p. 38 (BR): DragonImages/iStock/Getty Images Plus/Getty Images; p. 42: Rudi Von Briel/Photolibrary/Getty Images; p. iv (Unit 7), p. 44 (header): anyaivanova/iStock/Getty Images Plus/Getty Images; p. 44 (TR): MixAll Studio/Blend Images/Getty Images; p. 45: monkeybusinessimages/iStock/Getty Images Plus/Getty Images; p. 46 (CR): scyther5/iStock/Getty Images Plus/Getty Images; p. 46 (BR): Michele Falzone/AWL Images/Getty Images; p. 47: Maskot/Getty Images; p. 48 (speaker): Atsadej0819/iStock/Getty Images Plus/Getty Images; p. 48 (GPS): Peter Dazeley/Photographer's Choice/Getty Images; p. 48 (flash drive): Westend61/Getty Images; p. 48 (smartphone): milindri/iStock/Getty Images Plus/Getty Images; p. 48 (ATM): Volodymyr Krasyuk/iStock/Getty Images Plus/Getty Images; p. 49: Daren Woodward/iStock/Getty Images Plus/Getty Images; p. iv (Unit 8), p. 50 (header): ferrantraite/E+/Getty Images; p. 50 (Saint Patrick's Day): Sachin Polassery/Moment Editorial/Getty Images; p. 50 (Day of the Dead): Darryl Leniuk/Photographer's Choice/Getty Images; p. 50 (Chinese New year): WILLIAM WEST/AFP/Getty Images; p. 50 (Thanksgiving): Kathryn Russell Studios/Photolibrary/Getty Images; p. 51 (L): Hero Images/Getty Images; p. 51 (C): JGI/Jamie Grill/Blend Images/Getty Images; p. 51 (R): Blend Images - JGI/Jamie Grill/Brand X Pictures/Getty Images; p. 52 (TL): altrendo images/Getty Images; p. 52 (CR): Thinkstock Images/Stockbyte/Getty Images; p. 52 (B): huzu1959/Moment Open/Getty Images; p. 53 (Julia): Tara Moore/Stone/Getty Images; p. 53 (Anusha): Carlina Teteris/Moment/Getty Images; p. 53 (TR): Blend Images/Getty Images; p. 54: Tetra Images/Getty Images; p. 55 (TL): oversnap/iStock/Getty Images Plus/Getty Images; p. 55 (BR): ruslan117/iStock/Getty Images Plus/Getty Images; p. 56 (CR): vgajic/iStock/Getty Images Plus/Getty Images; p. 57 (TL): Dezein/iStock/Getty Images Plus/Getty Images; p. 57 (TC): artpartner-images/Photographer's Choice/Getty Images; p. 57 (TR): André Rieck/EyeEmGetty Images; p. 57 (BR): Satoshi Kawase/Moment/Getty Images; p. vi (Unit 9), p. 58 (header): Artur Debat/Moment/Getty Images; p. 58 (TL): Michael Fresco/Evening Standard/Hulton Archive/Getty Images; p. 58 (TC): Car Culture/Car Culture ® Collection/Getty Images; p. 58 (TR): Javier Pierini/The Image Bank/Getty Images; p. 59: Hero Images/Getty Images; p. 60 (CR): Jordan Siemens/Iconica/Getty Images; p. 60 (BR): RoBeDeRo/E+/Getty Images; p. 61: GH-Photography/iStock/Getty Images Plus/Getty Images; p. 62 (TR): Barry Austin Photography/Iconica/Getty Images; p. 62 (Ex 11a: photo 1): Hill Street Studios/Blend Images/Getty Images; p. 62 (Ex 11a: photo 2): Hill Street Studios/Blend Images/Getty Images; p. 62 (Ex 11a: photo 3): Hill Street Studios/Blend Images/Getty Images; p. 62 (Ex 11a: photo 4): Aziz Ary Neto/Cultura/Getty Images; p. 62 (Ex 11a: photo 5): Blend Images-Mike Kemp/Brand X Pictures/Getty Images; p. 63: Daniel Schoenen/LOOK-foto/LOOK/Getty Images; p. vi (Unit 10), p. 64 (header): Hero Images/Getty Images; p. 64 (BR): BJI/Blue Jean Images/Getty Images; p. 65: Caiaimage/Paul Bradbury/Caiaimage/Getty Images; p. 67 (disorganised): Stuart McCall/Photographer's Choice/Getty Images; p. 67 (hardworking): Dave and Les Jacobs/Blend Images/Getty Images; p. 67 (Ex 9a): adventtr/E+/Getty Images; p. 67 (Paula): Portra Images/Taxi/Getty Images; p. 67 (Shawn): PeopleImages/DigitalVision/Getty Images; p. 67 (Dalia): Jetta Productions/Blend Images/Getty Images; p. 69: Image Source/Getty Images; p. 71:

monkeybusinessimages/iStock/Getty Images Plus/Getty Images; p. vi (Unit 11), p. 72 (header): d3sign/Moment/Getty Images; p. 72 (Eiffel Tower): Kart Thomas/Photolibrary/Getty Images; p. 72 (Machu Picchu): mimmopellicola.com/Moment/Getty Images; p. 72 (Neuschwanstein Castle): Brian Lawrence/Getty Images; p. 72 (Mount Fuji): Christian Kober/robertharding/Getty Images; p. 72 (Statue of Liberty): Brian Lawrence/Getty Images; p. 72 (Big Ben): Joe Fox/Photographer's Choice/Getty Images; p. 73: Print Collector/Hulton Fine Art Collection/Getty Images; p. 74 (L): JTB Photo/Universal Images Group/Getty Images; p. 74 (C): PIERRE VERDY/AFP Creative/Getty Images; p. 74 (R): JLGutierrez/iStock/Getty Images Plus/Getty Images; p. 76 (TR): Radius Images/Getty Images Plus/Getty Images; p. 76 (CR): Jodi Jacobson/E+/Getty Images; p. 76 (BR): Photography Aubrey Stoll/Moment/Getty Images; p. 77 (TL): Hemant Chawla/The India Today Group/Getty Images; p. 77 (CR): Luis Javier Sandoval/Oxford Scientific/Getty Images; p. 77 (BL): EPA european pressphoto agency b.v./Alamy; p. vi (Unit 12), p. 78 (header): Timur Emek/Getty Images Europe/Getty Images; p. 78 (TL): JasnaXX/RooM/Getty Images; p. 78 (TR): Rodrigo Alvarez-Icaza/Moment Open/Getty Images; p. 78 (BR): James Woodson/Photodisc/Getty Images; p. 79 (TR): Michael Krinke/Vetta/Getty Images; p. 79 (BR): biglike/iStock/Getty Images Plus/Getty Images; p. 82: David Lees/Taxi/Getty Images; p. 83: Rachel Murray/WireImage/Getty Images; p. 84: Ben Pruchnie/Getty Images Europe/Getty Images; p. vi (Unit 13), p. 86 (header): spawns/iStock/Getty Images Plus/Getty Images; p. 86 (TL): Jim Spellman/WireImage/Getty Images; p. 86 (TR): Pictorial Press Ltd/Alamy; p. 86 (BR): Murray Close/Contributor/Moviepix/GettyImages; p. 87: Araya Diaz/WireImage/Getty Image; p. 89: Jon Kopaloff/FilmMagic/Getty Images; p. 90 (TR): Daniel Zuchnik/WireImage/Getty Images; p. 90 (BR): Valerie Macon/Getty Images North America/Getty Images; p. 91 (BL): Paul Hawthorne/Getty Images North America/Getty Images; p. 91 (TR): Alberto E. Rodriguez/Getty Images North America/Getty Images; p. vi (Unit 14), p. 92 (header): Joe Drivas/Photographer's Choice/Getty Images; p. 93 (Ex 4: photo 1): champja/iStock/Getty Images Plus/Getty Images; p. 93 (Ex 4: photo 2): Dahl Per/Getty Images; p. 93 (Ex 4: photo 3): Seymour Hewitt/The Image Bank/Getty Images; p. 93 (Ex 4: photo 4): Merbe/E+/Getty Images; p. 93 (Ex 4: photo 5): BJI/Blue Jean Images/Getty Images; p. 93 (Ex 4: photo 6): m-imagephotography/iStock/Getty Images Plus/Getty Images; p. 94: BJI/Blue Jean Images/Getty Images; p. 98: uniquely india/Getty Images; p. 99: GlobalStock/E+/Getty Images; p. vi (Unit 15), p. 100 (header): Tetra Images/Getty Images; p. 100 (TL): moodboard/Brand X Pictures/Getty Images; p. 100 (CL): Marcin Balcerzak/Hemera/Getty Images Plus/Getty Images; p. 100 (C): Erik Dreyer/The Image Bank/Getty Images; p. 100 (BR): Thomas_EyeDesign/E+/Getty Images; p. 102: pp76/iStock/Getty Images Plus/Getty Images; p. 104 (TR): Wavebreakmedia Ltd/Wavebreak Media/Getty Images Plus/Getty Images; p. 104 (CR): Ariel Skelley/Blend Images/Getty Images Plus/Getty Images; p. 105 (Jack): Frank Herholdt/The Image Bank/Getty Images; p. 105 (Sarah): Betsie Van Der Meer/Taxi/Getty Images; p. 105 (Maya): Caiaimage/Sam Edwards/Caiaimage/Getty Images; p. 105 (Dag): Dimitri Otis/Taxi/Getty Images; p. 105 (Andres): Ridofranz/iStock/Getty Images Plus/Getty Images; p. 105 (Marta): Mark Edward Atkinson/Tracey Lee/Blend Images/Getty Images; p. vi (Unit 16), p. 106 (header): Dan Dumitru Comaniciu/iStock/Getty Images Plus/Getty Images; p. 106 (TR): GK Hart/Vikki Hart/Stone/Getty Images; p. 107: ajr_images/iStock/Getty Images Plus/Getty Images; p. 108 (Gabriel): gradyreese/E+/Getty Images; p. 108 (Craig): Leland Bobbe/Image Source/Getty Images; p. 109 (Grant): Ezra Bailey/Taxi/Getty Images; p. 109 (Sayo): Sappington Todd/Getty Images; p. 109 (Diego): Fuse/Getty Images; p. 109 (Carrie): Jordan Siemens/Getty Images; p. 110: Jamie Grill/Photodisc/Getty Images; p. 111 (TR): Tom Le Goff/DigitalVision/Getty Images; p. 111 (CR): Ugurhan Betin/iStock/Getty Images Plus/Getty Images; p. 112: Moodboard Stock Photography Ltd./Canopy/Getty Images; screenshots on p. T-115–131 from Interchange Student's book 2, Jack C. Richards, Jonathan Hull and Susan Proctor.

Video still on p. xv (B) by Nesson Media Boston Inc.